The Taxation of
Income from Capital

A National Bureau
of Economic Research
Monograph

 **Institut für
Wirtschaftsforschung**

 Industriens
Utredningsinstitut

The Taxation of Income from Capital

A Comparative Study
of the United States, the
United Kingdom, Sweden,
and West Germany

Edited by   Mervyn A. King and
Don Fullerton

Country
Team
Directors

United Kingdom	Mervyn A. King
Sweden	Jan Södersten
West Germany	Willi Leibfritz
United States	Don Fullerton

Collaborating
Authors

Julian Alworth
David F. Bradford
Thomas Lindberg
Michael J. Naldrett
James M. Poterba

 The University of Chicago Press
Chicago and London

MERVYN A. KING is the Esmee Fairbairn Professor of Investment
at the University of Birmingham. DON FULLERTON is assistant professor of economics and public affairs at Princeton University and
a research associate of the National Bureau of Economic Research.

The University of Chicago Press, Chicago 60637
The University of Chicago Press, Ltd., London

Printed in the United States of America
91 90 89 88 87 86 85 84   5 4 3 2 1

Library of Congress Cataloging in Publication Data
Main entry under title:

The Taxation of income from capital.

  (A National Bureau of Economic Research monograph)
  Bibliography: p.
  Includes index.
  1. Saving and investment—Taxation—United States.
2. Saving and investment—Taxation—Great Britain.
3. Saving and investment—Taxation—Sweden. 4. Saving
and investment—Taxation—Germany (West) I. King,
Mervyn A. II. Fullerton, D. (Don) III. Alworth, J.
(Julian) IV. Series.
HJ4653.A3T39 1984   336.24′26   83-17884
ISBN 0-226-43630-6

Relation of the Directors to the
Work and Publications of the
National Bureau of Economic Research

1. The object of the National Bureau of Economic Research is to ascertain and to present to the public important economic facts and their interpretation in a scientific and impartial manner. The Board of Directors is charged with the responsibility of ensuring that the work of the National Bureau is carried on in strict conformity with this object.

2. The President of the National Bureau shall submit to the Board of Directors, or to its Executive Committee, for their formal adoption all specific proposals for research to be instituted.

3. No research report shall be published by the National Bureau until the President has sent each member of the Board a notice that a manuscript is recommended for publication and that in the President's opinion it is suitable for publication in accordance with the principles of the National Bureau. Such notification will include an abstract or summary of the manuscript's content and a response form for use by those Directors who desire a copy of the manuscript for review. Each manuscript shall contain a summary drawing attention to the nature and treatment of the problem studied, the character of the data and their utilization in the report, and the main conclusions reached.

4. For each manuscript so submitted, a special committee of the Directors (including Directors Emeriti) shall be appointed by majority agreement of the President and Vice Presidents (or by the Executive Committee in case of inability to decide on the part of the President and Vice Presidents), consisting of three Directors selected, as nearly as may be, one from each general division of the Board. The names of the special manuscript committee shall be stated to each Director when notice of the proposed publication is submitted to him. It shall be the duty of each member of the special manuscript committee to read the manuscript. If each member of the manuscript committee signifies his approval within thirty days of the transmittal of the manuscript, the report may be published. If at the end of that period any member of the manuscript committee withholds his approval, the President shall then notify each member of the Board, requesting approval or disapproval of publication, and thirty days additional shall be granted for this purpose. The manuscript shall then not be published unless at least a majority of the entire Board who shall have voted on the proposal within the time fixed for the receipt of votes shall have approved.

5. No manuscript may be published, though approved by each member of the special manuscript committee, until forty-five days have elapsed from the transmittal of the report in manuscript form. The interval is allowed for the receipt of any memorandum of dissent or reservation, together with a brief statement of his reasons, that any member may wish to express; and such memorandum of dissent or reservation shall be published with the manuscript if he so desires. Publication does not, however, imply that each member of the Board has read the manuscript, or that either members of the Board in general or the special committee have passed on its validity in every detail.

6. Publications of the National Bureau issued for informational purposes concerning the work of the Bureau and its staff, or issued to inform the public of activities of Bureau staff, and volumes issued as a result of various conferences involving the National Bureau shall contain a specific disclaimer noting that such publication has not passed through the normal review procedures required in this resolution. The Executive Committee of the Board is charged with review of all such publications from time to time to ensure that they do not take on the character of formal research reports of the National Bureau, requiring formal Board approval.

7. Unless otherwise determined by the Board or exempted by the terms of paragraph 6, a copy of this resolution shall be printed in each National Bureau publication.

(Resolution adopted October 25, 1926, as revised through September 30, 1974)

Contents

Preface

In early 1979 Martin Feldstein suggested that the general approach of Mervyn King's *Public Policy and the Corporation* (1977) could be used to compare effective marginal tax rates for several different countries. Since the existing studies had employed different methods, thus making inter-country comparisons hazardous, we decided to launch a study based on a common method that might shed light on the significant economic differences among the tax systems in four major economies that have experienced different degrees of economic success—the United States, the United Kingdom, Sweden, and West Germany. In this book we report the results of that enterprise, undertaken with the combined financial and human resources of the National Bureau of Economic Research (NBER) in Cambridge, Massachusetts, Institut für Wirtschaftsforschung (IFO) in Munich, West Germany, and the Industriens Utredningsinstitut (IUI) in Stockholm, Sweden. In addition, we gratefully acknowledge financial support from the National Science Foundation under grant numbers SES791420 and SES8025404.

Our first meeting was held at NBER in August 1979. This meeting included Helmut Laumer and Willi Leibfritz from IFO in Germany, Gunnar Eliasson and Jan Södersten from IUI in Sweden, Mervyn King and John Flemming from Britain, and several United States economists including Alan Auerbach, David Bradford, Larry Dildine, Martin Feldstein, Don Fullerton, Charles McLure, John Shoven, and Lawrence Summers. Subsequent meetings were held in Stockholm, June 1980, in Munich, November 1980, in Cambridge, August 1981, at the London School of Economics, January 1982, and again in London, June 1982. We received valuable comments and assistance from participants at each of these meetings.

In particular, though all authors participated in writing the whole manuscript, we would like to acknowledge the primary efforts made with respect to each chapter. The United Kingdom chapter was written primarily by Mervyn King of the University of Birmingham and NBER, by Michael J. Naldrett of the University of Birmingham and later of Princeton University, and by James Poterba of Nuffield College, Oxford, and NBER. We received invaluable assistance from E. B. Butler, R. M. Elliss, J. King, and P. Penneck of the Inland Revenue, from R. I. Armitage of the Central Statistical Office, and from J. S. Flemming and J. Ryding of the Bank of England.

The chapter on Sweden was written primarily by Jan Södersten of IUI and the University of Uppsala and by Thomas Lindberg of IUI. We are especially indebted to Villy Bergström, Göran Normann, Göran Råbäck, and Rolf Rundfelt for valuable assistance and helpful comments. Contributions were also made by participants of the research seminar of IUI and by Ragnar Bentzel, Christen Herzen, Sven-Olof Lodin, Gustav Sandström, and Leif Sundberg.

Primary authors of the chapter on Germany were Willi Leibfritz of IFO and Julian Alworth of the Bank for International Settlements in Basel, Switzerland. We are especially grateful to Heinz Ludwig of IFO for research assistance. Other helpful comments and assistance were received from Hans-Georg Jatzek, Robert Koll, Josef Körner, and Stephan Teschner. We are also grateful for statistical help from Christa Bronny and Christian Wagner, and from the Deutsche Bundesbank and the Statistisches Bundesamt.

Don Fullerton was the primary author of the United States chapter, though frequent assistance was provided by Yolanda K. Henderson. At several points during our progress we received help from Alan J. Auerbach, Larry L. Dildine, Daniel Feenberg, Martin Feldstein, Barbara M. Fraumeni, Roger H. Gordon, Dale W. Jorgenson, Lawrence B. Lindsey, Charles E. McLure, John B. Shoven, Martin A. Sullivan, Lawrence H. Summers, and William Vickrey.

Mervyn King had primary responsibility for the introductory chapters 1 and 2, and he began the computer programming with Michael Naldrett at the University of Birmingham. Later computer work was undertaken at Princeton University by Don Fullerton, Michael Naldrett, and Thomas Kronmiller. Fullerton had primary responsibility for writing chapter 7; tables for that chapter were drawn up by Thomas Kronmiller. David Bradford, also at Princeton, and Don Fullerton contributed their efforts as the primary authors of our concluding chapter. Particular mention must be made of Don Fullerton's efforts to produce results for each country from the Princeton computer according to a tight schedule.

Again, although we want to credit those responsible for each chapter, we also wish to emphasize that this book is a joint product, not a collection of separate papers. All authors participated in the drafting and redrafting of the manuscript and in the development of a common view on how best to tackle the problem we set ourselves.

Finally, we would like to express our thanks for remarkable efficiency and patience to those who typed various parts of the manuscript: Ingrid Hensel, Alice Pattersson, Jenny Saxby, Judy Weinberger, Michael Wickham, and Maja Woxen, and to Annie Zeumer of NBER for making life as easy as possible for the authors. A last word of thanks must go to Randall Mørck, who organized and shepherded the preparation of the final manuscript.

Glossary of Notation

This glossary includes notation defined in chapter 2 and used throughout the book. Notation that is specific to one country and used in a limited context is defined at the point where it is used.

A Present discounted value of tax savings from depreciation allowances and other grants associated with a unit investment.

A_d Present discounted value of tax savings from standard depreciation allowances associated with a unit investment.

A_z Present discounted value of depreciation allowances associated with a unit investment $(A_d = \tau A_z)$.

a Rate of tax depreciation on exponential basis.

a' Rate of exponential tax depreciation before switch ($= B/L$).

B Declining balance rate ($= 2$ for double declining balance).

b Proportion of funds allocated to investment funds that must be deposited in Central Bank (Sweden).

$b(n)$ Value age profile of an asset (Sweden).

C Effective cost of an asset.

c_d Tax on distributed profits (Germany).

c_u Tax on undistributed profits (Germany).

D An annual amount of economic depreciation (Sweden).

$d(n)$ Average age of retirement of machines (Sweden).

d_1 Dummy equals unity if corporate wealth taxes deductible from corporate income tax base; zero otherwise.

d_2 Dummy equals unity if asset is inventories; zero otherwise.

$f(n)$ Fraction of value of asset retained after n years (Sweden).

f_1 Proportion of cost of asset entitled to standard depreciation allowances.

f_2 Proportion of cost of asset entitled to immediate expensing.

f_3 Proportion of cost of asset entitled to cash grant.

G Total gross dividends paid.

g Rate of cash investment grant.

H Multiplicative coefficient (*Hebesatz*) for local business tax (*Gewerbesteuer*) (Germany).

i Nominal interest rate.

K Net capital stock (Sweden).

k Index for project combination.

L Asset life.

L_s Time of the asset's life for an optimal switch of depreciation method.

l Proportion of profits that may be allocated to the investment fund (Sweden).

M Base rate (*Messzahl*) for local business tax rate (Germany).

MRR Gross marginal rate of return on a project.

m Marginal personal tax rate.

m^{SB} Hypothetical tax rate where no initial tax credit is given (Sweden).

m^{SF} Equivalent tax rate (Sweden).

N Number of machines originally in a cohort of assets (Sweden).

n Period of fiscal depreciation (Sweden).

p Pretax real rate of return on a project.

$\bar{p}$ Mean of p.

q Ratio of market value to replacement cost (Tobin's q).

r Real interest rate.

$S(u)$ Survivor curve for capital assets (Sweden).

s Posttax real rate of return to the saver.

T Total tax liability.

t Marginal tax rate (w/p).

$\bar{t}$ Average marginal tax rate ($\bar{w}/\bar{p}$).

t_e Marginal tax rate on tax-exclusive basis (w/s).

u Index for time.

V Present discounted value of profits of a project.

v Proportion of inventories taxed on historical cost principles.

w Tax wedge ($p - s$).

$\bar{w}$ Mean of w.

w_c Rate of corporate wealth tax.

w_p Rate of personal wealth tax.

Y Corporate taxable income.

z Effective accrued tax rate on capital gains.

z_s Statutory rate of capital gains tax.

$z_s SF$ Equivalent tax rate on capital gains (Sweden).

α_k Proportion of net capital stock attributable to kth combination of asset, industry, source of finance, and owner.

β Growth rate in value of shares held by investment fund (Sweden).

γ Implied deduction against tax base of insurance company (Sweden).

δ Rate of exponential depreciation.

θ Opportunity cost of retained earnings in terms of gross dividends forgone.

λ Proportion of accrued gains realized by investors in each period.

μ Dividend yield of investment fund portfolio (Sweden).

π Rate of inflation.

ρ Rate at which firm discounts net of tax cash flows.

ρ_p Investor's nominal discount rate.

τ Rate of corporation tax.

τ_L Tax-inclusive effective local business tax rate (Germany).

τ_e Effective tax rate on insurance company (Sweden).

τ_s Statutory corporate tax rate (Sweden).

1   Introduction

A continuous increase in living standards is, in the long run, dependent upon a high level of investment. As the period of sustained economic growth enjoyed in the 1950s and 1960s has come to an end, governments in many countries have shown an increasing interest in policies designed to stimulate investment and productivity. One of the major weapons in the government's armory is the tax system. The impediments to savings and investment resulting from the tax system have been the focus of growing concern, especially in the periods of rapid inflation experienced in recent years.

It is not surprising, therefore, that a great deal of attention has been paid to analyzing the effects of the tax system on savings and investment. The failure of most of the developed economies to sustain high growth rates has led to an increased awareness of the lessons we may learn from each other. Is it true, for example, that countries with the highest rates of productivity growth have the lowest tax rates on capital income? The aim of the research described in this book is to compare the effective tax rates levied on capital income in the nonfinancial corporate sector in four major economies: the United States, the United Kingdom, Sweden, and West Germany. The study has entailed a collaborative effort by investigators working in each of the four countries to ensure as exact a comparison as possible. This is reflected in the fact that the project has produced a book rather than a series of papers by individual authors. As far as possible we have tried to ensure uniformity in our treatment and comparability of our estimates.

The existing literature on international comparisons of tax systems lacks a sharp focus, primarily because the statistics are produced for a multitude of purposes and are not designed to answer a clearly defined question. In this study we are attempting to answer the question, What is the distribution of tax rates levied on marginal investment projects in the corporate sector? In each country the tax system imposes a wedge between the rate of return on an investment project and the rate of return that can be paid to the investors who financed the project.

When we look at the present value of expected taxes relative to the expected income from a marginal investment under consideration, we measure what might be called a "marginal effective tax rate." We compare this rate with an "average effective tax rate," defined as the ratio of observed taxes to income from existing investments. Our results indicate that the two are very different. The average rate reflects cash flows and tax burdens, but the marginal rate is more appropriate for looking at incentives to save and invest. Also, many studies that measure either of these effective tax rates have looked only at corporate taxes on marginal or existing investments (see discussion and references cited in Fullerton 1983). Although we limit our study to investment in the corporate sector, we do not limit ourselves to corporate taxes. We measure a marginal effective total tax rate, in the sense that we include corporate taxes, personal taxes, and wealth taxes asociated with the income from each marginal investment.

In addition, we shall see that within each country the estimated marginal tax rate varies enormously among industries, among assets, among different sources of finance, and among different categories of original investors. A further important question we investigate is the sensitivity of the effective tax rate to changes in the rate of inflation. No particular relationship is necessary here, and indeed we find that the effect of inflation varies enormously from country to country.

Questions like these are both interesting and important for an analysis of the effects of taxation on investment, but they have a wider policy relevance as well. In three of the four countries involved in this project there have been major reports in recent years on the structure of the tax system. In the United States *Blueprints for Basic Tax Reform* was published in 1977. This official Treasury report examined the structure of the United States tax system and considered a number of major reforms. Simultaneously, under the sponsorship of the Institute for Fiscal Studies, the Meade Committee produced its report in the United Kingdom (Meade Committee 1978). This drew attention to the haphazard taxation of savings and investment in the United Kingdom and recommended that the tax system be reformed so that taxation would be based on expenditure rather than income. A similar conclusion was reached in a Royal Commission Report in Sweden in 1976 (Lodin 1976). Although these reports were produced quite independently, there is one striking fact about them. The phenomenon that all the reports identified as of fundamental importance for tax reform was the potential distortion of savings and investment decisions caused by the *unsystematic* tax treatment of income from capital.

To analyze this phenomenon requires a comprehensive treatment of both corporate and personal taxation. We attempt to provide this and to give empirical estimates of the size of the tax wedge between the return on investment and the return on savings. A study of this kind requires both a theoretical framework and a substantial amount of empirical work to ensure comparability of our estimates. Chapter 2 describes the theoretical framework we have used, and the individual country chapters (chaps. 3–6) provide the empirical basis for our estimates.

The economic performances of the four countries in our study have been rather different, and they provide a contrast in terms of both tax systems and institutional background. These four countries were chosen to provide a balance of economic and political structure and to represent countries with very different growth experiences. The study was limited to four countries to ensure feasibility of the project, although we hope that the methodology described in this book will be applied to other countries.

The approach we adopt is designed to complement existing comparisons of international tax systems. These are of two types. First, there are studies of the levels of revenue raised in different countries by different types of taxes. The best example of this type of study is the regular publication *Revenue Statistics of Member Countries* published by the Organization for Economic Cooperation and Development (OECD). This publication is designed to provide an accounting framework within which the total tax structures of member countries may be compared. It is not designed to answer any particular question, and the classification of taxes by category is inevitably a little arbitrary. For our purpose the problem is that the statistics are not collected with a view to providing information on the incentives offered by the tax system. Nevertheless, the figures published by the OECD do provide a useful starting point for an analysis of taxes, and they are used in the introductory section of each country chapter. The focus of our study, however, is the empirical estimation of the incentives to save and invest afforded by the different tax systems, and for this we need a theoretical framework.

The second type of international comparison usually consists of descriptions of the tax code in different countries as it affects particular assets or types of income. For example, there are studies of the differences in the tax treatment of dividends, of capital transfers, and of capital gains. Some of these studies have been the basis for policy recommendations. For example, the European Economic Community (EEC) has been trying to harmonize its treatment of corporate taxation with respect to dividends. The drawback to this approach is that to evaluate the economic effects of the tax system we need to take into account a very long list of provisions in the tax code. One of the problems with the EEC's attempts to harmonize corporate taxation has been that to date it has focused far more on the taxation of dividends than on the definition of the corporate tax base. Since the provisions for depreciation and allowances for inflation vary widely among member countries, such an approach is at best partial and at worst highly misleading. To examine the effects of the tax system on investment, we need to take account of a large number of details in the tax code, including the rate of corporation tax, the nature and scope of depreciation allowances, the extent to which these are indexed for inflation, investment tax credits or other cash grants for investment, regional grants and subsidies, the system of corporation tax (the classical versus the imputation system, for example), the personal tax treatment of dividends and interest income, capital gains taxation, wealth taxation, and the tax treatment of particular types of investors such as pension funds and insurance companies. An exhaustive description of the tax treatment of these different items in each country would be just as incomprehensible as the tax codes themselves, so in this study we have tried to set out a simple conceptual framework within which we may analyze the effective marginal tax rate on capital income. Not only does this framework enable us to bring together the different aspects of the tax code, it also allows us to compute the quantitative significance of the tax system as a whole.

The size of the marginal tax rate levied on investment depends upon the way the project is financed and the identity of the supplier of finance. We have attempted to compute distributions of marginal tax rates using as weights the proportions of net capital stock financed by particular owners and from particular sources. We have also examined the allocation of investment among industries and among different types of asset. This required an empirical study into the ownership of different types of securities and the financing of industry. In themselves these data requirements proved time consuming and are described in detail in individual country chapters. One of the by-products of our study is a good deal of detailed information about the financing and ownership of industry in each country and of the institutional background against which our results may be seen. As part of our study, we used very large data sets to compute a distribution of marginal tax rates on individual investors in each country, and we carried out the most systematic study to date of shareownership in West Germany.

We would stress, therefore, that the output of this research project should not be seen solely in terms of the tax rates we present in chapter 7. The individual country chapters contain a good deal of detail about the financing and ownership of the corporate sector and of tax systems so as to allow the reader to place our results in context. To make this detail more accessible, we have organized each country chapter in an identical fashion, as follows:

1. Introduction
2. The Tax System
   2.1 The Personal Income Tax
   2.2 The Corporate Tax System
   2.3 Tax Allowances for Depreciation and Inventories
   2.4 Estimates of Economic Depreciation
   2.5 Investment Grants and Incentives
   2.6 Local Taxes
   2.7 Wealth Taxes
   2.8 Household Tax Rates
   2.9 Tax-Exempt Institutions
   2.10 Insurance Companies
3. The Structure of the Capital Stock and Its Ownership
   3.1 Data Limitations
   3.2 Capital Stock Weights
   3.3 Sources of Financial Capital
   3.4 The Ownership of Equity
   3.5 The Ownership of Debt
4. Estimates of Effective Marginal Tax Rates
   4.1 Principal Results
   4.2 Recent Changes in Tax Legislation
   4.3 Comparison with 1960 and 1970
   4.4 Comparison with Average Tax Rates

This arrangement should enable readers who wish to compare the tax treatment of, for example, insurance companies in each country to do this by referring to section 2.10 in each country chapter. A glossary of notation is provided at the beginning of the book.

The work of the project fell into three parts. First, there was the development of the conceptual framework. Second, there was the collection of data on a comparable basis for the computation of effective marginal tax rates. Finally these rates were estimated using a common computer program. The bulk of the time was taken up in producing estimates of the parameters used in our calculations and in ensuring comparability of our estimates.

The plan of the book is as follows. The conceptual framework is described in chapter 2, and the data for the individual countries are discussed in chapters 3–6. Our main results concerning effective marginal tax rates may be found in chapter 7, and the main lessons of our study are summarized in chapter 8. Readers who wish to focus on the principal results are advised to start with chapters 1, 2, 7, and 8 and then return to the individual country chapters for a fuller explanation.

The discussion in chapter 7 compares the marginal effective tax rates in the four countries for 1980. In section 4 of each country chapter the results for 1980 are summarized, and their sensitivity to alternative assumptions is examined. For each country we also examine the effect of recent changes in tax legislation and provide two sets of comparisons. The first is with estimated marginal effective tax rates for 1960 and 1970, to give some idea of how tax rates have evolved over time. The second comparison is with an estimate of the average effective tax rate on income from corporate capital in 1980. This comparison shows the difference between marginal and average tax rates.

Our aim is to provide sufficient detail on both the methodology underlying our study and the data used so that other investigators may, first, replicate the calculations for the same sample of four countries and, second, extend the analysis to other countries. In time we hope to persuade governments or other bodies to adopt our methods so as to produce regular estimates of the incentive effects of taxation. The study should also be a useful compendium of information not only about the tax system in each country but also about the structure of the corporate sector.

It is more than two hundred years since Edmund Burke wrote that "to tax and to please, no more than to love and to be wise, is not given to men." Our results will not make it easier for governments to please their electorate, but we hope they will make voters and governments alike a little wiser about the true impact of tax legislation.

2   The Theoretical Framework

Our aim is to examine the incentives to save and invest in the private
nonfinancial corporate sector offered by the tax system in each country.
Clearly, taxes are only one of the determinants of capital formation, and
our four countries exhibit many important differences beyond differences
in the taxation of capital income. But the structure of the tax system is
often cited as an impediment to economic growth, and it is under the
direct control of government. Taxation can affect many economic decisions, including labor supply, work effort, enterprise, and risk taking, as
well as household savings and corporate investment in real assets. In this
study we focus on the flow of private savings into real corporate investment and the flow of profits that result from this investment back to
households. We do not explicitly discuss the effects of taxes on risk taking
or work effort, and our analysis is limited to the incentives to save and
invest. Since the exercise of "enterprise" usually involves some investment—that is, some sacrifice of present consumption for future returns—
our estimated effective tax rates bear closely on the incentives or disin-
centives provided by government to channel resources into entrepreneurship.

2.1   The Measurement of Effective Tax Rates

The measurement of effective tax rates is not straightforward. Popular
discussion tends to concentrate on the tax burden on corporate profits,
especially in periods of rapid inflation. This corporate tax burden (or
average effective corporate tax rate) may be a misleading measure for
two reasons. First, it ignores the interaction between personal and corporate taxation. For example, interest payments that are deductible at the
corporate level are taxed in the hands of the personal sector upon receipt.

7

The incentives to invest depend upon the combined weight of personal and corporate taxes. Second, the tax burden measures the observed tax rate on realized capital income. It does not measure the incentive for additional investment which is a function of the marginal tax rate. In what follows, we develop estimates of the effective *marginal* tax rate on capital income for each of the four countries.

To do this requires a precise definition of the margin involved. The margin considered here is a small increase in the level of real investment in the domestic nonfinancial corporate sector, financed by an increase in the savings of domestic households. An alternative marginal tax rate would be that applicable to an increase in profits that did not result from an addition to investment but that resulted, perhaps, from an unexpected increase in selling prices. Although the latter definition has its place, the former is preferred here because it is the margin relevant to the incentive effects of taxation.

The empirical study is restricted to domestic savings and investment. International capital flows are important in a number of areas, but the intricacies of double tax agreements and of the accounting behavior of multinational companies introduce complexities that are better deferred to a separate study. In any event, the bulk of investment in each of the countries studied here is financed domestically, and the effective tax rates presented below give a fairly accurate picture of the incentives provided by the different tax systems. Public-sector investment is also excluded from our study. Its determinants are unrelated to the tax system, and our focus is on taxation. Finally, we examine only corporate investment. This limitation means we ignore not only unincorporated business but also investment in residential housing. Again, most industrial investment is in the corporate sector. Details of the size of the corporate sector and the importance of foreign ownership of domestic capital are provided in the respective country chapters.

To assess the impact of taxation on investment, two approaches may be identified. The first is the econometric modeling of the process that generates time-series observations on savings and investment. A major problem with this approach is the complexity of the correct specification of tax variables, not to mention uncertainty, adjustment costs, and production lags. As a consequence, the very limited number of observations that are available, even with quarterly data, contain insufficient information for us to be confident of identifying the underlying process. Moreover, the relation between investment and taxation depends upon corporate financial policy and on the pattern of ownership of corporate securities. There is no unique cost of capital to the corporate sector that is independent of its ownership pattern and those other factors that determine its capital structure.

The second approach is to compute directly the tax "wedge" between the rate of return on investment and the rate of return on savings for a series of hypothetical marginal projects. In the absence of taxes, when the saver puts up money to finance a project he earns a rate of return equal to that earned on the project itself. With distortionary taxes the two rates of return can differ. The size of the tax wedge depends upon the system of corporate taxation, the interaction of these taxes with inflation, the tax treatment of depreciation and inventories, the personal tax code, the treatment of different legal forms of income (capital gains versus dividends, for example), the existence of wealth taxes, and a number of other details we examine below. It is clear, therefore, that the effective tax rate on an investment project depends upon the industry where it is located, the particular asset purchased, the way the investment is financed, and the identity of the investor who supplies the finance. In this study we shall compute estimates of the effective marginal tax rate for many different combinations of these factors. Such estimates are not to be regarded as a substitute for econometric analysis of investment behavior. Rather, they provide a description of the actual incentives offered by the tax system. We hope they will be useful as inputs to future econometric studies of investment and other aspects of corporate behavior. The effective tax rates calculated below are intended to summarize a very complicated tax code in a way that is intuitively appealing.

The tax wedge is the difference between the rate of return on investment and the rate of return on the savings used to finance the investment. We denote by p the pretax real rate of return on a marginal investment project, net of depreciation. It is the return society earns on a particular investment of one extra unit (dollar, pound, kroner, or mark). Let s denote the posttax real rate of return to the saver (whether a household or an institution) who supplied the finance for the investment. The tax wedge, w, is simply the difference between the two rates of return:

(2.1) $w = p - s.$

The effective tax rate, t, we define to be the tax wedge divided by the pretax rate of return:

(2.2) $t = \dfrac{p - s}{p}.$

This definition of the tax rate is a "tax-inclusive" measure in which the denominator includes the tax paid as well as the net income received. An alternative "tax-exclusive" measure would divide the tax wedge by the posttax return to the saver. This measure, t_e, is defined by:

(2.3) $t_e = \dfrac{p - s}{s}.$

In presenting our results, we shall use all three measures of the distortion caused by taxes, but we shall be concerned primarily with estimates of the effective tax rate in (2.2). Nevertheless, in some circumstances the tax wedge may be more informative than the tax rate (when p is small, for example).

The link between the saver and the company that carries out the investment is the rate of return the company pays on the saver's financial claims. For example, if the saver lends money to the company in the form of a fixed-interest loan, then the company must pay an interest rate on the loan. We denote the real rate of interest on such financial claims by r and the corresponding nominal interest rate by i. If π denotes the rate of inflation, then in terms of instantaneous rates

(2.4) $\qquad r = i - \pi .$

The interest rate r plays an intermediate role between the investment decisions by companies and savings decisions by households, and it is important in our analysis. For any given investment project we may ask the question, What is the minimum rate of return it must yield before taxes in order to provide the saver with the same net of tax return he would receive from lending at the market interest rate? This minimum pretax rate of return is called the cost of capital. It depends upon the asset and industry composition of the investment, the form of finance used for the project, and the saver who is providing the funds. For a given combination of these factors, we may express the relation between the cost of capital and the interest rate as

(2.5) $\qquad p = c(r).$

The cost of capital function, $c(r)$, depends upon the details of the tax code, and we derive explicit expressions below.

Condition (2.5) may be thought of in two ways. On the one hand, we may view it as an expression of capital market equilibrium that determines the marginal yield on real investment of different types, using different financial instruments that would be chosen by profit-maximizing firms in an economy with an interest rate r. In this case p is determined by r. On the other hand, we may think of (2.5) as indicating the maximum interest rate such that savers would be indifferent between lending at this rate and receiving the after-tax proceeds of a given type of project, financed in a particular way, yielding a pretax return of p. In this case, the causation runs from p to r. In our study we make use of both interpretations.

The relation between the market interest rate and the return to the saver depends on the tax treatment of personal income. In none of the four countries studied here is the personal tax base defined as real income from capital. Rather, tax is charged on receipt of nominal interest income. Hence the posttax real rate of return to the saver is given by

(2.6) $\qquad s = (1 - m)(r + \pi) - \pi - w_p ,$

where m is the marginal personal tax rate on interest income and w_p is the marginal personal tax rate on wealth. In the absence of taxes, $p = s = r$. Savers provide funds to companies, these sums are invested in physical assets, and the profits accruing on the project are then distributed either to bondholders in the form of interest or to stockholders in the form of dividends and share value appreciation. As a result, savers earn the same rate of return on their savings as companies earn on their investment. In practice, taxes drive a wedge between the return on investment and the return on savings, and this wedge can be measured by comparing equations (2.5) and (2.6).

Using this approach, we measure effective marginal tax rates for each of four countries. But even within a single country the tax rate varies from one project to another depending upon the asset and industry in which the funds are invested, the nature of the financial claims on the profits (equity versus debt), and the ultimate recipient of the capital income. To investigate the distribution of effective tax rates within each country, we consider a series of hypothetical projects, where each project corresponds to a particular combination of asset, industry, financial instrument, and owner. The first set of calculations is for the effective marginal tax rate on each project, where all projects are assumed to have the same pretax rate of return. We call this *the fixed-p case*. For each project we then compute the value of s, the real posttax return to savers the project could sustain, from equations (2.5) and (2.6). From the fixed value of p and the calculated value of s, we compute both the tax wedge w and the effective marginal tax rate t. To compare tax systems across countries, we use the same value for p in all countries, and in most of our calculations we take a value of 10 percent per annum. The relation between the assumed value of p and the tax rate is discussed further below.

Comparing the tax rates corresponding to a common value for p provides a picture of the incentives offered by the tax system for particular kinds of investment projects. In other words, the fixed-p calculations describe tax schedules facing different projects. But, in turn, we would expect that the effect of these varying tax rates would be to stimulate investment in low-taxed projects relative to more highly taxed investments. We would expect the allocation of capital among the various combinations to adjust until an equilibrium is established in which there exist no further opportunities for mutually profitable transactions. For a given individual saver, arbitrage would result in an equilibrium in which the same net rate of return was earned on each project. We might therefore calculate an effective tax rate for each combination for a common value for s rather than a common value for p. Arbitrage opportunities are limited, however, and in particular we do not think it reasonable to assume that differences in personal tax rates can be eliminated by arbitrage. This arbitrage might be possible for a husband and wife (in systems where spouses are taxed separately), but it is unlikely to occur between unrelated persons. I may love my neighbor, but not enough to transfer the legal ownership of my assets to his care. Moreover, a substantial fraction of capital income now accrues to tax-exempt institutions (such as pension funds), and if arbitrage could eliminate differences in personal tax rates, then the only possible equilibrium would be one in which all effective personal tax rates on capital income were zero. This does not seem to us to be a reasonable assumption.

In practice, governments impose limits on the flow of savings from households to institutions precisely to prevent full tax arbitrage. Hence, in a second set of calculations for this study we assume that arbitrage leads to an outcome in which all projects offer the same rate of return to savers before personal tax. In other words, we assume a common value of r for all combinations, and we call this *the fixed-r case*. For any given saver (that is, given values of personal income and wealth tax rates), this case implies that all projects yield the same value of s. But the value of s varies from one saver to another if they face different personal tax rates. It must be stressed that when arbitrage eliminates differences among projects in the real rate of interest there must be differences in the pretax rates of return on investment. Hence the tax system distorts the allocation of resources. The value of p in this case is *not* uniform across projects. Allowing for the possibility of arbitrage in the capital market equilibrium does not rule out inefficiencies in the allocation of resources.

With a linear tax schedule, that is, one in which the rate of tax is independent of the value of p (or, equivalently, r) at which it is evaluated, the tax rate on any given project will be the same in the fixed-p case as in the fixed-r case. Under a nonlinear schedule, as happens in practice, the size of the tax rate depends upon the value of p at which it is evaluated. If the value for r in the fixed-r case implies a value for p different from that assumed in the fixed-p calculations, then the two cases yield different values for the tax rate. This results solely from the nonlinearity of the tax schedule. More significant differences between the two measures arise when we examine a weighted average of hypothetical projects in order to assess the average marginal tax rate on investment in the corporate sector as a whole.

2.2   Combinations of Hypothetical Projects

For each hypothetical project we compute an effective marginal tax rate for both the "fixed-p" and the "fixed-r" cases. A hypothetical project is defined in terms of a particular combination of characteristics that affect the tax levied on the returns from the project. The characteristics we examine include the asset in which the funds are invested, the industry of the project, the way the project is financed, and the ultimate recipient or owner of the returns. Each hypothetical project is described by a unique combination of these four characteristics. For each characteristic we examine three alternatives. First, the three assets are

1. machinery
2. buildings
3. inventories.

The category for machinery includes plant and machinery, equipment, and vehicles. We shall not be concerned with investment in financial assets, research and development, or other intangibles such as a good managerial team, trade contacts, or advertising goodwill. The study is limited also to reproducible assets, so we ignore investment in land.

Second, our three industries are

1. manufacturing
2. other industry
3. commerce.

The precise definition of industrial sectors is as follows. Manufacturing forms a natural grouping and corresponds to the same description in standard industrial classifications (SIC). For the United States, standard industrial classification manufacturing comprises SIC numbers 13–64. The "other industry" group consists mainly of construction, transportation, communications, and utilities. It corresponds to SIC numbers 11, 12 and 65–68. The "commerce" sector includes nonfinancial services and distribution, which are SIC numbers 69 and 72–77. Those activities excluded are agriculture, extractive industries, real estate, government, and financial services.

Third, our three sources of finance are

1. debt
2. new share issues
3. retained earnings.

Debt is defined to include both bond issues and bank borrowing.

Finally, our three ownership categories are

1. households
2. tax-exempt institutions
3. insurance companies.

The first category includes indirect household ownership through taxed intermediaries such as mutual funds or banks. The second category includes indirect tax-exempt ownership through pension funds, the pension business of life insurance companies, and charities. The third category includes funds invested as part of contractual savings made by households via the medium of insurance companies, principally life insurance policies, which are not tax exempt but are taxed at special rates. Our choices for these categories of owner are motivated by their different tax treatment. Although personal tax rates clearly vary within the personal sector, the schedule is common to all households, and in the individual country chapters below we describe the distribution of personal marginal tax rates in the respective countries. More substantial differences exist in the tax-exempt status given to pension funds and charitable holdings. Although deemed "tax exempt," institutions in this category may end up paying some tax because of the asymmetric nature of the tax system. For example, both Britain and Germany have imputation credits as part of their corporate tax systems. In Britain the credit is refunded to tax-exempt stockholders, whereas in Germany the credit is not refunded. The effect of this difference is that tax-exempt institutions in Germany do effectively pay some personal tax on dividend income. Finally, insurance funds are often taxed in special ways, as described in country chapters below, and we take into account the tax treatment of premiums and distributions.

With three categories for each of four characteristics, the number of distinct combinations we identify is 3^4, a total of eighty-one for each country. In chapter 7 we compute the effective marginal tax rate for each combination as well as the distribution of tax rates. To plot the distribution of tax rates, we need to know the proportion of investment identified with any given combination. We assume that the marginal increase in investment under consideration is proportional to the existing distribution of net capital stocks among assets and industries. Further, we assume that the saving required to finance the investment is proportional to existing ownership patterns. It might be argued that a marginal investment would not be allocated in proportion to existing stocks and that not all ownership categories would provide the marginal finance. For example, the size of funds held by the tax-exempt category might be limited by legal ceilings on the sums households can invest in this favored manner. Such limits are usually related to income, however, and we prefer to consider a marginal increase in savings and investment that corresponds to an equiproportionate expansion of the economy. Additional savings are assumed to be made by all these ownership categories and are invested in proportion to existing net capital stocks. Marginal investment is assumed to be proportional to net capital stocks rather than gross investment flows because the former are representative of long-run asset requirements, while the latter are influenced by differing asset depreciation rates. Inventories, for example, form an important component of net capital stock, while they account for a very small share of gross investment. With steady growth, the use of net capital stocks is equivalent to the use of *net* investment flows for the allocation of our marginal investment.

This assumption about the nature of the marginal increment to savings and investment determines the weights we apply to each combination when we compute the distribution of marginal tax rates. The reader who wishes to make alternative assumptions about marginal savings or investment may use the basic data on effective tax rates for each of the eighty-one combinations to plot his own distribution. These data are provided in Appendix B.

The mean of the distribution provides an estimate of the overall marginal tax rate on the capital income generated from a small equiproportionate increase in the capital stock. Let k denote a particular combination of asset, industry, source of finance, and category of owner. Also, let α_k denote the capital stock weight for that combination $(\Sigma\alpha_k = 1)$. The mean tax wedge on the marginal capital income, $\bar{w}$, is

$$(2.7) \qquad \bar{w} = \sum_{k=1}^{81} (p_k - s_k)\alpha_k .$$

For the kth combination, p_k and s_k are the real rates of return on the investment and on savings, respectively. The additional capital income generated, $\bar{p}$, is given by

$$(2.8) \qquad \bar{p} = \sum_{k=1}^{81} p_k \alpha_k .$$

The overall mean marginal tax rate, $\bar{t}$, is

$$(2.9) \qquad \bar{t} = \frac{\bar{w}}{\bar{p}} \quad \frac{\displaystyle\sum_{k=1}^{81} (p_k - s_k)\,\alpha_k}{\displaystyle\sum p_k\alpha_k} .$$

In addition to the overall mean marginal tax rate, we calculate conditional means by summing over appropriate subsets of combinations. For example, we compute the mean marginal tax rate on investment in machinery by summing over all combinations that involve machinery and that correspond, therefore, to different industries, sources of finance, and owners. There are twenty-seven such combinations. The construction of the α_k weights is described in section 3 of each country chapter, while overall and conditional means of marginal tax rates are presented in section 4 of each country chapter. These tax rates are compared and analyzed in more detail in chapter 7.

The overall mean tax rate derived from these calculations is an aggregate statistic for the difference between the return to investment and the return to saving in the economy as a whole. In many ways, however, the distribution of marginal tax rates around the mean provides more information. The variance of this distribution reflects the distortion of the pattern of savings and investment created by the tax system. The variation in tax rates has further implications for our measure of the aggregate marginal tax rate itself. If the tax rate applicable to all combinations were the same, then the overall marginal tax rate would be equal to this common value, for both the fixed-p and the fixed-r cases. But when tax rates vary, the mean marginal tax rate will be different in the two cases. In the fixed-p case, where p_k is the same for all combinations, equation (2.9) reduces to

(2.10) $\bar{t} = \Sigma \alpha_k t_k$,

where t_k is the marginal tax rate for combination k. In the fixed-r case, the same equation reduces to

(2.11) $\bar{t} = \dfrac{\underset{k}{\Sigma} \alpha_k p_k t_k}{\underset{k}{\Sigma} \alpha_k p_k}$.

The mean marginal tax rate in the fixed-p case is a weighted average of the individual tax rates, where the weights are the capital stock weights for each combination. In the fixed-r case, the weights are the product of the capital stock proportions and the pretax rates of return for each combination. In order to produce the same value of r, the more heavily taxed combinations require a higher value of p, and therefore they receive a higher weight ($\alpha_k p_k$) in the fixed-r case. Hence the mean marginal tax rate will be higher in the fixed-r case than in the fixed-p case.

The difference between the two means reflects the variance in tax rates among different combinations. To illustrate this argument, consider a simple example. Suppose there are two possible combinations and the capital stock weights are one-half for each combination. Suppose, further, the tax rate on the first combination is zero and that on the second is 50 percent. Then in the fixed-p case,

$$\bar{t} = .5(0) + .5(.5) = \frac{1}{4}.$$

If there are no personal taxes, then $r = s$ from equation (2.6). In other words, assume that the difference in the tax rates comes solely from the corporate tax treatment of the two combinations. Since $t_k = (p_k - r)/p_k$ in the fixed-r case, we have

(2.12) $p_k = \dfrac{r}{1 - t_k}$.

Substituting this into (2.9) yields

(2.13) $\bar{t} = 1 - \left(\Sigma \dfrac{\alpha_k}{1 - t_k} \right)^{-1}$.

For our example, we then have

$$\bar{t} = 1 - (0.5 + 1.0)^{-1} = \frac{1}{3}.$$

The greater weight given to the more heavily taxed combination produces a mean marginal tax rate of one-third in the fixed-r case, compared with one-quarter in the fixed-p case. The difference between the two measures can be large when some combinations are taxed and other combinations receive subsidies. Returning to our example with two equally weighted combinations, suppose one combination is taxed at 50 percent and the other receives a subsidy of 50 percent. In the fixed-p case the mean tax rate is zero. But in the fixed-r case the mean is equal to one-quarter, from equation (2.13). The fixed-r case uses weights given by $\alpha_k p_k$, the additional pretax profits that result from the marginal increment to the capital stock. If both combinations are to earn the same r, then the taxed combination must have a higher share of the additional pretax profits than of the capital stock.

The choice between the fixed-p and the fixed-r distributions of marginal tax rates depends upon whether we are more interested in the tax schedule facing potential investors or in the proportion of marginal factor income that is taxed away. Both are of interest, and we present results for both distributions. The fixed-p calculations are a better guide to the schedule of tax rates levied on different combinations, and it is this distribution of marginal tax rates that determines the welfare losses resulting from the distortionary nature of the taxation of capital income. In contrast, the weighted averages in the fixed-r case are a better guide to the ratio of additional taxes paid to additional profits earned that results from a small increase in the corporate sector capital stock. If the tax schedule for each combination was linear, then the fixed-r weighted average tax rates would always exceed the fixed-p weighted averages. But in a nonlinear schedule it is possible (though it occurs only infrequently in our calculations) that the fixed-p tax rate exceeds the fixed-r tax rate for a given combination by enough to offset the fact that in the fixed-r case greater weight is given to combinations with high tax rates. Since our primary interest is in the effects of taxation on the incentive to invest, we focus mainly on the fixed-p results.

In recent years, the interaction between inflation and the tax system has been one of the most important aspects of the effect of taxes on savings and investment. The expected rate of inflation enters into both the determination of p in equation (2.5) and s in equation (2.6). We examine the effect of inflation in detail below, and we calculate effective tax rates for three different rates of inflation. First, a zero rate provides a benchmark against which to judge other figures, and it describes the impact the tax system would have if it were fully indexed. Second, we look at an inflation rate of 10 percent per annum, a midpoint in the historical experiences of our group of countries in the decade 1970–79. We hope it is not too optimistic to regard this rate as an upper bound on inflation for the next decade. This second rate enables us to compare tax systems across countries for a common, and significantly positive, rate of inflation. Finally, for each country we take the actual annual rate of inflation experienced in the decade 1970–79. This actual rate varied from 4.2 percent for Germany to 13.6 percent for Britain. The rate we take for each country is an average of the rates of increase of the price deflators for consumer goods and for investment goods in that country. Our interest is in the level of inflation, not in relative price changes, so we use a common inflation rate for all sectors of the economy.

2.3   The Cost of Capital Function

Given a value for p or, alternatively, given a value for r, we use equations (2.5) and (2.6) to compute a value for the effective tax rate. We therefore need an expression for the cost of capital function, $c(r)$, for each combination. In these expressions we shall assume that statutory tax rates are known and constant over time, that there is perfect certainty, and that inflation is uniform over time. Consider an investment project with an initial cost of one unit (a dollar, pound, mark, or crown). Let MRR denote the gross marginal rate of return to this increment to the capital stock, and assume that the asset depreciates at a constant exponential rate δ. The rate of return net of depreciation is

(2.14) $p = \text{MRR} - \delta$.

For convenience, we assume economic depreciation is exponential, but we distinguish carefully between economic depreciation and tax depreciation. The latter is not generally exponential (or, in discrete time, declining balance). For the moment we ignore corporate wealth taxes and the tax treatment of inventories. If the corporate tax rate is denoted by τ, and the rate at which the company discounts cash flows in nominal terms is denoted by ρ, then the present discounted value of the profits of the project, net of taxes, is[1]

$$V = \int_0^\infty (1 - \tau)\text{MRR} \; e^{-(\rho + \delta - \pi)u} \, du$$

(2.15) $$= \frac{(1 - \tau)\text{MRR}}{\rho + \delta - \pi}.$$

Nominal profits increase at the rate of inflation, fall in value at the rate of depreciation, and are discounted at the rate ρ. The value of the discount rate is endogenous and depends not only on the real interest rate

---

1. To ensure convergence of the integral, we assume that $\rho + \delta - \pi$ is strictly positive. In the fixed-r case, this assumption places restrictions on the feasible range of values for r. Still, for apparently plausible values for r, the restrictions are violated in a few instances. The reader is referred to the country chapters for details. When p tends to zero, then the tax wedge w is a much more informative guide than the tax rate t that has p as its denominator.

and the inflation rate, but also on the source of finance, as we shall see below. The cost of the project is unity, the initial payment for the asset, minus the present discounted value of any grants or tax allowances given for the asset. The present value of such grants and allowances we denote by A. Hence the cost of the project is

$$(2.16) \qquad C = 1 - A.$$

For any given discount rate, the value of MRR that equates V with C is the return the project must earn if it is to be an attractive investment. Looking at it the other way round, if MRR is a given return on a marginal project, then the net of tax interest rate the firm could afford to pay on the finance obtained to purchase the asset is the value of ρ that equates V with C. Setting V from equation (2.15) equal to C from (2.16) and using equation (2.14), we solve to obtain the following relation between p and ρ:

$$(2.17) \qquad p = \frac{(1 - A)}{(1 - \tau)}(\rho + \delta - \pi) - \delta.$$

To derive an expression for A, we assume that grants and allowances for investment take one of three forms. These are: (1) standard depreciation allowances; (2) immediate expensing or free depreciation; and (3) cash grants (equivalent to tax credits). The proportion of the cost of an asset that is entitled to "standard" depreciation allowances is denoted by f_1, and the present value of tax savings from standard depreciation allowances on a unit of investment is A_d. If f_2 denotes the proportion of the cost of the project qualifying for immediate expensing at the corporate rate τ, then the tax saving from this write-off is $f_2\tau$. Finally, suppose that the proportion qualifying for grants is denoted by f_3, and that the rate of grant is g. Then

$$(2.18) \qquad A = f_1 A_d + f_2\tau + f_3 g.$$

There is no need to restrict the sum of f_1, f_2, and f_3 to unity. At certain times it exceeds unity (for example, when accelerated depreciation does not reduce the base for standard depreciation allowances). Equation (2.18) is capable of describing the full range of tax allowances and investment incentives in the four countries studied here. The value of standard depreciation allowances will depend upon the pattern allowed for tax depreciation. Common examples are declining balance, straight line, and other schemes under which the firm may switch from one method of calculation to another partway through the asset's life. In each case the present discounted value may be computed from the parameters of the relevant legislation. Consider a simple example in which tax depreciation is granted at an exponential rate equal to a (this is the continuous-time version of declining-balance depreciation), and suppose that tax depreciation allowances are computed at historical cost. The value of standard depreciation allowances is given by

$$(2.19) \qquad A_d = \int_0^\infty \tau a \, e^{-(a+\rho)u} \, du = \frac{\tau a}{a + \rho}.$$

There are other assets (buildings in Germany and the United Kingdom, for example) for which the tax system usually provides straight-line depreciation. In this case a tax lifetime, L, is specified for each asset, and the asset may be written down for tax purposes by $1/L$ per unit in each year until L years have elapsed. With straight-line depreciation,

$$(2.20) \qquad A_d = \int_0^L \tau \left(\frac{1}{L}\right) e^{-\rho u} \, du = \frac{\tau(1 - e^{-\rho L})}{\rho L}.$$

There exist more complicated depreciation formulas such as the United States allowances for double declining balance with a switch to sum-of-the-years'-digits partway through the tax life of the asset. Where relevant, these formulas are described in section 2.3 of each country chapter. For computational purposes we simply note that the value of A_d is a nonlinear function of the firm's discount rate, which in turn is a function of the real interest rate.

We turn now to the effect of wealth taxes on corporations and to the tax treatment of inventories in periods of inflation (which itself is akin to a wealth tax). Consider first a tax on the net worth of the company such that an addition to the net capital stock of one unit raises the wealth tax base by a unit. If the rate of corporate wealth tax is w_c, then in the absence of a tax on corporate profits the wealth tax reduces the marginal rate of return from MRR to MRR $- w_c$. When there is a tax on profits at the rate τ, and the wealth tax is not deductible for corporation tax purposes, the net of tax return to the company is reduced to $(1 - \tau)\text{MRR} - w_c$. When the wealth tax is deductible from the corporate profits tax base, the posttax return is $(1 - \tau)(\text{MRR} - w_c)$. Equation (2.10) now becomes

$$V = \int_0^\infty [(1 - \tau)\text{MRR} - (1 - d_1\tau)w_c] \, e^{-(\rho + \delta - \pi)u} \, du$$

$$(2.21)$$

$$= \frac{[(1 - \tau)\text{MRR} - (1 - d_1\tau)w_c]}{\rho + \delta - \pi},$$

where $d_1 = 1$ if corporate wealth taxes are deductible against the corporate tax base, and
$= 0$ if wealth taxes are not deductible.

The remaining issue in the specification of the cost of capital function is the tax treatment of inventories in periods of inflation. During each accounting period, the book value of inventories changes for two reasons.

First, there may be an increase in the volume of inventories; second, there may be a rise in the price of inventories. In part, this latter component of the increase in book value reflects general inflation and would not be taxed under a corporate tax system based on real profits. But in some countries the use of historical cost accounting means that the inflationary gain on inventories is taxed as current profits when inventories are turned over. This realization of inventory profits for tax purposes can occur fairly soon if traditional FIFO (first in, first out) accounting is used, or it can be postponed almost indefinitely if LIFO (last in, first out) accounting is used. We assume that v denotes the proportion of inventories taxed on historical cost principles. Then a marginal investment of one unit of inventories, if there are no relative price changes, will incur an additional tax of $\tau v \pi$ per annum. This modifies equation (2.21), resulting in the general form

$$(2.22) \qquad V = \frac{[(1 - \tau)\mathrm{MRR} - (1 - d_1\tau)w_c - d_2\tau v\pi]}{\rho + \delta - \pi},$$

where d_2 equals unity for inventories and zero for other assets. We may summarize our discussion on the cost of capital by noting that if we combine equation (2.22) with the definition of p, then the relation between the pretax real rate of return on a project and the firm's discount rate is given by

$$(2.23) \qquad p = \frac{1}{(1 - \tau)}[(1 - A)(\rho + \delta - \pi)$$
$$+ (1 - d_1\tau)w_c + d_2\tau v\pi] - \delta.$$

It can easily be checked that, when there are no taxes, the values of both p and s as given by equations (2.23) and (2.6), respectively, are equal to the real interest rate.

The final step in our calculations is to relate the firm's discount rate to the market interest rate. With perfect certainty and no taxes, the two would be equal. In a world of distortionary taxes, however, the discount rate will differ from the market interest rate and, in general, will depend upon the source of finance. For debt finance, since nominal interest income is taxed and nominal interest payments are tax deductible, the rate at which firms will discount after-tax cash flows is the net of tax interest rate. In other words, for the case of debt finance,

$$(2.24) \qquad \rho = i(1 - \tau).$$

For the two other sources of finance, the discount rate depends upon both the personal tax system and the corporate tax system. We define the corporate tax system in terms of two tax variables. The first, defined above, is the basic corporate tax rate τ, the rate of tax paid if no profits are distributed. The second variable measures the degree of discrimination between retentions and distributions. The tax-discrimination variable is denoted by θ and is defined as the opportunity cost of retained earnings in terms of gross dividends forgone. Gross dividends are dividends before deduction of personal income tax. Hence θ equals the additional dividends shareholders could receive if one unit of post-corporate-tax earnings were distributed. For a detailed discussion of these issues, see King (1977, chap. 3).

Under a classical system[2] of corporation tax (such as that in the United States), no additional corporate tax is collected (or refunded) when dividends are paid out, so the value of θ is unity. With an imputation system (such as that in the United Kingdom), a tax credit is attached to dividends paid out, so the value of θ exceeds unity. From the definition of θ, we know that if one unit of profits is distributed, θ is received by shareholders as dividends and $(1 - \theta)$ is collected in tax. Hence the additional tax per unit of gross dividends is equal to $(1 - \theta)/\theta$. The total tax liability of the company—that is, total taxes excluding personal income tax on both dividends and interest and excluding any capital gains tax on retained earnings—is given by

$$(2.25) \qquad T = \tau Y + \left(\frac{1 - \theta}{\theta}\right) G,$$

where Y denotes taxable income and G denotes gross dividends paid by the company.

With an imputation system of corporation tax, part of the company's tax bill is imputed to the stockholders. If the rate of imputation is c, then the stockholder receives a dividend before personal tax equal to the cash dividend plus the tax credit of $c/(1 - c)$ per unit dividend. Hence, $(\theta - 1)$ equals the tax credit per unit, and $\theta = 1/(1 - c)$. When full imputation at the corporate tax rate is granted (such that dividends are fully deductible against profits for corporate tax purposes,[3] as in West Germany), then $\theta = 1/(1 - \tau)$.

Consider now the appropriate discount rate for the firm when financing investment by new share issues. Potential investors would require a rate of return on the money they subscribe to the company equal to $i(1 - m)$, where i is the nominal market interest rate. Suppose the project yields a return net of corporate income tax of ρ. Then this required yield (that is, the firm's discount rate) must be such as to equate the net of tax dividend yield with the investor's opportunity cost rate of return. The former is

2. Our taxonomy of corporate tax systems follows the convention established by the debate in the European Economic Community. For a full discussion, see King (1977, chap. 3).

3. A system where dividends are fully deductible at the corporate level and fully taxed at the personal level is equivalent to a system where tax is collected on all profits at the corporate level but is rebated to individuals on dividends received at the personal level. Recipients are taxable on gross dividends $\theta = 1/(1 - c)$, but they receive credit for $c/(1 - c)$, the amount paid at the corporate level on those profits.

equal to $(1 - m)\theta\rho$, and the latter is $(1 - m)i$. This means that for new share issues the firm's discount rate is given by

$$(2.26). \qquad \rho = \frac{i}{\theta}.$$

The use of retained earnings enables investors to accumulate at a rate of return that is taxed by capital gains tax rather than income tax. This is often attractive because the effective rates of capital gains tax are usually significantly lower than income tax rates. If the yield of a project is ρ, then the investor would require a yield such that $\rho(1 - z) = i(1 - m)$, where z is the effective tax rate on accrued capital gains. The discount rate for the retained earnings is, therefore, given by[4]

$$(2.27) \qquad \rho = i\left(\frac{1 - m}{1 - z}\right).$$

In practice, capital gains are taxed only on realization, and to allow for the benefit of this deferral of tax, we must convert the statutory rate, z_s, into an effective accrued tax (or EAT) rate. For this purpose we use a simple model of investor behavior. Let λ be the proportion of accumulated accrued gains realized by investors in a particular tax bracket in each period. That is, a capital gain of one unit accruing in period one will lead to a realized gain of λ in period one and an unrealized gain of $1 - \lambda$. In the second period realizations are equal to $\lambda(1 - \lambda)$. In the third period, realizations are $\lambda(1 - \lambda)^2$, and so on. If we assume that λ is constant, then the present discounted value of the stream of tax payments resulting from a unit of accrued gain is given by

$$(2.28) \qquad z = \lambda z_s \sum_{j=0}^{\infty} \left(\frac{1 - \lambda}{1 + \rho_p}\right)^j = \frac{\lambda z_s}{\lambda + \rho_p},$$

where ρ_p is the investor's nominal discount rate. In general, the investor's nominal discount rate is equal to $s + \pi$.

When computing marginal tax rates, we substitute the expression for z from (2.28) into equation (2.27). The EAT rate z is thus endogenous to the calculations, because of its dependence on the market interest rate. The tax treatment of capital gains is described in the appropriate sections

---

4. In practice, we often have data for the personal tax rate on dividend income that is different from the tax rate on interest income. This difference occurs because holders of equity are typically in higher tax brackets than holders of debt (and not because of different tax schedules for interest and dividends). A potential investor in equity, with a single personal tax rate m_e, would receive $(1 - m_e)\theta\rho$ on dividends, $(1 - z)\rho$ on retained earnings, or $(1 - m_e)i$ on alternative investments. Hence equations (2.26) and (2.27). His value for s is $i(1 - m_e) - \pi - w_p$, and we have enough information to find both p and s for any combination involving equity finance. A potential investor in debt, with personal tax rate m_d, would receive a net return $s = i(1 - m_d) - \pi - w_p$. The firm's discount rate for debt finance is $i(1 - \tau)$, from equation (2.25), and again we can calculate the difference between p and s.

of each country chapter. Except where capital gains are taxed as they accrue (as for insurance companies in Sweden), we take a value of 0.1 for λ. This value implies that corporate shares have a mean holding period of ten years (King 1977, chap. 3).

There is one further point to note concerning retained earnings. For this source of finance the cost of capital is a function of personal tax rates. The required rate of return on a hypothetical investment project depends upon the tax rate of the investor. Yet by their very nature, retained earnings cannot be attributed to only one group of stockholders (given the restrictions on the tax treatment of stock dividends), and so the cost of capital for a firm financing out of retained earnings must be the same for all stockholders. There are several ways out of this dilemma. One would be to consider a hypothetical project carried out by a firm owned entirely by a single investor whose tax rate would uniquely determine the cost of capital. Another would be to examine an equilibrium of the capital market in which high tax rate investors owned equity and low tax rate investors owned debt. A segmented equilibrium of this kind is sometimes known as a "Miller equilibrium" (Miller 1977; Auerbach and King 1983). Neither approach, however, is consistent with the fact that in all four countries both tax-exempt investors and individuals facing the highest marginal tax rates own corporate equity. A marginal project financed out of retained earnings will use funds attributable to all types of investors in proportion to their stockownership. Hence, we assume that for retained earnings the cost of capital is a weighted average of the values given by expression (2.27), where the weights are the shareownership proportions of the different investors.[5]

2.4   Computing Effective Tax Rates

The equations above enable us to calculate the tax wedge w and the marginal tax rate t for each combination. In the fixed-r case, we first

5. Further intuition for these equations is provided in section 7.4 (in the comparative results chapter), where we look at the simple case with economic depreciation allowances, no investment tax credits, no corporate wealth taxes, and no inflation. In this simple case, equation (7.2) shows that discount rates for debt, new shares, and retained earnings reduce to $r(1 - \tau)$, r, and $r(1 - m)$, respectively. Equation (7.6) shows that effective tax rates reduce to m for debt, $\tau + m(1 - \tau)$ for new shares, and τ for retained earnings. An interpretation for new share issues is that the investment earns corporate profits taxed at rate τ and that the after-tax profits $(1 - \tau)$ are distributed and taxed again at rate m. It is not necessary, however, to assume that the income is actually distributed. Rather, the dividend tax is relevant because it must be paid anytime profits are distributed. For retained earnings finance, on the other hand, the dividend tax is not relevant because it must ultimately be paid whether these funds are reinvested or not. (See Auerbach 1979; Bradford 1980; King 1977.) Finally, we might note that chapter 8 further discusses how the assumption of arbitrage at the personal level implies discount rates that differ by source of finance at the firm level. An alternative assumption of arbitrage at the firm level would imply rates of return that depend on source of finance at the personal level. These differences might be resolved in a model with uncertainty, but in this model they provide a further reason to emphasize the fixed-p case rather than the fixed-r case (which must choose a particular kind of arbitrage).

compute s from (2.6), and then the firm's discount rate from equations (2.24) through (2.28). With the resulting value of ρ, we compute p from (2.23). In the fixed-p case, however, the calculations are more complicated. Given a value for p, we solve (2.23) for the discount rate, but iteration is required because the discount rate enters the expression for depreciation allowances in a nonlinear fashion. For complicated depreciation schemes the function is highly nonlinear, but we have checked that our solution is unique in the feasible range. Then, given a discount rate, we solve for the market interest rate. (In the case of retained earnings, further iteration is required because the capital gains tax rate depends upon the interest rate.) Then we solve for the posttax real rate of return to savers, s.

The functional relationship between p and s is, in general, nonlinear. The values of the tax wedge and the tax rate thus depend upon the values of p and r at which they are evaluated. We investigate these relationships in chapter 7. For most of our tax rate calculations, we use a value of 10 percent per annum for p, or 5 percent per annum for r.

One of the important relationships we investigate is the effect of inflation on effective marginal tax rates. In the fixed-p case, we assume the same 10 percent value for p, the real pretax return, at all inflation rates. But in the fixed-r case we must be more careful. With an unindexed personal tax system, higher inflation generally widens the dispersion of effective tax rates. A tax-exempt investor remains tax exempt, but a taxed investor pays tax not only on the real return but on the inflation premium as well. This increased dispersion of effective tax rates is an inevitable consequence of the arbitrage mechanism underlying our fixed-r assumptions, in which all differences in posttax rates of return are arbitraged away, *except* for those resulting from differences in personal tax rates. With an unindexed personal tax system, therefore, an arbitrage equilibrium is characterized by the dispersion of effective tax rates being an increasing function of the inflation rate.

When comparing different projects at a given inflation rate in the fixed-r case, arbitrage requires a constant real rate of return r. This arbitrage argument is not relevant, however, when making ceteris paribus comparisons among different inflation rates. It would be possible to assume that r is fixed across inflation rates, but this real rate of return $(i - \pi)$ is relevant to tax-exempt investors only. Since nominal interest is taxed, other investors would experience a real after-tax return s that is a decreasing function of the inflation rate. Instead, as our benchmark, we choose to assume that the average value of s over *all* ownership groups is a constant across inflation rates. As a consequence, the value of r is held constant across projects at any one inflation rate, but it is not held constant across different inflation rates. (This assumption and its alternatives are further investigated in section 7.5.)

It is evident from (2.6) that if the average value of s over ownership groups is to be independent of the inflation rate, then the nominal interest rate implied by our fixed-r calculations must rise with each percentage point increase in inflation by a factor equal to unity divided by unity minus the average personal tax rate. We stress that this is not an assumption about how inflation actually affects nominal market interest rates. There has been a great deal of debate about the effect of inflation on interest rates, but our assumption is merely a ceteris paribus decision about the value of r at which to measure tax rates. While alternative assumptions are explored in chapter 7, the results for the fixed-r case in each country chapter are based on the benchmark described here.

It is clear from the equations above that the effective marginal tax rate depends upon the particular asset in which an investment is made, and upon the industry, source of finance, and category of owner. To obtain the solution to the system of equations for each combination, and to compute the weighted averages, it is necessary to resort to a computer program. Yet it is possible in simple cases to illustrate how the equations operate and to demonstrate that they accord with our intuition. To proceed, we consider two very special tax systems. Consider first a personal expenditure tax on all investors combined with a cash flow corporation tax in which all investment outlays are immediately expensed (with negative tax payments where required) and in which interest payments are not tax deductible. We know that this tax regime imposes no tax wedge between the return to savers and the return to investors (for example, King 1977, chap. 8). With a cash flow corporation tax and no interest deductibility, the firm's discount rate will be equal to the market interest rate for all sources of finance. With this regime of immediate expensing for all types of investment, then, $f_1 = f_3 = w_c = v = 0$. Also, f_2 equals unity, and hence $A = \tau$. The result is that the value for p in each combination is equal to the real market interest rate $(i - \pi)$. With a personal expenditure tax, $m = z = w_p = 0$, and hence $s = p$. Thus the tax wedge and the marginal tax rate are both equal to zero.

The other special case we consider is that of complete integration of the corporate income tax and personal income tax and indexation of the resulting integrated tax system. No corporate taxes as such are levied in this case, and the investors' discount rate becomes that of the firm. With an indexed tax system, this rate is equal to $(1 - m)r + \pi$. There are no wealth taxes and no taxation of inflationary gains on inventories. Tax allowances are given only for true economic depreciation at replacement cost. Hence $f_2 = f_3 = 0$, and f_1 equals unity, so $A_d = m\delta/(\delta + \rho - \pi)$. With this expression it is easy to see from equation (2.17) that $p = r$, the real market rate of interest.[6] It is also clear that $s = r(1 - m)$. Hence, for every

---

6. When $f_2 = f_3 = 0$, $f_1 = 1$, and $A_d = \dfrac{m\delta}{\delta + \rho - \pi}$, then (2.17) becomes

combination, the effective marginal tax rate is equal to the investor's personal tax rate.

In practice, as we shall see, the complex tax systems that all of our four countries levy on corporate income mean not only that the effective marginal tax rate differs from the standard of either an income tax or an expenditure tax, but that the tax rates vary enormously from one combination to another. One of the major aims of our study is to document this phenomenon empirically and to provide estimates of the magnitude of the effect and of the proportion of investment that is channeled through each of the combinations. These estimates enable us to compute a distribution of marginal tax rates.

We conclude this chapter by noting a number of detailed points concerning our methodology. First, we have omitted taxes on gifts and estates from our calculations. These taxes may well be important in particular instances where the principal motive for saving is to pass on wealth to succeeding generations. Much saving, however, is channeled through contractual schemes for life-cycle saving, and there are well-known opportunities for avoiding taxes on gifts and estates. In each country chapter we set out some relevant information concerning these taxes, but their rates are not incorporated into our calculations.

We assume that all relevant tax allowances can be claimed. We assume that firms engaging in our hypothetical investment projects have positive taxable profits or, equivalently, that the tax system is symmetric in that it makes refunds on losses at the same rate at which it taxes profits. In practice, there are firms with negative taxable profits that are unable to claim allowances. Tax losses can be carried forward, and in some cases backward, so the fact that taxable income is currently negative need not mean that the tax allowances are lost forever. However, in the cases of Britain and Sweden there are grounds for believing the problem cannot be overlooked. Simulations of marginal tax rates for companies that have exhausted tax allowances are contained in section 4 of those two country chapters. One of the main reasons for the rapid growth of leasing has been the wish of "tax-exhausted" firms to lease assets from companies

---

$$p = \left(\frac{1 - \dfrac{m\delta}{\delta + \rho - \pi}}{1 - \tau} \right) (\rho + \delta - \pi) - \delta$$

$$= \frac{\delta(1 - m) + \rho - \pi}{1 - \tau} - \delta.$$

In the integrated system, $\rho = (1 - m)r + \pi$ (see text) and $\tau = m$. In this case,

$$p = \frac{\delta(1 - m) + r(1 - m) + \pi - \pi}{1 - m} - \delta$$

$$= r.$$

with positive taxable profits who could claim the tax allowances. Where this is possible the effectiveness of tax allowances is not diminished.

We have made no explicit allowance for risk in our calculations, and the equations above assume perfect certainty. In itself this is not a significant assumption, in that the effect of risk is mainly to alter the required rate of return on an investment project. A project that is unusually risky will require a high rate of return, particularly if it has a high covariance with other projects, thus reducing its value as an investment hedge. These differences mean that the value of r we choose to use in the fixed-r calculations might differ for projects with varying degrees of risk. But we wish to evaluate the incentives provided by the tax system, and it seems sensible to use a common value of r (or p) for all projects. Risk might vary from one industry to another or one asset to another, and it is possible that our investor groups would have different degrees of risk aversion and would choose different portfolios accordingly. These considerations mean that we might wish to evaluate marginal tax rates at different values for the real rate of return required by savers, but they do not alter the principles underlying calculations of the magnitude of the wedge the tax system imposes between a given rate of return on a project and the rate of return that can be paid out to the supplier of finance.

The definition of tax-exempt institutions includes pension funds. The tax treatment of contributions to pension funds does indeed imply a zero marginal tax rate on capital income, provided the income tax rate against which contributions may be deducted is equal to the income tax rate at which ultimate pension benefits are taxed when paid out. In practice, individuals may have higher tax rates during their working life when making contributions than during retirement when receiving pension benefits. To the extent that tax rates fall after retirement, the effective tax on capital income from pension funds is negative rather than zero. Our calculations slightly overstate the true marginal tax rate on capital income in this case.

One difficult problem concerns the tax treatment of funds deposited by households (or institutions) in banks and then lent by banks to companies. This indirect form of debt finance, in contrast to direct purchase of corporate bonds, has been growing in recent years. We assume in our calculations that the banking system acts as a competitive financial intermediary and that, at the margin, it earns no monopoly profits on interest receipts. Hence the only taxes we assume are collected on interest receipts in connection with corporate borrowing from banks are personal taxes levied on investors' interest income. At this point we draw a distinction between time deposits and checking accounts. The former pay interest at market rates (except in the United States, where legal restrictions hold rates down; see chap. 6 for further discussion of the tax treatment in this case), and investors pay income tax on such interest income. For time deposits, we assume that interest payments are taxed at investors' marginal tax rates. But where funds lent to firms originate from an addition to checking accounts, then, in those countries where checking accounts do not pay interest, the income accrues to households in the form of tax-free banking services. On accounts of this type we assume that the effective personal tax rate is zero. We assume that a marginal investment financed by bank borrowing would come from the two types of accounts in proportion to their existing deposits, such that the average marginal personal tax rate on interest paid to banks is a weighted average of zero (for checking accounts) and the investor's marginal tax rate (for time deposits). A diagrammatic illustration of our assumptions concerning the tax treatment of debt finance is given in chapter 3, where this issue is first discussed with reference to a particular country. Refer to that discussion for an empirical analysis of the taxation of interest income.

Net trade credit is excluded from our definition of debt finance. This exclusion causes the magnitude of debt finance to be understated, particularly for the "other industry" sector in Sweden. The matter is discussed further in individual country chapters.

Finally, we have estimated rates of true economic depreciation for use in our calculations. In our exposition, it was convenient to assume that assets decayed exponentially, but in most countries national accounts estimates of depreciation and capital stocks employ the assumption of straight-line depreciation with lifetimes obtained from surveys or other sources. To exploit these sources of data concerning asset lives, we ask, What rate of exponential depreciation would give the same present discounted value of the depreciation stream as is implied by straight-line depreciation with an asset life of L years? If we discount at the real interest rate (we are measuring real flows here), then the answer to this question is the exponential rate δ given by

(2.29) $$\frac{\delta}{r+\delta} = \frac{1}{rL}(1 - e^{-rL}).$$

Rearranging this yields

(2.30) $$\delta = \frac{r(1 - e^{-rL})}{rL - (1 - e^{-rL})}.$$

Although the value of δ in equation (2.30) depends upon the real discount rate, a good approximation may be found in cases where the product of the real discount rate and the asset life is small. Formally, it is possible to show that[7]

(2.31) $$\lim_{r \to 0} (\delta) = \frac{2}{L}.$$

7. Applying L'Hôpital's rule twice.

Table 2.1   **Exchange Rates, End of 1980**
                       (units of row currency per unit of column currency)

	United States	United Kingdom	Sweden	Germany
United States	1.000	2.385	0.229	0.510
United Kingdom	0.419	1.000	0.096	0.214
Sweden	4.373	10.417	1.000	2.230
West Germany	1.959	4.680	0.448	1.000

Source: International Monetary Fund, *International Financial Statistics.*

We use the asset lives provided by national accounts data and convert to equivalent rates of true economic depreciation using equation (2.31).

2.5   Data Requirements

The data requirements for our study are as follows. First, we need a detailed description of the statutory tax rates embodied in the tax system and a detailed description of the parameters embodied in the rules that enter into the definition of the cost of capital equations. Given these data, we calculate effective marginal tax rates for all eighty-one combinations. Second, we need weights for the proportion of total net capital stock that can be identified with each combination. The construction of both kinds of data is described in detail in each country chapter. The first section of each chapter contains an introduction to the tax system and general background on its rules. The tax system itself is described in section 2. The capital stock weights are described in section 3. All data refer to the calendar year 1980, or to the nearest tax year if the fiscal year differs from the calendar year. To enable the reader to compare monetary values across countries, we show in table 2.1 the matrix of exchange rates ruling at the end of 1980. Our aim is to provide sufficient information about the methods employed and the data used in our computations so that other investigators may, first, repeat our calculations to confirm the results and, second, extend the coverage to earlier time periods and to a wider range of countries.

3   The United Kingdom

3.1   Introduction

Income tax was first introduced to Britain during the Napoleonic Wars, but it became a permanent feature of the tax system only in 1842. Although there has been an increase both in tax rates and in the number of taxpayers, much of the administrative structure of the system has remained unchanged. This superficial continuity, however, masks far-reaching changes in the economic effects of the tax system, especially since the Second World War. Many of these changes concern the taxation of income from capital.

A government with an overall parliamentary majority finds it easy to alter both the structure and the rates of tax. Most finance acts in recent years have contained significant innovations. Since the Second World War there have been four major reforms of corporation tax, the introduction and subsequent major overhaul of a capital gains tax, a reform of capital transfer taxation, and a rapid growth in tax-exempt saving via financial intermediaries (such as pension funds and life insurance companies). One of the principal motives for these changes was a desire to increase the incentives to save and invest, in an effort to raise the growth rate of industrial productivity. From a situation in which the tax system could be said to approximate a tax on economic income, Britain has moved over the past thirty years to a situation in which many types of investment attract 100 percent first-year allowances. There has been a gradual move from an income-based tax system to an expenditure-based tax system, albeit an uncoordinated change based on a series of ad hoc reforms.[1] Part of this shift resulted from attempts to adjust the tax system

1. There have been occasional hiccups, but these have usually proved temporary. The latest move away from an expenditure tax treatment is the change in stock relief (see section 3.2.3).

for the effects of inflation. In the decade 1970–79 the average annual rate of increase of the consumption goods deflator was 12.76 percent, and that for the investment goods deflator was 14.37 percent. The average of 13.57 percent was high in comparison with that of Britain's major competitors and led to concern about the effects of inflation on the taxation of corporate profits and investment income in general. At the corporate level, investment incentives were gradually extended, and a system of "stock relief" was introduced to remove the inflation-induced increase in inventory values from the tax base. The effects of inflation on personal investment income were ameliorated by an expansion of investment in tax-exempt forms, the introduction of government index-linked bonds, and (in 1982) the partial indexation of capital gains tax by an adjustment to the asset's acquisition cost.

Some of the other major changes in the postwar period include the introduction of value-added tax (replacing purchase tax) in 1973, the

Table 3.1   Sources of Tax Revenue, United Kingdom, 1960–79

Revenue Source	Share of Total Receipts (%)			Total Receipts (£ million)
	1960	1970	1979	1979
Taxes on personal incomes	27.8	31.1	31.3	20,169
Wages and salaries			25.2	16,251
Dividend, interest, trading income			3.9	2,535
Capital gains			0.6	413
Other			1.5	970
Taxes on corporate incomes	9.7	9.2	7.6	4,918
Social security contributions	12.6	13.9	17.3	11,169
By employers			10.4	6,666
By employees			6.6	4,237
By self-employed			0.4	266
Payroll taxes	0	4.4	4.4	2,853
Property taxes	15.2	12.5	12.2	7,849
Value-added tax[a]	7.3	6.5	10.3	6,617
Taxes on specific goods and services	25.6	19.9	14.9	9,601
Alcohol			3.7	2,638
Tobacco			3.8	2,474
Petroleum			4.3	2,777
Other			3.1	1,982
Miscellaneous taxes	1.9	2.5	1.9	1,214
Total receipts	100.0	100.0	100.0	64,390
Gross domestic product (£ million)	25,520	50,780	189,270	
Share of taxes in GDP (%)	28.15	35.85	34.02	

Source: Revenue Statistics of OECD Member Countries, 1965–1980 (Paris, 1981), table 59; International Monetary Fund, International Financial Statistics.
[a]For 1960 and 1970, purchase tax.

reduction in the higher rates of personal tax in 1979 such that the top rate of tax on earned income is now 60 percent, and the gradual reduction in the deductibility of interest payments. With few exceptions, the only interest payments that are tax deductible in the United Kingdom are payments on loans for business purposes or for the purchase or improvement of a principal residence. There is, in fact, a limit on the latter in that (in 1982) only interest on loans up to £25,000 was tax deductible, and this nominal limit had remained constant for a number of years. If the nominal limit remains constant, then the effective deduction of interest payments for home purchase will be further reduced. There is no taxation of imputed rental income of owner-occupied housing (schedule A taxation of imputed rental income was abolished in 1963), and so housing is one of the assets most favorably treated for tax purposes. It is therefore not surprising that most net personal saving has in recent years been channeled into owner-occupied housing, pension funds, and savings through life insurance companies.

The relative importance of different taxes in the United Kingdom in 1979 is shown in table 3.1. The share of total tax revenue in gross domestic product is 34 percent, a figure similar to the average for the OECD countries. Only a small proportion of total revenue is derived from taxes on income from capital, and there has been an increasing reliance on receipts from value-added tax and social security contributions, which brings the United Kingdom more into line with its Common Market partners. These aggregated figures, however, give little indication of the effective marginal tax rates on income from capital, and it is to the calculation of such rates that we now turn.

3.2 The Tax System

3.2.1 The Personal Income Tax

The principal characteristics of personal taxation in the United Kingdom are, first, the relatively small number of allowances against taxable income; second, the high initial tax rate (currently 30 percent); and, third, the broad band of income that is taxed at the basic rate of income tax. All taxpayers receive a personal allowance that is the amount of income they can receive free of tax. In fiscal years 1980–81 and 1981–82 this allowance was £1,375 per annum for the single taxpayer. All income beyond this amount is subject to tax. The first band of taxable income is taxed at the basic rate, and the band is so broad that most taxpayers face a marginal tax rate equal to the basic rate. In 1980–81 the first £11,250 of taxable income was taxed at this basic rate of 30 percent.

The degree of progression in marginal rates is shown in table 3.2, which sets out the tax rates and the bands of taxable earned income to which

Table 3.2   Rates of Income Tax 1980–81 and 1981–82

	Slice of Taxable Income (£)	Rate of Tax. (%)
Basic rate	1–11,250	30
Higher rates	11,251–13,250	40
	13,251–16,750	45
	16,751–22,250	50
	22,251–27,750	55
	27,751 upward	60

Source: Inland Revenue Statistics, 1981, table A.2.

they applied in the period 1980–82. The maximum marginal tax rate on earned income is 60 percent. Fewer than 5 percent of taxpayers pay tax at a marginal rate greater than the basic rate (in 1980/81 the proportion was 3.4 percent), so that for the vast majority of taxpayers the United Kingdom income tax approximates a "linear" tax system.

In addition to income tax, social security (National Insurance) contributions are levied on earned income. In 1980–81 the combined rate on employer and employee was 13.45 percent of pretax income. Since the social security system is not an insurance system in any genuine sense, these rates are equivalent to additional marginal tax rates on earned income. The effective marginal tax rate on labor costs, for someone paying tax at the basic rate, is (30 + 13.45) divided by labor costs. Since the employer's contribution of 9.2 percent is not taxable income to the employee, these total labor costs consist of pretax earnings of 100 and employer's contributions of 9.2. Thus the marginal rate is 39.8 percent. The contribution rates quoted are those for taxpayers contracted out of the State Earnings-Related Pension Scheme, who are in consequence in a private occupational pension scheme.

Investment income is subject to the same schedule of rates as earned income, although if investment income in total is greater than a certain value it is subject to additional rates of tax. In the period 1980–82, if net investment income exceeded £5,500, that excess was subject to an investment income surcharge at the rate of 15 percent. This means that the highest marginal tax rate on investment income was 75 percent. But this rate applied only to those persons with a total taxable income in excess of £27,750 and more than £5,500 of investment income.

Deductibility of interest payments is much more restrictive in the United Kingdom than is typically the case elsewhere (except for West Germany, as seen in chap. 5). There is therefore an asymmetry in the tax treatment of investment income in that receipts of interest and dividends are taxed whereas, in general, payments of interest on loans taken out to purchase securities are not deductible.

Capital gains are taxed at a special tax rate. The tax is levied only upon net realized gains (that is, realized gains less realized losses), and in 1980–82 the first £3,000 of such gains was not liable for tax. The remainder was taxed at 30 percent. In 1980 no allowance was made for inflation, but in 1982 a major change in capital gains tax took place in the wake of the availability of index-linked government securities to all investors (domestic and foreign investors, taxed and tax exempt alike). Capital gains tax was indexed by allowing the acquisition cost of an asset to be adjusted by the increase in the retail price index that occurred after the asset had been held for one year (or after April 1982 for assets purchased before April 1981). Hence, apart from inflation during the first year of ownership, the indexation for inflation is complete.[2] In addition, the threshold was raised such that the first £5,000 of gains in any one year is free of tax. Since capital gains are now defined in real terms, the rationale for such a high threshold is unclear. It had previously been defended as a substitute for indexation.[3] The revenues from capital gains tax are likely to become very small in the long run. More important, there is an unresolved issue as to how long the system will be able to function with one channel of rewards taxed on an indexed basis and other channels (such as interest income on debt) taxed on an unindexed basis.

The taxation of households has been subject to a good deal of debate, and the present system is unlikely to remain unchanged for long. The basic premise of the tax system is that a wife is a dependent of her husband. A wife's income is therefore added to her husband's to obtain their joint income, and the husband is liable for the resulting tax payment. In recognition of the husband's responsibility for his wife, he receives a married man's allowance (in 1981–82, £2,145 per annum), which has in the past been approximately 1.5 times the single person's allowance. In addition, if a wife receives earned income in her own right, then she receives a single person's allowance against that income. Consequently, a married couple receives a higher tax allowance than two single people living together. But if their joint income is high, the fact that the income is aggregated and may be subject to higher rates of tax means that the benefit of the additional allowance may be more than offset by the burden of the higher rates. To deal with this, the tax code permits a husband and wife to elect to be taxed separately on their earned income. In this case the earned income of each partner is taxed individually. The husband forgoes the married man's allowance and receives a single

2. The adjustment for inflation cannot, however, give rise to an allowable loss.
3. The present defense of the high threshold appears to be that it is a substitute for making indexation retrospective to 1965, when capital gains tax was introduced.

person's allowance instead. Investment income continues, however, to be taxed jointly, though not symmetrically, and a wife's investment income is added to the total income of her husband.

Debate about this system centers on two aspects. First, the married man's tax allowance affords generous tax treatment of two-earner couples. Second, the system is not symmetrical between husband and wife in the sense that the total tax liability of the household is a function of whether it is the husband or the wife who receives a particular amount of income.[4] Debate on both these points has been lively.[5] Although it is improbable that totally separate taxation of all income will be introduced, the likely outcome is the introduction of separate taxation of earned income with the phasing out of the married man's allowance, and a symmetrical treatment of aggregate investment income.

Since the introduction of child benefit (cash allowances for children), there have been no child tax allowances (apart from certain transitional arrangements and allowances for children living overseas). There is, however, a special allowance for the head of a one-parent family to ensure that such a person receives an allowance equal to that of a married man rather than that of a single person.

The degree of progression implied by the rate structure depends upon the pattern of average tax rates, whereas the disincentive to work is a function of the marginal tax rate.[6] Both average and marginal rates at different levels of earnings are shown in table 3.3. Part A of the table shows the tax rates for a married man receiving tax allowances of £2,000 (for mortgage interest payments) in addition to the married man's allowance in the period 1978–82. Each row shows the marginal and average tax rate for a constant level of money income throughout the period. More realistic perhaps is the comparison of tax rates on constant real income levels, and in part B of table 3.3 we show the tax rates on constant levels of money income at 1982 prices (but holding nominal mortgage interest constant). The table shows clearly the reduction in tax rates made by the incoming Conservative government in 1979 when the basic rate of income tax fell from 33 to 30 percent, and the top rate on earned income was reduced from 83 to 60 percent. But part B of the table shows also that average tax rates were higher in 1982 than before the 1979 budget for almost all earners, except those at the very top of the distribution, earning more than £30,000 per annum. Moreover, these figures include neither National Insurance contributions nor value-added tax, both of

---

4. This is because investment income, of either partner, is always aggregated with the earned income of the husband and hence taxed at a rate determined by the size of the husband's earnings rather than by the earnings of either the household or the higher earner.

5. The government's view of alternative schemes has been set out in a green paper, "The Taxation of Husband and Wife" (Cmnd. 8093, London: HMSO, 1980).

6. Strictly speaking, it is the pattern of marginal tax rates over the range of earnings opportunities that is relevant.

Table 3.3   **Income Tax Rates 1978–82**
(%)

A. Constant Money Incomes

Gross Income, All Earned (1982 £)	Marginal Tax Rate			Average Tax Rate		
	1978–79	1979–80	1980–82	1978–79	1979–80	1980–82
5,000	33	30	30	9.7	7.1	5.1
10,000	33	30	30	21.3	18.6	17.6
15,000	55	40	30	27.9	22.9	21.7
20,000	70	50	45	36.4	28.5	26.7
25,000	75	55	50	43.7	33.1	31.2
30,000	83	60	55	49.6	36.9	34.6
50,000	83	60	60	63.0	46.1	44.8
100,000	83	60	60	73.0	53.1	52.3

B. Constant Real Incomes

Gross Income (1982 £)	Marginal Tax Rate				Average Tax Rate			
	1978–79	1979–80	1980–81	1981–82	1978–79	1979–80	1980–81	1981–82
5,000	0	25	30	30	0	0.002	2.3	5.1
10,000	33	30	30	30	14.6	14.7	16.2	17.6
15,000	33	30	30	30	20.7	19.8	20.8	21.7
20,000	45	40	45	45	25.0	23.4	24.7	26.7
25,000	60	50	50	50	30.8	27.8	29.1	31.2
30,000	70	50	55	55	36.4	31.5	32.7	34.9
50,000	83	60	60	60	52.9	42.1	43.1	44.8
100,000	83	60	60	60	67.9	51.0	51.5	52.3

Source: Own calculations based on *Inland Revenue Statistics*, 1981, tables A.1 and A.2; *Economic Trends*, March 1982, p. 42.

Note: Tax rates are those applying to a married man with allowances of £2,000 plus the married man's allowance. In panel B the income level at 1982 prices was converted to a money income for each year by the general index of retail prices for the third quarter of the year (midpoint of the fiscal year). The actual tax schedule was then applied to the computed money income level.

which have risen since 1979 and both of which contribute to the tax
"wedge" between work and leisure. Marginal tax rates have, however,
fallen for individuals in the top two percentiles of the earnings distribution.

The degree of progression in the 1980–82 rate structure is illustrated
also in figure 3.1, which shows marginal and average tax rates for a
married man. The figure shows the effect of the broad basic rate band on
the average rate curve, the slope of which changes nonmonotonically as
income rises.[7] The effect of the rate structure may be illustrated also in
terms of the net income elasticity curve, which shows the percentage
increase in net income corresponding to a 1 percent increase in gross
(pretax) income for a married man at different earnings levels.

3.2.2   The Corporate Tax System

The United Kingdom provides an excellent case study for examining
the effects of different corporate taxes because of the frequent changes of
system since the war. In this respect the United Kingdom experience is
unique and may afford lessons for other countries.

The continuing debate on corporate taxation has been concerned with
three main issues. First, the relative taxation of dividends and capital
gains, and hence the incentives to use internal as opposed to external
finance, has been a matter on which successive governments have felt
sufficiently concerned to change the system of corporation tax. Since the
war, four different tax systems have been used. Second, the tax has
gradually been changed from one based on a measure of profits in the
direction of one based on cash flow. Concern about low levels of investment, particularly in manufacturing, has led successive governments to
increase tax allowances for capital investment in fixed assets. From a
position after the war in which tax allowances approximated "economic
depreciation," the United Kingdom has now arrived at a point where a
large proportion of investment qualifies for 100 percent first-year allowances. In addition, investment in particular "depressed" areas qualifies
for cash grants. Depreciation allowances and investment grants are discussed further in sections 3.2.3 and 3.2.4, respectively. Third, the inflationary experience in the 1970s raised questions about the appropriate
definition of the corporate tax base. By then the tax base had already
moved far enough from any concept of economic profits that the issue of
adjusting profits for inflation was confused with the desirability of moving
to a cash flow basis of corporation tax. Inflation causes particular problems for the taxation of inventory profits, and a temporary system of

---

7. The nonmonotonicity would be even more apparent were national insurance contributions included. Because of the ceiling on the level of earnings on which contributions
are paid, the marginal tax rate actually falls at a level of earnings below that on which the
higher rates of tax are charged.

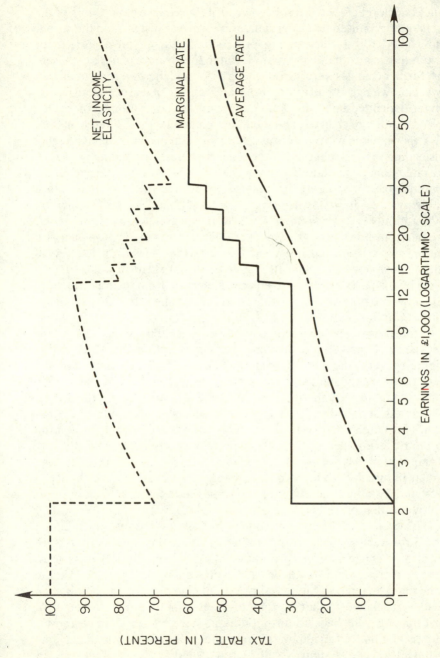

Fig. 3.1 Income tax structure in the United Kingdom, 1980–82: married man. From *Inland Revenue Statistics*, 1980, chart 1.5.

relief (stock relief) was introduced in 1974. Successive chancellors of the exchequer promised that a permanent reform was just around the corner and waited for the accounting profession to agree on a system for accounting in an inflationary period. But in the absence of a clear consensus, further changes were introduced in 1981, and the government implicitly acknowledged that the appropriate reform of corporation tax no longer depended upon the deliberations of the accounting profession.

The number of changes, and their size, mean that the United Kingdom has experimented with corporate taxation in so many ways that it is highly misleading to represent the effects of the corporate tax system by a single tax rate, namely the statutory rate of tax. We discuss below the economic consequences of some of the changes. Nor have the changes led to a stable system. In 1982 the government published a green paper on corporation tax (*Corporation tax* 1982), which set out a number of avenues for reform. The green paper drew attention to the problems with the present system, but it is clear that a further period of debate will precede any new legislation. It is likely that future reform will be undertaken by the party or parties to emerge victorious from the next election. The only safe prediction is that there will indeed be future legislation on corporation tax.

In the postwar period, four corporate tax systems have been tried. Between 1947 and 1958 a two-rate system was in force, in which undistributed profits were taxed at one rate of profits tax and distributed profits were taxed at a higher rate. The second system, in force between 1958 and 1965, abolished the differential element in profits taxation. Both distributed and undistributed profits were taxed at a single rate. In addition, shareholders were given credit for tax paid on dividends at the corporate level. In effect, this was an imputation system in which the rate of imputation was set equal to the basic rate of income tax. Although similar in principle to the two-rate system, the system in force between 1958 and 1965 had the effect of reducing the tax burden on dividends relative to that on retentions.

The advent of a Labour government in 1965 saw the introduction of a straightforward system of corporation tax. Under this system profits were taxed at a single rate of corporation tax, and the shareholders were charged income tax on dividends and capital gains tax (introduced at the same time) on realized capital gains. The change raised the tax burden on dividends relative to that on retentions. But in 1973 the Conservative government went back to an imputation system with a single rate of corporation tax and an imputation rate equal to the basic rate of personal income tax. This system is still in force, and since 1974 the rate of corporation tax has been constant at 52 percent. The rate of imputation is, in practice, kept equal to the basic rate of tax to reduce the number of taxpayers from whom additional tax on dividends must be sought and to whom refunds must be paid. Shareholders whose marginal tax rates are greater than the basic rate thus pay additional personal taxes on dividends, and shareholders whose personal tax rates are less than the basic rate receive refunds. The only shareholders for whom the marginal tax rates are less than the rate of imputation are those with a zero tax rate, and the bulk of these consist of pension funds and the pension business of life insurance companies. Such bodies receive regular and substantial refunds from the Inland Revenue under the imputation system. The principle of the system is that part of the corporate tax bill is regarded as income tax at the basic rate on distributions of dividends.

To prevent tax avoidance, companies must pay income tax at the basic rate to the Inland Revenue when dividends are distributed. Such payments are made in advance of the date when corporation tax would normally be paid, and since they are also part of the corporate tax bill, they are termed advance corporation tax (ACT). Since part of the corporate tax bill is effectively income tax at the basic rate on distributed profits, it makes sense to regard this part of company taxes as really personal taxation. This element, which is equivalent to advance corporation tax, would be paid as income tax even if corporation tax were abolished. Hence the total of company taxes minus ACT is usually termed "mainstream" corporation tax, and it is this figure that is equivalent to the revenues from corporate income tax under a classical system.

The imputation system provides credit to the shareholders for tax paid on their behalf by the company. But when companies have no tax liability it is necessary for the prevention of tax avoidance that imputation relief be withdrawn. This is now a serious problem in the United Kingdom because, in any year, approximately half of all companies have no mainstream corporate tax liability. This arises from the generous first-year allowances and the deductibility of nominal interest payments. To prevent tax avoidance, the Inland Revenue must collect "advance corporation tax" on dividends that, for companies with zero mainstream tax liabilities, cannot then be credited against payments of corporation tax (although the unrelieved ACT can be carried forward). This unrelieved ACT has been the subject of great concern, but the concern has been largely misplaced. The principle of imputation is that relief can be granted only for tax paid by the company. To do otherwise would create further possibilities for tax avoidance (for a detailed analysis see King 1977, chap. 4). The problem of unrelieved tax liabilities has nothing to do with ACT as such but concerns the result of an asymmetric tax system that taxes positive profits but does not provide refunds on tax losses. Of course such losses may be carried forward, but in the United Kingdom there are many companies with substantial cumulative losses that have no immediate prospect of seeing a positive taxable income. In the absence of full loss offset, unrelieved ACT will continue.[8] Even for companies that do not pay dividends (and hence do not pay ACT), unrelieved losses will be a serious problem. This is one of the practical problems that are likely to stimulate the demand for reform in the future. An imputation system is difficult to reconcile with a tax base under which many companies have no positive taxable income.

For small companies there are special lower rates of corporation tax, and special rates apply also to cooperative and building societies and to insurance companies. The taxation of insurance companies is discussed below in section 3.2.10. In 1980, small companies whose total profits were less than £80,000 were taxed at the lower rate of 40 percent. Since the floor for the full rate is low and the difference in rates is small, we shall take the basic statutory rate of 52 percent as the marginal tax rate on the corporate sector in 1980.

To illustrate the effects of the frequent changes in the corporate tax system, we present two series of tax rates in table 3.4. The first is the marginal tax rate on retained earnings (defined as τ in chap. 2), and the second is the opportunity cost of retained earnings in terms of gross dividends forgone (defined as θ in chap. 2). This latter variable relates to the relative tax burden on dividends and retained earnings. The table shows the values of these two variables over the period 1947–80. There has clearly been substantial variation in both rates during this time. The figures shown in the final row for 1980 are those used in our comparative study. As discussed in chapter 2, the value of θ is unity divided by unity minus the rate of imputation. In the United Kingdom, the rate of imputation has been set equal to the basic rate of income tax, and at a rate of 30 percent this implies a value for θ of $1/(1 - 0.3) = 1.429$.

3.2.3   Tax Allowances for Depreciation and Inventories

The effective rate of corporate taxation on investment income depends critically upon the depreciation allowances granted both on fixed investment and on investment in inventories. The United Kingdom system is complicated by the multiplicity of ways depreciation is treated. For many years depreciation allowances have been becoming more and more generous, and now 100 percent of all investment in plant, machinery, ships, and aircraft can be written off in the first year of purchase (immediate expensing). Industrial buildings received a first-year allowance of 50 percent in 1980 (increased to 75 percent in 1981), and in addition special cash grants are available for investment in the assisted regions for both

8. Unrelieved ACT could continue also for companies with substantial overseas income on which they were entitled to a credit for foreign tax paid. For companies that are not "tax exhausted" but pay gross dividends in excess of taxable profits, there is a further restriction on the amount of ACT that can be recovered.

Table 3.4   **Corporate Tax Rates, United Kingdom, 1947–80**

Year	τ	θ	Year	τ	θ
1947	0.50500	1.581	1965	0.40000	1.527
1948	0.50500	1.581	1966	0.40000	1.000
1949	0.50500	1.570	1967	0.41875	1.000
1950	0.52750	1.550	1968	0.44375	1.000
1951	0.52750	1.361	1969	0.43125	1.000
1952	0.51000	1.356	1970	0.40625	1.000
1953	0.51500	1.333	1971	0.40000	1.000
1954	0.45000	1.311	1972	0.40000	1.257
1955	0.45000	1.277	1973	0.49000	1.460
1956	0.45375	1.190	1974	0.52000	1.515
1957	0.45500	1.183	1975	0.52000	1.538
1958	0.47000	1.521	1976	0.52000	1.527
1959	0.48750	1.633	1977	0.52000	1.504
1960	0.50625	1.633	1978	0.52000	1.460
1961	0.53125	1.633	1979	0.52000	1.429
1962	0.53750	1.633	1980	0.52000	1.429
1963	0.53750	1.633			
1964	0.56250	1.667			

Source: Own calculations as described in the text.

machinery and industrial buildings. No depreciation allowances, however, are given for land and commercial buildings (except for hotels and commercial buildings in enterprise zones), because such assets are assumed to retain their value. The effect is that most investment by industrial companies qualifies either for immediate expensing or for greatly accelerated depreciation. When combined with the fact that nominal interest payments are deductible, this means that the treatment of such investment where it is debt financed is exceedingly generous.

In terms of the notation in chapter 2, for the asset machinery the value of f_2 equals unity and f_1 equals zero in all three industry groups. This is because machinery receives 100 percent first-year allowances and hence receives no annual depreciation allowances. In the case of buildings, as already noted, a distinction is made between industrial and commercial structures. Industrial buildings receive a first-year allowance at an accelerated rate, and the remaining amount is depreciated for tax purposes on a straight-line basis (currently 4 percent per annum). We assume, therefore, that for buildings in the manufacturing and other industrial sectors, the values for both f_1 and f_2 are 0.5. In the commercial sector we assume a value of zero for both parameters for all investments in buildings other than hotels. The latter receive an initial allowance of 20 percent, and 4 percent per annum write-down allowances on the remainder. Inland Revenue data suggest that 5 percent of new commercial buildings are new hotels. Hence we take f_1 to be 0.04 and f_2 to be 0.01 in commerce.

For most of the postwar period, inventories were taxed on a FIFO basis (first in, first out). Both accounting and tax systems were based on historical cost accounting principles. But the experience of rapid inflation in the late 1960s and throughout the 1970s led to increasing concern over the appropriate tax treatment of inventories. Over the decade 1970–79, as mentioned earlier, the average annual rate of increase of the consumption goods deflator was 12.8 percent, and that of the investment goods' deflator was 14.3 percent. This represents an inflation rate significantly higher than the rates for the other countries in our study. The government appointed an inflation accounting committee (the Sandilands Committee), which reported in 1975. This report led to a continuing debate in the accounting profession, and the government postponed permanent reform of the tax system in the hope that the accounting profession would come up with an agreed set of principles. Because the tax system is not based on profits anyway (one difference being accelerated depreciation for tax purposes), the relevance of a new accounting standard to the tax base is unclear. In 1974 some temporary relief for the tax burden on inventories was introduced. Significant changes to this temporary scheme were introduced in 1981, and these affected liabilities for the year 1980–81. Before 1980, companies were allowed to deduct for tax purposes the excess of the change in the book value of inventories over 15 percent of trading profits measured after depreciation allowances for tax purposes.[9] The increase in the book value of inventories in any one year consists of the inventory valuation adjustment (termed stock appreciation in the United Kingdom) plus the value of the net physical investment in inventories. The initial idea was to take the former component out of the tax base but to leave in the latter. Since no simple method could be introduced quickly for distinguishing between the two components, the temporary scheme merely gave relief for the whole of the increase in the book value beyond a figure that was thought to be a rough average of the value of physical investment in inventories for the economy as a whole. This figure was taken to be 15 percent of net trading profits. At the margin, however, the scheme not only offered relief for the effect of inflation, but also granted immediate expensing on the purchase of inventories. In this period it is appropriate to assume that inventories were taxed according to LIFO principles (last in, first out) and that the value of f_2 was equal to unity. The other depreciation rate variables are set to zero.

---

9. When stock relief was first introduced in 1974, the allowable deduction was the change in the book value of inventories less 10 percent of trading profits measured before tax depreciation allowances.

The scheme was modified in 1980 because immediate expensing of marginal purchases of inventories means that, when inventories are run down, the relief is "clawed back." The prospect of clawed-back relief threatened to reduce corporate cash flow when there was substantial disinvestment in inventories in 1980–81, and so the scheme was altered. Under the modified scheme no relief on physical increase in inventories was allowed as a tax deduction, and a method of restricting relief to the increase in book value resulting only from inflation was introduced. The rate of inflation used in these calculations is not an average rate of inflation but a rate relating to inventories themselves: companies must use an "all inventories index" the government has devised for the purpose. Relief is then calculated by multiplying the closing value of inventories at the end of the preceding year (less a small de minimus amount) by the proportionate increase in the index. As explained in chapter 2, our calculations assume a uniform inflation rate, and we ignore changes in relative prices. Given this assumption, the new scheme is equivalent to a system under which inventories are taxed on LIFO principles but in which the increase in the volume of inventories is no longer deductible. Hence the value of f_2 is zero. The tax treatment of inventories does not vary from one industry to another.

The above system of depreciation allowances for fixed assets and for inventories is supplemented by a system of cash grants for investment in particular regions. We discuss these schemes in section 3.2.5.

3.2.4   Estimates of Economic Depreciation

The extent to which the tax system acts as a deterrent or an incentive to investment depends to a large extent on the relation between tax allowances for depreciation and the true or "economic" rate of depreciation. The former were analyzed in section 3.2.3, and here we discuss the construction of estimates of economic depreciation for the different types of asset examined in this study.

In chapter 2 we assumed that assets depreciate at a constant exponential rate, denoted by δ, and showed that, if economic depreciation did in fact follow a different path, it could be approximated by an equivalent rate of exponential decay. For example, if economic depreciation is truly straight line (which means that an asset depreciates by a constant amount $1/L$ each year for L years), then the equivalent rate of exponential decay can be approximated by $2/L$ (see chap. 2). This result is useful because the United Kingdom national accounts assume straight-line depreciation when capital stock estimates are made. Given lifetimes for each asset, we can compute equivalent exponential rates of depreciation.

Since there exists the possibility of replacing parts of a machine and thereby modifying or improving its operation, the definition of the service life of an asset is not unambiguous. Nevertheless, assumed average service lives have been estimated in the United Kingdom for the purposes of the national accounts, although the source of these estimates is not always clear. Before the Second World War, the Inland Revenue occasionally surveyed businessmen and engineers to determine average service lives of capital goods. These estimates were used to construct a schedule of declining balance rates at which fixed assets could be depreciated for tax purposes (these are given in Board of Inland Revenue 1953). In his pioneering study of capital stock in the United Kingdom, Redfern (1955) used the Inland Revenue data, together with figures used for accounting purposes in some publicly owned industries, to compute capital consumption and the net capital stock. The Redfern estimates have become the basis of national accounts statistics, in part because of the absence of other studies and in part because of the irrelevance of tax allowances that now bear no relation to economic depreciation.

In the mid-1960s the Central Statistical Office reviewed the assumptions about asset lives using a range of miscellaneous data such as surveys conducted by trade associations and information provided by engineers and accountants (see Griffin 1975, 1976). The surprising feature of this review was that there appeared to have been no significant reduction in asset lives over the previous thirty years. This is an important finding because the asset lives assumed in the United Kingdom are undoubtedly longer than those used in the construction of national accounts in some other countries (see for example King and Mairesse 1982). One explanation is that the rate of growth of real labor costs in manufacturing has been much lower in the United Kingdom than in most of her competitors, and so the age at which it is optimal to scrap a machine is higher in the United Kingdom. In addition, as Griffin (1976) points out, "the United Kingdom has a reputation for making its machinery last."

To compute asset lives for the different assets and industries in our classification, we used data on asset lives for a large number of assets both in manufacturing (Griffin 1976) and in nonmanufacturing (supplied by the Central Statistical Office). For almost all buildings in every industry, the average lifetime is assumed to be eighty years. This implies that the equivalent annual rate of exponential decay is equal to $(2/80) = 0.025$. In the case of machinery, however, there are wide variations in the composition of investment among industries. Machinery is not a homogeneous quantity, and asset lives vary across industries. The importance of vehicles, which typically have shorter lives than fixed plant, varies from industry to industry, and within the category "vehicles" there are differences between trucks, ships, and aircraft. Lack of data on the composition of investment in vehicles led us to assume that all such investment had a life of ten years. This is too short for aircraft and ships, but much investment of this kind is in the public sector and so is excluded from our study. The assumed equivalent annual rate of exponential decay for vehicles is therefore equal to 0.20.

Table 3.5   Assumed Lifetimes of Machinery Excluding Vehicles

Life Length (L)	Depreciation Rate (2/L)	Share of Fixed Plant	
		Manufacturing	Commercial
5	.400	.047	0
16	.125	.018	.060
19	.105	.058	0
25	.080	.181	.540
34	.059	.503	.280
50	.040	.193	.120
		1.000	1.000

Weighted average depreciation rates
Manufacturing .079
Commerce   .072

Source: Own calculations, based on unpublished Central Statistical Office data.

Investment in machinery excluding vehicles is classified into any one of several lifetime categories. The proportion of net capital stock in both the manufacturing and the commercial sectors corresponding to each lifetime is shown in table 3.5. Column 2 shows the equivalent depreciation rates for each lifetime, and the average depreciation rate was computed by weighting the individual depreciation rates by their share in net capital stock.[10] The weighted averages are 0.079 for manufacturing and 0.072 for the commercial sector. Data were not available for "other industry," and we have assumed that the rate was the same as that for manufacturing. Finally, the rates for vehicles and for machinery excluding vehicles were averaged using their shares in net capital stock as weights. These are shown in the final column of table 3.6. The depreciation rate is much higher in the other industrial sector because of the relative importance of vehicles in this sector, particularly in construction.

The matrix of depreciation rates by asset and industry (see Appendix A) contains the estimates for machinery, our assumed values of 2.5 percent per annum for buildings, and an assumed rate of zero for inventories.

3.2.5 Investment Grants and Incentives

The experience with investment grants and incentives in postwar Britain has been one of continuous change and experimentation. Both the magnitude and the nature of incentives to investment have altered frequently, with use being made of cash grants as well as increasingly generous tax allowances. In particular, all investment in manufacturing, construction, and extractive industries qualified for investment grants

10. Note that it is the depreciation rates (2/L) that are averaged, not the asset lives.

Table 3.6   Depreciation Rates for Machinery Including Vehicles

| | Machinery | | Vehicles | | Total |
Sector	Share in Capital Stock	Depreci-ation Rate	Share in Capital Stock	Depreci-ation Rate	Average Depreciation Rate
Manufacturing	.976	.079	.024	.20	.0819
Other industry	.384	.079	.616	.20	.1535
Commerce	.913	.072	.087	.20	.0831

Source: Own calculations, based on unpublished Central Statistical Office data.

between 1966 and 1970, when grants ranging between 20 and 45 percent were available. In section 3.2.3 we described the current regime of tax allowances for investment, and here we focus on cash grants. At present most grants available in the United Kingdom arise from two types of help for industrial investment, regional assistance and national selective assistance. Grants are nontaxable receipts.

As its name implies, the purpose of regional assistance is to stimulate industrial investment in those areas suffering from high unemployment—the so-called depressed areas. Certain areas have been designated assisted areas (of which there are several categories), and regional assistance is provided only for fixed investment within the designated areas. The major form of this aid is given in the form of regional development grants, which amounted to £490.5 million in the financial year 1980–81. The designated assisted areas are classified into three categories: special development areas, development areas, and intermediate areas. In 1979 the incoming Conservative government announced a gradual reduction of the geographical size of these assisted areas (principally of the intermediate areas), although the scheme itself was maintained. In all assisted areas grants are made toward capital expenditure on new buildings that are used for "qualifying activities." In terms of our industrial classification, qualifying activities fall principally within the manufacturing sector, with the exception of construction, which is in the "other industrial" sector. In addition, in the special development areas and development areas, grants are awarded for capital expenditure on new machinery employed on the premises and used for the same "qualifying activities." Unlike other forms of assistance (regional or national), regional development grants are given at fixed statutory rates, the values of which are shown in table 3.7.

In addition to regional development grants, which are available automatically on qualifying expenditure, investment projects undertaken in assisted areas may be eligible for discretionary selective assistance under section 7 of the 1972 Industry Act. Similarly, on a national basis, invest-

Table 3.7   **Rates of Regional Development Grants**
                              (%)

		Rate of Grant	
Asset	Area	Before 31 July 1980	From 1 August 1980
Machinery	Special development area	22	22
Machinery	Development area	20	15
Machinery	Intermediate area	0	0
Buildings	Special development area	22	22
Buildings	Development area	20	15
Buildings	Intermediate area	20	0

Source: Department of Trade and Industry.

ment, wherever undertaken, may qualify for discretionary support under section 8 of the 1972 Industry Act. These discretionary grants are usually awarded at a rate of between 5 and 15 percent of the initial investment. During the year 1980–81, new assistance under section 7 amounted to £105.5 million, and that under section 8 amounted to £7.5 million. This total of £113 million is only 21 percent of the amount provided for regional development grants. Many of the selective assistance schemes have been eliminated since 1979, and actual payments over recent years have been higher than the figure for section 8 assistance shown above, reflecting the gradual withdrawal of the scheme.

A new scheme of enterprise zones, as yet very limited in scope, was introduced in the 1980 budget. The aim of the scheme is to offer a range of tax concessions to encourage businesses (particularly small businesses) to generate activity in derelict areas of the urban conurbations. Within these enterprise zones, companies are exempt from rates (property taxes) and receive 100 percent tax allowances for investment in buildings in addition to the allowances on machinery to which all companies are entitled. They are also exempt from the need to comply with a range of administrative procedures on planning, industrial training, and certain other matters. Because the amount of investment in such zones is still negligible in relation to total investment, we shall ignore these incentives in our calculations. It is also plausible that, given the size of enterprise zones, the incentives are capitalized into land values and hence rents. But the idea of enterprise zones has attracted interest in the light of concern with inner-city problems, and the success of the scheme will be watched closely in coming years.

Grants and subsidized loans for particular investment projects are also available from a variety of other sources, including the EEC and government agencies such as the National Enterprise Board, the British Steel

Corporation (Industry), Ltd., and a range of Scottish, Welsh, and Northern Irish government bodies. The approach taken here is, however, to make a conservative assumption about the grants firms expect would be forthcoming on additional investment projects. We shall ignore *all* discretionary grants and analyze only grants paid at fixed statutory rates on well-defined activities. Only regional development grants satisfy these conditions. This means we shall be understating the magnitude of investment grants that would, in practice, be paid out and hence overstating the effective marginal tax rate on capital income. But regional development grants are far and away the most important and dependable form of assistance to investment provided through channels other than the tax system.

Using the notation of chapter 2, therefore, f_3 is equal to the proportion of investment made in the assisted areas, and g is equal to the average rate of regional development grant. For the commercial sector, the value of f_3 is zero for all three assets. None of the qualifying activity is contained in this sector. (Note that the value of g is irrelevant when f_3 equals zero.) No grants are paid on investment in inventories, which leaves industrial investment in both machinery and buildings.

For manufacturing and other industrial companies, data are available on the amount of grant paid, classified according to qualifying activity, by area and by asset. This information, together with the rates of grant shown in table 3.7, allow us to make an estimate of the average rate of grant and the amount of investment within the assisted areas for each asset. These data were obtained from the annual reports of the Industry Act of 1972. For each asset in each industry, the grants paid were grossed up by the statutory rate of grant to obtain an estimate of total qualifying investment expenditure. The statutory rates were taken to be a simple average of the figures in the two columns of table 3.7, because the date when the rates changed was roughly halfway through the financial year 1980–81, to which the figures on grant payments refer. These statutory rates were then weighted by the investment shares in the different areas to obtain an average rate of grant for each asset. It was not possible to do this separately for manufacturing and for other industrial groups, and the distribution of qualifying investment by type of area was assumed to be the same for the two sectors. The resulting estimates of the effective rates of regional development grant are 19.46 percent for machinery and 14.76 percent for buildings. To obtain the proportions of investment expenditures that were eligible for the grant, we computed the ratio of total qualifying investment expenditure to the value of investment as a whole (from the national accounts) in each asset and industry. These calculations are shown in table 3.8. The values of f_3 and g used in later calculations are shown in table 3.9.

Table 3.8   **Investment Eligible for Regional Development Grants, 1980**
(£ million)

	Machinery	Buildings
Eligible investment		
Manufacturing	1,826.8	873.5
Other industry	12.00	8.5
Total investment		
Manufacturing	5,659.0	1,064.0
Other industry	3,385.0	1,157.0
Proportion eligible (f_3)		
Manufacturing	0.323	0.821
Other industry	0.004	0.007

Source: Own calculations based on "Annual Report of the Industry Act, 1972, for the year ended 31 March 1981," HMSO, July 1981 (appendix 2, table 1). *National Income and Expenditure*, 1981, tables 6.3 and 10.8.

Table 3.9   **Investment Grant Parameters**

Sector	Machinery	Buildings	Inventories
A. Rate of Grant			
Manufacturing	.1946	.1476	0
Other industry	.1946	.1476	0
Commerce	0	0	0
B. Proportion of Investment Receiving Grant			
Manufacturing	.323	.821	0
Other industry	.004	.007	0
Commerce	0	0	0

Source: Own calculations as described in the text.

3.2.6   Local Taxes

The only local tax in the United Kingdom is called "rates." Rates are levied by local authorities on "immovable property," which, apart from very small amounts of immovable plant, consists of buildings. They differ from conventional property taxes in that they are a tax on the benefit of occupation and can be avoided by leaving a building empty.[11] The reform of the rating system attracts perennial interest, and there have been frequent discussions about the implications of moving to alternative sources of revenue for local authorities, such as a local income tax.

11. The picture is a little more complicated in that local authorities have discretion to levy a rate on unoccupied property (after six months of nonoccupation for a new building and three months for a building previously occupied). About half of local authorities take advantage of this discretion.

The basis of rates is the "net annual value" of the property, which is intended to be the amount for which the property might be let if the tenant was responsible for all repairs. A single rate of tax is then set that applies to all property within a particular local authority. It is a strictly proportional tax, so that the marginal tax rate is equal to the average rate. There are two difficulties in estimating the average tax rate for the nation. First, the tax rate varies from one local authority to another, and there is almost no information on the distribution of capital stock by asset and industry among authorities. Second, the basis of the tax is not current market values, because the ratable value of a property is revised only periodically, and the last revaluation was in 1973.[12]

The method used to estimate the average marginal tax rate was to divide the yield of total nondomestic rates by the net stock of buildings valued at current replacement cost in the private industrial and commercial sectors. In 1980–81 commercial and industrial rates were £3,408.6 million (figure supplied by the Chartered Institute of Public Finance and Accountancy). The value of private net capital stock in buildings other than dwellings at the end of 1980 was £138.4 billion (table 11.11 of *National Income and Expenditure*, 1981). This gives an average corporate wealth tax rate on buildings of 2.46 percent. We shall assume that the tax rate was the same in the corporate as in the unincorporated sector, and that the buildings of all three of our industrial sectors were identically distributed among the various local authorities, so that the rate of tax may be assumed to be the same for each industry.

The economic effects of rates on a marginal investment project are assumed to be equal to that of a tax on corporate wealth held in the form of buildings. This makes no assumption about the incidence of the tax, but it does ignore any additional benefits the companies might receive by way of publicly provided services such as sewerage or new roads. The rates of corporate wealth tax assumed in our study are therefore equal to 2.46 percent for wealth in the form of buildings and zero for wealth in machinery and inventories.

3.2.7   Wealth Taxes

There are no personal wealth taxes in the United Kingdom, and the value of the wealth tax parameter, w_p, is therefore equal to zero for all three ownership groups. Furthermore, apart from local authority rates (discussed in the previous section), there are no corporate wealth taxes.

The distinction between taxes on income and taxes on capital is not clear-cut. Our study, however, does not require such a distinction provided all of the appropriate taxes are taken into account in our computa-

---

12. In contrast to the United States, though, revaluations have always been synchronized and made on a consistent basis.

tions. Since our formulas include taxes on capital gains, taxes on investment income (including the inflationary component), and taxes on wealth, this objective is attained. The only tax omitted is that on transfers of wealth, in the form of either taxes on inheritances or taxes on gifts.

The taxation of transfers was reformed in Britain in 1975 with the introduction of capital transfer tax. One important change was made at this time, namely the extension of the taxation of estates to cover inter vivos gifts. Before 1975 lifetime gifts were not taxed, but to prevent gifts made "in contemplation of death" from avoiding tax altogether it was necessary to include gifts made just before death in the taxable estate. Before it was replaced, estate duty included gifts made within seven years of death in the tax base, albeit on a sliding scale. Since then a number of concessions have been introduced, and lifetime gifts are now taxed at much lower rates than transfers on death. For most of the rate bands, lifetime transfers are taxed at one-half the rate applying to transfers on death, except at the highest levels, where the maximum rates are 50 percent for lifetime transfers and 75 percent for estates. But these high marginal rates are reached only on transfers of more than £2.5 million, and this takes no account of the substantial concessions that exist for particular types of asset. These concessions are largely for small businesses and agricultural property. The net effect of these changes in legislation since 1975 has been to render capital transfer tax as ineffective a tax as the estate duty it replaced. The revenue has been falling in real terms, and changes between 1979 and 1982 will lead to further reduction. For further discussion of capital transfer taxation in the United Kingdom, see Kay and King (1983) and Sutherland (1981).

3.2.8   Household Tax Rates

In this section we describe the calculations of marginal tax rates on both dividend and interest income and also on capital gains received by the personal sector. Investment income is liable to income tax at the basic and higher rates, and also to an investment income surcharge on income over a certain amount (see section 3.2.1). Capital gains are liable to capital gains tax.

To compute average marginal tax rates in the household sector, it was necessary to examine income tax and investment income surcharge separately. To calculate the average marginal income tax rate on investment income, we need a distribution of both dividend and interest income by taxable income. Then, given the tax schedule, we can compute the distribution of marginal tax rates. The available data, however, provide a distribution of dividend and interest income only by "total net income" rather than by taxable, or assessed, income. Total income is income less certain deductions for tax purposes but before allowable interest deductions, life insurance premium relief, and personal allowances. Hence we require a correspondence between levels of total income and levels of assessed income.

To construct this correspondence, we assume that the ranking of individuals by total net income is the same as by assessed income. Observations on the two distributions may be obtained from *Inland Revenue Statistics*, which provides the distribution of taxpayers by assessed income and by total net income. The aim of the exercise is to find the level of total income that corresponds to each tax threshold level. In this way the distribution of investment income can be reclassified as a distribution by bands of taxable income. In each band there is a unique marginal tax rate, and the distribution provides weights from which we may calculate the average marginal tax rate.

To construct the correspondence between the two distributions, we need a continuous distribution, and we follow the assumption of Orhnial and Foldes (1975) and King (1977, Appendix A) that income is distributed according to a Pareto distribution. Thus, if the logarithm of income is plotted against the logarithm of total number of people with incomes in excess of each level of income, the result is approximately a straight line. We obtained two separate straight lines—one for the distribution of assessed income and the other for the distribution of total income. Together these lines enable us to read off the level of total net income that corresponds to any given level of assessed income. In turn, this enables us to express the tax thresholds for each band in terms of total net income, and we further assume that all persons who fell below the threshold for the higher rates of tax were liable to tax at the basic rate. It is unlikely that a substantial proportion of investment income accrued to people whose total taxable income was below the personal allowance, but to the extent that such income existed we have slightly overestimated the marginal tax rates applicable to personal sector receipts of dividend and interest income. The average marginal tax rates on dividend and interest income were calculated as the weighted average of the marginal tax rates, with weights given by the proportions of dividend and interest income, respectively, accruing to recipients in each tax bracket.

Data on the distributions were obtained from *Inland Revenue Statistics* for 1980 and the *Survey of Personal Incomes* for 1977/78. A distribution for dividend income is given, but the distribution for interest income we used was that for "investment income taxed at source other than dividend income and building society interest." This category of income includes not only interest income from corporate securities but also interest from government bonds. But there is no alternative source of data to enable us to obtain a distribution of interest income from the corporate sector alone. The latest year for which data on the relevant distributions were available was the tax year 1977–78.

Using the method above, the estimated average marginal tax rate on dividend income was 48.6 percent. To obtain the values for later years, we assumed that the real distribution of dividend and interest income remained unchanged. The distribution for 1977–78 was increased in money terms by the percentage increase in total dividend payments in each year, and, using the relevant tax schedules, we computed a new distribution of marginal tax rates for subsequent tax years. In the tax year 1980–81, we obtained estimates of 39.0 percent for the average marginal income tax rate on dividend income and 38.2 percent for that on interest income. These are clearly substantially below the values for 1977–78, and the reason is the reduction in the top income tax rate and the increase in thresholds for the higher rates of tax introduced in the 1979 Conservative budget.

The next step is the computation of effective rates of investment income surcharge. There are no reported distributions of dividend or interest income by range of investment income surcharge. We computed the effective marginal rates indirectly by calculating the average marginal rate of surcharge on total investment income and using this as the appropriate rate. Data are available on the distribution of total investment income, and also on the amount of investment income surcharge paid on it, by total net income. These may be converted into distributions by assessed income rather than total income using the method described above. In addition, *Inland Revenue Statistics* provides the number of taxpayers liable to each of the different rates of surcharge classified by assessed income. Using this information, along with knowledge of the rate schedule, it is possible to compute the average marginal rate of investment income surcharge for each of the assessed income brackets. From these rates an overall average marginal rate may be computed as follows. Let the investment income surcharge schedule be parameterized by the most general form used in practice:

Range of Net Investment Income, Lower Limit £	*Rate of Surcharge (%)*
0	t_1
R_1	t_2
R_3	t_3

Note that t_1 is typically zero, and let

n_1 = the number of income tax payers liable to a marginal rate of t_1
n_2 = the number of income tax payers liable to a marginal rate of t_2
n_3 = the number of income tax payers liable to a marginal rate of t_3
SC = total amount of surcharge paid

I_1 = the amount of total investment income received by persons taxed at a marginal rate of t_1

I_2 = the amount of total investment income received by persons taxed at a marginal rate of t_2

I_3 = the amount of total investment income received by persons taxed at a marginal rate of t_3,

with $I = I_1 + I_2 + I_3$.

Now the average marginal rate of surcharge, m_a, is:

$$m_a = \frac{I_1 t_1 + I_2 t_2 + I_3 t_3}{I}.$$

Also:

$$SC = I_1 t_1 + R_1 n_2 t_1 + (I_2 - R_1 n_2)t_2 + R_1 n_3 t_1 + (R_2 - R_1)n_3 t_2 + (I_3 - R_2 n_3)t_3.$$

Therefore, in terms of observable variables,

$$m_a = \{SC - [R_1 n_2 + R_1 n_3]t_1 - [(R_2 - R_1)n_3 - R_1 n_2]t_2 + R_2 n_3 t_3\}/I.$$

The final calculation is to allow for the fact that the distribution of dividend (or interest) income by assessed income will not, in general, be the same as that for total investment income. We have made some adjustment for this by computing the average marginal rate of surcharge for dividend and interest income as a weighted average of the average marginal rates of surcharge on total investment income for each of the assessed income brackets. The weights used in this calculation were those for the distributions of dividend and interest income by assessed income, respectively, described above. Applying this method to the 1977–78 observations, the average marginal rate of investment income surcharge on dividend income was calculated as 9.29 percent and that on interest income as 8.74 percent.

Since this method of calculation is specific to the particular investment income surcharge schedule, it does not lend itself conveniently to extrapolation of effective marginal surcharge rates for the subsequent years in which the schedule was different. This makes it difficult to estimate the 1980–81 marginal tax rates with any great accuracy. The major change was that the 1979–80 schedule was different from those in previous years. The changes between 1977–78 and 1978–79 and again between 1979–80 and 1980–81 were small in real terms. Given the reduction in the number of investment income surcharge payers (*Inland Revenue Statistics*, 1980), we estimated the effective average marginal rates of surcharge in 1980 as 6.0 percent on dividend income and 5.5 percent on interest income.

The total average marginal rate of income tax applicable to dividends is the average marginal income tax rate of 39.0 percent plus the average marginal rate of investment income surcharge of 6.0 percent. Together these give a total marginal tax rate of 45.0 percent. The average marginal tax rate on debt interest income is equal to 38.2 percent plus 5.5 percent, which equals 43.7 percent. These figures are, in total, about twelve percentage points below their respective values for 1977–78, before the reductions in the 1979 budget. This estimate for the absolute reduction in the effective tax rate on investment income is marked, and it contributes substantially to the change in effective marginal tax rates on capital income between the early 1970s and the early 1980s.

The Inland Revenue kindly performed for us some calculations with their tax model and obtained a similar result, with a fall of twelve percentage points in the marginal income tax rates on dividends between 1977–78 and 1979–80. The figures from the Inland Revenue tax model were some five or six percentage points higher in each year than our estimates. Part of this difference may arise from a different treatment of the investment income surcharge, and so in section 3.4 we examine the sensitivity of our results to the difference in estimated marginal tax rates. In any event, it is comforting that the results concerning the fall in the marginal tax rate in recent years are similar. In the results of section 3.4 we shall use the figures 45.0 percent and 43.7 percent as the standard values for the effective marginal tax rates of the household sector on dividend and interest income, respectively. Part of the interest income of households is received from banks, and the appropriate tax treatment of this income is discussed in section 3.3.5 below.

The final task in this section is to compute the average marginal rate of capital gains tax for the tax year 1980–81. We first calculate the nominal tax rate, then convert it to an effective rate of tax on accrued capital gains. Computation of the nominal rate was made using a distribution of realized gains on corporate securities by a range of total net realized gains (as given in *Inland Revenue Statistics*, 1980).

Using this distribution, we may compute the average marginal capital gains tax rate by knowledge of the rate schedule. Again, however, the latest data are for the tax year 1977–78, and we assume that the real distribution of gains remained unchanged between 1977 and 1980. The money values of total net realized gains were adjusted by the change in the "all share index" (*Financial Statistics*). This produced an average rate of capital gains tax of 28.32 percent, very close to the maximum rate of 30 percent.

The second step is to convert this nominal rate into an effective accrued tax rate (EAT rate). We employ the simple model of investor behavior described in chapter 2, which is used in our model to calculate endogenously the ratio of the effective to the statutory rate. The model makes the assumption that a constant proportion of accrued gains will be realized in each year and that the expected nominal rate of capital gains tax is stationary. We use a value of 0.1 for the proportion of accrued gains realized in each year (see King 1977 for an empirical justification of this assumption). To illustrate the calculations, suppose that the discount rate is equal to the observed 13.68 percent gross redemption yield on long-dated government securities during the tax year 1980–81. Then, using the formula for the EAT rate of chapter 2, we obtain an effective accrued tax rate of 13.6 percent. In the results presented in section 3.4, the interest rate used to compute the effective accrued rate is endogenous and depends upon the particular combination being analyzed.

3.2.9   Tax-Exempt Institutions

One of the most significant developments in the taxation of capital income since the Second World War has been the extraordinarily rapid growth of the asset holdings of tax-exempt institutions. In large part this represents the growth of pension funds and the pension business of life insurance companies. From relatively small beginnings in the postwar period, these funds now account for a substantial proportion of total corporate securities, and this change is documented in detail in section 3.3.4. In addition to pension funds, the tax-exempt group of institutions includes charities and nonprofit bodies. The size of such bodies has remained fairly stable and hence has been declining as a proportion of the tax-exempt group.

The comparative advantage of investment via the medium of tax-exempt institutions depends upon the extent to which households are allowed to channel their private savings into such forms and upon the tax burden imposed on the income accruing to directly invested personal savings. The Inland Revenue has tried to limit tax concessions for private savings to schemes associated with contractual savings through either pensions or life insurance policies. But a great deal of complex anti-avoidance legislation has proved necessary to deal with "bogus" life insurance policies involving only a very tenuous connection with insurance against loss of life. Changes in the personal tax system have altered the relative advantage of tax-exempt institutions, and just as important has been the change in the effective tax rate on capital income levied on the personal sector by an unindexed tax system. The consequences of this will be seen clearly in the results of section 3.4.

One of the main aims of this comparative exercise is to estimate the effective marginal tax rates on capital income. Although the tax-exempt ownership group might appear by definition to pay a zero tax rate, we shall see that this is far from true. The effective tax rate on capital income depends upon taxes collected at all stages, and the interaction between the corporate and the personal tax systems means that, although the tax-exempt group may pay no tax at one particular stage, the overall effective tax rate may be either positive or negative. In particular, high personal tax rates in times of inflation have raised the pretax rate of return to levels such that tax-exempt owners received, in practice, a substantial subsidy on capital income.

3.2.10   Insurance Companies

The third category of owner analyzed in our study is insurance companies. Insurance business is divided into three categories for tax purposes: nonlife "ordinary" insurance business, life insurance business, and pension business. Nonlife insurance business income is taxed as ordinary corporate income. Pension business is, as we have seen, tax exempt. Life insurance business is taxed in a special way that distinguishes it both from pension business and also from direct personal ownership by households. In sections 3.3.4 and 3.3.5 we attempt to separate the pension and life insurance components of insurance company holdings.

When a life insurance company purchases shares or other securities of unit value for its policyholders, the effective acquisition cost to the policyholder is only $1 - \epsilon$, because tax relief is granted to the individual on premiums paid to life insurance companies at rate ϵ. The value of ϵ has varied from year to year and has usually borne a stable relation to the basic rate of income tax. In recent years it has been 50 percent of the basic income tax rate. The 1981–82 figure was $\epsilon = 0.15$. Although relief is granted on policyholders' premiums only provided the premiums do not exceed a certain proportion of income, we shall ignore this restriction. It is unlikely to be binding on many investors, because of the additional possibilities of tax-exempt contributions to pension funds.

When the income on the initial investment accrues to the insurance fund it is taxed at a special rate, which for some time has remained at 37.5 percent. But on dividend income no corporate tax is paid, and the effective tax rate is simply the basic rate of income tax deducted at source by the company paying the dividend. We shall denote this special rate of tax on life business by τ_I. Hence, if the fund earns a posttax return of $1 - \tau_I$ on its initial investment, this is equivalent to a posttax return of $(1 - \epsilon)(1 - \tau_e)$ on the policyholder's investment, where τ_e is the *effective* tax rate on the capital income accruing to the policyholder. This implies that

$$(1 - \epsilon)(1 - \tau_e) = 1 - \tau_I.$$

Therefore,

$$\tau_e = \frac{\tau_I - \epsilon}{1 - \epsilon}.$$

The equation above defines the effective tax rate on capital income obtained through the medium of a life insurance policy in terms of the statutory corporate tax rate on insurance companies and the rate at which premiums may be deducted against tax by policyholders. Given the relevant values for τ_I of 37.5 percent on interest income and 30 percent on dividends, and given the value of 0.15 for ϵ, the effective tax rates for ownership by life insurance companies are 26.47 percent on interest and 17.65 percent on dividend income. We shall use these values for the tax rates of the ownership group "insurance companies."

The effective capital gains tax rate is derived in exactly the same way, with the one difference that capital gains are taxed at the rate of 30 percent rather than the special corporate tax rate applicable to insurance companies. Hence the effective nominal tax rate on the capital gains obtained through life insurance companies is given by the formula above with τ_I set equal to 0.3. This gives a nominal tax rate of 17.65 percent, which is the same as that applying to dividends.

3.3   The Structure of the Capital Stock and Its Ownership

3.3.1   Data Limitations

The data described in the previous section may be used to compute the effective tax rates on income from capital for any given combination of asset, industry, source of finance, and category of owner. These give eighty-one different tax rates. Although the distribution of tax rates is interesting in itself and will be described in detail in section 3.4, we shall also compute weighted average marginal tax rates. To do this we need weights for the relative importance of the different combinations. We shall now describe the construction of the weights.

In the ideal outcome it would be possible to estimate individual weights for all eighty-one combinations. Unfortunately, however, the cross-tabulations required for this are not available. In section 3.3.2 we describe the construction of a matrix of proportions of capital stock tabulated by asset and industry for the nonfinancial corporate sector. Although we can obtain a classification of capital stock by asset and industry, it is not possible to allocate these across sources of finance and categories of owner. The data on sources of finance (see section 3.3.3) refer to the whole nonfinancial corporate sector, and we have not tried to impute a particular source of finance to a particular type of investment. Similarly, although we can produce a cross-tabulation by category of owner and source of finance (distinguishing between the ownership of debt and equity), we are unable to obtain a classification of ownership by industry or asset. Nevertheless, the weights constructed below provide a broadly accurate picture of the relative importance of the different combinations in terms of the proportions of the capital stock for which they account.

3.3.2 Capital Stock Weights

In calculating weights for each of the routes by which savings may be channeled into investment, the first step is to compute weights for the net capital stock in different assets and industries. The aim is to produce a cross-tabulation of net capital stock by industry and asset.

Estimates of the capital stock are made by the Central Statistical Office using the perpetual inventory method (for a fuller description see Griffin 1975). Depreciation is assumed to occur on a straight-line basis, and, as discussed in section 3.2.4, the assumed asset lives have changed very little since Redfern's (1955) study. For all manufacturing industries, for example, buildings are assumed to have a life of eighty years, and most types of machinery are assumed to have a lifetime of twenty-five years or more. In table 3.10 we show the breakdown of net capital stock valued at current replacement cost by four asset types (buildings, equipment, vehicles, and inventories) classified by three industrial groups (manufacturing, other industry, and distributive trades and other services, which here includes financial institutions). Figures for the financial sector are shown separately because these are used below to make an adjustment for leased assets.

Several difficulties arise in using the basic data in a way compatible with the aims of our study. The most important concerns the treatment of leased assets. These assets are typically purchased by financial institutions but used by manufacturing and other industrial firms. The principal motive for leasing is to enable the lessor to claim tax allowances on purchased assets (which, as we have seen, are generous in the United Kingdom) that manufacturing companies might not have been able to claim because of an insufficient level of taxable profits. Figures given in *National Income and Expenditure*, 1981 (p. 131), show that the total volume of investment leased in 1980 was £2.8 billion. Unfortunately these data cover leasing of buildings by property companies and do not provide

Table 3.10   **Corporate Capital Stock in United Kingdom, End 1980**
(£ billion)

Sector	Buildings	Machinery	Vehicles, Ships, and Aircraft	Book Value of Inventories
Manufacturing	45.1	73.3	2.9	35.5
Other industry	5.7	5.6	18.1	1.3
Distributive trades and				
other services	52.4	23.2	7.2	15.9
Financial institutions	15.7	7.0	2.2	0.001

Source: Unpublished data provided by the Central Statistical Office; *National Income and Expenditure*, 1981, table 12.4.

sufficient information to enable us to make an accurate reallocation of leased assets from sector of ownership to sector of use. We have therefore used the following approximation in order to allocate investment to the sector in which it is used.

From table 3.10 we see that about 30 percent of the net capital stock of the sector "distributive trades and other services" is owned by the financial sector. Some of these assets are leased to nonfinancial companies, and others are used as inputs to the production of financial services (machinery and buildings of banks and financial institutions). The discussion in *National Income and Expenditure*, 1981, which covers leasing activity in connection with the purchase of machinery and vehicles, suggests that in total 2 percent of the net capital stock of these assets in the manufacturing sector is leased from other sectors. The original capital stock figures were then adjusted by adding 2 percentage points to the net capital stock of the manufacturing sector as a whole and allocating this addition only to the category machinery. The capital stock of our commercial sector was assumed to be 70 percent of the assets of the "distributive trades and other services" sector, except for inventories where a figure of 100 percent was imputed to the commercial sector because the holdings of inventories by financial institutions are negligible. Table 3.11 shows the adjusted figures for the net capital stocks and the corresponding weights for the share of each asset in each sector.

Of the nonfinancial corporate sector capital stock, slightly less than half is invested in machinery, one-third in buildings, and one-fifth in inventories. The relative magnitudes for different assets vary according to industry, with machinery being more important for the manufacturing sector

Table 3.11   Net Capital Stock at Current Replacement Cost, United Kingdom, End 1980

	Asset			
Sector	Machinery	Buildings	Inventories	Total
A. Levels (£ billion)				
Manufacturing	78.6	45.1	35.5	159.2
Other industry	23.7	5.7	1.3	30.7
Commerce	21.2	36.7	15.9	73.8
Total	123.5	87.5	52.7	263.7
B. Percentage Shares				
Manufacturing	29.8	17.1	13.5	60.4
Other industry	9.0	2.2	0.5	11.7
Commerce	8.0	13.9	6.0	27.9
Total	46.8	33.2	20.0	100.0

Source: Own calculations based on table 3.1 and unpublished data provided by the Central Statistical Office.

and buildings for the commercial sector. The figures above refer to the corporate sector, and in table 3.12 we show the division of the national capital stock among the corporate, personal, and public sectors. In total, the corporate sector accounts for only just over one-third of the capital stock, with the remainder accounted for by dwellings (both privately and publicly owned), nationalized industries, public administration and services, and the unincorporated business sector. But the corporate sector accounts for most of the "business" assets, such as machinery and inventories, as shown in part B of table 3.12.

3.3.3   Sources of Financial Capital

For British corporations there are three important sources of funds by which savings may be channeled from the household to the corporate sectors: retained earnings, new share issues, and borrowing. Other sources of finance do exist (principally import and other credit and overseas capital issues), but 89 percent of corporate finance is raised from these three major sources. In what follows, we shall focus on these three sources.

Our aim is to estimate weights for the marginal contribution of the three sources to the financing of new investment projects. By its nature, all we can observe are historical average weights for sources of finance. If it were true that firms attempted to maintain some long-run debt-to-equity ratio in their capital structure, then we could estimate it from data

Table 3.12   **National Capital Stock, United Kingdom, End 1980**
(£ billion)

A. Net Fixed Assets at Current Replacement Cost

By Sector		By Asset	
Personal	174.7	Vehicles, ships, and aircraft	39.2
Corporate	252.7	Machinery	168.1
Nationalized industries	127.9	Dwellings	232.3
Central and local government	189.6	Other buildings	305.3
Total	744.9	Total	744.9

B. Cross-Tabulations

Machinery		Inventories at Book Value	
Personal	8.3	Personal	7.8
Corporate	105.7	Corporate	54.7
Nationalized industries	48.5	Nationalized industries	4.7
Central and local government	5.6	Government	1.7
Total	168.1	Total	68.9

Source: National Income and Expenditure, 1981, tables 11.11 and 12.4.

on the market values of debt and equity outstanding. We shall assume that the marginal investment projects relevant to our study would be financed in the same proportions as the average capital structure of the corporate sector. The market value of debt, defined as the market value of debentures and loan stock plus net short-term borrowing (bank advances less liquid assets), is shown in columns 1–3 of table 3.13. The table reports also the market value of common and preferred equity outstanding, and the implied debt/equity ratio. At the end of 1980 the debt/equity ratio for industrial and commercial companies was 0.263, and the implied share of debt in the total capital structure was 0.208.

Equity finance may be obtained from retained earnings or by the issue of new shares to equity holders. Table 3.14 shows the relative importance of retentions and new share issues over the period 1975–80. During this period, new share issues accounted for 5.43 percent of total equity finance. This is consistent with the broad historical trends documented in King (1977). By combining the information on the corporate sector debt/equity ratio and the split of equity finance between internal and external sources, the shares of the different sources of finance may be computed. These are shown in table 3.15. They are average figures for the period 1975–80 and show that the weights are 0.193 for debt, 0.763 for retentions, and 0.044 for new share issues.

The assumption that the average and marginal debt/equity ratios are equal may be examined in the light of tables 3.13 and 3.14. The share of debt issues and borrowing in the total sources of funds of nonfinancial companies averaged 26.8 percent during the period 1975–80. This figure is only slightly higher than the figure for the average debt/equity ratio shown in the capital structure of the nonfinancial corporate sector in table 3.13.

The one significant trend, which is shown clearly in table 3.14, is that there has been a marked shift from long-term debt finance to short- and medium-run bank borrowing during the 1970s. In fact, between 1973 and 1980 bond redemptions exceeded new issues in five of the eight years, and in the remaining three years only very small net amounts were raised. The collapse of the corporate bond market was partly the result of uncertainty about future inflation, and hence interest rates, which made companies reluctant to enter into long-term fixed-interest contracts, and partly the result of the authorities' discouragement of attempts to issue index-linked securities. Now that the public sector is itself issuing index-linked securities, and given that capital gains tax has been indexed, it is possible that new forms of corporate borrowing will appear. But in the recent past, variable interest rate borrowing from banks has seemed attractive. This shift has had important consequences for the ownership of corporate debt and, in particular, for the effective taxation of capital income, as we shall see in section 3.3.5.

Table 3.13   **Capital Structure of Nonfinancial Companies, 1975–80**
(£ million)

Year	Market Value of Debenture and Loan Stock (1)	Net Bank Borrowing (2)	Net Debt (3) = (1) + (2)	Market Value of Equity		Equity (6) = (4) + (5)	Debt/ Equity Ratio (7) = (3)/(6)
				Ordinary (4)	Preference (5)		
1975	5,113	7,196	12,309	43,709	451	44,160	0.279
1976	5,280	8,705	13,985	41,708	547	42,255	0.331
1977	6,927	8,213	15,140	66,511	767	67,278	0.225
1978	6,562	8,722	15,284	87,539	736	88,275	0.173
1979	6,273	12,260	18,533	109,626	781	110,407	0.168
1980	6,324	14,538	20,862	78,576	815	79,391	0.263

Source: Unpublished data provided by the Bank of England.
Note: The average debt/equity ratio in 1975–80 was 0.240.

Table 3.14   Sources of Funds of Nonfinancial Companies, 1975–80
                                (£ million)

Year	Undis-tributed Profits (1)	New Equity Issues (2)	Debt (3)	Loans and Bank Borrowing (4)	Total (5)
1975	9,057	1,003	202	3,211	13,473
1976	12,563	785	42	4,872	18,262
1977	15,064	730	−67	4,958	20,685
1978	16,777	829	−71	4,747	22,282
1979	20,406	906	−22	6,859	28,149
1980	15,781	897	423	9,549	26,650

Source: Financial Statistics, October 1981, table 9.2.

Table 3.15   Sources of Corporate Finance
                    (%)

Debt	19.3
Retentions	76.3
New share issues	4.4
Total	100.0

Source: Tables 3.4 and 3.5.

3.3.4 The Ownership of Equity

Given data on the distribution of tax rates by category of owner and on the relative shares of the different sources of finance, the final set of information we require is the distribution of source of finance by category of owner. In this section we examine the ownership of equity, and in section 3.3.5 we examine the ownership of debt. In neither case was it possible to obtain information on ownership separately for each industry group, and so we assumed that the ownership of debt and equity by type of owner was the same for each of our three industry groups.

Statistics on ownership of corporate equity have been collected in various surveys of company registers for the years 1957, 1963, 1969, and 1975 (see *Economic Trends*, September 1977, for a discussion of these surveys). The major problem encountered in examining shareownership is the need to distinguish between registered nominee and beneficial ownership. There are institutions such as banks and nominee companies that hold securities purely as intermediaries. The surveys attempted as far as possible to trace back all nominee holdings to their ultimate beneficial owners, and it is for this reason that the results of such surveys are unique. Other sources of information on United Kingdom ownership suffer from the problem of nonallocation of nominee holdings. The size of nominee

Table 3.16   **Beneficial Share Ownership, United Kingdom, 1957–75**
(%)

Category of Owner	1957	1963	1969	1975
Persons	79.44	71.09	65.95	54.02
Tax-exempt institutions	5.89	9.64	12.64	21.63
Insurance companies	9.78	11.34	13.90	18.01
Overseas	4.89	7.94	7.52	6.34
Total	100.00	100.00	100.00	100.00

Source: Own calculations based on *Economic Trends*, September 1977, p. 100.

Note: Columns may not sum to total shown because of rounding errors. Tax-exempt institutions comprise mainly pension funds but also include charities and nonprofit bodies. Persons include unit and investment trusts. The proportions owned by "other" groups (banks, corporations, and the public sector), about 10 percent of the total, were ignored in calculating the figures in this table. The surveys refer to ownership on 31 December each year except for 1957, when the date is 1 July.

holdings is by no means negligible. In 1975 individuals owned 32 percent of total registered equity holdings, but their beneficial ownership was 38 percent (*Economic Trends*, September 1977). There has been no study imputing nominee holdings to their beneficial owners since 1975. Table 3.16 summarizes the existing information on shareownership in the United Kingdom based on the four postwar surveys. It reveals marked trends in shareownership. There has been a sharp decline in the fraction of equity owned by the household sector, with a corresponding increase in holdings by tax-exempt institutions and life insurance companies. The proportion of equity held by pension funds has increased dramatically—it rose by more than 150 percent between 1963 and 1975.

To construct beneficial shareownership weights for 1980, we extrapolated from 1975. The first assumption was that the fraction of equity held by overseas investors remained constant at 6.5 percent.[13] For two of our three ownership categories—life insurance companies and pension funds—information on the total market value of ordinary shareholdings is available for the period 1975–80. These figures are shown in table 3.17 together with the total market value of outstanding equity of industrial and commercial companies. From this table we see that the total market value of equity rose by 123 percent during 1975–80, while that of pension funds increased by no less than 265 percent and that of life insurance companies by 138 percent. These figures imply that the ownership share of pension funds in total equity rose by 63.6 percent between 1975 and 1980, and that the ownership share of life insurance companies rose by 6.6 percent. Because the total funds of life insurance companies comprise two components, life insurance and pension business, that are taxed in

13. At the time of writing, no data on foreign ownership of United Kingdom equity after 1975 was available. A stock exchange survey was due to be completed in early 1983.

Table 3.17   **Market Value of Equity Holdings**
                                       (£ million)

Year	Total Market Value of Nonfinancial Corporate Equity	Value of Equity Held by Pension Funds	Value of Equity Held by Life Insurance Companies		
			Total	Life Insurance	Pension Business
1975	51,912	6,515	5,962	4,550	1,412
1976	49,594	7,455	5,740	4,382	1,358
1977	77,429	11,310	8,930	6,815	2,115
1978	105,469	15,622	9,835	7,506	2,329
1979	142,557	17,436	10,593	8,084	2,509
1980	115,894	23,800	14,206	10,841	3,365

Source: Unpublished data provided by the Bank of England, with reallocation for share of life insurance holdings (9/38) attributable to pension business.

different ways, it is important to distinguish between them. Although such a division is necessary for the tax liability of an insurance company to be computed, no statistics are published on the relative sizes of life insurance and pension business of insurance companies. This failing was criticized by the Wilson Committee (1980), which produced its own estimates of the division (pp. 532 and 579) and suggested that pension business accounted for £9 billion of the total assets of life insurance companies out of £38 billion at the end of 1978. We use this figure to reallocate a proportion of insurance company assets from our ownership group "insurance companies" to the group "tax-exempt institutions." The two components of life insurance company equity holdings are shown in table 3.17.

The figures above enable us to compute new values for the shareownership weights at the end of 1980, and these are reported in table 3.18. Adjusting for the assumed constant share of overseas owners yields the share of the personal sector as a residual. Because we are interested in the shares of total equity owned by domestic investors, we recompute the shares excluding holdings by overseas investors, and the final set of shareownership weights used in our study is shown in the last column of table 3.18.

3.3.5   The Ownership of Debt

In analyzing the ownership of debt, we must take into account the two distinct ways companies may obtain debt finance—issues of debentures and net bank borrowing. It is important to distinguish between these components because of the different assumptions we make about the taxation of income deriving from the two sources. Income from debenture loan stock is taxed at ordinary personal tax rates, whereas income

Table 3.18   Shareownership Weights

Category of Owner	1975 Weight	Growth Factor, 1975–80	1980 Weight	Weight after Business Allocation	1980 Weight in Domestic Ownership	
					Without Reallocation	With Reallocation
Households	0.540	0.755	0.408	0.408	0.435	0.435
Tax-exempt institutions	0.216		0.337	0.382	0.360	0.407
Pension funds	0.190	1.636	0.311	0.356	0.332	0.380
Other	0.026	1.000	0.026	0.026	0.028	0.028
Insurance companies	0.180	1.066	0.192	0.147	0.205	0.157
Overseas investors	0.063	1.000	0.063	0.063	—	—
Total[a]	1.000		1.000	1.000	1.000	1.000

Source: Own calculations based on tables 3.7 and 3.8.

[a]Columns may not sum to total shown because of rounding errors.

obtained from savings channeled to the corporate sector via banks is taxed in a more complicated way. We must therefore distinguish between the way debt finance is made up, on the one hand, of debentures and borrowing from banks and, on the other hand, of the two types of bank deposits. As discussed in chapter 2, we shall assume that income accruing to sight deposits (checking accounts) is in the form of bank services provided free of charge and untaxed. Interest income on time deposits will, in contrast, be assumed to be taxed at ordinary rates.

The composition of debt finance is illustrated in figure 3.2, which shows

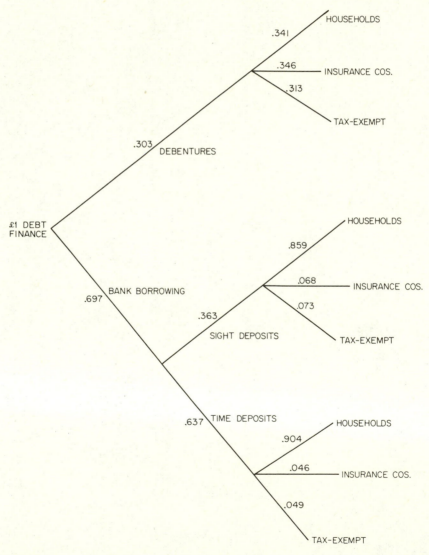

Fig. 3.2   The structure of debt finance.

the way the three ultimate categories of owner may contribute to a unit increase in total debt finance. The proportion of an increase in debt finance coming from each category of owner along the different routes may be calculated by multiplying the numbers shown along each route. For example, at the end of 1980 debenture finance accounted for 30.3 percent of nonfinancial corporate sector debt finance (table 3.13). This figure is shown in the diagram along the path corresponding to debenture finance. We shall show below that the proportion of debentures owned by the personal sector was 34.1 percent, which also is shown on the appropriate path in the diagram. Hence the proportion of an increase in debt finance accounted for by personal sector ownership of debentures was $0.303 \times 0.341 = 0.103$.

We examine first the ownership of the debenture stock. Table 3.19 shows the ownership of debentures and loan stock for several types of owners, principally the personal sector and a number of financial institutions that include building societies, trustee savings banks, finance houses, pension funds, and life insurance companies. Figures are shown separately for unit trusts and investment trusts because we include these in our definition of the household sector, whereas in the official statistics they are included in a category of financial institutions. Hence the final two rows of table 3.19 show the holdings for the "adjusted" household sector, which includes unit and investment trusts, and the "adjusted" other financial institutions, which excludes these two types of owners.

At the end of 1980 the proportion of debenture and loan stock owned by the household sector was 34.1 percent. The division of the remaining 65.9 percent among different financial institutions was possible using data provided by the Bank of England. These are shown in table 3.20 and indicate the holdings of debt by life insurance companies and by pension funds at the end of 1980. Holdings by the category "other financial institutions" seem to be extremely small, and these have been neglected. We show figures also for a reallocation of insurance company holdings to pension business using the proportion described in section 3.3.4. That the

Table 3.19   **Debenture Holdings by Sector 1976–80**
(£ million)

Sector	1976	1977	1978	1979	1980
Household sector	1,686	2,364	2,158	1,585	1,379
Unit trusts	18	22	18	8	15
Investment trusts	84	95	71	42	30
"Adjusted" household sector	1,788	2,481	2,247	1,635	1,424
Other financial institutions	2,750	3,208	2,930	2,657	2,762

Source: Economic Trends, July 1981; *Financial Statistics*, October 1981, tables 8.11 and 8.12.

Note: The "adjusted" household sector includes unit and investment trusts; "other financial institutions" excludes them.

Table 3.20   **Debenture Holdings by Insurance Companies**
                  and Pension Funds, End 1980

	Amount (£ million)		Share	
	Before Pension Reallocation	After Pension Reallocation	Before Pension Reallocation	After Pension Reallocation
Life insurance companies	2,023	1,544	0.688	0.525
Pension funds	918	1,397	0.312	0.475
Total	2,941	2,941	1.000	1.000

Source: Unpublished data provided by the Bank of England, and own calculations.

total holdings of insurance companies and pension funds shown in table 3.20 sum to more than the total shown in table 3.19 appears to be the result of the inclusion of a small amount of foreign debt instruments, and we have assumed that such securities were owned in equal proportions by pension funds and insurance companies. Hence, of the 65.9 percent of debentures owned outside the personal sector, 52.5 percent (34.6 percent of the total) were attributed to life insurance companies and the remaining 47.5 percent (31.3 percent of the total) to the tax-exempt group, which consists primarily of pension funds and the pension business of insurance companies. These numbers are shown in the top half of figure 3.2.

To determine the weights applicable to bank finance, we assume that an increase in bank borrowing by the corporate sector is financed by an equiproportionate increase in both time and sight deposits. We shall therefore focus on the two types of bank deposits held by our three ownership groups. Table 3.21 shows the total value of both sight and time

Table 3.21   **The Ownership of Bank Deposits, End 1980**
                  (£ million)

	Sight Deposits		Time Deposits	
Group	Value	Share	Value	Share
Households	9,745.4	.859	17,984.4	.904
Insurance companies	768.3	.068	919.1	.046
Pension funds[a]	824.8	.073	987.0	.049
Total	11,338.5	.363	19,890.5	.637

Source: Own calculations based on *Financial Statistics*, January 1982, tables 8.11 and 8.12, and unpublished data provided by the Bank of England. For pension funds the ratio of sight to time deposits was assumed to be the same as that for insurance companies; a separate breakdown was unavailable.

[a]Includes pension business of insurance companies.

deposits for the three groups. Again, part of insurance company holdings were reallocated to tax-exempt institutions as described above. It is clear that the household sector holds the bulk of time deposits and almost as high a proportion of sight deposits. Of bank deposits held by our three groups in total, 36 percent were in the form of sight deposits. The proportionate shares of the different sources of bank finance given by table 3.21 are shown also in figure 3.2.

Using figure 3.2, we may now compute effective tax rates for debt finance applicable to each ownership group. The tax rate applied to interest income from debt finance for each ownership group is a weighted average of the group's marginal tax rate (as estimated in section 3.2.8) and zero, where the respective weights are the share of the group's ownership of debenture finance and time deposits and its share of total sight deposits. As explained in chapter 2, income received via sight deposits is deemed to be taxed at a zero rate. For both time deposits and debenture interest, we use the appropriate marginal tax rate. The proportions of total debt finance attributable to the three groups in both taxable and nontaxable form are shown in table 3.22. The final row of the table shows the weights we use for each ownership group for debt finance. The marginal tax rates applicable to debt finance for each ownership group are equal to the product of the marginal tax rates derived in sections 2.8–2.10 above and the fraction of the group's total debt ownership that is in taxable form (given by the ratio of its entry in row 1 in table 3.22 to the sum of rows 1 and 2). The estimated effective tax rates on debt income are as follows: 30.55 percent for the household sector, 23.28 percent for insurance companies, and zero for pension funds.

That the household tax rate on debt interest is lower than that on dividends compensates for the smaller fraction of debt held by the tax-exempt institutions and insurance companies. The result is that the weighted average marginal tax rate on dividend income over all ownership groups is 22.4 percent, and that on interest income is 25.3 percent.

Table 3.22   **Debt Ownership Proportions**
(%)

	Households	Insurance Companies	Pension Funds	Total[a]
Debentures and time deposits	50.01	12.77	11.87	76.69
Sight deposits	21.79	1.72	1.85	25.31
Total[a]	71.80	14.49	13.72	100.00

Source: Own calculations based on figure 3.1.

[a]Rows and columns may not sum to totals shown because of rounding errors.

3.4   Estimates of Effective Marginal Tax Rates

This section describes the results for the United Kingdom. Summary results for the base-case parameter values for 1980 are presented in section 3.4.1. The effect of recent changes in legislation is discussed in section 3.4.2, and estimates for two earlier years, 1960 and 1970, are presented in section 3.4.3. In section 3.4.4 we compare our estimates of marginal tax rates with a calculation of the average tax rate on capital income in the nonfinancial corporate sector. This shows the relation between our "forward-looking" measure of the tax rate on new investment and a "backward-looking" measure of the tax revenues collected on past investment. Further discussion of the results is postponed until chapter 7, where comparisons are made with the other countries in our study.

3.4.1   Principal Results

Using the values of the tax parameters described in section 3.2, the marginal tax rates on capital income may be computed for each of the eighty-one combinations. These values may be aggregated using the capital stock weights described in section 3.3. In table 3.23 we show the marginal tax rates for the fixed-p case, in which each hypothetical

Table 3.23   **Effective Marginal Tax Rates,**
United Kingdom, 1980, Fixed-p Case
(%)

	Inflation Rate		
	Zero	10%	Actual (13.6%)
Asset			
Machinery	− 24.2	− 33.3	− 36.8
Buildings	41.5	41.0	39.3
Inventories	50.5	42.7	39.5
Industry			
Manufacturing	− 1.7	− 6.9	− 9.6
Other industry	4.6	− 2.3	− 5.4
Commerce	46.8	39.5	36.6
Source of finance			
Debt	− 29.6	− 81.7	− 100.8
New share issues	7.6	− 0.9	− 4.2
Retained earnings	23.5	29.3	30.6
Owner			
Households	26.6	38.3	42.0
Tax-exempt institutions	− 5.1	− 33.5	− 44.6
Insurance companies	8.7	− 2.1	− 6.7
Overall	12.6	6.6	3.7

investment project is assumed to earn a pretax real rate of return of 10 percent per annum. Each column of the table corresponds to an assumed rate of inflation, and we consider three particular values: zero, 10 percent, and the actual annual average in the period 1970–79. Comparison of the first two columns illustrates the effect of an increase in the inflation rate on the effective marginal tax rate. This effect may be compared across countries (see chap. 7). Comparing the first and third columns reveals the effect of the actual inflation rate over the 1970s. Each row of table 3.23 corresponds to a particular subset of the full set of eighty-one combinations. For example, the row for machinery gives the weighted average marginal tax rate over the combinations containing machinery (twenty-seven in all).

A striking feature of table 3.23 is the contrast between the effective subsidy given to investment in machinery and the high tax rates levied on investment in buildings and inventories. This is reflected in the relatively low tax rates in manufacturing and other industry (in the former there is a small subsidy on average) compared with the high rax rate in commerce. Given the relative decline of United Kingdom manufacturing, these figures are all the more surprising.

There are also marked differences in the tax rates on the different sources of finance, with debt finance receiving a substantial subsidy, new share issues being taxed at a rate close to zero, and positive tax rates existing only for retained earnings. The imputation system of corporation tax lowers the cost of new share issues below that of retained earnings for all investors other than those with very high personal tax rates and so produces the ranking of source of finance by marginal tax rate shown in table 3.23. As expected, the differences among the categories of owner are significant. For investment financed by savings channeled directly from households to companies, the tax system produces an effective marginal tax rate on capital income only a little below household marginal tax rates. At the actual inflation rate, the difference is small. But for investment financed by savings channeled indirectly through tax-exempt institutions and insurance companies, the position is very different. For insurance companies the tax rate is close to zero, and tax-exempt institutions receive a substantial subsidy, particularly at high rates of inflation. An increase in inflation increases the dispersion of tax rates among different types of owner because it increases the advantage of a tax-exempt institution over a household that pays tax on nominal interest income.

The overall average marginal tax rate is only 12.6 percent at zero inflation, 6.6 percent at a 10 percent rate of inflation, and 3.7 percent at the actual inflation rate. In practice, therefore, the United Kingdom tax system approximates an expenditure tax as far as the corporate sector as a whole is concerned. The average marginal tax rate on capital income is close to zero. But this average conceals a very wide dispersion of marginal tax rates, which would not be a feature of a true expenditure tax. Interestingly, the overall tax rate declines with inflation. The generous depreciation allowances for investment and the deductibility of nominal interest payments at the corporate level more than offset the failure to index the personal tax system.

Table 3.24 shows the pattern of marginal tax rates in the fixed-r case, with a common rate of return to investors (before personal tax) of 5 percent per annum on all projects. As explained in chapter 2, this calculation gives much greater weight to projects subject to high tax rates, and this is particularly marked for the United Kingdom. Projects that are subsidized receive a low weight because the required pretax return on the project is much lower, and this is responsible for the figure of about 30 percent for the overall average marginal tax rate. The relative magnitudes of the tax rates are the same as in the fixed-p case, and the overall marginal tax rate is again a decreasing function of the inflation rate. In the case of debt finance for the two positive rates of inflation, the tax rate is not shown because the value of the real rate of return on an investment project required to produce a 5 percent return to investors is actually negative. The incentives to invest and the tax advantages of debt

Table 3.24   **Effective Marginal Tax Rates, United Kingdom, 1980, Fixed-r Case** (%)

	Inflation Rate		
	Zero	10%	Actual (13.6%)
Asset			
Machinery	− 32.0	− 47.4	− 57.5
Buildings	56.1	57.0	56.4
Inventories	53.0	48.7	45.9
Industry			
Manufacturing	15.3	13.7	10.7
Other industry	17.9	15.0	12.0
Commerce	59.1	56.5	55.0
Source of finance			
Debt	3.8	—	—
New share issues	27.3	8.3	− 1.8
Retained earnings	40.0	47.0	48.2
Owner			
Households	48.1	87.5	104.6
Tax-exempt institutions	19.6	− 19.4	− 34.5
Insurance companies	31.7	20.4	14.5
Overall	34.9	32.4	30.0

finance are so great that the revenue generated by the project need not cover even depreciation costs to produce the stipulated rate of return. Very low, even negative, real rates of return (net of depreciation) may be consistent with equilibrium in the capital market, with investors earning positive real returns on their savings.

Tables 3.23 and 3.24 summarize the principal results for the United Kingdom using our standard values for the parameters. We shall investigate the sensitivity of our results to two particular assumptions. The first is that all tax allowances may be claimed by the company. In practice, United Kingdom companies have found it increasingly difficult to use all their tax allowances—the problem of "tax exhaustion." By 1982 about half of all companies had no mainstream corporation tax liability in any given year. Of course unused tax losses may be carried forward (and backward), but for many companies it is possible that the marginal incentives were different from those illustrated in table 3.23. We show in table 3.25, again for the fixed-p case, the estimated marginal tax rates under the assumption that the company does not claim tax allowances and never pays mainstream corporation tax ($\tau = 0$). Under this assumption, imputation relief is withdrawn (that is, θ becomes unity) because no mainstream tax is collected. ACT would continue to be collected and

Table 3.25   Effective Marginal Tax Rates, United Kingdom, 1980: The Case of Tax Exhaustion
(%)

	Inflation Rate		
	Zero	10%	Actual (13.6%)
Asset			
Machinery	4.8	12.9	15.5
Buildings	27.7	36.2	38.9
Inventories	11.9	20.1	22.7
Industry			
Manufacturing	9.2	17.3	20.0
Other industry	16.0	24.2	26.8
Commerce	23.0	31.4	34.1
Source of finance			
Debt	26.9	52.2	61.3
New share issues	24.0	46.4	54.4
Retained earnings	1.0	13.0	13.7
Owner			
Households	35.4	67.1	78.2
Tax-exempt institutions	−13.7	−35.5	−43.7
Insurance companies	8.9	11.7	12.4
Overall	13.9	22.1	24.7

would become income tax on dividends deducted at source. Unrelieved ACT was about £30–35 billion in 1982, and table 3.25 shows the incentives to invest under these conditions. The most interesting feature of the table is that the tax rate is now an *increasing* function of inflation. At zero inflation the overall marginal tax rate remains almost unchanged at 13.8 percent, but at 10 percent inflation it reaches 22 percent. It is the interaction between inflation and tax exhaustion that raises tax rates rather than the phenomenon of tax exhaustion as such. This is reflected in the sharp increase in the tax rate on projects financed by debt, which are no longer able to benefit from the deductibility of nominal interest payments. In turn, the burden of the increased tax rate falls on projects financed by households and life insurance companies, leaving tax-exempt institutions no more heavily taxed than in table 3.23.

The second sensitivity test we shall carry out relates to household marginal tax rates. In section 3.2.8 we estimated the marginal tax rate on dividend income as 45.0 percent and that on interest income as 30.5 percent. These estimates are somewhat lower than those implied by the Inland Revenue tax model, which, under our assumptions, would give a tax rate on dividends of 51.0 percent and on interest of 34.7 percent. In turn, these imply overall effective marginal tax rates in the fixed-*p* case of

Table 3.26   **Effective Marginal Tax Rates, United Kingdom, before 1980 Change in Stock Relief, Fixed-*p* Case**
(%)

	Inflation Rate		
	Zero	10%	Actual (13.6%)
Asset			
Machinery	−24.2	−33.3	−36.8
Buildings	41.5	41.0	39.3
Inventories	−5.2	−14.1	−17.6
Industry			
Manufacturing	−14.2	−19.6	−22.3
Other industry	2.2	−4.7	−7.8
Commerce	34.9	27.2	24.0
Source of finance			
Debt	−45.8	−97.9	−117.0
New share issues	−3.9	−12.4	−15.8
Retained earnings	13.7	19.2	20.4
Owner			
Households	17.3	28.9	32.5
Tax-exempt institutions	−18.6	−47.3	−58.5
Insurance companies	−2.9	−13.9	−18.6
Overall	1.4	−4.8	−7.7

13.4, 8.6, and 6.1 percent for zero, 10 percent, and actual inflation rates, respectively. In the fixed-r case, the overall effective tax rates rise very slightly to 35.4, 33.6, and 31.5 percent for the three rates of inflation.

3.4.2   Recent Changes in Tax Legislation

In this section we shall illustrate the effect of a number of recent changes to the tax treatment of capital income in the United Kingdom. One of the most important, though unheralded, changes was the reform of stock relief in 1980 that withdrew immediate expensing on marginal investment in inventories (see section 3.2.3). At the time, attention was focused on the average corporate tax burden, but the effect on the marginal tax rate is shown clearly in table 3.26. A comparison with table 3.23 reveals that the reform had the effect of converting a small subsidy into a positive tax rate of about 40–50 percent. As a result, the overall marginal tax rate on capital income rose by about ten percentage points. This was a marked change, though it went virtually unnoticed at the time.

Several other changes to the taxation of capital income were made after the election of the Conservative government of Mrs. Thatcher in 1979. In tables 3.27 and 3.28 we show the pre- and post-Thatcher effective marginal tax rates. After the 1979 election, reductions in income tax

Table 3.27   **Effective Marginal Tax Rates, United Kingdom, Pre-Thatcher, Fixed-p Case**
(%)

| | | Inflation Rate | |
	Zero	10%	Actual (13.6%)
Asset			
Machinery	−23.5	−30.4	−33.0
Buildings	36.1	38.0	37.2
Inventories	−3.2	−9.8	−12.4
Industry			
Manufacturing	−16.2	−19.3	−21.1
Other industry	3.4	−1.3	−3.6
Commerce	35.0	29.5	27.0
Source of finance			
Debt	−37.2	−76.1	−90.4
New share issues	−4.2	−9.7	−12.0
Retained earnings	10.2	15.2	16.3
Owner			
Households	27.6	52.7	61.3
Tax-exempt institutions	−31.5	−69.4	−83.9
Insurance companies	−12.8	−30.5	−37.6
Overall	0.4	−3.6	−5.6

produced a significant fall in the personal tax rates on dividends and interest. Using the methods explained in section 3.2.8, we estimate that the pre-Thatcher tax rates on dividends and interest were 57.9 and 39.5 percent, respectively, for households. In addition, the value of θ was 1.5 (reflecting the higher basic rate of income tax), the wealth tax rate on corporate investment in buildings was 2.0 percent, and the rates of investment grant in manufacturing and other industry were 21 percent for machinery and 18 percent for buildings. As discussed above, immediate expensing was available on investment in inventories. For the post-Thatcher comparison we use the standard parameter values with two adjustments. First, in 1981 the first-year allowance for investment in industrial buildings was raised to 75 percent. Second, major changes were made to capital gains tax. The tax base was indexed to the retail price index, and the threshold below which gains were tax exempt was raised to £5,000 per annum (see section 3.2.1). To a large extent these changes eliminated liability to capital gains tax for many investors, and we assume that the effective accrued tax rate on capital gains was zero for the post-Thatcher calculations.

From tables 3.27 and 3.28 it is clear that the differences between pre- and post-Thatcher tax rates are small. For low rates of inflation, the

Table 3.28   **Effective Marginal Tax Rates, United Kingdom, Post-Thatcher, Fixed-*p* Case**
(%)

	Inflation Rate		
	Zero	10%	Actual (13.6%)
Asset			
Machinery	−29.9	−41.2	−45.3
Buildings	27.7	20.8	17.8
Inventories	47.2	36.2	32.2
Industry			
Manufacturing	−12.1	−21.3	−24.8
Other industry	−2.2	−12.5	−16.4
Commerce	43.7	32.9	28.9
Source of finance			
Debt	−34.4	−88.1	−107.4
New share issues	4.2	−5.4	−8.9
Retained earnings	14.5	15.9	16.2
Owner			
Households	20.9	30.1	33.2
Tax-exempt institutions	−16.0	−49.6	−61.9
Insurance companies	0.3	−14.5	−20.0
Overall	4.6	−5.1	−8.8

post-Thatcher rates are higher than the pre-1979 tax rates. The relative advantage of investment financed from tax-exempt institutions and insurance companies has been reduced, and the tax rate on households is lower than in 1979. But, although there are changes in the effective tax rates on different assets (a higher tax on inventories and lower tax on buildings, for example), the overall weighted average marginal tax rate has changed little.

3.4.3   Comparison with 1960 and 1970

To illustrate the trend in effective tax rates over time, we show in tables 3.29 and 3.30 marginal tax rates for both 1960 and 1970. These may be compared with the 1980 rates shown in table 3.23. For comparison, we have used the 1980 capital stock weights in the construction of the 1960 and 1970 effective tax rates so that any trends that may be apparent from the tables are the result of changes in the tax system rather than changes in the pattern of investment. Similarly, we have evaluated the effective tax rates at the same three inflation rates as before—zero, 10 percent, and 13.6 percent. The values of the tax parameters used in the 1960 and 1970 calculations are shown in tables 3.31 and 3.32.

The changes over time are striking. The overall marginal tax rate has

Table 3.29   **Effective Marginal Tax Rates, United Kingdom, 1960, Fixed-p Case**

(%)

	Inflation Rate		
	Zero	10%	Actual (13.6%)
Asset			
Machinery	12.5	26.6	28.7
Buildings	61.0	58.6	56.1
Inventories	46.2	92.4	8.9
Industry			
Manufacturing	30.8	47.9	51.9
Other industry	24.6	43.0	46.2
Commerce	49.7	58.8	61.3
Source of finance			
Debt	16.7	7.3	1.5
New share issues	30.8	39.8	40.9
Retained earnings	40.3	61.9	67.8
Owner			
Households	52.5	90.0	1.9
Tax-exempt institutions	13.1	−1.1	−8.8
Insurance companies	32.2	43.2	45.1
Overall	35.3	50.4	53.8

declined sharply, particularly at the higher inflation rate. At a 10 percent rate of inflation the overall marginal tax rate fell from 50.4 percent in 1960 to 27.7 percent in 1970 and 6.6 percent in 1980. The other notable change is that in 1980 the overall tax rate was a declining function of the inflation rate, whereas in 1960 and 1970 the tax rate increased sharply with inflation. The move to immediate expensing and the change in the tax treatment of inventories are mainly responsible for this reversal of the relation between tax rates and inflation. The most significant change between 1960 and 1980 was the introduction of more and more generous investment incentives in the form of higher tax allowances and cash grants. Although investment in machinery was especially favored, all assets received higher allowances of some sort. The one major exception to the general rule that tax rates have declined uniformly over time is the treatment of the different sources of finance. The introduction of a classical corporate tax system in 1965 meant that between 1960 and 1970 the tax rate on investment financed from new share issues rose relative to that financed from retained earnings (tables 3.29 and 3.30). This was reversed when the imputation system of corporation tax was introduced in 1973 (tables 3.23 and 3.30).

Table 3.30	Effective Marginal Tax Rates, United Kingdom, 1970, Fixed-p Case (%)		
	Inflation Rate		
	Zero	10%	Actual (13.6%)
Asset			
Machinery	−40.4	−19.2	−13.5
Buildings	53.0	59.2	60.2
Inventories	43.5	85.0	99.6
Industry			
Manufacturing	3.6	23.4	29.1
Other industry	−19.5	−0.9	3.9
Commerce	26.9	48.9	55.7
Source of finance			
Debt	−10.4	−3.0	−1.6
New share issues	32.3	75.5	90.1
Retained earnings	10.5	32.7	39.2
Owner			
Households	34.7	78.9	93.8
Tax-exempt institutions	−27.6	−38.0	−43.6
Insurance companies	1.3	16.3	20.2
Overall	7.4	27.7	33.6

3.4.4 Comparison with Average Tax Rates

The calculations presented to date have considered the effective tax rates on a hypothetical project that might be undertaken by a United Kingdom corporation. These estimated marginal tax rates may, however, be substantially different from the average tax rate actually paid on corporate income. To provide some means of comparing our estimates with published data on tax collections, in this section we examine the average tax burden on corporate porfits.

To calculate the average tax rate on corporate source income requires data on both total tax receipts and the real profits of industrial and commercial companies (ICCs). We define the real operating profits of the ICCs as gross trading profits less capital consumption and stock appreciation, *plus* payments of rates. The correction for capital consumption removes the real depreciation cost of physical capital from reported profits, and the adjustment for stock appreciation removes from profits nominal gains on inventories and work in progress. Our correction for rates is necessary because the national income accounts reflect rates as a

Table 3.31   **Tax Rates in 1960, United Kingdom**
$(\tau = 0.50625; \theta = 1.633; v = 1.0)$

	m	z
Households		
Debt	0.3812	—
Equity	0.5610	0
Insurance companies		
Debt	0.2296	—
Equity	0.2604	0

		Investment Incentives				
Asset	Industry	f_1	f_2	f_3	a	g
Machinery	Manufacturing	0.9	0.3	0	0.153	0
	Other industry	0.9	0.3	0	0.153	0
	Commerce	0.9	0.3	0	0.153	0
Buildings	Manufacturing	0.95	0.15	0	0.02[a]	0
	Other industry	0.95	0.15	0	0.02[a]	0
	Commerce	0	0	0	0	0
Inventories	Manufacturing	0	0	0	0	0
	Other industry	0	0	0	0	0
	Commerce	0	0	0	0	0

Source: King (1977), Appendix A.
Note: All other parameter values as in standard case.
[a]Straight-line basis.

current item expenditure. We treat rates as a tax liability, to be deducted from real profits, and as a payment out of the factors income accruing to capital.

Our calculation of the tax liability proceeds in three stages. First, we define the flow of corporate tax payments as corporation tax accruals, plus rates, less the value of investment and regional development grants to ICCs. This defines the net tax liability of corporations. Dividend payments and interest charges of the ICCs are reported in the national income accounts, and we use this information to define real retained earnings as the residual after dividends and interest have been subtracted from real operating profits. The calculation of real retained earnings for 1978–80 is shown in table 3.33. We assume that the value of shareholders' equity rises by the amount of real retained earnings.

The second step in our tax liability calculation was to assess tax liabilities on dividends and interest payments. Using the estimated marginal tax rates calculated in section 3.2, and assuming that all income flows are subject to tax at these marginal rates, we computed the tax liabilities shown in table 3.34. This assumes that dividends and interest receipts are regarded as marginal sources of income. The estimated capital gains tax

Table 3.32 **Tax Rates in 1970, United Kingdom**
$$(\tau = .40625; \ \theta = 1.0; \ v = 1.0)$$

	m	z
Households		
Debt	.3941	—
Equity	.5800	.268
Insurance companies		
Debt	.2257	—
Equity	.2560	.1667

Asset	Industry	Investment Incentives				
		f_1	f_2	f_3	a	g
Machinery	Manufacturing	.8	.2	.93	.2	.261
	Other industry	.8	.2	.84	.2	.261
	Commerce	.8	.2	.69	.2	.261
Buildings	Manufacturing	.7	.3	0	.04[a]	0
	Other industry	.7	.3	0	.04[a]	0
	Commerce	.7	.3	0	0	0
Inventories	Manufacturing	0	0	0	0	0
	Other industry	0	0	0	0	0
	Commerce	0	0	0	0	0

Source: King (1977), Appendix A; "Investment Grants Annual Report," HMSO (1971).
Note: All other parameter values as in standard case.
[a]Straight-line basis.

Table 3.33   **Corporate Profits and Their Appropriation,**
                    United Kingdom, 1978–80
                    (£ million in current prices)

	1978–80 Average
Real operating profits	15,669
Corporate taxes	5,740
Interest payments	6,054
Dividend payments	4,981
Real retained earnings	−1,106

Definitions

Real operating profits: Gross trading profits *less* capital consumption *less* stock appreciation *plus* rates (property taxes).

Corporate taxes: Corporation tax (accruals) *less* ACT *less* regional development and investment grants *plus* rates.

Interest payments: Debenture and loan and other interest.

Dividend payments: Dividends on ordinary and preference shares including ACT.

Real retained earnings: Real operating profits *less* corporate taxes *less* interest payments *less* real retained earnings.

Source: National Income and Expenditure, 1981, tables 5.2, 5.4, 8.1, and 11.9.

Note: A figure of £100 million for preference dividends was assumed (see King 1977, Appendix B). The figure for rates was computed by applying the increase in total rates to the figure for industrial and commercial companies given in section 3.2.6.

Table 3.34   **Average Tax Rate on Real Corporate Profits**
                    (£ million in current prices)

	1978–80 (Average)	Percentage (of Profits)
Total taxes	8,308	53.02
Corporate taxes	5,740	36.63
Taxes on		
Interest payments	1,532	9.78
Dividend payments	1,116	7.12
Real retained earnings	−80	−0.51
Personal wealth	0	
Real operating profits	15,669	
Average tax rate (%)	53.02	
Average profit rate (%)		
Gross of tax	7.03	
Net of tax	3.30	

Source: Table 3.33 and *National Income and Expenditure*, 1979, 1980, and 1981.

Note: The profit rate is the ratio of real operating profits to the average value of the end-78 and end-79 capital stock, which is defined to be the net capital stock at current replacement cost plus the book value of inventories.

liability is found by multiplying the calculated EAT rate by real retained earnings to capture the change in share values. Since these earnings were negative, we assume full loss offset and deduct the tax rebate shareholders would receive from total tax collected. Since the EAT rate is low, the estimates are not sensitive to this. As shown in table 3.34, these calculations yield a total tax burden of £8,308 million or 53.02 percent of corporate earnings. This must be compared with the 30.0 percent estimate of the overall marginal tax rate from our calculations in the fixed-r case (table 3.24). The increases in investment incentives mean that the forward-looking marginal tax rate is significantly below the backward-looking average rate.

One by-product of our calculations is an estimate of the pretax rate of return on corporate capital. This is defined as the ratio of real operating profits to the ICCs' net capital stock. For 1978–80 this rate of return was 7.03 percent per annum. After deducting the total tax payments we attribute to corporate source income, posttax earnings averaged 3.30 percent of the net capital stock over 1978–80.

4   Sweden

4.1   Introduction

During the postwar period, the total tax yield in Sweden increased dramatically from 25 percent of GNP in 1955 to 50 percent in 1979. As shown in table 4.1, this increase was accompanied by substantial changes in the tax structure. Social security contributions, mainly by employers, accounted for roughly half of the twenty-five percentage point increase, thereby raising employers' share of total tax receipts more than tenfold. The share of taxes on personal incomes and corporate profits, on the other hand, fell markedly.

The structural changes in the tax system, apparent from table 4.1, reflect the growth of the public sector and a marked shift in the direction of fiscal policy from the 1950s to the 1970s. The large devaluation of the Swedish crown in 1949 greatly improved the international competitiveness of Swedish industry. Through moderate wage increases the favorable relative cost position was preserved for more than a decade, making the 1950s a period of high rates of profit and steadily expanding business investment. In this situation, stabilization policy during periods of excess demand was directed mainly at containing private investment. The statutory corporate tax rate was raised, and free depreciation allowances for machinery and equipment were gradually phased out. The rules of inventory valuation were tightened, and in two instances, in 1952–53 and 1955–57, special investment taxes were introduced to reduce the rate of private capital formation.

Toward the end of the 1950s this type of fiscal policy was abandoned as economic growth became a more central economic objective. Several changes in the tax system shifted the burden of the stabilization mechanism from corporate investment to private consumption. The system of investment funds was revised and put to active use. Household taxation

Table 4.1 Sources of Tax Revenue, Sweden, 1955–79

Revenue Source	Share of Total Receipts (%)						Total Receipts (BSEK)[a]
	1955	1960	1965	1970	1975	1979	1979
Taxes on personal incomes (including capital gains)	53.1	52.4	48.3	49.6	46.0	42.4	97.209
Taxes on corporate incomes	13.8	8.8	6.1	4.4	4.3	3.1	7.065
Social security contributions	2.1	4.3	12.0	14.9	19.5	27.1	62.135
Employers	2.1	1.7	8.8	11.7	18.3	25.9	59.477
Employees	—	2.6	1.8	2.0	—	—	0.0
Self-employed	—	—	1.4	1.2	1.2	1.2	2.658
Payroll taxes	0.0	0.0	0.0	1.1	4.4	2.6	5.868
Property taxes	2.4	2.2	1.8	1.5	1.1	0.9	2.089
Value-added tax	—	1.9[b]	10.3[b]	10.2	11.9	13.3	30.580
Taxes on specific goods and services	26.6	28.4	19.9	16.6	11.1	9.1	20.927
Alcohol	n.a.	n.a.	5.0	4.2	3.3	2.6	5.916
Tobacco	n.a.	n.a.	2.8	2.4	1.5	1.1	2.582
Energy	n.a.	n.a.	5.3	4.2	3.2	3.3	7.578
Other	n.a.	n.a.	6.8	5.8	3.1	2.1	4.851
Miscellaneous taxes	2.0	2.0	1.6	1.7	1.7	1.5	3.357
Total receipts (%)	100.0	100.0	100.0	100.0	100.0	100.0	
Total receipts (BSEK)[a]	12.957	19.604	40.385	69.480	132.233	229.230	
Gross domestic product (BSEK)[a]	50.800	72.190	113.450	169.902	298.915	456.007	
Share of taxes in GDP (%)	25.51	27.16	35.60	40.89	44.24	50.27	

Source: Revenue Statistics of OECD Member Countries, 1965–80 (Paris, 1981).
[a]Billions of Swedish crowns.
[b]Refer to sales taxes.

was raised through a general sales tax in 1960 as well as a new payroll tax for social security. As a result, the budget surplus increased dramatically.

With the emergence of balance-of-payments deficits from the mid-1960s, expansion of industrial investment received greater emphasis in policymaking. There was a liberalization of the rules for fiscal depreciation and also a more frequent use of the special Swedish scheme of subsidizing investment—that is, the investment funds system (described in detail in section 4.2.5). In addition, the investment tax component of commodity taxation was abolished when the general sales tax was replaced by a value-added tax in 1969.

The external imbalances, which first arose in the mid-1960s, were much aggravated by the oil crises a decade later. The problem was further worsened by the rapid wage increases and the exchange rate policies of the second half of the 1970s. The long-term policy for eliminating the balance-of-payments deficit has remained one of promoting industrial growth. This has meant, for example, that firms during the second half of the 1970s and the early 1980s have been able to count on using their investment funds almost continuously for new investment. Several kinds of ad hoc measures, such as extra investment allowances, have also been used to stimulate investment. Other recent changes in the tax system include further mitigation of the double taxation of dividends and special tax concessions to household savings.

In the past twenty years there have been major changes in the redistributive role of the Swedish tax system. During the 1960s interest in economic growth gave way to concern about income distribution. The individual income tax became more progressive after the mid-1960s. A major reform of the income tax was enacted in 1971, involving, among other things, a shift from joint to individual taxation of spouses. The reform resulted in a marked increase in progressivity combined with the abolition of the deduction allowed for the local government income tax. The latter meant that an increase in local income tax no longer automatically implied a reduction of national income tax liability. As a result, effective marginal tax rates rose.

The enhanced progressivity built into the tax schedule by the reform of 1971 and the simultaneous rapid increases in local income tax rates and, in particular, of high rates of inflation caused a "marginal tax problem" for the rest of the 1970s. To secure a given increase in real after-tax earnings, it was necessary to ask for large increases in nominal pretax wages. During the early 1970s the government attempted to solve this problem by annual ad hoc adjustments to the taxation of earned income, carried out before the rounds of central collective bargaining. These adjustments, which involved reductions in income tax and increases in the payroll tax, made possible increases in real after-tax earnings at rates acceptable to the largest groups of wage earners. At the same time, the tax adjustments were designed to achieve a further redistribution of income. (For a discussion of this period, see Normann 1978, 1981).

The policy of making annual ad hoc adjustments to the tax schedule was changed in 1979 as part of the new tax policy of the nonsocialist government that came into power in 1976. The income tax schedules were indexed to the consumer price index. In addition, some small steps were taken toward a lowering of marginal tax rates.

The beginning of the 1980s witnessed some important changes in attitudes, with a growing concern about possible detrimental effects of high marginal tax rates. More emphasis was placed on efficiency and incentives and less on the goal of an equitable distribution of income. A manifestation of this was the agreement in April 1981 between two of the three parties in the nonsocialist coalition government and the opposition Social Democratic party to a major reform of personal income taxation. The reform, enacted by Parliament in June 1982, is scheduled to be fully implemented by 1985, after a two-year phase-in period. It is designed to cut marginal income tax rates for the majority of full-time wage earners to a maximum of 50 percent, while simultaneously lowering the value of interest deductions for earners in the higher marginal rate brackets to 50 percent (see section 4.2.1 for a more detailed account of this tax reform).

4.2 The Tax System

4.2.1 The Personal Income Tax

The personal income tax in Sweden consists of two parts: a flat-rate local income tax and a progressive central government income tax. Local and national income taxes are assessed on similar bases. Before the tax reform of 1971, however, local income tax payments were deductible from the base of the national income tax.

An important feature of the reform of 1971 was the change from joint to individual taxation of spouses. Individual taxation applies to so called A-income, that is, income from wages and salaries, farms, and unincorporated businesses. Income from other sources—for example investment income, which is labeled B-income—is, however, still taxed jointly beyond a certain amount—at present 2,000 Swedish crowns (SEK).

For the calculations of taxable income, several kinds of deductions may be made. First, all individuals are entitled to a basic deduction. During the second half of the 1970s this deduction amounted to 4,500 SEK, but the rules have recently been changed. The basic deduction is now confined to local income taxation, and the amount has been raised to 6,000 SEK. Households with children are entitled to an "employment deduction," which means that the secondary worker of the family may deduct 25 percent of his or her earned income up to a maximum of 2,000 SEK.

Single persons with children are allowed the same deduction. We note, finally, a minor remnant of the old system of joint taxation of spouses. A household with only one income earner is granted a credit against the income tax liability of 1,800 SEK.

As already pointed out, investment income in Sweden is regarded as B-income and is taxed on a joint basis if over 2,000 SEK. B-income is added to the income of the primary (highest) income earner and taxed according to her or his marginal rate of income tax. (Note, however, that the first 4,500 SEK of income of each spouse is treated as A-income, regardless of source. As explained, A-income is taxed individually.)

Swedish tax laws exempt a limited amount of investment income from tax. In 1980 this tax-free amount was 1,600 SEK for a married couple and 800 SEK for a single person. Apart from this, the tax rules are symmetrical in the sense that interest payments are deductible with no upper limit. As a result of the tax reform due to be implemented by 1985, this principle of symmetry will be broken for high-income earners. Technically this will be accomplished by dividing the national income tax into two parts, the basic tax and the supplementary tax. The tax base for the basic tax will be determined according to existing rules, which include in the base net investment income and net income from homeownership (usually a negative amount after deductions for mortgage interest). The marginal tax rate rises to a maximum of 20 percent at an income of 64,000 SEK in 1981 prices. The base of the supplementary tax is defined differently in one important respect, namely that *negative* net investment income and *negative* income from homeownership may not be used as an offset against wage income. The marginal tax rates for the supplementary tax run from zero at 102,400 SEK to a maximum of 30 percent at 288,000 SEK (in 1981 prices).

During the past few years, the tax base has been further eroded by some concessions to specific forms of household savings. Savings in special bank accounts (with an annual upper limit of 4,800 SEK) and special funds for shares (with an annual maximum of 7,200 SEK) are granted a tax-free return over a five-year period. The annual savings under this scheme are further entitled to a credit against income tax liability amounting to 20 percent for bank account savings and 30 percent for savings put into the special funds for shares. Another recent change was the introduction of a temporary scheme to reduce the tax burden on dividends. Starting in 1981, and pending a possible introduction of an imputation system, shareholders are allowed a credit against their income tax liabilities of 30 percent of dividends received. This credit, however, may not exceed, 4,500 SEK for a married couple (2,250 SEK for a single person).

Capital gains are taxed in Sweden, although only upon realization. A fraction of capital gains is included in the income tax base. For long-term gains the inclusion rate ranges from zero on personal property to 100 percent on real estate, and for financial assets, such as shares, it is 40 percent (further details may be found in section 4.2.8).

Over the past decade there has been a growing concern in Sweden about the efficiency effects of the present system of taxing capital income. There is a widespread belief that the tax system diverts savings into "unproductive" investments such as art, antiques, gold, and consumer durables at the expense of financial assets such as bank accounts and corporate securities, which are used to channel savings into business investment in fixed capital. Residential investment in owner-occupied housing and summer cottages is also favored by the tax system. Owner-occupied housing provides a noteworthy exception to the general principle of taxing only realized income. Homeownership—including summer cottages—in Sweden is taxed by imputing an income at a rate of 2 percent (with higher rates on more expensive houses) on the tax-assessed value of the house. This imputed income is included in the income tax base of the owner. The tax-assessed values are approximately 75 percent of the market values at the time they are set, and the assessments are changed at intervals of about five years. Mortgage interest is fully deductible in computing the personal income tax base. Real capital gains on housing (defined by indexing the acquisition cost) are taxed upon realization, with an inclusion rate of 100 percent. New rules enacted in 1981 imply a partial departure from the principle of taxing real capital gains by disallowing indexation of the acquisition cost for the first four years of ownership.

For more than a decade, the national income tax schedules have been changed almost annually. Since 1979 these revisions have been based on changes in the consumer price index. It would, however, be wrong to conclude that personal income taxation in Sweden is fully indexed. The basic deductions and allowances described above are all defined as fixed nominal amounts, and changes in these deductions and allowances have been implemented only ad hoc. Moreover, the taxation of capital income is unindexed, and tax is charged on nominal capital gains (except for housing) and nominal interest receipts.

The income tax schedule in Sweden is highly progressive. The degree of progressivity may be expressed in terms of the elasticity of net of tax income (the percentage change in posttax income resulting from a 1 percent change in pretax income). With a proportional tax schedule the elasticity is unity, whereas under a progressive tax system it is less than unity. During the 1950s and 1960s, the elasticity was about 0.8 for the largest groups of wage earners and varied little between different income levels. But as a result of the major tax reform of 1971, progressivity was increased, and since the beginning of the 1970s the elasticity has been about 0.6.

Figure 4.1 shows marginal and average tax rates and elasticities of

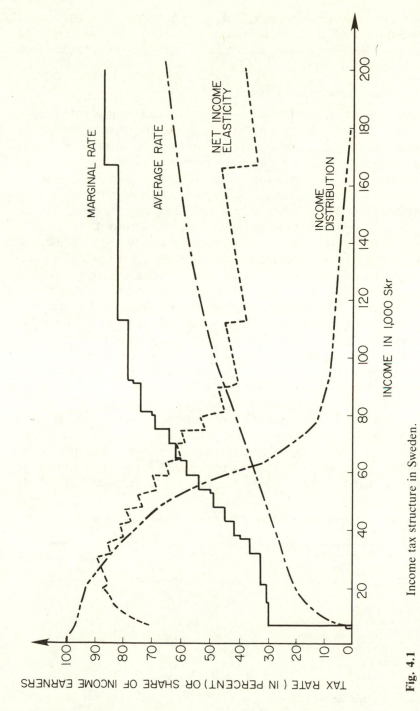

Fig. 4.1   Income tax structure in Sweden.

posttax income for different levels of pretax income in 1979. The income distribution curve shows the fraction (percentage) of the total number of income earners in income brackets with an average income of no less than the indicated amount.

4.2.2   The Corporate Tax System

The corporation is by far the most important legal form of enterprise in Sweden. Table 4.2, which is based on a special investigation carried out for this study by the Swedish Central Bureau of Statistics (SCB), shows the share of sales originating from corporations in several industry groups. The proportion of total sales originating from corporations in 1979 is less than 90 percent only for wholesale and retail trade. This industry group also exhibits large shares of partnerships and so-called economic associations (a cooperative form of enterprise).

Corporations pay both local and national income tax. The national income tax at present amounts to 40 percent of taxable profits. The local income tax varies between different communities, averaging about 29 percent in 1980. Local income tax payments are deductible (with one year's lag) from the national tax assessment, making the total statutory tax burden on corporate net profits approximately 57 percent. This statutory tax rate is used in section 4.2.5 to compute the parameter value for τ, the tax rate on corporate profits. As will be explained, its value depends also on the rules for the investment funds system, allowing firms to deduct up to 50 percent of their profits.

The Swedish corporate income tax may be described as a classical system of company taxation. Corporations pay a flat rate of tax on all taxable profits, and the shareholders in their turn are liable to income tax on dividends. Since the early 1960s, however, some mitigation of the double taxation of dividends has been offered at the firm level through the so-called Annell legislation. According to the rules in force in 1980,

Table 4.2   **Corporate Share of Total Sales in Each Industry, 1979**
(%)

Industry	All Corporations	Privately Owned Corporations
Manufacturing	92	84
Electricity, gas, water	95	40
Building and construction	98	96
Wholesale and retail trade	77	70
Transportation	92	82
Private services[a]	91	78
Total	86	78

Source: Central Bureau of Statistics (SCB).
[a]Only part of private services are included.

firms are allowed to deduct against current profits dividends on newly issued shares for a maximum of twenty years following a new share issue. The sum of deductions taken may not exceed the amount raised by the issue, and the annual deduction is further restricted to a maximum of 10 percent of the issue. The Annell rules in force in 1970 were less generous than those applying in 1980, allowing a maximum deduction of 5 percent for ten years. No mitigation of double taxation was offered in 1960.

Formally, this can be described in the following way. Let h be the rate of Annell deduction per dollar of new issue and assume this deduction to be taken for ω years ($h\omega = 1$). Annual tax savings are τh, and the present discounted value of the tax savings will then be

$$(4.1) \qquad \tau h \int_0^\omega e^{-\rho u} du = \frac{\tau h}{\rho} [1 - e^{-\rho \omega}],$$

where ρ is to be the firm's discount rate.

Note that this expression is the present value of tax saved per dollar of new issues. To incorporate the Annell deduction into the theoretical framework of our study, it must be transformed into an equivalent tax saving per dollar of gross investment. This necessitates a rather formal treatment, which is relegated to Appendix C. We show there that the economic effect of the Annell deduction may be modeled by adding, in the case of new share issues, an additional term to the expression for A (the present value for tax allowances) reflecting the value of the deduction. This is given in equation (C.5) of Appendix C. When the Annell deduction is incorporated in this way the value of θ ("the opportunity cost of retained earnings in terms of dividends forgone") is set equal to unity.

4.2.3   Tax Allowances for Depreciation and Inventories

The effective tax burden on corporate profits depends upon the rules governing the valuation of inventories and the depreciation allowances for fixed assets. Firms are required to value inventories at acquisition cost or market value, whichever is lower, and this means that for tax purposes profits are calculated according to the principle of "first in, first out" (FIFO). As an offset to this, a deduction is allowed up to a maximum of 60 percent of the value of net purchases of inventories. This main rule is inter alia supplemented by an additional rule ("supplementary rule I") that makes it possible for firms reducing their inventories to base inventory write-down on the average size of inventories for the past two years.

Construction firms receive a special tax treatment for that part of their inventories that consists of buildings either not yet completed or only recently completed. On assets of this kind, inventory write-down is limited to approximately 15 percent.

The Swedish rules for taxing inventories imply that $v = 1$ for all industry groups, and $f_2 = 0.6$ for inventories in manufacturing and commerce.

For other industry (which includes construction) the weighted average value for f_2 is 0.193.

The rules of inventory write-down described above were supplemented in 1980 by a scheme that allowed firms to defer corporate taxes by making allocations to a "profit equalization fund." The size of the fund is limited to 20 percent of the firm's total wage costs, and the amount allocated for one year is included with taxable income for the following year unless offset by a new allocation. If use is made of this scheme, regular inventory write-down is limited to 45 percent compared with the normal 60 percent.

The stated motive for the introduction of this new scheme in 1980 was to give firms with either no inventories or limited inventories an opportunity to defer corporate taxes. Judging from the empirical investigations carried out by the Government Committee on Business Taxation in the mid-1970s and by Rundfelt (1982), however, it seems clear that for the three industry groups included in this study the "representative" firm has continued to use the regular rules of inventory write-down rather than the new scheme. The rules of the "profits equalization fund" have therefore not been taken into account in our calculations.

As far as machinery and equipment are concerned, the acquisition cost may be depreciated for tax purposes at a rate of 30 percent per annum on a declining balance basis (the "30 rule"). This means that $f_2 = a = 0.3$, since the first allowances may be taken in the year of acquisition, and $f_1 = 1 - f_2 = 0.7$, in terms of the notation of chapter 2. At any time, though, firms have an option to choose instead—for the entire stock of machines—the accounting value that would result from five years' straight-line depreciation. In other words, a firm is free to write off an amount needed to bring the remaining value down to what it would have been had the firm from the outset written off 20 percent of the original amount invested. For a *single* investment it is profitable to switch to the "20 rule" after the third year. A growing firm, however, with many young vintages of capital, would always stick to the "30 rule." Our assumptions about f_2 and a for investments in machinery therefore may be thought of as applying to such a firm.

Fiscal depreciation of buildings is generally carried out on a straight-line basis. The lifetime for tax purposes varies between buildings of different types and different uses, according to special guidelines issued by the tax authorities. A comparison between these guidelines and the actual composition of investments in buildings—as reflected in the calculations of capital stocks carried out by the Central Bureau of Statistics (see section 4.2.4)—indicates that buildings within the "manufacturing industry" are typically written off using a lifetime of twenty-eight years, compared with thirty-three years for "other industry" and thirty-six years for "commerce." Buildings completed since 1970, however, are treated more favorably. During the first five years, firms are allowed to deduct an additional 2 percent per year, which shortens the tax lifetime of the asset.

The rules of tax depreciation for buildings may be expressed in terms of the present discounted value of depreciation allowances, A_z, which is given by

$$(4.2) \qquad A_z = 0.02 + \frac{1}{L} + \left(0.02 + \frac{1}{L}\right)\int_0^4 e^{-\rho u} du + \frac{1}{L}\int_4^n e^{-\rho u} du,$$

where L is the tax lifetime.

The first term of this expression reflects the fact that the first allowances may be taken in the year of acquisition. Depreciation is carried out for n years, where n is determined so as to make the sum of all allowances equal to the acquisition cost:

$$(4.3) \qquad 0.02 + \frac{1}{L} + 4\left(0.02 + \frac{1}{L}\right) + (n-4)\frac{1}{L} = 1.$$

This gives $n = 0.9L - 1$ for use in the calculations. Before 1970 no "primary deductions" were allowed, and the period of fiscal depreciation was therefore $n = L - 1$.

4.2.4 Estimates of Economic Depreciation

It is generally believed that the Swedish rules of fiscal depreciation are generous—at least in times of stable prices—allowing firms to defer corporate tax payments. The extent of accelerated write-off is, however, difficult to determine owing to lack of reliable studies on rates of economic depreciation.

The most ambitious attempt to calculate economic depreciation in Sweden is that of the Central Bureau of Statistics (SCB), and our assumptions about rates of economic depreciation correspond to those implicitly used by the SCB. The purpose of this section is to describe the rather complicated procedure employed by the SCB in estimating net capital stocks and economic depreciation. The implied rates of economic depreciation are shown in table 4.3.

For each specific category of asset for which capital stocks are estimated—a machine of a certain type used in a certain industry—the SCB assigns a time pattern, according to which the assets of a given cohort are retired from service, and an assumed mean value for the age at which the asset is retired. The retirement patterns have been obtained from the set of survivor curves estimated by Winfrey (1935) for the United States during the 1930s, whereas the assumptions on average retirement age are based on a number of Swedish sources. The main source for the assumptions on average retirement age is Wallander (1962).

Table 4.3   **Rates of Economic Depreciation**
                          (%)

	Manu-facturing	Other Industry	Commerce
Machinery[a]	7.7	19.7	18.2
Equipment	7.1	12.2[c]	11.7
Vehicles	46.7	37.0	40.3
Buildings	2.6	2.3	1.8
Total[b]	5.4	7.1	7.7

Source: Own calculations based on estimates of economic depreciation and net capital stocks of the Central Bureau of Statistics (SCB).

[a]Machinery is a weighted average of equipment and vehicles in each industry.

[b]The row for total is a weighted average of machinery and buildings in each industry.

[c]The major explanation for this rather high figure is the fast depreciation of equipment in the building and construction sector (one-third of all equipment in other industry). The average depreciation rate for this kind of asset is nearly 22 percent (drilling machines, grinding machines, cement mixers, bulldozers, and similar heavy equipment subjected to very rough usage).

The Winfrey survivor curves combined with the SCB assumptions on average retirement age form the basis for perpetual-inventory estimates of gross capital stocks. These estimates of gross capital stocks can be thought of as implying a "sudden death" assumption for each single asset, which means that an asset maintains full productive efficiency until the moment it is retired. The time of retirement varies among the different assets of a vintage, however, as reflected by the survivor curve.

The SCB also provides estimates of economic depreciation based on unpublished calculations of net capital stocks. Net capital stocks are calculated by adjusting the gross capital stocks to allow for the fact that the *value* of an asset declines as it approaches the age of retirement. The approach chosen by the SCB for this purpose can be explained in the following way. Assume that a cohort of assets of a given vintage originally consists of N machines, each of unit value. The number of machines remaining in service after u years is then $S(u)N$, where $S(u)$ represents the "normalized" survivor curve, which takes the value of unity for a new vintage. At time u, $-\dot{S}(u)N$ machines are retired from service. The average retirement age of the assets of this cohort is therefore

$$(4.4) \qquad d(0) = \frac{1}{S(0)N} \int_{0}^{\omega} -u\, \dot{S}(u)N\, du,$$

where ω represents the maximum age of the cohorts (implying that $S(\omega) = 0$). For those assets that still remain in service after n years (at time $u = n$), the average age of retirement is

(4.5) $$d(n) = \frac{1}{S(n)N} \int_n^\omega -u\dot{S}(u)N \, du.$$

The average expected remaining life of the assets surviving after n years is therefore $d(n) - n$.

Now the SCB simply assumes that an asset still in service after n years retains a fraction $f(n)$ of its original value equal to the ratio between the average expected remaining life $[d(n) - n]$ and the average total expected life $d(n)$:

(4.6) $$f(n) = \frac{d(n) - n}{d(n)}.$$

The "valuation coefficient" $f(n)$ takes the value unity for a new vintage ($n = 0$) and declines to zero at the maximum age of the cohort ($n = \omega$). By multiplying $f(n)$ by the number of assets surviving, the SCB obtains a value-age profile ($n = 0, \ldots, \omega$) for a cohort of assets of a given vintage.

(4.7) $$b(n) = S(n)Nf(n), \qquad n = 0, \ldots, \omega.$$

For manufacturing industry, the most frequently used survivor curve for machinery (the Winfrey S_1 curve) has an assumed average retirement age of twenty-five years. The corresponding $b(n)$ curve is then almost linear for the first one-third of the maximum life and approximately geometric for the remaining two-thirds.

This approach forms the basis for perpetual-inventory estimates of net capital stocks. Economic depreciation is then obtained as the difference between gross investment and the change in the net capital stock. To determine the actual rates of depreciation implicit in the calculations performed by the SCB, we have related economic depreciation, D, to the corresponding values of the net capital stocks, K. (Data on net capital stocks are not published by the SCB. Our calculations on rates of economic depreciation are therefore based on unpublished tables at the four-digit level, obtained directly from the SCB.) We define the rate of economic depreciation to be

(4.8) $$\delta_u = \frac{D_u}{K_u}.$$

The parameter δ_u combines the effects of retirement from service (assuming no in-place loss of efficiency) and decline in value as assets approach the time of retirement. Our calculations, covering a thirty-year period ending in 1979, indicate a remarkable constancy of the implicit δ_u.

The degree of constancy is particularly striking for buildings, with practically no variation over time. As a good approximation, therefore, the SCB estimates of economic depreciation are equivalent to estimates based on the simple case of geometric depreciation with a constant δ.

Our estimated depreciation rates are shown in table 4.3. These are an average of the implicit rates described above for the years 1970–79. The marked differences between the industry groups in the depreciation rates for machinery are largely explained by the different proportions of rapidly depreciating vehicles.

It is interesting to compare the estimates with the results of a recent survey carried out by the Industriens Utredningsinstitut (IUI) and the Federation of Swedish Industries (Wallmark 1978). According to this survey, manufacturing firms estimated the average length of life of newly installed machinery as 14.3 years and that of new buildings as 28.7 years. The exact meaning of these answers is unclear. Assuming, however, that the pattern of depreciation is geometric, which implies that the average length of life is the inverse of the rate of depreciation, these numbers may be interpreted as average rates of depreciation of 7.0 and 3.5 percent, respectively. These rates are not far from those implicit in the SCB estimates of economic depreciation for manufacturing.

4.2.5   Investment Grants and Incentives

An important feature of the Swedish corporate income tax is the investment funds system (IF). The idea behind the system is to induce firms to reserve profits during boom years to be used for investment during subsequent recessions. The IF system was introduced in 1938 but did not gain importance until 1955, when the rules were changed. In that year firms started to make tax-free allocations to investment funds, and in the 1958 recession funds were released for the first time. Since then, releases of investment funds have been more and more frequent. In particular, the efforts during the 1970s to promote industrial growth meant that firms were able to use the IF system almost continuously for new investment. Since the mid-1960s the IF system has also been used extensively for regional policy purposes.

The investment funds system works as follows. Each year a firm can deduct up to 50 percent of its tax profits by "allocating" an equivalent amount to its investment fund (appearing as an entry on the balance sheet). Since the IF allocation takes the form of a deduction against taxable profits, tax payments are reduced by an amount equal to the allocation times the (statutory) corporate tax. However, 50 percent of the allocation must be deposited interest-free at the Central Bank (the remainder may be used for any purpose). Hence, even if the funds are never used again, IF allocations provide an attractive alternative to paying profits tax: 50 percent is paid to the Central Bank rather than 57 percent to the government as profits tax.

When the investment funds are released, for example during a recession, firms are allowed to withdraw from the Central Bank deposits corresponding to 50 percent of the cost of investments considered to be financed by the IF. Depending on the rules set up for a particular release, firms are sometimes also granted an extra investment allowance in the tax assessment amounting to 10 percent of the IF used. (This refers to a so-called 9 : 1 release that was in effect at the end of the 1970s and beginning of 1980s.) Investments financed by IF, on the other hand, are considered to be fully written off for tax purposes. Firms lose, therefore, the possibility of deducting fiscal depreciation.

As pointed out, the IF system was put to extensive use during the 1970s. Available data indicate, though, that the firms in the industry groups included in our study financed less than 20 percent of their investments by investment funds. It seems reasonable to assume, therefore, that the *marginal* investment considered for this study must be written off according to the regular rules of fiscal depreciation rather than through the IF system.

This view does not imply, however, that the profitability of the marginal investment is unaffected by the IF system. As explained, Swedish corporations are allowed to reduce the income tax base by allocating up to 50 percent of taxable profits to an IF. This means that 50 percent of the profits from the marginal investment will be taxed at the statutory corporate tax rate of 57 percent, while the remaining 50 percent will be untaxed. There is, however, an implicit cost to the firm of the allocation, and this cost equals the interest forgone on the 50 percent of the allocation that must be deposited with the Central Bank plus the increased tax payments owing to the loss of regular depreciation allowances on assets financed by the IF.

By this line of argument, it seems reasonable to define the *effective* corporate tax rate τ to be used for our model calculations as a weighted average of the statutory tax rate τ_s (which is 57 percent in 1980) and the implicit cost of the IF allocation. To put the expression for the effective corporate tax rate in a general form, we may introduce the following notation: let ℓ be the proportion of profits that may be allocated to the IF and b be the proportion thereof that must be deposited with the Central Bank. The IF allocation is used after n years, at which time the firm can withdraw the Central Bank deposit. The effective corporate tax rate then becomes

(4.9) $$\tau = (1 - \ell)\tau_s + b\ell(1 - e^{-\rho n}) + \ell A_d \, e^{-\rho n},$$

where τ_s is the statutory corporate tax rate and ρ the firm's after-tax rate of discount (which depends on the source of finance). The second term of the equation then represents the present value of the interest forgone on the Central Bank deposit and the third term the present value of increased tax payments owing to forgone depreciation allowances. During the second half of the 1970s and the beginning of the 1980s, firms were allowed to use the IF system almost continuously for new investment. For 1980 it seems reasonable, therefore, to assume a zero time lag between allocation and use of the IF ($n = 0$). The cost to firms of IF allocations would then be limited to the loss of regular depreciation allowances on the acquired assets. In this case equation (4.9) simplifies to

$$(4.10) \qquad \tau = (1 - \ell)\tau_s + \ell A_d.$$

Both 1960 and 1970 represent peak years of the business cycle, and, with a cycle length of four to five years, firms would expect a time lag of about two years before the IF allocations could be used. We assume, therefore, that $n = 2$ for 1960 and 1970. The details of the IF system given above imply, furthermore, that ℓ has a value of 0.5 for 1980. For 1960 and 1970 ℓ equals 0.4. In 1980, 50 percent of an IF allocation had to be deposited with the Central Bank, which means that b equals 0.5. For 1960 and 1970 b takes the value 0.46.

Considering that the present discounted value of regular depreciation allowances per unit of investment is lower for buildings than for machinery, it seems reasonable to assume that a tax-minimizing firm would use its investment funds for investments in buildings rather than machinery. This assumption will be used here, and the definition of A_d in equation (4.9) is therefore (see section 4.2.3):

$$(4.11) \qquad A_d = \tau\left[0.02 + \frac{1}{L} + \left(0.02 + \frac{1}{L}\right)\int_0^4 e^{-\rho u}du \right.$$

$$\left. + \frac{1}{L}\int_4^{0.9L-1} e^{-\rho u}du\right].$$

The effective corporate tax rate τ, as defined by (4.9), is a function of the firm's after-tax discount rate ρ, and this means that it depends on the source of finance used in connection with future IF releases. However, to reduce the programming work involved for our numerical estimates, we use the same parameter value for τ for all sources of finance. This value is computed by using for ρ a weighted average of ρ (as obtained for the "fixed-r" case) for each source of finance. The weights correspond to the 1980 proportions of debt, new share issues, and retained earnings for the three industry groups aggregated. This procedure makes it possible, in turn, to approximate equation (4.9) by a linear function of the inflation rate (π). This means that $\tau = 0.449 - 1.06\pi$ for 1980 and $\tau = 0.410 - 0.41\pi$ and $\tau = 0.454 - 0.49\pi$ for 1960 and 1970, respectively. At 9.4 percent inflation, which is the rate of inflation actually experienced in

Sweden over 1971–80, the effective corporate tax rate τ is therefore 34.9 percent, compared with the statutory corporate tax rate (τ_s) of 57 percent. For 1960 and 1970, statutory corporate tax rates were 49 and 53 percent, and (at the same inflation rate) effective corporate tax rates were 37 and 41 percent, respectively.

On occasions there have been special and temporary improvements of depreciation rules and special tax reductions to stimulate investment. These types of stimuli appear to have been used more frequently in recent years. Thus, in 1976–78 firms were offered an extra investment allowance of 25 percent for machinery and equipment, for national income tax purposes. Regular fiscal depreciation was not affected by this extra allowance. This investment allowance was reintroduced in 1980, and the rate was then set at 20 percent for both the local and national tax assessments. A 10 percent allowance was granted for buildings. With a statutory corporate tax rate of 57 percent, these investment allowances are equivalent to investment grants of 11.4 percent for machinery and 5.7 percent for buildings. We assume, therefore, $f_3 = 1$ and $g = 0.114$ for machinery, and $f_3 = 1$ and $g = 0.057$ for buildings.

In addition to the grants and tax allowances discussed above, large subsidies were extended to manufacturing firms during the recession of the late 1970s. These were provided ad hoc, to a large extent in the form of rescue operations to maintain employment. The magnitude of payments is discussed in section 4.4.4. For this reason we have not included such subsidies in our calculations and have restricted our attention to statutory rates of allowances and grants.

The general sales tax that was in effect in Sweden between 1959 and 1969 included gross investments in its base. Tax payments were deductible against the corporation income tax base. In 1960 the general sales tax was levied at the rate of 4 percent and the corporate tax rate was 49 percent. Therefore the sales tax was equivalent to a *negative* investment grant of 2 percent ($f_3 = 1$ and $g = -0.02$ in 1960).

4.2.6   Local Taxes

The local income tax in Sweden applies not only to individuals but also to corporations. The tax on individuals was discussed in section 4.2.1. The base of the corporate tax—which is similar to that of the national corporation income tax—is defined by the central government, while the rates are determined by the local authorities. The same rate is applied to companies as to individuals. In 1980 the countrywide average was 29 percent.

A Swedish corporation is not liable for property taxes as usually defined. For local income tax purposes, however, a firm must declare an amount corresponding to 2 percent of the assessed value of its buildings and real estate. This "guarantee amount" is deductible from profits for the local income tax assessment, but taxable income cannot fall below the guarantee amount. The effect of this is to levy a minimum tax on firms equal to the product of the tax rate and 2 percent of the value of their real estate. We have ignored this provision (which is not relevant to marginal investment in machinery and inventories) and assumed that firms investing in buildings have taxable profits above the guarantee amount.

4.2.7   Wealth Taxes

The Swedish wealth tax applies only to individuals. Capital values of insurance policies and individually acquired pension rights are excluded from the tax base. The 1980 schedule (unchanged since 1975) levied a zero tax rate on net wealth (assets less liabilities) below 200,000 SEK, a 1 percent rate on wealth between 200,000 and 275,000, 1.5 percent between 275,000 and 400,000, 2 percent between 400,000 and 1,000,000, and 2.5 percent on wealth exceeding 1,000,000 SEK.

A detailed description of the distribution of household wealth in Sweden for 1975 is presented in Spånt (1979), and this study makes it possible to estimate the marginal wealth tax rates implied by a hypothetical 1 percent increase in household wealth. Spånt shows the holdings of various assets such as real estate, bank accounts, and shares for thirteen different classes of taxable net wealth. Using this information and the marginal tax rates for each class of net wealth, as implied by the tax schedule, we have obtained separate estimates of the weighted average marginal tax rates on the holdings of equity and debt. For 1975 the marginal wealth tax rate on equity turned out to be 1.5 percent, compared with 0.4 percent on bank account holdings. Since there is almost no direct lending (through bonds, for example) from households to the business sector, the tax rate on bank account holdings has been used as our estimate of the marginal wealth tax rate on debt.

The different marginal tax rates on equity and debt obviously reflect the differences in the distribution of the holdings of shares and bank accounts among households. Wealthy households have invested a larger proportion of their net wealth in shares than have less wealthy households. An additional indication of this fact is that 35 percent of the total amount of shares owned by households are held by households paying the top marginal wealth tax rate, whereas for bank account holdings the corresponding figure is barely 4 percent. On the other hand, households with taxable net wealth below the tax-exempt limit own 10 percent of household shareholdings and 26 percent of total bank holdings.

With an average rate of inflation of nearly 10 percent since the mid-1970s, it is reasonable to expect the marginal wealth tax rates to be higher in 1980 than in 1975. Assuming the average net wealth within each wealth class to increase at the rate of inflation and the relative distributions of bank account and shareholdings to be unchanged, we have estimated that the marginal tax rate on equity actually rose from 1.5 percent in 1975 to 1.9 percent in 1980, compared with an increase from 0.4 to 0.8 percent on debt.

The wealth tax schedule, introduced in 1975 and still in force in 1980, was changed in 1981. This revision reduced the estimated marginal tax rates to their 1975 level. Because the revision of the schedule in 1981 effectively reestablished the marginal tax rates of 1975, we have chosen as our estimates for 1980 the average of the 1975 values (which equal the 1981 values) and 1980 values. The assumed marginal wealth tax rate is therefore 1.7 percent on equity and 0.6 percent on debt.

4.2.8   Household Tax Rates

Average marginal income tax rates on investment income of households are shown in table 4.4 for the years 1960, 1970, and 1980 and for the proposals due to be implemented in full by 1985.

The figures for 1980 are based on a special investigation carried out for this study by the Central Bureau of Statistics (SCB). Since the mid-1970s the SCB has collected detailed information on household income based on a sample survey of tax returns and other sources. This data base (HINK), which consists of approximately 28,000 individuals from a population of 8.2 million, has been used to estimate the relative distributions of dividends and interest receipts over different income brackets in 1978. (The Swedish term for the income concept used is *sammanräknad nettoinkomst.*) To obtain reliable estimates, it has been necessary, furthermore, to combine the regular HINK data base with a supplementary sample of wealthy households.[1] This supplementary sample was not available for 1979 and 1980.

Since the basic data were available only for 1978, we have assumed that the "real" distributions (that is, adjusted for changes in the price level) of dividends and interest receipts were the same in 1978 and 1980. The average incomes of each of the nineteen income classes employed in 1978 were translated into corresponding nominal amounts for 1980. Marginal tax rates for the different levels of income were obtained from the IUI model of the System of Personal Income Taxation (see Jakobsson and Normann 1974). The marginal tax rates were then weighted together to obtain average marginal tax rates.

The first row of table 4.4 shows the weighted average marginal income tax rates for households that receive dividends and interest income, respectively. These numbers may, however, exaggerate the tax burden on a marginal increase of investment income, since all households are

---

1. The HINK data base is described in annual publications from the SCB (see Statistical Reports N1981:8.1). The procedure of using a supplementary sample of wealthy households is explained in Spånt (1979).

Table 4.4   **Average Marginal Income Tax Rates (m) and**
                   Statutory Capital Gains Tax Rates (z_s)
                   of Household Investors
                               (%)

| | m | | |
Year	Debt	Equity	z_s
1980	52.2	65.2	26.1
1980[a]	49.9	64.0	25.8
1970	48.0	58.0	15.0
1960	34.0	45.0	0
"New rules" 1985	43.9	57.2	22.9

Source: Own calculations as aescribed in the text.
[a]With the exemption limit for investment income taken into account.

allowed a limited amount of investment income free of tax (see section
4.2.1). We have therefore also calculated the share of dividends and
interest receipts, respectively, going to households whose *net* investment
income (dividends, interest receipts, etc., *less* interest costs) exceed the
maximum tax-free amount. The adjusted tax rates obtained by multiplying these shares by the corresponding marginal tax rates for each
income bracket then reflect the fact that some households do not pay any
tax on marginal increases in investment income. As shown by the second
row of the table, these calculations reduce the weighted average marginal
tax rates by two and one percentage points, respectively.

   For purposes of comparison, table 4.4 also includes estimates of average marginal tax rates for 1970 and 1960. The estimates are based on our
own calculations using a 1966 study of the distributions of ownership of
shares and bank account holdings over different income brackets (Statens
Offentliga Utredningar 1969). These distributions were used, in turn, as
proxies for the distributions of dividends and of interest receipts.

   The calculations assume that the real distributions of dividends and
interest receipts over income class were the same in 1960 and 1970 as in
the year of the study, 1966. The mean incomes for the income classes
employed in the 1966 study were translated into corresponding nominal
amounts for 1960 and 1970, using tax assessment statistics. As for 1980,
marginal tax rates were obtained from the IUI tax model.

   Table 4.4 shows the statutory marginal tax rates on realized capital
gains on shares. Taxation of long-term capital gains on shares was first
introduced in Sweden in 1966 (see Rundfelt 1982). According to the rules
in force in 1970, 10 percent of the proceeds of the *sale* of shares were
included in the personal income tax base of the seller.

   Assuming that investors expect capital gains to accrue at the nominal
rate of 5 percent per annum (the average increase in the stock market

index at the time), and assuming a holding period of ten years, this "sales tax" is equivalent to a statutory rate of tax on realized capital gains of 15 percent. The rules were then changed in the mid-1970s to define a tax on realized nominal capital gains. The new rules require that 40 percent of realized long-term nominal gains (in excess of a tax-free amount of 3,000 SEK) be included in the taxable income of the owner. This means that, at the margin, the capital gains tax rate equals 40 percent of the income tax rate. Long-term gains are gains on assets held for more than two years. Short-term capital gains on assets held for less then two years are fully taxed as income.

Finally, the last row of table 4.4 shows marginal income tax rate for the tax reform due in 1985 but introduced into legislation in June 1982. The figures shown are the tax rates that would have applied had the reform been in full effect in 1980. The rules of the 1985 system have not been incorporated into the IUI tax model, and the numbers reported are therefore approximate. In addition, the 1985 tax system poses special problems because of the division of the national income tax into a basic tax and a supplementary tax. For the supplementary tax, *negative* income from financial investments and homeownership (*underskottsavdrag*) may not be used to offset wage income, and available information on the distribution over income class of this negative income is not fully comparable with the data used for table 4.4.

Chapter 2 of this book (as well as the country chapters for the United Kingdom and the United States) discusses in some detail the problems posed by the fact that households may hold debt instruments in a non-interest-bearing form (such as sight deposits). It is assumed that non-interest-bearing accounts yield a return in the form of bank services provided free of charge. Income from non-interest-bearing deposits is therefore deemed to be taxed at a zero rate. This implies, in turn, that the marginal tax rate on income from debt instruments must be calculated as a weighted average of the ordinary marginal tax rate (as shown in table 4.4) and the zero rate on non-interest-bearing deposits.

Household holdings of non-interest-bearing debt instruments are much less important in Sweden than in other countries. Furthermore, Swedish households do, as a rule, earn interest income on sight deposits (such as checking accounts), albeit at a lower rate than on time deposits. Income accruing to sight deposits in Sweden, therefore, will be considered to take the form of both interest income (which is taxed at ordinary tax rates) and untaxed bank services. According to our approximate calculations, the proportion of total household income on debt instruments accruing as untaxed bank services was only 1.4 percent, leaving 98.6 percent of total debt income in taxable form. The marginal tax rates of households applicable to debt finance are therefore equal to the tax rates appearing in table 4.4 times 0.986. The 1980 marginal tax rate on interest earnings of 49.9 percent is then reduced to 49.2 percent, and the 1985 tax rate is reduced from 43.9 to 43.3 percent.

The numbers appearing in the second column of table 4.4 represent the average marginal *income* tax rates of household equity investors. As will be explained below, it is important to distinguish between changes in the tax system that affect these marginal income tax rates and changes that affect the marginal tax burden on *dividends* alone. One reason for distinguishing between the two is illustrated by the operation of the 30 percent dividend tax credit scheme introduced in 1981. The tax credit (against personal income tax and therefore relevant only to households) applies only to the first 15,000 SEK of dividend income for a married couple (the limit is 7,500 SEK for a single person). The effect on marginal tax rates for dividends has therefore been estimated in a way similar to that used when calculating the effects of exempting from tax certain amounts of investment income. We have thus determined the share of a marginal increase in dividends in each income bracket that would qualify for the credit. According to these calculations, the new dividend tax credit did reduce the 1980 average marginal tax rate on dividends by eleven percentage points, from 64.0 to 53.0 percent. Alternatively, if the 1985 tax schedule had been in effect in 1980, the dividend tax credit system would have reduced the marginal tax burden on dividends from 57.2 to 47.3 percent.

As mentioned in section 4.2.1, household taxation of investment income has also been affected by concessions to some special forms of savings—on special bank accounts and special funds for shares—introduced at the end of the 1970s. There is unfortunately no obvious way to translate the rules governing the "tax-savings" schemes into single "tax rates" comparable to the marginal tax rates on regular forms of interest receipts or dividends. The numbers reported below thus reflect several somewhat arbitrary assumptions.

Consider an investor who puts one crown into a qualified special bank account. He immediately receives a credit against his income tax liability of twenty öre (20 percent), and no tax is charged on interest earnings provided the crown—including compound interest—is kept in the account for a full five years. After the required five years, the account turns into a regular bank account with a taxable return. We shall assume, therefore, that the investor withdraws his money (amounting to e^{i5}, including compound interest) after five years. This assumption does not limit the time horizon of the "representative" investor to five years, however. As long as the annual savings in the scheme are below the maximum sum allowed, the investment pattern described here may well be repeated any number of times. We may assume, therefore, that upon withdrawing the amount e^{i5} in year five, the investor immediately returns one crown to the special bank account and receives an additional tax credit of twenty öre. The present value of the (negative) tax payments from repeating this procedure x times will then be

(4.12) $$T = -0.2 \sum_{u=0}^{x} e^{-i(1-m)5u},$$

where 0.2 is the tax credit per crown of qualified savings, $i(1-m)$ is the after-tax rate of discount of the "representative" investor, and u denotes time.

Now imagine an alternative hypothetical arrangement where no initial tax credit is provided, but the investor has the option of paying tax (or, rather, of receiving the subsidy involved) at the rate m^{SB} on his annual interest earnings from the special bank account. The same investment pattern in assumed, implying that the investor puts one crown into the account at time zero and then makes additional deposits between years zero and five to keep the same amount of money in the account as with the scheme described above. The investment is repeated x times, and m^{SB} is set so as to yield the same present value of tax payments (subsidies),

(4.13) $$\left[\int_{0}^{5} m^{SB} i e^{iu} \cdot e^{-i(1-m)u} du \right] \sum_{u=0}^{x} e^{-i(1-m)5u} = T,$$

where T is defined by equation (4.12) above. The expression under the integral sign of (4.13) is the present value of tax (subsidy) payments for each five-year period, discounted to the beginning of each period. It is immediately clear from (4.12) and (4.13) that the holding period of the investor (denoted by the parameter x) does not affect m^{SB}.

Given the underlying assumptions, equations (4.12) and (4.13) can be used to obtain the value of the "equivalent tax rate" m^{SB}. To an individual with a marginal tax rate (m) of 49.9 percent, the special bank savings scheme thus turns out to be equivalent to a tax of minus 3.3 percent on the annual return on the investment plan, assuming a market interest rate (i) of 15 percent. The value of 15 percent was chosen to be representative of nominal market rates at the time, although the equivalent tax rate is rather insensitive to changes in the assumed value for i.

The effects on household tax rates of the concessions to savings in the special funds for shares were estimated in a similar manner. There are at present seven funds in operation (six of which are run by banks) that acquire shares on the stock market. Savings channeled into these funds must be kept for five years, and all dividends received by the funds must be reinvested. The individual is granted a credit against his income tax liability of 30 percent of his annual savings made under the scheme, and no taxes are charged on dividends and capital gains accruing within five years.

An immediate question here is whether the 30 percent tax credit granted by the scheme should be regarded as an offset to tax payments on dividends or on capital gains. We have settled this question by considering two funds. One of the funds is assumed to specialize in shares from corporations paying all their after-tax profits as dividends. No capital gains are thus expected on the portfolio of this fund. The other fund acquires shares from corporations that retain all their profits. The return on the portfolio of this fund would then accrue only as capital gains.

On the basis of these two polar cases, the "equivalent" tax rates on dividends and capital gains can be determined. Consider the first fund specializing in shares from corporations paying all their profits as dividends. Let the dividend yield on the portfolio of this fund be μ. Since all dividends are reinvested, one crown put into the fund at time zero will earn dividends of $\mu e^{\mu u}$ at time u. The "equivalent tax rate" m^{SF} may then be derived in exactly the same way as m^{SB} above, that is, from the equation

$$(4.14) \qquad \int_0^5 m^{SF} \mu e^{\mu u} e^{-i(1-m)u} \, du = -0.3,$$

where 0.3 is the tax credit per crown of savings in the special funds for shares. Assuming the pretax rate of discount and the return on the portfolio of the fund to be 15 percent ($i = 0.15$, $\mu = 0.15$), the "equivalent tax rate" m^{SF} would then be -4.7 percent for a "representative" equity investor with a marginal tax rate of 64 percent ($m = 0.64$; see table 4.4).

The second fund, by assumption, specializes in corporate shares paying no dividends. Let the rate of growth in the value of the shares of this fund be β. At the end of the tax-free five-year period, therefore, the investor withdraws an amount $e^{\beta 5}$ per crown of initial savings. The "equivalent tax rate" z_s^{SF} may then be defined as the rate of tax (subsidy) that would yield the same present value of capital gains tax payment (subsidy) if applied to the conventionally defined capital gain of $e^{\beta 5} - 1$ as the 30 percent tax credit provided by the special funds scheme:

$$(4.15) \qquad z_s^{SF}(e^{\beta 5} - 1) \, e^{-i(1-m)5} = -0.3.$$

Assuming $\beta = i = 0.15$, the "equivalent tax rate" z_s^{SF} is then -35.2 percent.

The tax savings schemes discussed here have not been taken into account for the "standard case" estimates of effective tax rates for 1980 (presented in section 4.4.1). We have chosen instead to consider the tax savings schemes as part of the "new 1981 rules," which also include the dividend tax credit system described above. This requires an assumption about the weight to be attached to the tax savings schemes in estimating household tax rates.

Both types of tax savings schemes were introduced in 1978, but interest initially was largely confined to the special bank accounts. At the end of 1979, 8 percent of taxpayers participated, and, of those, only one in ten chose to put his or her savings into the special funds for shares. The average annual savings amounted to almost 70 percent of the maximum amounts allowed. During 1980 the rules of the special funds for shares were changed, increasing the initial tax credit from 20 to 30 percent and the maximum amount of qualified annual savings from 4,800 to 7,200 SEK. After these changes, savings in the special funds for shares grew rapidly. By mid-1981 the participation rate for the two schemes together had risen to 15 percent of eligible taxpayers and, of those, almost 30 percent used the special funds for shares. Average annual savings still amounted to about two-thirds of the maximum sums allowed.

It is notable that households on average have not used the "tax savings" schemes to the maximum extent. It seems reasonable, therefore, to expect that an increase of household savings, of the kind assumed when defining the "margin" in this study, would be directed both through regular channels—for example, bank accounts and the stock market—and through the "tax savings" schemes. With this view, an assumption must be made regarding the proportion of total household savings in banks that would be channeled through the special bank accounts and the proportion of household equity investments that would be put into special funds for shares.

In mid-1981 the market value of the holdings of the special funds for shares amounted to approximately 3 percent of total household share-holdings. Holdings in the special bank accounts (including compound interest) were also about 3 percent of total household bank holdings. These numbers may give an unduly conservative picture of the importance of the "tax savings" schemes, however. Considering that the schemes were introduced as late as 1978, it seems more appropriate to use flow data. For 1981 the flow of deposits into special bank accounts amounted to 10 percent of the total increase in household bank holdings. As for the special funds for shares, by mid-1981 household deposits had risen to an annual rate corresponding to 6 percent of the total amount of equity capital obtained by the nonfinancial sector by way of new issues and (gross) retained earnings. These numbers, 10 and 6 percent, respectively, have been used as weights when determining the effects of the tax savings schemes on household marginal tax rates on interest income, dividends, and capital gains.

The "tax savings" scheme is therefore assumed to reduce the marginal tax rate on interest income from 49.2 to 44.0 percent ($= 0.9 \times 0.49 + 0.1$ (-0.033)). As mentioned above, the 1981 dividend tax credit system alone effectively reduces the marginal tax rate on dividend receipts from 64.0 to 53.0 percent. Considering the special funds for shares, this marginal tax rate is further reduced to 49.5 percent ($0.94 \times 0.53 + 0.06 \times$

(-0.047)). Similarly, the capital gains tax rate is reduced from 26.1 percent to 22.4 percent ($0.94 \times 0.261 + 0.06 \times (-0.352)$).

As already pointed out, the reduction in the marginal tax rate on dividends (m_d) brought about by the dividends credit system and the "tax savings" scheme must be distinguished from a reduction in the statutory marginal income tax rate (m) of the equity investors. The expressions for the cost of capital with equity finance derived in chapter 2 of this book assume the existence of a market for alternative financial investments where the nominal rate of return is taxed as income at the marginal rate of income tax (m). This after-tax rate of return represents the rate of discount used for determining the cost of capital for equity-financed corporate investments in fixed capital. Measures that affect only the taxation of corporate dividends, such as the Swedish dividend credit system, leave unaffected the rate of discount used by equity investors.

To incorporate the difference between the tax rates m and m_d into the analytical framework set out in chapter 2, consider a marginal investment in fixed capital of unit value financed by a new share issue at the beginning of a year. To simplify notation we will abstract from inflation, initial allowances, investment grants, and so forth, and assume that the rate of fiscal depreciation equals the rate of true economic depreciation, δ. The gross return on investment is MRR, which accrues at the end of the year. The firm then immediately sells the asset and repays the money put up by the shareholders at the beginning of the year. Assuming that the firm, by selling the asset, obtains an amount equal to the replacement value, $1 - \delta$, there remains an amount

$$(4.16) \qquad (\text{MRR} - \delta)(1 - \tau)$$

to be distributed to the shareholders as a dividend. This dividend is taxed at the marginal tax rate m_d, and, to make it worthwhile for the shareholders to participate in the new issue, the net dividend must equal the after-tax return the shareholders could obtain on alternative financial investments:

$$(4.17) \qquad (\text{MRR} - \delta)(1 - \tau)(1 - m_d) = i(1 - m),$$

where i is the investors' pretax opportunity cost of funds, which we take to be the market interest rate. Hence

$$(4.18) \qquad \text{MRR} = \frac{i(1 - m)}{(1 - \tau)(1 - m_d)} + \delta.$$

The corresponding expression in chapter 2 is

$$(4.19) \qquad \text{MRR} = \frac{i}{(1 - \tau)\theta} + \delta,$$

which implies that

$$(4.20) \qquad \theta = \frac{1 - m_d}{1 - m}.$$

Before the dividend credit system was introduced as part of the personal income tax in 1981, m_d was equal to m, and the "opportunity cost of retained earnings in terms of dividends forgone," θ, therefore took the value of unity. The "new 1981 rules," which reduced m_d from 0.640 to 0.495, then raised the value of θ to 1.403. However, since the dividend credit system as well as the tax savings scheme applies only to households, θ still takes the value of unity for the categories "tax-exempt institutions" and "insurance companies."

For the 1985 tax schedule m is reduced from 0.640 to 0.572. In combination with the 1981 dividend credit system, the marginal tax rate on dividends m_d is then 0.473, and this implies that θ for households takes the value 1.23.

4.2.9   Tax-Exempt Institutions

Tax-exempt institutions by definition pay no tax on interest receipts, dividends, or capital gains. This category of owner includes different kinds of charities, scientific and cultural foundations, and foundations for employee recreation set up by companies. It also includes the equivalent of pension funds for supplementary occupational pension schemes.

One line of business of Swedish life insurance companies is to provide individual or collective pension plans. Such pension plans belong to tax category P ("pension insurance"), which exempts the insurance companies from tax on the yield of policy reserves. Contributions to individual pension plans are deductible against the personal income tax base up to a limit of 10 percent of earned income.

Contributions by employers to occupational pension schemes—determined by national collective bargaining—are likewise excluded from the taxable income of employers. Pension payments received are fully taxable to individuals. Savings for pension purposes under the rules described here thus receive the equivalent of consumption tax treatment.

The occupational pension scheme for white-collar workers in the private sector (the PRI/FPG system) is rather differently organized. Under this system pension payments are handled by the participating firms themselves, and these firms are required to account for their pension obligations by entering an item called "pension debt" on their balance sheets (see table 4.19 below). The size of the pension debt of each individual firm is determined by the Pension Registration Institute (PRI) according to conventional actuarial principles.

As the size of the estimated and required pension reserve changes, the firm must make a corresponding allocation to its pension debt. This allocation—which does not affect cash flow and does not require any earmarking of the money retained—reduces reported profits and hence the base of the corporation income tax. Pension payments are likewise deductible against taxable profits.

These special features of the PRI/FPG system obviously do not affect the size of the required pension reserve or pension payments. Had the pension plan instead been administered by a separate insurance company—as is the case for blue-collar workers—pension reserve allocations and pension payments would be covered by employer contributions and by the earnings on the pension reserve. These earnings would be tax exempt under the regulations of tax category P, described above. Employer contributions would also be tax deductible for the participating firms.

The PRI/FPG system, allowing firms to exclude allocations to pension debt and pension payments from their taxable income, therefore effectively accords the same tax treatment to pension savings as is accorded to the "category P" pension schemes described above. The PRI/FPG savings have thus been included in the category of tax-exempt institutions.

4.2.10   Insurance Companies

This category of owner includes property insurance companies, the nonpension life insurance (category K) business of insurance companies, and labor market organizations. We consider these in turn.

Property insurance companies—for the most part mutual companies—pay a 29 percent local tax and a 40 percent national tax on the net income of the business, including interest receipts, dividends, and capital gains. Local tax payments, however, are deductible from the national tax assessment with a one-year lag, making the total statutory tax rate approximately 57 percent.

It is important to note that the financial investments of insurance companies are treated as inventories by the tax authorities. The implication is that the accruing nominal changes in value of the investments (for example, changes in the market value of shares) constitute taxable income.

The effective tax rate on property insurance companies is, however, reduced below the statutory tax rate of 57 percent by some provisions affecting the tax base. First, companies are allowed to undervalue their financial investments for tax purposes. Shares are valued at 60 percent of their market value, and as a result taxable income is reduced by 0.4 when a company acquires a share of unit value. As the market value of the share changes, 60 percent of the accruing capital gain (or loss) is included in the tax base. Financial investments in debt instruments are valued at 90 percent of market value. Second, a return of 4 percent on the investment is effectively exempt from tax. This exemption is accomplished by allowing the companies to annually allocate an amount equal to a return of 4 percent on the insurance fund to a tax-free reserve.

The effective tax rate on the capital income of insurance companies can then be determined in the following way. Let the statutory tax rate be τ_s, and assume that a company acquires a financial investment of unit value that is written down to $1 - \gamma$ for tax purposes. The net cost of investment is then $1 - \gamma\tau_s$, since the undervaluation implies a deduction against the tax base of γ. Assume, furthermore, that the market value of the investment grows at a rate β with a dividend yield of μ.[2] The taxable income on the investment at time u will then equal dividends received plus the accruing change in the tax accounting value of the investment, $(1 - \gamma)\beta\, e^{\beta u}$, less the tax-exempt return, $\eta e^{\beta u}$ (where in practice η equals 4 percent). The after-tax internal rate of return, j, on this investment is defined by the following equation (where the last term is the present value of after-tax proceeds from selling the investment at time ω):

$$(4.21) \qquad 1 - \gamma\tau_s = \int_0^\omega [\mu - \tau_s[\mu + (1 - \gamma)\beta - \eta)]e^{\beta u - ju}du$$

$$+ (1 - \gamma\tau_s)e^{\beta\omega - j\omega}.$$

This gives

$$(4.22) \qquad j = (\mu + \beta)\left(\frac{1 - \tau_s}{1 - \gamma\tau_s}\right) + \frac{\tau_s\eta}{1 - \gamma\tau_s}.$$

Now the effective tax rate τ_e is defined as

$$(4.23) \qquad \tau_e = \frac{(\mu + \beta) - j}{\mu + \beta},$$

which gives

$$(4.24) \qquad \tau_e = \frac{\tau_s(1 - \gamma)}{1 - \gamma\tau_s}\left[1 - \frac{\eta}{(\mu + \beta)(1 - \gamma)}\right].$$

As explained, τ_s is 0.57, and γ equals 0.4 for shares and 0.1 for debt instruments. A return of $\eta = 0.04$ is exempt from tax. The effective tax rate depends also on the actual yields to the insurance companies. For 1980 we have assumed a nominal rate of return $(\mu + \beta)$ of 11.8 percent on investments in shares and a 9.4 percent return on debt instruments. These rates of return correspond to the average effective yield for 1971–80 on the Stockholm Stock Exchange and on long-term industrial bonds, respectively. Equation (4.24) then gives an effective tax rate on dividends

---

2. These parameters are defined and used similarly in section 4.2.8.

and accrued capital gains of 19 percent and an effective tax rate on interest receipts of 28 percent.

It should be noted that the tax-exempt yield η is fixed in nominal terms, and therefore the effective tax rate will depend on the inflation rate. The 1980 effective tax rates of 0.19 and 0.28 thus reflect the actual rate of inflation used in our calculations for 1980, which is 9.4 percent. It is obviously difficult to know what rates of return insurance companies would have earned on their investments in 1980 in a hypothetical situation with no inflation. Equation (4.24) indicates that the effective tax rate would be zero if the returns on equity and debt instruments did not exceed 6.7 and 4.4 percent, respectively. It seems reasonable to assume that the rates of return with zero inflation would be below these critical values. We have assumed, therefore, an effective tax rate of zero in the case of no inflation.

The second type of tax treatment of insurance companies relates to nonpension life insurance business. Investment in this kind of policy belongs to the K category (*Kapital-insurance*) for tax purposes. Premiums are paid out of after-tax income, and the proceeds of such policies are not taxable. The insurance companies are liable for a 29 percent local tax and a 10 percent national tax on their net business income, including interest receipts, dividends, and capital gains. Because local tax payments are deductible against the base of the national tax, the combined result is a statutory tax rate of approximately 36 percent. This tax rate is then effectively reduced by some special provisions affecting the tax base. First, 5 percent of net capital income is exempt from taxation, and, second, companies are allowed to reduce their tax base by a factor of 0.003 times a "base" amount (*basbelopp*) for each policy. This amount was 16,000 SEK at the end of 1980. This last provision, however, is not taken into account here because its effects are assumed to be intramarginal. The total statutory tax rate on the return on insurance policies of category K is therefore 34 percent (0.95×0.36).

As is the case for property insurance companies, the financial investments of the life insurance companies are treated as inventory holdings, and the same rates of undervaluation for tax purposes apply. The provision that exempts from tax a 4 percent return on the insurance fund, however, is not extended to life insurance companies. The effective tax rate on capital income is therefore

$$(4.25) \qquad \tau_e = \frac{\tau_s(1 - \gamma)}{1 - \gamma\tau_s}.$$

With $\tau_s = 0.34$, the effective tax rate is 24 percent on dividends and accrued capital gains and 32 percent on interest receipts.

Finally, our category "insurance companies" includes labor market organizations. These pay a 29 percent local tax and a 15 percent national tax on dividends and interest receipts, making a total tax rate of 40 percent (allowing for the deductibility of local tax payments). Capital gains are taxable according to the same schedule as for individuals (see section 4.2.8). For 1980, therefore, the tax rate on realized capital gains equals 40 percent of the marginal income tax rate—that is, 16 percent.

The marginal tax rates on insurance companies are summarized in table 4.5. The rates for the three groups—property insurance, nonpension life business, and labor market organizations—were weighted together using 1980 ownership proportions. These were 0.67, 0.17, and 0.16, respectively, for equity, and 0.68, 0.22, and 0.10 for debt.

The effective tax rates of table 4.5 reflect the assumption that property insurance companies earn a nominal rate of return of 11.8 percent on their equity investments and 9.4 percent on debt instruments. The same yield assumptions are used for 1960 and 1970 in order to focus interest on the changes in tax legislation rather than on the combined effect over time of changes in tax legislation and actual market yields. The rules of undervaluation (expressed in the parameter γ) have applied since 1960, and the increases in the marginal effective tax rates from 1960 through 1980 are explained by the increases in the statutory tax rates caused by the gradual increases over time in local income tax rates.

The (weighted average) effective marginal tax rates of insurance companies depend on the rate of inflation, to the extent that nominal yields to property insurance companies are affected by inflation. The numbers appearing in table 4.5 reflect the "actual rate of inflation" of 9.4 percent, experienced over 1971–80. As explained above, it seems reasonable to assume that the market yields to property insurance companies at zero inflation would be sufficiently low to imply a zero marginal tax rate on investment income. Our estimates of the effective (weighted average) marginal tax rates of insurance companies at zero inflation, shown in table 4.6, have been obtained using this assumption. The effective tax rates for 10 percent inflation have been estimated by simply extrapolating

Table 4.5	Average Marginal Income Tax Rates (m) and Statutory Capital Gains Tax Rates (z_s) of Insurance Companies at 9.4 Percent Inflation (%)			

		m		
	Year	Debt	Equity	z_s
	1960	23.8	17.4	12.9
	1970	26.8	20.2	15.4
	1980	31.0	24.4	19.1

Source: Own calculations as described in the text.

Table 4.6   Average Marginal Income Tax Rates (m) and
Statutory Capital Gains Tax Rates (z_s)
of Insurance Companies at Zero Inflation
($\%$)

	m		
Year	Debt	Equity	z_s
1960	6.8	7.1	2.3
1970	8.5	8.8	3.7
1980	11.0	10.6	5.0

Source: Own calculations as described in the text.

the rate of change in the effective tax rates between zero and 9.4 percent inflation.

Swedish insurance companies (as well as households and tax-exempt institutions) hold debt instruments in both interest-bearing and non-interest-bearing forms. According to our estimates, non-interest-bearing debt accounted for 4.7 percent of the total debt holdings of insurance companies in 1980, and, as explained in section 4.2.8, we assume that income from non-interest-bearing debt (accruing as bank services) is taxed at a zero rate. The marginal tax rate of insurance companies applicable to debt finance (to be used for the calculations presented in section 4.4 below) is therefore obtained by multiplying the marginal tax rate derived in this section, and shown in tables 4.5 and 4.6, by $(1 - 0.047)$.

4.3   The Structure of the Capital Stock and Its Ownership

In section 4.2 we presented the parameters needed to estimate the wedge between the pretax rate of return on a marginal investment project and the posttax return on the savings made to finance the investment. We analyze this tax wedge for three kinds of real assets, three industry groups, three sources of finance, and three categories of owners, implying eighty-one possible combinations of a hypothetical marginal investment. The purpose of this section is to describe the construction of the weights for these eighty-one combinations. These weights, in turn, are used for the estimates of the weighted average marginal tax rates presented in section 4.4.

4.3.1   Data Limitations

Data limitations prevented us from computing separate numbers for more than thirty out of the eighty-one possible combinations. One obvious reason for the seemingly modest achievement is the difficulty in linking the real and financial activities of firms. We were forced to assume that, within an industry, investment in the three types of assets was financed by debt, new share issues, and retained earnings in the same proportions.

Another difficulty was to identify the beneficial owners of financial securities in the different industries. We managed to produce rough estimates of the shares of financial liabilities in the respective industries held by each of the ownership groups, but we did not succeed in finding industry-specific equity ownership data.

We distinguish between three industry groups: manufacturing, other industry, and commerce. Restricting the analysis to these three industrial sectors implies a restricted coverage of overall activity in the economy. The three groups accounted for about 56 percent of total GDP in 1980, as seen in row 4 of table 4.7. The table shows also the importance of the public sector in Sweden. The "cost of production" in civil service departments, public authorities, and so on (government services, line 8) and the

Table 4.7   Distribution of Value Added in Sweden, 1980

Sector	Billions of Swedish Crowns		%
1. Manufacturing		113.3	24.1
2. Other industry		72.5	15.4
a. Electricity, gas, water	14.3		3.1
b. Building and construction	35.0		7.4
c. Transport and storage	23.2		4.9
3. Commerce		75.5	16.0
a. Wholesale and retail trade	52.6		11.2
b. Other services	22.9		4.8
4. Total included industries		261.3	55.5
5. Excluded business sectors		92.4	19.6
a. Agriculture, forestry, fishing	16.0		3.4
b. Mining and quarrying	2.4		0.5
c. Restaurants and hotels	4.0		0.8
d. Communication (public)	8.4		1.8
e. Finance, insurance, real estate	61.6		13.1
6. Other domestic services, discrepancies		5.0	1.1
7. Total industry		358.7	76.2
a. Public enterprises	22.6		4.8
b. State business agencies	22.3		4.7
8. Government services		112.1	23.8
9. Gross domestic product		470.8	100.0

Source: National accounts of the Central Bureau of Statistics (SCB). Factor values exclude indirect taxes but include subsidies, in current prices. Lines 7a and 7b are estimates from annual reports of the included enterprises.

value added in publicly owned industry (lines 7a and 7b) together account for approximately one-third of total value added.

We have also excluded from our study nationalized industries, enterprises where the public interest is predominant, and unincorporated businesses. The implications of considering only the corporate sector are illustrated in table 4.8 for the year 1979. From column 1 of this table, state business agencies were excluded to obtain column 2. This adjustment affects other industry particularly, because of the state-owned electricity company (Vattenfall) and the railroad company (Statens Järnvägar). Second, legal forms of organization other than corporations were excluded to obtain column 3. These units—for example, family businesses in the form of partnerships—are, as one could expect, most common in wholesale and retail trade. Finally, we excluded state and local government corporations—for example, the large holding company Statsföretag. Summarizing the table, we see that the three industry groups defined in our study account for no more than 38 percent of GDP (column 4, row 10). This limited coverage must be borne in mind when evaluating the results presented in section 4.4.

The importance of confining the analysis to private corporations is further demonstrated in table 4.9, which shows various characteristics of the total business sector divided according to legal form of organization. The table reveals the existence of substantial differences among the types of organization. For example, public corporations invested three times more than private corporations, as seen in the fifth row, but these investments were internally financed to a much lesser extent than in private industry (row 4). Nevertheless, the experience of private corporations (in column 3) was very similar to that for "all firms" (in column 1). The corporate form has, in fact, strengthened its dominant position during the past fifty years, as seen from table 4.10. The table reveals, furthermore, a rather dramatic decrease in "individuals" (mainly single proprietorships), from almost one-third of total operating income at the beginning of the 1930s to about 10 percent in 1979.

Suitable data on capital stocks, sources of financial capital, and ownership of debt and equity for our three industry groups are not readily available from official statistics. The numbers presented below are based on information from a number of sources, of which the most important was the annual publication *Enterprises, Financial Accounts of the Central Bureau of Statistics* (SCB). Unfortunately, information of acceptable quality on real capital stocks is not available from this source, and for this reason we have used an additional classification scheme based on the national accounts. Thus we have had to interface two partly separate industrial classifications. Yet a third system of classifying business activity is used in Financial Statistics of the SCB, an important source for tracing

Table 4.8   **Value Added by Industries, 1979**

Industry	National Accounts Total		Financial Accounts Total		Financial Accounts, Nonfinancial Corporations		Financial Accounts, Private Nonfinancial Corporations	
	BSEK	%	BSEK	%	BSEK	%	BSEK	%
1. Manufacturing	102.9	100	100.8	98	97.3	95	89.7	87
2. Electricity, gas, water	11.8		3.8		3.7		1.7	
3. Building and construction	31.8		19.0		18.5		18.1	
4. Transport and storage	21.0		14.0		12.9		9.9	
5. Other industry (2 + 3 + 4)	64.6	100	36.8	57	35.1	54	29.7	46
6. Wholesale and retail trade	47.5		43.8		35.2		32.8	
7. Other services	20.7		9.3		8.5		7.2	
8. Commerce (6 + 7)	68.2	100	53.1	78	43.7	64	40.0	59
9. Total included (1 + 5 + 8)	235.7	100	190.7	81	176.1	75	159.4	68
10. In % of GDP (416.0 BSEK)	56.7		45.8		42.3		38.3	

Source: Enterprises, Financial Accounts, 1979 of the Central Bureau of Statistics (SCB), and unpublished data.
Note: BSEK = billions of Swedish crowns.

Table 4.9   **Economic Characteristics of Different Parts of Industry, All Industrial Sectors, 1979**

	All Firms	Corporations			Local Government	Partnerships	Associations	Other Legal Forms
		All	Private	State				
1. Value added (BSEK)[a]	207.5	190.3	171.3	14.7	4.3	4.9	11.8	0.6
2. Gross operating profit/ Value added	21.5	21.0	21.5	10.3	38.2	39.4	22.8	12.6
3. Retained earnings/ gross operating income	4.2	4.3	4.3	3.2	11.0	8.9	2.1	5.3
4. Retained earnings/ gross investment	117.7	113.8	134.6	36.9	80.4	266.4	121.7	112.5
5. Gross investment/ value added	13.4	13.4	11.3	31.5	34.5	12.8	13.8	11.8
6. Value added/fixed assets	155.7	154.8	183.9	65.1	59.5	252.3	150.5	90.9
7. Machinery/net capital stock	23.7	24.1	23.9	20.6	46.1	32.8	15.6	10.1
8. Buildings/net capital stock	25.2	24.7	21.5	38.4	39.8	13.9	32.9	80.2

Source: Enterprises, Financial Accounts, 1979, and special computations from SCB. Note that the capital stocks are measured at book value, not replacement cost.

[a]Value added is in billions of Swedish crowns. All other figures are percentages.

Table 4.10   **Distribution of Gross Operating Income by Legal Form of Organization, All Industrial Sectors**
(%)

Form of Organization	1930	1950	1972	1979
Corporations	53.1	60.7	74.1	75.3
Partnerships	5.1	2.6	2.0	2.1
Economic associations	6.4	11.3	11.7	10.4
Individuals	30.1	19.9	6.3	} 12.2[a]
State business and other legal forms	5.3	5.5	5.9	
Total	100.0	100.0	100.0	100.0

Source: The 1931, 1951, and 1972 Census of Enterprises and Enterprises, Financial Accounts, 1979. The 1979 figures are not fully comparable with those for earlier years.
[a]No data are available for individuals and state business agencies in 1979, so we use the same share of gross operating income as for 1972.

the ownership of securities. Finally, we note that in some instances the latest year for which data were available was 1979.

4.3.2   Capital Stock Weights

Net capital stocks are estimated for two reasons. First, with values for real capital, financial assets, and debt we are able to determine debt/ equity ratios from the stock side, treating equity capital as a residual. These ratios are then used in constructing weights for the different sources of finance (section 4.3.3). Second, real capital stock figures are required in order to estimate the distribution of assets among the three industry groups. Our estimates of the proportions for machinery and buildings are based on unpublished tables of net capital stocks from the Central Bureau of Statistics (SCB). As described in section 4.2.4, the SCB calculates these stocks using the perpetual-inventory method (see also Cederblad 1971). The SCB estimates refer to activity as a whole and are scaled down to the corporate sector using data on value added for national accounts enterprises, on the one hand, and for private corporations on the other. Inventory values for nonfinancial private corporations are obtained from Enterprises, Financial Accounts. These inventories are valued according to certain legal rules and are normally not very different from replacement cost values. The written-down book values (for tax purposes) are, of course, much lower, as seen in section 4.2.3.

Table 4.11 shows the distribution of the corporate capital stock among assets and industries in 1980. The corresponding matrix of the nine asset-by-industry capital stocks and proportions is shown in table 4.12. Two remarks should be made in connection with table 4.12. The first has to do with the concept of inventories in the "building and construction" part of other industry. As can be seen from the table, inventories constitute a remarkably high share, more than 50 percent, of the capital

**Table 4.11   Proportions of Nonfinancial Capital Stock by Asset
              and Industry, 1980: Private Corporations Only**

Asset	Industry		
	Manufac-turing	Other Industry	Commerce
Machinery	.2635	.0253	.0345
Buildings	.2127	.0662	.0620
Inventories	.1496	.0957	.0905

Source: National accounts and Enterprises, Financial Accounts, and own calculations.

in that particular sector. This is, however, merely a reflection of the fact that inventories include buildings either under construction or recently completed but not yet sold.

The second remark concerns the rapidly growing use of *leasing* as a way of expanding capacity. The SCB assigns such investments to the sector of ownership (mainly financial companies). It should be noted, however, that assets acquired by leasing in Sweden, in contrast to many other countries (e.g., the United Kingdom), still seem to account for an insignificant part of the total capital stock—less than 1 percent. There may, however, be some potentially important tax advantages to leasing. For example, a firm with positive taxable profits could purchase assets and claim the 20 percent investment allowance (see section 4.2.5), then lease the assets to firms with zero taxable profits. This could enable firms with zero taxable profits to take advantage of the investment allowance. Since 1982 this particular arrangement can no longer be used. According to the new rules, the investment allowance can be claimed only by the "final users" of assets.

The alternative approach to measuring capital stock weights would be to compute proportions using data on investment flows. To demonstrate the differences between the stock and flow methods, we have put together, in table 4.13, the resulting asset proportions for manufacturing, had they instead been based on gross investments. As can be seen, the pattern is much changed, with machinery receiving a larger weight. In a steady-state situation with no net investment, we would expect this outcome, since machines in general depreciate faster than buildings and therefore have to be replaced sooner. The reader is referred to the discussion of this point in chapter 2.

4.3.3   Sources of Financial Capital

To estimate market value debt/equity ratios, the following approach was used. The first stage was to estimate the replacement cost value attributable to equity. Using the net capital stock calculations—at current

Table 4.12   **Private Corporate Capital Stock, 1980**

	Manufacturing		Other Industry		Commerce		Total	
	BSEK[a]	%	BSEK	%	BSEK	%	BSEK	%
Machinery	121.168	42.1	11.628	13.5	15.891	18.5	148.687	32.3
%	81.5		7.8		10.7		100.0	
Buildings	97.807	34.0	30.422	35.4	28.495	33.1	156.724	34.1
%	62.4		19.4		18.2		100.0	
Inventories	68.772	23.9	44.018	51.1	41.618	48.4	154.408	33.6
%	44.5		28.5		27.0		100.0	
Total	287.747	100.0	86.068	100.0	86.004	100.0	459.819	100.0
%	62.6		18.7		18.7		100.0	

Source: National accounts and Enterprises, Financial Accounts, and own calculations.

[a]Billions of Swedish crowns.

Table 4.13   **Proportions of Capital and of Gross Investment in Manufacturing**
(%)

	Net Capital Stock 1980	Investments 1970–80	Investments 1980
Machinery	42.1	65.5	62.8
Buildings	34.0	23.7	19.7
Inventories	23.9	10.8[a]	17.5[a]
Total	100.0	100.0	100.0

Source: National accounts and Enterprises, Financial Accounts, and own calculations.
[a]Changes in stocks of inventories.

replacement cost—and balance sheet data on financial assets and liabilities together with our own calculations of the contingent tax liability resulting from accelerated depreciation and inventory write-down, the replacement cost value of equity was determined as a residual. Net trade credit was excluded. In the second stage we estimated the market value of equity using a sample of thirteen major engineering corporations (or conglomerates), accounting for 40 percent of sales in manufacturing and 25 percent of the market value of the Stockholm Stock Exchange in 1980. The ratio of market value to replacement cost (the "q ratio") for the thirteen large corporations is shown in table 4.14. Our calculations indicate that equity in 1960 had a market value very close to its estimated replacement value. The "q ratio" fell to 0.6 in 1970 and further to 0.3 in 1980, reflecting the poor performance of the Swedish stock market. These q ratios were assumed to be representative of the three industry groups. The market values of equity were then computed as q times the estimates of the replacement cost value of equity, using the 1970–80 average value of q equal to 0.51.

   In judging this method for calculating the market value of equity, it should be noted that, in view of the preferential tax treatment of capital gains, it may be quite rational for a firm to undertake investments that produce less than a dollar's worth of capital gains for the marginal dollar of retention, leading to a value for q of less than unity (Bergström and Södersten 1976). In equilibrium, shareholders would be indifferent between a dollar of dividends and $(1 - m)/(1 - z)$ dollars worth of capital gains, if dividends were taxed at the rate m and (accrued) capital gains at the rate z. For $m = 0.409$ and $z = 0.096$, representing weighted average marginal tax rates for equity investors in 1980, this "marginal rate of substitution of dividends for capital gains" takes the value of 0.65. This analytically derived value for "marginal q" is well in line with the q ratios appearing in table 4.14 for the first half of the 1970s.

   The debt/equity ratio was estimated as the ratio of the market value of debt to the market value of equity. For the former we used data on the

Table 4.14   **"q Ratios" for Thirteen Major Engineering Corporations**
(%)

Year	q	Year	q
1970	59.3	1976	48.0
1971	73.6	1977	37.3
1972	74.3	1978	34.3
1973	62.8	1979	29.4
1974	50.8	1980	31.3
1975	57.2		

Source: Own calculations. The underlying capital stocks were constructed assuming a geometric rate of depreciation of 5.4 percent, corresponding to the average rate for machinery and buildings in manufacturing. See section 4.2.4. The last three years are measured directly, and the preceding years are estimates. The corporations are: Alfa Laval, ASEA, Atlas Copco, Bahco, Bulten-Kanthal, Electrolux, ESAB, Flaktfabriken, Ericsson (LME), PLM, Saab-Scania, SKF, and Volvo.

Note: The q ratio is the ratio of market value to net worth.

book value of debt because very little debt is marketable. The market for corporate bonds is rather thin in Sweden, and the share of bonds in total net debt held by beneficial owners is less than 5 percent.

The division of equity finance between retained earnings and new share issues was estimated from sources of funds data, and we used a three-year average (1978–80). Since new share issues to acquire an existing company (*apportemission*) do not constitute a source of net new finance, such issues were excluded from our calculations. The three-year average was necessary to prevent cyclical fluctuations in both retained earnings and new issue activity from biasing the results. Table 4.15 summarizes the result of this exercise. We were able to separate manufacturing in this table but not able to distinguish commerce from other industry. Making use of the data on identical enterprises with more than fifty employees in 1979 and 1980, we managed to extrapolate the 1979 data for private corporations to 1980.

Finally, the shares of different sources of corporate finance were obtained by adjusting both debt and equity for intermediate ownership. The adjustment coefficients are given in sections 4.3.4 and 4.3.5, and the final weights for the different sources of finance appear in table 4.16. The first thing to notice from the table is that the proportion of total finance from new share issues is, as in other countries, very small. Another striking feature is the high degree of indebtedness in other industry and commerce. The higher debt ratio in the former industry is explained by the fact that buildings in progress, which are included in inventories in table 4.12, are typically financed by short-term debt, and that inventories make up a particularly large share of the net capital stock. This is illustrated by the approximate figures on the maturity structure of debt

Table 4.15   Equity Finance, 1971–80

Year	Manufacturing			Other Industry/Commerce		
	New Issues[a]	Retained Earnings[a]	New Issues as % of Equity Finance[b]	New Issues[a]	Retained Earnings[a]	New Issues as % of Equity Finance[b]
1980	1.362	17.478	7.23	1.539	18.790	7.57
1979	1.252	15.654	7.41	1.077	16.719	6.05
1978	0.313	11.057	2.75	1.054	11.360	8.49
1977	0.344	5.437	5.95	1.291	10.587	10.87
1976	1.060	11.950	8.15	2.766	11.435	19.48
1975	1.214	13.447	8.28	1.034	9.997	9.37
1974	0.949	17.099	5.26	0.549	10.521	4.96
1973	0.268	11.541	2.27	0.345	8.067	4.10
1972	0.488	7.098	6.43	0.371	6.220	5.63
1971	0.329	6.146	5.08	0.361	5.292	6.39
1971/80	7.579	116.907	6.09	10.387	108.988	8.70
1978/80	2.927	44.189	6.21	3.670	46.869	7.26
1978/80 adjusted	1.850	44.189	4.02	2.319	46.869	4.71

Source: New issues (cash payments) are from the Central Bank and the Registration Office for Enterprises (PRV). Retained earnings are from Enterprises, Financial Accounts. Manufacturing also includes mining. Other industry/commerce is "other companies" (excluding bank and credit institutions, manufacturing, mining, agriculture and forestry). In the row "1978/80 adjusted," new issues have been corrected for intermediate purchases (see table 4.18).

[a]In billions of Swedish crowns.

[b]$100 \times$ (new issues)/(new issues + retained earnings).

Table 4.16   **Sources of Finance in Each Industry, 1980**
                                                (%)

Source of Finance	Manufacturing	Other Industry	Commerce
		Industry	
Debt	40.5	81.2	62.5
New share issues	2.4	0.9	1.8
Retained earnings	57.1	17.9	35.7
Total	100.0	100.0	100.0

Source: Own calculations as described in the text.

given in table 4.17. Long-term debt accounted for 66.8 percent of total borrowing in manufacturing, but only 51.6 percent in commerce and 33.4 percent in other industry.

4.3.4   The Ownership of Equity

We would like to obtain ownership weights for equity that reflect beneficial ownership—that is, intermediate holdings should be excluded. There is unfortunately no information readily available about such indirect or *nominee* ownership. In table 4.18 the numbers showing the distribution of owners in 1979/80 have therefore been obtained from many different sources; the main source was a report to the Commission on Wage-Earners Funds (Boman 1982), but substantial complementary calculations of our own were necessary.

The major drawback of these ownership distributions is that they refer only to shares quoted on the Stockholm Stock Exchange. Unquoted

Table 4.17   **Maturity Structure of Private Corporate Debt in Each Industry, 1980**

Industry	Long-Term Debt as % of Net Financial Debt
1. Manufacturing	66.8
2. Other industry	33.4
Electricity, gas, water	96.5
Building, construction	13.3
Transportation	72.9
3. Commerce	51.6
Wholesale, retail trade	50.9
Private services	57.8

Source: Own calculations based on unpublished data from the national accounts and Enterprises, Financial Accounts.

Table 4.18   **Shareownership in Sweden 1979/80 and 1975/76**
                        in Billions of Current Swedish Crowns
                        (proportions in parentheses)

Category of Owner	1979/80	1975/76
1. Households	23.2	22.0
	(0.604)	(0.724)
Direct ownership	21.9	21.5
In share funds	1.0	0.5
In tax-sheltered funds	0.3	—
2. Tax-exempt institutions	11.6	6.0
	(0.302)	(0.197)
Life insurance (type P)	4.3	2.2
Charities and foundations	7.3	3.8
3. Insurance companies	3.6	2.4
	(0.094)	(0.079)
Property insurance	2.4	2.0
Life insurance (type K)	0.6	0.3
Labor market and other		
taxable organizations	0.6	0.1
Total	38.4	30.4
	(1.000)	(1.000)
4. Other ultimate owners		
Government	2.3	0.4
Other organizations	0.5	0.2
Foreign owners	3.0	2.0
Total ultimate owners	44.2	33.0
(1 + 2 + 3 + 4)		
5. Intermediate owners	16.6	12.0
Investment companies	8.5	7.0
Other companies	8.1	5.0
6. Total stock of shares	60.8	45.0

Source: Boman (1982), Carlsson (1976), Spånt (1979), Aktiv Placering, and own calculations.

shares are not included, since there are few data with which to determine their ownership, and valuation is difficult in the absence of an active market. If we assume that the relation between book and market values for unquoted companies was the same as for quoted companies, then these unlisted corporations would, as a group, have a market value exceeding the value of all listed corporations by approximately 50 percent. We also know that intermediate ownership is much larger for unlisted companies. Roughly half the shares in these companies are owned by other firms, and between 15 and 20 percent belong to the public sector, leaving one-third to direct beneficial owners (compared with two-thirds of the quoted shares, table 4.18). The lion's share of these holdings is held by households, nonprofit bodies, and the like, rather than by pension funds and insurance companies.

If the ownership of these unquoted shares were included in our study, it is quite plausible that the share of households would be larger than the 60 percent figure in table 4.18. Our calculations, however, are solely based on the ownership of shares listed on the Stockholm Stock Exchange, the only stock market in Sweden. Considering the relative smallness of this market, we have not attempted to construct industry-specific ownership proportions. Although the quoted sector accounts for roughly 40 percent of all private corporate sales and an even larger share of gross profits, it is heavily dominated by manufacturing, with few firms from industries such as construction, transportation, and commerce.

In table 4.18 we see that the principal owner of equity is the household sector, accounting for 60 percent of total beneficial ownership. There has, however, been a significant downward trend in the fraction of equity owned by households.

The decreasing household ownership has, of course, a counterpart in the growing importance of institutions as shareholders. Classifying all but households as institutions, we notice a ten percentage point increase during the latter half of the 1970s for this group. The growth is especially marked for government institutions (e.g., the AP fund explained below), insurance companies, and tax-exempt institutions. Foreign ownership has, on the other hand, stayed rather constant during the period. In 1981, however, there was a marked increase in foreign investors' interest in the Swedish stock market. This interest was partly due to the abolition in 1979 of some formal obstacles to "export" of Swedish shares, and for the first time a surplus was registered for this type of portfolio investment in the capital account.

Foreign ownership of Swedish industry is more important than indicated by the stock-market figures of table 4.18, however. The reason for this is that the greater part of foreign ownership is accounted for by direct investment rather than by portfolio investment. Foreign investors' total share of (beneficial) equity ownership in Sweden amounts to nearly 10 percent.

Investment companies, shown in the table as intermediate owners, have held a fairly constant share of the ownership of listed corporations. These Swedish investment trusts are of the "closed end" type—that is, the share capital is not freely variable. A major feature of the investment trusts from a tax point of view is that dividends are exempt from tax provided at least 80 percent of the receipts are redistributed.

Table 4.18 shows that the beneficial owners included in our study account for 63.2 percent of the total value of the Swedish stock market (38.4 out of 60.8 BSEK). This share is the adjustment coefficient referred to in section 4.3.3. It is used to adjust available data on new share issues and retained earnings before estimating the shares of different sources of corporate finance.

4.3.5   The Ownership of Debt

Table 4.19 shows the ownership of financial debt in our three sectors. The estimates are based mainly on unpublished primary tables from Enterprises, Financial Accounts (covering *all* enterprises with more than fifty employees, industry by industry). The industry-specific parameters for beneficial ownership of corporate debt are shown in the top half of the table. Beneficial ownership accounts for 28, 29, and 40 percent of total debt in manufacturing, other industry, and commerce, respectively. These proportions are the adjustment coefficients for debt used in section 4.3.3 to estimate the shares of different sources of finance.

In keeping with our general approach we exclude public ownership, and hence the ownership weights calculated from the table exclude direct government lending and "special government lending." "Special lending" denotes the lending activities carried out by a number of finan-

Table 4.19   **Liabilities of Swedish Enterprises, 1980,
in Billions of Current Swedish Crowns**
(proportions in parentheses)

Category of Owner	Manufacturing	Other Industry	Commerce
1. Households	7.9	18.1	9.2
	(0.252)	(0.750)	(0.482)
Through banks	7.0	17.3	5.8
Direct lending	0.9	0.8	3.4
2. Tax-exempt institutions	21.1	4.8	9.1
	(0.672)	(0.199)	(0.476)
Pension debt (PRI)	16.1	2.1	4.5
Life insurance (type P)	3.9	1.9	1.0
Charities and foundations	1.1	0.8	3.6
3. Insurance companies	2.4	1.2	0.8
	(0.076)	(0.051)	(0.042)
Property insurance	1.8	0.9	0.4
Life insurance (type K)	0.5	0.2	0.1
Labor market organizations	0.1	0.1	0.3
Total beneficial owners	31.4	24.1	19.1
	(1.000)	(1.000)	(1.000)
4. Other domestic	57.7	52.0	26.0
"Special" lending	5.5	2.0	2.2
ATP	12.2	4.0	1.7
Government	5.8	25.0	1.9
Short-term financial debt	34.2	21.0	20.2
5. Foreign owners	22.8	7.5	2.8
Loans	16.1	6.8	2.8
Bonds	6.7	0.7	—
6. Total financial debt	111.9	83.6	47.9

Source: Enterprises, Financial Accounts, and own calculations.

cial institutions funded via the state budget. These institutions provide debt finance on terms that often are more favorable than those prevailing in the regular capital market.

The National Supplementary Pension Plan (ATP) is by far the most important scheme of occupational pensions in Sweden. The ATP plan, enacted in 1960 and financed by employers' contributions, is basically a "pay as you go" system where total contributions each year are supposed to cover that year's pension payments. However, during the introductory years of the system the rates of employer contributions were set by Parliament at such a high level that a fund of considerable size was created. There is no connection in the ATP plan between the size of this fund (or its earnings) and the pension benefits. The idea behind creating a fund during the period of introduction was rather "(i) to make possible a gradual introduction of the plan without creating inequity between different age groups, (ii) to compensate for an expected decline in private insurance savings, (iii) to make possible a general increase in capital formation without raising taxes and (iv) to enhance the ability of the economy to fulfill pension commitments in a future with a greater number of retired persons to be supported by the plan" (Bentzel and Berg 1983, p. 169). Thus, the ATP plan may be schematically described as a "pay as you go" system combined with a payroll tax that earmarks part of the revenue for financial investment. These characteristics motivate the exclusion of the ATP fund investments from our ownership weights.

Furthermore, we exclude "short-term financial debt" and foreign owners from our ownership weights. Under the heading "short-term financial debt" we include interfirm debt and value-added tax liabilities and income taxes deducted at source but not yet paid to the government. Finally, bank holdings of corporate debt—advances and bonds—have been imputed to households, insurance companies, and other owners according to the respective ownership categories' shares of total bank deposits, regarding banks or financial intermediaries.

4.4 Estimates of Effective Marginal Tax Rates

This section presents the effective marginal tax rates on capital income in the corporate sector in Sweden. It is organized in the following way. Section 4.4.1 summarizes the results of the "base case," which represents our best estimates of the parameter values for the tax system and for the capital stock weights in 1980. As explained in earlier sections of this chapter, however, some important changes in tax legislation, including a new dividend tax credit system and a reduction in personal income tax rates, have been made in recent years. In section 4.4.2 the effects of these changes are analyzed. For comparison, calculations of effective tax rates are presented also for 1960 and 1970 in section 4.4.3. Finally, in section 4.4.4 we present a comparison between calculations of effective marginal tax rates and average tax rates on the return to capital invested in the nonfinancial sector.

4.4.1   Principal Results

Table 4.20 shows the marginal effective tax rates on private nonfinancial corporate investment in Sweden in 1980 for the fixed-p case in which all assets earn a pretax real annual rate of return of 10 percent. Each column of the table corresponds to a specific assumption about the inflation rate. Three assumptions are explored—a zero rate of inflation, the actual average rate of inflation of 9.4 percent experienced in 1971–80, and a 10 percent rate of inflation.

The first three rows of the table show the marginal tax rates for machinery, buildings, and inventories. These are average marginal tax rates where the average has been taken over all industry groups, sources of finance, and categories of owner.

The variation in effective tax rate by asset is striking. As far as investment in machinery is concerned, the present tax system approximates an expenditure tax (equivalent to a zero tax rate on capital income). It is, in fact, more favorable than an expenditure tax at a zero inflation rate, providing a net subsidy to investment in machinery. For other assets the tax rate is higher. With a fully indexed comprehensive income tax, the

Table 4.20   **Effective Marginal Tax Rates, Sweden, 1980, Fixed-p Case**
(%)

	Inflation Rate		
	Zero	10%	Actual (9.4%)
Asset			
Machinery	− 18.1	1.5	0.2
Buildings	28.9	37.3	36.6
Inventories	26.5	71.0	68.8
Industry			
Manufacturing	8.1	28.3	27.1
Other industry	29.6	62.6	60.5
Commerce	12.1	40.7	39.2
Source of finance			
Debt	− 12.9	6.4	5.0
New share issues	44.2	93.2	90.4
Retained earnings	40.9	69.5	68.2
Owner			
Households	57.1	108.0	105.1
Tax-exempt institutions	− 39.2	− 52.8	− 51.8
Insurance companies	− 16.0	22.0	18.9
Overall	12.9	37.0	35.6

marginal tax rates corresponding to table 4.20 would equal an average of marginal income tax rates. In 1980 the average marginal income tax rate of households (taken over debt and equity) was 57.3 percent, and apart from investment in inventories when inflation is high, the present tax system is more favorable than an income tax.

The differences in effective tax rates among the industry groups are explained mainly by differences in the composition of their capital stock. Inventories constitute twice as large a share of the total net capital stock in other industry and commerce as in manufacturing, and inventory investment is the most heavily taxed type of real investment. The average allowed rate of inventory write-down is only 19.3 percent for other industry compared with 60 percent for manufacturing and commerce, as seen in section 4.2.3, and this contributes to the dispersion of tax rates.

The effective marginal tax rate differs markedly among the different sources of finance. The relatively lower tax rates on debt finance are explained by the combined effect of allowing companies to deduct the nominal cost of debt and the fact that the average marginal income tax rate on interest income is lower than that on dividends and capital gains. New share issues constitute the most heavily taxed form of equity finance, despite the special scheme to mitigate the "double taxation" of dividends (see section 4.2.2).

There are dramatic differences in effective tax rates among the three categories of owners. Investment financed by savings channeled through tax-exempt institutions receives a substantial subsidy. The effective tax rate of minus 51.8 percent means that for a 10 percent rate of return on real investments undertaken by corporations, tax-exempt institutions earn a posttax real rate of return of 15.2 percent on their savings. This seemingly paradoxical result is explained by the interaction between personal and corporate taxation and the fact that the corporate tax system provides a subsidy to real investment.

The taxation of the return to savings channeled directly to companies by households represents the case opposite to that of tax-exempt institutions. At the inflation rate actually experienced in 1971–80, the wedge between the pretax and posttax rates of return corresponds to more than 100 percent of the pretax rate of return.

The last row of table 4.20 shows the overall average marginal tax rates, where the average is taken over source of finance, category of owner, industry, and type of asset. At the actual rate of inflation in 1971–80, this overall tax rate of 35.6 percent is considerably below the average marginal income tax rate of households of 57.3 percent.

On *average*, therefore, the present tax system is more favorable than a comprehensive income tax, and at low rates of inflation it is closer to an expenditure tax than to an income tax. An important difference between the present system and either an expenditure tax or a comprehensive income tax is, of course, the wide dispersion of effective tax rates around the mean and their sensitivity to inflation. Both of these issues are investigated further in chapter 7.

A comparison of the different columns of table 4.20 reveals the effects of inflation on effective tax rates. The Swedish tax system is not indexed, and it is often assumed that this causes the effective tax burden to rise as the rate of inflation increases. This belief is, for Sweden, confirmed by our study. An increase in the inflation rate from zero to 10 percent almost triples the overall effective tax rate. Several factors combine to explain this remarkable result. The real value of historical cost depreciation is undermined by inflation, and FIFO accounting rules make corporations pay tax on purely nominal capital gains on inventory holdings. Inflation reduces also the real value of the special Swedish scheme to mitigate the "double taxation" of dividends (the Annell deduction). Inflation increases the nominal market interest rate, and the resulting increase in nominal interest receipts is included with the income tax base of households and insurance companies. Insurance companies are further affected by inflation because inflation reduces the real value of nominally fixed deductions for reserves (see section 4.2.10). These tax-increasing effects of inflation are partly offset by the fact that nominal interest costs are fully deductible against the taxable income of corporations. This last provision actually outweighs the taxation of nominal interest receipts to investors, since the (effective) corporate tax rate, τ, exceeds the personal rate, m, averaged over investors. The difference between the two rates is reduced by inflation, however, and the reason for this is that the effective corporate tax rate is reduced by inflation (see section 4.2.5).

Tax-exempt institutions provide a striking exception to the rule that inflation raises tax rates. In the "fixed-p" case, we calculate the maximum nominal rate of return the company can afford to pay on the financial claims of investors. Under the Swedish corporate tax system, a ceteris paribus increase in inflation leads to an increase in the real market yield that can be paid to investors. For tax-exempt institutions this raises the real rate of return on savings. For households and insurance companies, however, the increase in real market yields is not enough to compensate for the income taxation of the nominal returns to debt and equity.

It is interesting that inflation increases the dispersion of effective tax rates dramatically. The tax differential between machinery and inventories increases from 45 percentage points at zero inflation to 70 percentage points at 10 percent inflation. Similarly, the tax differential between households and tax-exempt institutions increases from 96 percentage points at zero inflation to 161 percentage points at a 10 percent rate of inflation.

The results for the "fixed-r" case are shown in table 4.21. By assuming that the yield to investors before personal tax is the same for all invest-

Table 4.21   **Effective Marginal Tax Rates, Sweden, 1980, Fixed-*r* Case**
(%)

	Inflation Rate		
	Zero	10%	Actual (9.4%)
Asset			
Machinery	−113.9	2.8	−0.7
Buildings	33.6	49.2	48.5
Inventories	37.8	73.4	72.5
Industry			
Manufacturing	12.5	46.2	45.1
Other industry	32.6	78.7	77.0
Commerce	12.7	54.9	53.7
Source of finance			
Debt	−25.5	13.4	11.5
New share issues	40.8	94.1	92.9
Retained earnings	50.3	91.2	89.6
Owner			
Households	74.0	143.6	141.0
Tax-exempt institutions	−58.2	−69.6	−68.8
Insurance companies	−28.5	30.9	26.9
Overall	16.7	54.9	53.6

ment projects, the tax rates obtained are in general higher than those in the "fixed-*p*" case. The reasons for this difference were explained in chapter 2. Note, however, that the variation in effective tax rates according to asset, industry, source of finance, and category of owner is just as true for the "fixed-*r*" case as for the "fixed-*p*" case.

4.4.2   Recent Changes in Tax Legislation

Several changes in the taxation of investment income have been introduced or proposed during the last few years. These include the so-called tax savings scheme, the dividend tax credit introduced in 1981, and the proposed "1985 system" of personal income taxation. The details of these changes were presented in sections 4.2.1 and 4.2.8 above.

We consider first the "new rules of 1981," defined to include the tax savings scheme and the dividend tax credit. They imply that (*a*) the average marginal tax rate on the interest income of households is reduced from 49.2 to 44.0 percent; (*b*) θ, the opportunity cost of retained earnings in terms of dividends forgone, for households is raised from unity to 1.403 but remains at unity for institutional investors; (*c*) there is a minor reduction in the statutory capital gains tax on households from 26 to 22 percent (arising from the tax savings scheme). Table 4.22 shows the effects of these new rules for the "fixed-p" case. Their main effect is to bring about a considerable reduction in the marginal effective tax rate on savings channeled through new share issues. Depending on the rate of inflation, the effective tax rate on new share issues is reduced by between 10 and 17 percentage points, making new share issues less heavily taxed than retained earnings at zero inflation. New issues remain, however, the most heavily taxed source of equity capital at higher rates of inflation because the effect of the scheme to mitigate the double taxation of dividends, the Annell deduction, is undermined by inflation (see section 4.2.2).

The 1981 "new rules" apply only to households, but the reduction in the average effective marginal tax rate on households is small. Depending on the rate of inflation, the reduction ranges from 3.5 to 6 percentage points. The explanation for this limited effect on household taxation is, of course, the relative unimportance of new share issues as a means of channeling household savings into real investment.

A major reform of personal income taxation was decided upon by the Swedish Parliament in June 1982 and is due to come into full effect in 1985. It implies a reduction in the average marginal income tax rate of household equity investors from 64.0 percent in 1980 to 57.2 percent. The statutory marginal tax rate on capital gains, which equals 40 percent of

Table 4.22   **Effective Marginal Tax Rates, Sweden, 1981 Rules, Fixed-p Case**
(%)

| | Inflation Rate | | |
	Zero	10%	Actual (9.4%)
Asset			
Machinery	− 19.9	− 1.1	− 2.3
Buildings	27.3	34.1	33.5
Inventories	24.5	67.8	65.7
Industry			
Manufacturing	7.1	26.9	25.7
Other industry	25.7	55.2	53.4
Commerce	9.8	36.9	35.4
Source of finance			
Debt	− 16.7	0.8	− 0.5
New share issues	34.6	75.8	73.5
Retained earnings	41.0	70.2	68.8
Owner			
Households	53.6	102.0	99.2
Tax-exempt institutions	− 39.2	− 52.8	− 51.8
Insurance companies	− 16.0	22.0	18.9
Overall	11.1	34.1	34.7

the marginal income tax rate, is therefore reduced from 26 to 23 percent. The average marginal income tax rate of household investors' debt is cut from 49.2 percent in 1980 to 43.3 percent, taking into account that 98.6 percent (see section 4.2.8) of household income on debt instruments is in taxable form. The combination of the cut in the marginal income tax rate of equity investors and the dividend tax credit system implies that the tax discrimination variable θ takes the value of 1.23 for household investors. (The tax savings scheme is not considered part of the "1985 system.")

As shown in table 4.23, the 1985 rules reduce the overall average effective tax rate at 10 percent inflation by no more than three percentage points compared with the 1981 rules. Only household investors are affected, however. Depending on the rate of inflation, their tax reduction ranges from four to eight percentage points.

The third and final alternative considered in this section represents a change in tax legislation of a different kind. We shall examine the effects of abolishing the corporation income tax (and associated grants and allowances). This represents an interesting case not only because the abolition of the separate tax on corporate profits has been suggested in Sweden as an alternative to tax reform, but also because it brings out clearly the importance of the corporation tax for the results presented above. Furthermore, in practice many Swedish corporations do not pay

Table 4.23   **Effective Marginal Tax Rates, Sweden, 1985 Rules, Fixed-*p* Case**
(%)

	Inflation Rate		
	Zero	10%	Actual (9.4%)
Asset			
Machinery	−21.7	−4.4	−5.6
Buildings	26.2	31.5	30.9
Inventories	23.4	65.7	63.7
Industry			
Manufacturing	5.7	23.9	22.9
Other industry	24.6	53.1	51.3
Commerce	8.7	34.6	33.2
Source of finance			
Debt	−16.7	−0.3	−1.5
New share issues	33.0	73.0	70.7
Retained earnings	39.1	65.7	64.5
Owner			
Households	49.6	93.9	91.4
Tax-exempt institutions	−39.2	−52.8	−51.8
Insurance companies	−16.0	22.0	18.9
Overall	9.8	31.4	30.1

any corporation income tax as a result of the combination of low pretax earnings and the existing extensive possibilities to reduce taxable profits. Another important group of companies with low pretax earnings pay corporation tax just sufficient to meet the requirement in Swedish law that dividends be paid out of current or accumulated book profits (which in turn are approximately equal to tax-accounting profits). For these companies, an additional investment project may not affect total tax payments, provided tax allowances on existing assets have not been fully used. (For further discussion of this point, see section 4.4.4.) The effective marginal tax rates in the fixed-p case for $\tau = 0$ and $g = 0$ appear in table 4.24.

Comparing tables 4.24 and 4.20 makes it clear that eliminating the corporate income tax would bring about a considerable increase in the overall effective tax rate. The explanation for this increase is that the range of tax concessions to investment is sufficiently great that taken together they more than offset the effects of the tax. The required rate of return on a project is a decreasing function of the corporate tax rate. Readers looking for a full discussion of this point are referred to the second part of Appendix C. In the case of debt finance, the effective tax rate falls as the corporate tax rate rises if the tax allows full interest deductibility and depreciation allowances beyond the value of true eco-

Table 4.24   **Effective Marginal Tax Rates, Sweden,
with the Corporation Tax Abolished, Fixed-p Case**
(%)

	Inflation Rate		
	Zero	10%	Actual (9.4%)
Asset			
Machinery	25.4	45.7	44.0
Buildings	27.6	50.3	48.8
Inventories	29.4	54.1	52.6
Industry			
Manufacturing	23.7	42.1	40.9
Other industry	39.6	75.3	73.1
Commerce	28.1	51.7	50.2
Source of finance			
Debt	25.3	50.4	48.8
New share issues	49.9	92.3	89.7
Retained earnings	29.1	47.9	46.7
Owner			
Households	62.8	112.3	109.3
Tax-exempt institutions	−11.9	−26.0	−25.2
Insurance companies	−7.0	23.6	20.7
Overall	27.5	50.1	48.7

nomic depreciation. When interest payments are not deductible, the tax rate falls only when allowances and grants for investment are worth more than 100 percent first-year allowances (immediate expensing). The same argument applies to equity finance, with the condition about deductibility of interest payments replaced by a condition about the deductibility of dividends (imputation credit). With immediate expensing and no imputation credit for dividends, the corporate tax reduces the net cost of investment by the same proportion as it reduces the present value of the earnings from the investment. Hence, when the tax system allows deductions that have a value greater than that implied by immediate expensing, companies pay a negative tax on equity-financed marginal investments.

As shown in tables 4.24 and 4.20, abolishing the corporation tax would result in a sharp rise in the effective tax rate on debt-financed investments. With the exception of the rate on new issue finance at zero inflation, abolishing the corporate income tax would reduce the effective tax rate on the return to equity-financed investment. This indicates that the combined effect of the available deductions and grants on average is less favorable than free depreciation. Inspection of the results for the eighty-one individual combinations in Appendix B makes it clear, however, that the depreciation allowances for machinery in combination with the 11.4 percent investment grant are more favorable to firms than free depreciation. The corporation tax therefore provides a subsidy to marginal investments in machinery irrespective of the source of finance, although it is a positive tax as far as other assets are concerned.

4.4.3   Comparison with 1960 and 1970

Promotion of industrial growth by means of generous investment incentives at the corporate level has been a paramount policy objective of Swedish governments for more than two decades. During this period there has been a rapid growth of total taxes, from 27 percent of GDP in 1960 to 41 percent in 1970, and to 50 percent in 1979 (see table 4.1 above). It is particularly interesting to examine the changes over time in the incentives to save and invest, as measured by the effective marginal tax rates on capital income, in the light of this growing tax burden.

Brief accounts of the derivation of the parameter values for 1960 and 1970 were given in section 4.2. In 1960 Sweden had a classical system of corporate taxation, whereas in 1970 some mitigation of double taxation had been introduced through the Annell legislation. By 1980 the Annell deduction had increased further. The rules of inventory valuation and of fiscal depreciation of machinery have not been changed since the mid-1950s, whereas for buildings an extra 2 percent allowance was introduced in 1970. In 1960 investment in machines and buildings was taxed under the sales tax at a rate equivalent to an investment grant of *minus* 2 percent. No investment grants were available in 1970, whereas in 1980 investment in machinery and buildings qualified for allowances equivalent to investment grants of 11.4 percent and 5.7 percent, respectively. The rules of the investment funds system (IF) were altered during the late 1970s, and the system was also put to more active use. At the margin, as explained in section 4.2.5, the IF system effectively reduces the corporate tax rate below the statutory tax rate. As a result, the effective corporate tax rate (as defined in section 4.2.5 and assuming a 9.4 percent inflation rate) was 37 percent in 1960, 41 percent in 1970, and 35 percent in 1980, compared with the statutory corporate tax rates for the three years of 49, 53, and 57 percent. The statutory corporate tax rate increased over time as a result of gradual increases in local income tax rates.

The 1960s and 1970s brought considerable increases in household tax rates. The average marginal tax rates on household investors in debt and equity rose from 34 and 45 percent in 1960, respectively, to 48 and 58 percent in 1970, and to 50 and 64 percent in 1980. Taxation of capital gains on household shareholdings was introduced in the mid-1960s, and by 1970 and 1980 the average marginal statutory tax rates had risen to 15 and 26 percent, respectively.

As a result of increases in local income tax rates, the marginal tax rate on insurance companies (estimated at a 9.4 percent inflation rate) rose from 24 percent in 1960 to 27 percent in 1970 and to 31 percent in 1980 for investment in debt, whereas the marginal tax rate on dividends increased from 17 percent in 1960 to 20 percent in 1970 and 24 percent in 1980. Capital gains taxes were increased from 13 percent in 1960 to 15 percent in 1970 and 19 percent in 1980.

The results of our calculations of effective marginal tax rates on capital income in 1960 and 1970 are shown in tables 4.25 and 4.26. The combined effect of the rising marginal tax rates on investors and of the more generous investment incentives has been to leave the overall effective marginal tax rate, at a 9.4 percent inflation rate, practically the same in 1980 as in 1960. The zero inflation effective tax rate was almost halved between 1960 and 1980. A comparison between tables 4.25, 4.26, and 4.20 reveals, furthermore, that the effective tax rates rose between 1960 and 1970 and fell again between 1970 and 1980. This development is explained by the fact that most of the increases of personal taxes occurred between 1960 and 1970, whereas the reduction in corporation tax was concentrated in the period 1970–80.

There are some noteworthy differences in the changes in effective tax rates over time between the three categories of owners. For tax-exempt institutions, the effective cuts in the corporation tax have brought about a considerable reduction in the effective tax rate over time, whereas for households the greater investment incentives have been insufficient to counteract rising marginal tax rates. We note also that the tax discrimina-

Table 4.25   **Effective Marginal Tax Rates, Sweden, 1960, Fixed-*p* Case**
(%)

	Inflation Rate		
	Zero	10%	Actual (9.4%)
Asset			
Machinery	16.2	16.8	16.7
Buildings	31.3	28.1	28.3
Inventories	19.9	58.2	56.1
Industry			
Manufacturing	21.5	30.8	30.3
Other industry	29.5	45.8	44.9
Commerce	19.1	35.9	35.0
Source of finance			
Debt	2.1	1.3	1.3
New share issues	58.4	99.9	97.6
Retained earnings	44.4	69.6	68.3
Owner			
Households	50.2	82.3	80.4
Tax-exempt institutions	− 10.0	− 26.7	− 25.6
Insurance companies	4.6	29.5	27.3
Overall	22.6	34.6	33.9

tion against new share issues was more pronounced in 1960 than in 1980, and the explanation for this is that in 1960 there was no mitigation of double taxation. The variation in effective tax rate by asset was less striking in 1960 and 1970 than in 1980. The main reason for this difference is that the investment grants available in 1980, but not available in 1960 and 1970, favored investment in machinery over investment in buildings.

A final observation concerns the sensitivity to inflation of the effective tax rates. Inflation causes the overall effective tax rate to rise for both 1960 and 1970, but the tax-increasing effects of inflation are less dramatic than in 1980. While historical cost depreciation and FIFO accounting rules provide explanations common to all three years for the increase in effective tax rates with inflation, the differences in the sensitivity to inflation are mainly explained by the fact that the purely nominal increases in market yields to investors were taxed at lower rates in 1960 and 1970 than in 1980. It should be noted, finally, that for 1960 the effective tax rate on the return to debt-financed investment falls as the rate of inflation increases, whereas the opposite is true for both 1970 and 1980. In 1960 the tax-reducing effect of deducting interest costs at the (effective) corporate tax rate of 37 percent outweighs the tax-increasing effect of taxing nominal interest receipts to all three categories of owners.

Table 4.26   **Effective Marginal Tax Rates, Sweden, 1970, Fixed-p Case**
(%)

	Inflation Rate		
	Zero	10%	Actual (9.4%)
Asset			
Machinery	15.2	20.3	19.9
Buildings	33.1	34.5	34.4
Inventories	24.1	72.5	69.9
Industry			
Manufacturing	21.7	35.6	34.8
Other industry	36.1	63.2	61.6
Commerce	21.2	45.9	44.5
Source of finance			
Debt	2.0	8.4	7.9
New share issues	55.6	103.7	100.9
Retained earnings	48.4	79.1	77.5
Owner			
Households	60.6	106.4	103.7
Tax-exempt institutions	−18.3	−37.6	−36.3
Insurance companies	−0.3	27.6	25.1
Overall	24.3	42.7	41.6

4.4.4   Comparison with Average Tax Rates

It is of interest to compare the calculations of marginal effective tax rates presented above with estimates of the average tax rates implied by actual tax payments. The calculations presented in this section all refer to the national accounts sector of nonfinancial enterprises. In addition to our three industry groups (manufacturing, other industry, and commerce) the national accounts data also cover mining and quarrying, agriculture, forestry and fishing, real estate, and business services. Public business agencies (for example, the State Railway Company) as well as other nonprivate and unincorporated enterprises are included. The choice of the nonfinancial enterprises sector for our calculations has been dictated by the lack of suitable alternative data.

The 1970s represented a period of dramatic change for the Swedish economy. After the 1971–72 recession and the oil crisis of 1973, Swedish firms—in particular manufacturing firms—experienced a boom in profits of an intensity not witnessed since the Korean War. The subsequent downturn, beginning in 1976, was equally dramatic, with the severest profits crisis for manufacturing industry since the 1930s. Business conditions improved again in 1979 and 1980, though profits remained low compared with their previous long-term average. This is clearly reflected in table 4.27, which shows corporate profits and their appropriation among corporate taxes, interest payments, dividend payments, and retained earnings. As a result of low profits, retained earnings net of economic depreciation were negative in 1978–80. A significant feature of the government's response to the difficulties facing business was large subsidies to industry (Carlsson, Bergholm, and Lindberg 1981). This policy, which included both rescue operations on a massive scale and ad hoc investment subsidies, is reflected in the second row of table 4.27. Corporate taxes of minus 2,078 million SEK are here defined as the sum of corporate tax payments of 4,170 million and ad hoc subsidies of no less than 6,248 million SEK. It should also be noted that, despite the downturn in profits, payments of corporation tax and payments of dividends from the nonfinancial sector continued to increase in 1978–80 compared with earlier years.

The average effective tax rate for the nonfinancial sector is defined here as the ratio of total taxes on capital income originating in the sector to real operating profits (net of economic depreciation). Its calculation is summarized in table 4.28. Data on actual tax payments are available only for the corporation tax. The actual amounts of income tax paid by the owners of debt and equity on interest receipts and dividends cannot be observed. Investment income is included with earned income for assessment of tax, and it is not possible to determine whether investment income comes "first" or "last." We have estimated tax payments on interest receipts and dividends by simply multiplying the interest and dividend payments of the sector by the weighted average marginal tax rates on interest income and dividends, respectively, using the ownership proportions presented in sections 4.3.4 and 4.3.5 as weights. The 1980 average marginal tax rates were 25.3 percent on interest income and 40.9 percent on dividend income.

Table 4.27   **Corporate Profits and Their Appropriation, Sweden 1978–80**
(billions of current Swedish crowns)

	1978–80 Average
Real operating profits	14.224
Corporate taxes (including subsidies)	−2.078
Interest payments[a]	19.932
Dividend payments	3.833
Real retained earnings	−7.463

Source: Own calculations based on National Accounts, 1980.

[a]Nonfinancial firms pay dividends and interest on debt both to other firms within the same sector and to recipients outside the sector. Firms likewise receive dividends and interest earnings from both within and outside the sector. By interest payments we mean the sum of all interest costs less the sum of all interest receipts. Dividend payments are defined analogously.

Table 4.28   **Average Tax Rate on Real Corporate Profits**
(billions of current Swedish crowns)

	1978–80 Average	Percentage of Profits
Total taxes		
Including subsidies	4.184	29.42
Excluding subsidies	10.432	73.34
Corporate taxes	−2.078	−14.61
Corporate tax payments	4.170	29.32
Ad hoc subsidies	−6.248	−43.93
Taxes on		
Interest payments	5.043	35.45
Dividend payments	1.568	11.02
Real retained earnings	−0.719	−5.05
Personal wealth	0.370	2.60
Real operating profits	14.224	
Average tax rate (%)		
Including subsidies	29.4	
Excluding subsidies	73.3	
Average profit rate (%)		
Gross of tax	2.0	

Source: Own calculations as described in the text.

Retained earnings are taxed as capital gains to the extent that profit retention causes the market value of equity to rise. We assume here that the tax rate on retained earnings can be approximated by the effective rate of tax paid by the owners of equity on accrued capital gains.

As explained in section 4.2, the effective capital gains tax rate of insurance companies is 19 percent, and for simplicity we have taken the effective accruals tax (EAT) rate of households to be one-half the statutory tax rate of 26 percent. This gives a weighted average tax rate on the retained earnings of the nonfinancial sector of 9.6 percent.

The Swedish wealth tax is assessed on the net wealth (assets less liabilities) of households, and there is no obvious way to allocate wealth tax payments among various assets. It is possible, however, to obtain rough estimates of the amounts of wealth taxes paid on account of the holdings of equity and debt of nonfinancial enterprises. In his recent study of household wealth, Spånt (1979) gives a detailed account of the distributions of financial and real assets of various kinds, as well as household debt, over different size classes of net (taxable) wealth. This information makes it possible to estimate the wealth tax payments of each class, using the tax schedule presented in section 4.2.7. We then simply assume that the wealth tax payments can be allocated proportionately among the various assets of each class. If, for example, shares make up 30 percent of total assets of a specific class of net wealth, 30 percent of the wealth tax payments of this class are allocated to the shares. This approach is obviously equivalent to assuming that within a specific class of net wealth assets of all kinds are financed by debt in the same proportion.

Using this approach, we estimate that approximately 25 percent of total wealth tax payments may be attributed to equity holdings and 13 percent to the ownership of bank deposits. Since only some 35 percent of bank lending goes to the nonfinancial sector, we attribute only 5 percent of total wealth tax payments to household ownership of debt. Hence, in total, 30 percent of wealth tax payments are attributed to the nonfinancial corporate sector, and the resulting 370 million SEK figure is shown in table 4.28.

Our estimates of the average effective tax burden on capital income from the nonfinancial sector appear in table 4.28. When the ad hoc subsidies extended to the business sector during the crisis are treated as negative taxes, the average tax rate turns out to be 29.4 percent. This is six percentage points lower than the overall average marginal tax rate for 1980, at the actual average rate of inflation. If, on the other hand, the 6.2 billion SEK of subsidies are excluded, the average tax rate rises to 73.3 percent. Considering the very low level of business profits in 1978–80, it is of interest to compare these numbers with corresponding figures for earlier years. For 1973—the year preceding the profits boom of 1974–75—we estimate the average effective tax rate to be 35.4 percent including subsidies and 42.2 percent when ad hoc subsidies are excluded.

For the comparison with the results of section 4.4.1, however, there are several observations to be made. As already pointed out, the tax rate in table 4.28 reflects actual tax payments and profits associated with both old and new assets held by firms, whereas the effective tax rates of section 4.4.1 refer to a set of hypothetical "marginal" investments. With a corporate tax system that allows firms extensive possibilities to defer tax payments through various schemes of accelerated depreciation, actual tax payments and the share of profits paid as corporate income tax become endogenous. They depend on the rate of growth of real investment and on the firms' (average) rate of return (see Södersten 1975, 1978).

The theoretical calculations of effective tax rates in this study are all based on the crucial assumption that corporations take full advantage of depreciation allowances and rules of inventory undervaluation. This implies either that the "representative" firm has sufficiently large profits, or that the tax laws provide for full loss offset on "tax accounting" losses. Empirical studies on a large number of Swedish firms indicate, however, that most firms have not been able to fully use the existing extensive possibilities to reduce or defer corporate tax payments. There is, in fact, a strong correlation between the use of accelerated depreciation, and so forth, and the (before-tax) rate of return of individual firms. As a result, high-profit firms have a lower effective annual tax burden than low-profit firms.

A possible explanation for this result is the combined effect of the requirement of Swedish law that dividends be paid out of current or accumulated book profits and of the close connection between book and tax accounting profits. Within the limits set by tax legislation, Swedish firms may themselves decide the size of the profits reported on the books, through a more or less intensive use of accelerated depreciation, variations in the valuation of inventories, and allocations to investment funds. If a policy of stable dividends is to be maintained, a firm with low profitability may not be able to make full use of these possibilities of tax deferral. This means the effective (annual) tax burden will be high in comparison with a more profitable firm that is able to use all its tax allowances.

5 West Germany

5.1 Introduction

The basic structure of the present German tax system emerged at the end of World War I. Taxes on income and net wealth, which before this time had been the principal sources of revenue for the states (*Länder*), came under federal control in 1920. Since then, legislation in the field of taxation has been primarily a federal matter, although the states have continued to play an important role in the administration of the tax system.[1]

As can be seen from table 5.1, taxes on personal incomes, including social security contributions, have been the main source of government revenue since the mid-1950s. In 1979 these taxes accounted for 63 percent of total revenue (44 percent in 1955), taxes on corporations accounted for only 6 percent of total revenue (10 percent in 1955), and the value-added tax (before 1968 the turnover tax) accounted for about 16 percent of all taxes (36 percent in 1955). Total revenue increased as a proportion of GDP. About two-thirds of the increase in the ratio of tax revenue to GDP, from about 31 percent in 1955 to about 37 percent in 1979, can be attributed to higher social security contributions.

These figures do not, however, bring out the numerous changes in policy that have occurred since the Second World War. These changes have been due partly to historical circumstances—the allied occupation, the needs of reconstruction, the prolonged recession of the mid-1970s—and partly to changes in the objectives of public policy. It is convenient to divide the postwar years into four distinct periods:

1. For a description of the historical development of the German tax system, see Gumpel and Boettcher (1963).

Table 5.1   Sources of Tax Revenue, Germany, 1955–79

Revenue Source	Share of Total Receipt (%)				Total Receipts (DM million) 1979
	1955	1960	1970	1979	
Taxes on personal incomes	19.2	22.5	26.6	28.9	151.208
Wages and salaries	7.5	8.5	15.8	18.6	97.067
Assessed income tax	7.5	9.5	7.2	7.2	37.551
Withholding except wages and salaries	0.6	0.9	0.9	0.7	3.809
Enterprise tax	3.6	3.6	2.5	2.4	12.781
Other			0.3		—
Taxes on corporate incomes	9.8	9.3	5.7	6.0	31.497
Corporation tax	5.4	6.9	3.9	4.4	22.912
Enterprise tax	4.4	2.5	1.6	1.6	8.520
Other			0.1	0.0	.064
Social security contributions	24.5	27.5	30.4	34.1	178.110
By employers	14.2	14.9	16.6	18.3	95.520
By employees	9.8	11.8	13.5	15.2	79.230
By self-employed	0.6	0.9	0.3	0.6	3.360
Payroll taxes	0.8	0.7	0.6	0.6	3.324
Property taxes	8.8	6.0	4.2	2.7	14.187
General taxes on goods and services	19.8	17.0	17.1	16.1	84.206
Taxes on specific goods and services	14.7	14.1	12.9	9.3	48.755
Alcohol	1.8	1.9	1.6	1.1	5.769
Tobacco	4.5	3.7	2.9	2.0	10.701
Petroleum	2.0	2.8	5.2	4.0	21.140
Other	6.4	5.7	3.1	2.1	11.145
Miscellaneous taxes	2.4	2.7	2.5	2.2	11.513
Total receipts	100.0	100.0	100.0	100.0	522.800
Gross domestic product (DM million)	182.0	302.8	678.8	1400.2	1,400.200
Share of taxes in GDP (%)	30.8	31.3	32.8	37.3	

Source: Revenue Statistics of OECD Member Countries 1965–1980 (Paris 1981).

1. Immediately after the war, the Allied Control Council introduced high personal income tax rates (up to 90 percent) and corporation tax rates (50 percent, raised to 60 percent in 1951). Favorable depreciation allowances, however, reduced the effective tax burden.

2. During reconstruction there were successive reductions in personal tax rates (1948, 1953, 1954). In 1958 a new rate structure was introduced that, despite subsequent modification, has been largely maintained. This structure comprised a low exemption level, a bracket with a constant marginal tax rate, a second bracket with progressive rates, and a final bracket with a constant marginal tax rate. During this period the major change in the corporation tax was the introduction of a "split-rate system" in 1953 (see below). Tax rates on retained earnings and dividends were changed repeatedly (1953, 1955, 1958). It is interesting that, along with the general reduction in tax rates, depreciation allowances were reduced, apparently in the hope of forcing firms to seek external finance for new investments by restricting cash flows.

3. With the end of the reconstruction period (mid-1960s) governments showed increased concern with demand management and the existing pattern of income distribution. It was often stated (especially by the advisory board of the Ministry of Finance) that tax policy toward investment should be employed to smooth cyclical fluctuations or to assist certain types of activity (regional development, R&D, etc.). Moreover, as in the case of grants, the instruments applied should attempt to be as neutral as possible among firms of different size. Hence surcharges on income and corporate taxes (in 1970–71, 1973–74), an investment tax (1973), and a temporary tax-free investment grant (1974–75) were introduced at different times. Investment grants were provided for regional development, for research, for environmental protection, and for energy saving.

4. Since the mid-1970s there has been a change of climate in favor of establishing a "better general framework" for investment. In 1977 the new corporate tax system was introduced that abolished (for residents) double taxation of distributed earnings by introducing a system with full imputation of corporate tax payments at the recipient level (see section 5.2.2). Wealth tax rates were lowered in 1978, after they had been increased in 1975. Exemption limits were raised for the local business tax, and in 1980 one component of the local business tax—the local payroll tax—was abolished. Furthermore, depreciation allowances were increased in 1977 and 1981, which seemed to indicate a departure from previous attitudes toward the tax treatment of investment.

Since 1975 no fewer than four income tax "reforms" have been carried out (1975, 1978, 1979, 1981). These changes are summarized in table 5.2, which shows the development of marginal tax rates on earnings.

Inflation has been a less serious problem in Germany than in other

Table 5.2   Development of Individual Income Tax Rates, 1974–81

Gross Annual Wages and Salaries (DM)	Average 1977[a] Wages and Salaries within Income Interval	Marginal Tax Rates					Change between 1974 and 1981
		1974	1977	1978	1979	1981	
Below 2,400	1,176	0.0	0.0	0.0	0.0	0.0	0
2,400–4,800	3,575	19.0	22.0	22.0	0.0	0.0	−19.0
4,800–7,200	5,950	19.0	22.0	22.0	22.0	22.0	3.0
7,200–9,600	8,401	19.6	22.0	22.0	22.0	22.0	2.3
9,600–12,000	10,773	23.1	22.0	22.0	22.0	22.0	−1.1
12,000–16,000	13,990	27.3	22.0	22.0	22.0	22.0	−5.3
16,000–20,000	18,102	32.0	32.8	32.8	25.6	22.1	−9.9
20,000–25,000	22,591	36.1	36.7	36.7	32.3	27.9	−8.2
25,000–36,000	30,051	40.7	42.0	42.0	40.0	35.7	−4.9
36,000–50,000	42,269	44.6	47.1	47.1	46.5	44.4	−0.1
50,000–75,000	58,471	48.1	50.1	50.1	50.1	50.1	1.9
75,000–100,000	84,212	50.6	53.7	53.7	53.7	53.7	3.1
100,000 and above	140,052	53.0	56.0	56.0	56.0	56.0	3.0
Total[b]	27,281	41.6	43.2	43.2	41.5	39.2	−2.3

Source: Tax laws in Germany.
Note: Entries are marginal tax rates that apply at specified wage and salary levels if the taxpayer has no other income. The wage and salary distribution of 1977 has been used to weight marginal rates among income intervals.
[a]Preliminary figures.
[b]Weighted average.

countries. The average annual inflation rate for consumption and investment goods between 1970 and 1980 was 4.2 percent in Germany, and this is the measure we use for the "actual" expected rate of inflation. The general increase in prices has had, consequently, somewhat less impact on the tax system, although there has still been "fiscal drag." From the point of view of this study, the more interesting effect of inflation relates to the definition of the tax base and the need for "capital income indexation." Although the base has not been adjusted in this way, the raising of depreciation allowances in 1977 and 1981 may be considered as partial compensation for the erosion of allowances that occurs under historic cost depreciation.

5.2   The Tax System

5.2.1   The Personal Income Tax (*Einkommensteuer*)

Individual residents in Germany are liable, in principle, to a single income tax on all sources of income. Assessment is, however, carried out according to a schedular system that specifies seven separate forms of income.[2]

1. From agriculture and forestry
2. From trade and business
3. From independent personal services
4. From employment
5. From capital
6. From rents and royalties
7. Miscellaneous income, including annuities and other recurrent payments of benefits, "speculation gains," and a few other sources of income.

Income for the first three categories is measured, with some adjustment, as the difference in net worth between the beginning and end of the accounting year as measured by book values. For the remaining categories income is measured as the difference between gross receipts and expenses.

Except for preferential tax rates on certain items (e.g., "extraordinary income," described below) tax is computed at graduated rates on the total aggregate amount of the taxpayer's income, net of all the allowable deductions and exemptions. Married couples are entitled to income splitting, whereby the tax charged is twice the amount that would be due on half the joint taxable income. In 1981 there were four clearly defined bands of tax rates:

---

2. The taxpayer is permitted to offset losses (or the excess of income-related expenses over gross income) from one or several sources against income from other sources.

The first DM 4212 (DM 8424, for married persons jointly assessed) of the tax base is exempt.

For taxable income above DM 4212 (DM 8424) and below DM 18,000 (DM 36,000), the tax is 22 percent.

For taxable income between DM 18,001 (DM 36,002) and 129,999 (259,999), the tax is computed by means of two complicated formulas that raise the marginal tax rate from 22 percent to 56 percent.[3]

Above DM 130,000 (DM 260,000) the tax rate is 56 percent.

A rough idea of the distribution of the tax rates on wages and salaries among the various income classes is presented in table 5.2, and the distribution of wages and salaries is shown in table 5.3.

Tax allowances for children were abolished in 1975. They have been replaced by uniform monthly cash payments made by the labor office. These monthly payments are respectively DM 50 for the first child, DM 100 for the second child, and DM 220 for each child after the first two.

Withholding taxes, the most important of which are the wage taxes (*Lohnsteuer*), are an important part of the German tax system. Most forms of capital income (including dividends and convertible bonds) are also subject to a flat-rate withholding tax of 25 percent, and for some forms—not of direct interest to the present study—a 30 percent rate represents a final payment of tax. Most bonds are, however, exempt from withholding taxes. The withholding tax is considered an advanced payment of income tax for residents. Credit against income tax and refunds, if payments exceed income tax due, are obtainable against amounts withheld. Not all tax-exempt institutions are able to reclaim the refund, and this produces the anomalous result that some institutions bear a rather heavy tax burden on particular forms of investment income.

In general, individuals are *not* taxed on capital gains. Sales and certain "dispositions" of property held for short periods are, however, treated as "speculative gains" and included in the individual's taxable income. If the holding period exceeds six months for securities and two years for real property, gains are not taxed. We have therefore assumed, for the purpose of this study, that there is no tax on capital gains ($z = 0$).

The German tax system allows many deductions for work-related expenses (*Werbungskosten*) and other expenses (*Sonderausgaben*) in computing taxable income.[4] For work-related expenses the taxpayer may choose to itemize deductions or take standard deductions for some categories of income.[5] The standard deductions include also a flat-rate

---

3. The formulas are: (a) DM 18,000–DM 59,999: $\{[(3.05y - 73.76)y + 695]y + 2200\}y + 3034$, where y is 1/10,000 of the amount that exceeds DM 18,000; and (b) DM 60,000–DM 129,999: $\{[(0.09y - 5.45)y + 88.13]y + 5040\}y + 20018$, where y is now 1/10,000 of the amount that exceeds DM 60,000.

4. We omit discussion of certain special allowances granted either for particular groups of taxpayers or exceptional expenses (*Aussergewöhnliche Belastung*).

5. These are as follows: income from employment (DM 564), for capital income (DM 100/joint assessment DM 200), annuities, and pensions (DM 200).

Table 5.3   Distribution of Gross Annual Wages and Salaries by Income Class, 1950–77

Gross Annual Wages and Salaries (DM)	Share of Total Wages and Salaries (%)						
	1950	1961	1965	1968	1971	1974	1977
Below 2,400	18.5	3.2	1.9	1.2	0.6	0.3	0.3
2,400–4,800	59.9	12.3	5.1	2.4	1.2	0.8	0.6
4,800–7,200	14.1	26.9	11.3	4.8	1.9	1.0	0.8
7,200–9,600	3.8	26.7	19.8	9.2	3.2	1.5	0.9
9,600–12,000	1.6	12.5	23.1	14.2	5.1	2.0	1.3
12,000–16,000	—	8.8	20.8	24.6	13.9	5.5	3.0
16,000–20,000	1.5	3.9	7.8	17.5	17.9	9.3	4.8
20,000–25,000	0.3	2.2	4.3	13.1	18.8	15.2	10.1
25,000–36,000	—	1.5	3.1	8.5	24.8	29.6	26.5
36,000–50,000	—	0.6	1.0	2.2	8.4	22.1	25.9
50,000–75,000	—	0.4	0.6	0.9	2.7	9.3	18.8
75,000–100,000	—	0.1	0.2	0.3	0.5	1.6	4.0
100,000 and above	—	0.4	0.4	0.4	0.6	1.1	2.4
Total	100.0	100.0	100.0	100.0	100.0	100.0	100.0

Source: Körner (1981).

supplementary allowance for employment income (DM 480), a "Christmas" allowance (DM 600), and a 40 percent allowance for income from pensions (with an upper limit of DM 4,800). In addition, a special "saver's exemption" (DM 300/DM600) is allowed for capital income.

Special expenses (*Sonderausgaben*) are personal or family expenditures not incurred in connection with the generation of income. Among others they include charitable contributions, the church tax, expenses for professional education, and donations to political parties.[6] The most important provisions, however, regard certain types of savings: life insurance policies; insurance policies covering civil liability, accidents, and health; social security contributions (including those paid by the employer); and, within certain limits, contributions to savings and loan associations. A standard allowance is granted for insurance premiums (*Versorgungspauschbetrag*). For wage and salary earners the standard allowance (which depends on income, marital status, and number of children) is incorporated in the wage tax schedule (*Vorsorgepauschale*). This allowance is granted even if the actual insurance premiums are lower. If higher, the actual premiums are deductible only up to certain limits, which depend again upon family composition (*Sonderausgabenhöchstbeträge*). These upper limits are adjusted from time to time.

In practice this system implies that the difference between the maximum allowance and the allowance incorporated in the tax schedule (*Vorsorgepauschale*), is rather small for most people. The *Vorsorgepauschale* becomes equal to the maximum allowance for single taxpayers above an annual income of DM 26,000 and for married taxpayers above DM 52,000 (if both spouses are employed and there are no children). If one spouse is employed the maximum allowance is higher than the allowance that is given automatically, although the difference is small in the middle and higher income brackets. Additional savings in life insurance policies are therefore in most instances not especially favored by the tax system.

There have been a number of other subsidies to saving, but these have recently been reduced. Between 1948 and 1958, all savings made under special "savings contracts" were deductible (*Sonderausgaben*). From 1959 to 1980, cash grants proportional to savings were available up to a certain limit. To encourage a wider distribution of wealth and workers' participation in enterprises, savings of employees and contributions by employers to special schemes are subsidized. Under this scheme a 30 percent cash grant is provided on maximum savings up to DM 624.[7] These

6. The church tax is a regular levy on individuals who declare themselves members of the Roman Catholic church or Protestant churches.
7. The rate of grant is 40 percent for families with three or more children. The maximum amount of savings (DM 624) includes the grant element, so the employee may place only DM 436.80 of his wage and salary income into this scheme. If the employer pays additional wages into the savings promotion scheme, his income (or corporate) tax is lowered by 30 percent of this amount (up to a maximum of DM 6,000).

cash grants are limited to employees with a maximum taxable income of less than DM 24,000 if they are single or DM 48,000 if they are married. There is no restriction on the form of the savings.

The tax treatment of owner-occupied housing distinguishes "one family houses" from "two or more family houses." If classified in the second category (at least one apartment has to be let by the owner), the investment is treated the same as a business investment—that is, interest payments are fully deductible and depreciation is deductible also at rates of 5 percent in the first eight years, 2.5 percent from the ninth to the fourteenth year, and 1.25 percent from the fifteenth to the fiftieth year (see section 5.2.3). On the other hand, both rent received and the imputed rent from owner occupancy are taxed. For a "one family house," interest payments for mortgages generally are not deductible, but there is no taxation of imputed rent. (For houses built between 1983 and 1986, interest payments are deductible up to 10,000 DM per annum during the first three years.) There are, however, favorable depreciation allowances at rates of 5 percent in the first eight years and 2.5 percent for the remaining years, subject to an upper limit of DM 200,000 for the depreciation base. In contrast to many other countries, interest payments on consumer loans are not deductible.

Government interest in savings subsidies seems to have waned in recent years. In 1980 the general savings bonus system was abolished, and grants for savings in residential construction were reduced. The importance of these schemes as a percentage of household saving is summarized in table 5.4.

5.2.2   The Corporate Tax System

In Germany the corporate sector accounts for about 35–40 percent of total turnover of all enterprises. The corporation tax, however, does not constitute a large proportion of tax revenues. In 1977 a new system of company taxation was introduced that virtually eliminated the double taxation of dividends. This was accomplished by combining the basic features of the split-rate system, whereby retained earnings and dividends are taxed at different rates, with an imputation system that provided for a dividend credit. Under this system corporation tax on profits is levied at a rate of 56 percent on retained earnings and 36 percent on distributed profits.[8] The shareholder then receives full credit for this 36 percent when his income tax liability is computed.

8. We shall limit the discussion here to industrial companies. Public credit institutions and savings banks are taxed at rates of 46 percent and 44 percent, respectively. The system separates distributable earnings into three categories: those that have to bear a tax at a rate of 56 percent, those taxed at 36 percent, and those that pay no tax. In most instances the last two categories apply respectively to domestic intercompany dividends and to income from foreign subsidiaries. There is no reduction in tax if dividends are distributed from earnings deemed to come from the 36 percent group, and, indeed, if profits are distributed from the no-tax group, the tax burden is increased to 36 percent.

Table 5.4   Direct and Indirect Savings Promotion Measures
(amount of each subsidy as % of total household savings)

| Period | Total of All Subsidy Schemes | Residential Housing Promotion | | | | | Savings Bonus Scheme | Wealth-Promotion Scheme for Employees |
| | | Savings Promotion | | | Other | | | |
		Total	Bonus Scheme	Tax Reductions	Special De-preciations	Land Tax Exemptions		
1949–53	9.7	7.6	0.5	2.9	2.5	1.7	2.1	—
1954–59	11.0	8.1	1.9	1.5	2.6	2.0	3.0	—
1960–70	9.9	8.1	2.6	1.8	1.9	1.7	1.4	0.5
1971–74	11.8	7.0	3.4	1.0	1.5	1.1	1.2	3.5
1975–78	13.1	7.0	2.3	0.7	2.8	1.3	2.7	3.3

Source: Ministry of Social Affairs, Statistical Office, and own calculations.

In practice, the credit is computed as follows. Dividends received are grossed up by the 36 percent rate to determine a notional gross dividend; that is, the shareholder includes 36/64 = 9/16 of the cash dividend received as well as the dividend itself in his taxable income. The grossed-up dividends are applied to the appropriate income tax schedule, and a credit equal to 9/16 of the cash dividend is available to offset the tax liability. Refunds are paid to individual shareholders whose credits exceed income tax liabilities.[9] Refunds are, however, not completely available to tax-exempt institutions (see section 5.2.9). The lower tax on dividends is therefore virtually a form of deduction at source for the income tax on dividends.

The basic rate of corporation tax is 56 percent. The effect of this split-rate and dividend credit system is that distributed profits are not taxed by the corporation tax but bear only the shareholder's personal rate of income tax. In other words, the system operates as if it were an imputation system where the rate of imputation is the basic rate of corporation tax. In chapter 2 we showed that with an imputation system the tax discrimination variable θ is equal to $1/(1-c)$ where c is the rate of imputation. Hence in Germany $\theta = 1/(1-0.56) = 2.2727$.

The advantages granted to domestic taxpayers are not given to foreigners. This means that foreigners have to bear the full tax burden on distributions as well as the additional dividend withholding tax. In the case of a 25 percent dividend withholding tax rate, the total tax burden on investment income for foreigners is $0.36 + 0.25 (1.00 - 0.36) = 52$ percent. In the case of double tax treaties where the dividend withholding tax is reduced to 15 percent, the total burden on foreigners is $0.36 + 0.15 (1.00 - 0.36) = 45.6$ percent.

Before the introduction of the present system of dividend relief, the German corporation tax was based on a split rate system that provided partial relief for the double taxation of dividends at the corporate level. Under this system, profits distributed to shareholders were subject to a tax rate of 15 percent, whereas retained profits were taxed at 51 percent. During the 1970s, both rates were subject to a 3 percent surcharge, making them 15.45 and 52.45, respectively. If we denote the tax rates on distributed and undistributed profits by c_d and c_u, then the tax discrimination variable θ is equal to $1/(1 + c_d - c_u)$, as described in King (1977, chap. 3). For Germany this gives a value for θ, before the new corporate tax system, of 1.589.

Apart from the supplementary surcharge of 3 percent (*Ergänzungsabgabe*), levied from January 1968 until the introduction of the new corporate tax system, two other temporary surcharges were introduced as

9. There is also a withholding tax of 25 percent of the cash dividend that is also credited. It is, however, not part of the imputation system and is not discussed here. But see section 5.2.9.

short-term stabilization measures. The "demand pressure surcharge" (*Konjunkturzuschlag*) was a temporary and repayable surcharge between 31 July 1970 and 1 July 1971 and was equal to 10 percent of tax liabilities. It was repaid after 15 June 1972. The "stabilization surcharge" (*Stabilitätsabgabe*) was a temporary surcharge that lasted from 1 July 1973 until 30 June 1974 and was also charged at a rate of 10 percent. Finally, all interest payments are deductible for corporate tax purposes, and in Germany there are taxes on corporate wealth (see section 5.2.6 and 5.2.7).

5.2.3   Tax Allowances for Depreciation and Inventories

The basis for computing depreciation allowances is historical cost. Firms have a choice between two main methods for computing depreciation:[10] (*a*) straight line, allowed on all assets and mandatory for buildings (with an exception to be discussed below), and (*b*) declining balance, at a rate equal to three times the value of the straight-line rate, with a maximum of 30 percent (before 30 June 1981, the rate was 2.5 times the straight-line rate, with a maximum of 25 percent). Changes in these rates are summarized in table 5.5.

There are other methods of depreciation that can be used in special cases: (*a*) The "production" method, based on output and utilization, is allowed for business assets whose use and physical wear and tear are subject to fluctuations. (b) Special depreciation possibilities exist for some sectors (mining, private hospitals, agriculture), some capital goods, environmental protection, and investment goods used for ships or aircraft or in certain areas (Berlin, eastern frontier area).

There are detailed depreciation tables with service lives for individual investment goods. These are compulsory and form the basis of the capital stock values presented in corporate financial balance sheets. Since depreciation rates vary considerably, the values employed in this study are averages based on our own calculations from data from the Statistical Office. These values take account of changes in tax laws and in the composition of the asset category.[11] As can be seen from table 5.6, there has been a shortening of the economic and tax lives of both buildings and equipment.

The present value of depreciation allowances with straight-line depreciation per dollar of investment (A_z) is (see chap. 2)

---

10. Straight-line and declining-balance depreciation are considered to be ordinary (*planmässige*) methods. The other methods mentioned and the special provisions are said to be "extraordinary" (*ausserplanmässige*).

11. The calculation of the tax lives was based on the same method employed for the actual service lives shown below and on an average adjustment factor provided by the Statistical Office for the present study.

Table 5.5   **Development of Maximum First-Year Allowances for Assets with Different Service Lives**
(%)

Service Life (years)	First-Year Allowance If Straight Line Depreciation	First-Year Allowance If "Accelerated" Depreciation					
		1953-57	1 January 1958 –8 March 1960	9 March 1960– 31 December 1960	1 January 1961– 31 August 1977	1 September 1977 –29 June 1981	Since 30 June 1981
1	100.0	100.00	100.00	100.00	100.00[a]	100.00	100.00
2	50.00	Accelerated depreciation not allowed	25.00	20.00	20.00	25.00	30.00
3	33.33		25.00	20.00	20.00	25.00	30.00
4	25.00		25.00	20.00	20.00	25.00	30.00
5	20.00		25.00	20.00	20.00	25.00	30.00
6	16.67		25.00	20.00	20.00	25.00	30.00
7	14.29		25.00	20.00	20.00	25.00	30.00
8	12.50		25.00	20.00	20.00	25.00	30.00
9	11.11		25.00	20.00	20.00	25.00	30.00
10	10.00	28.31	25.00	20.00	20.00	25.00	30.00
11	9.09	26.59	22.73	18.18	18.18	22.73	27.27
12	8.33	25.09	20.83	16.67	16.67	20.83	25.00
13	7.69	23.78	19.23	15.38	15.38	19.23	23.07
14	7.14	22.61	17.86	14.29	14.29	17.86	21.43
15	6.67	21.57	16.67	13.33	13.33	16.67	20.00
16	6.25	20.63	16.00	16.00	12.50	15.63	18.75
17	5.88	19.78	16.00	16.00	11.76	14.71	17.65
18	5.56	19.00	16.00	16.00	11.11	13.89	16.67
19	5.26	18.30	15.79	15.79	10.53	13.16	15.79
20	5.00	17.65	15.00	15.00	10.00	12.50	15.00
25	4.00	15.04	12.00	12.00	8.00	10.00	12.00
30	3.33	13.18	11.67	11.67	6.67	8.33	10.00
40	2.50	10.63	8.75	8.75	5.00	6.25	7.50
50	2.00	8.97	7.00	7.00	4.00	5.00	6.00
100	1.00	5.20	3.50	3.50	2.00	2.50	3.00

Source: Tax laws in Germany.

[a]Accelerated depreciation was not allowed from 6 June 1970 to 31 January 1971, or from 9 May 1973 to 30 November 1973.

Table 5.6   **Development of Average Actual Service Life and Tax Life for Machinery and Buildings, 1960–78**

| | Period of Service (years) | | | |
| | Machinery | | Buildings[a] | |
Year	Economic (1)	Tax Allowance (2)	Economic (3)	Tax Allowance (4)
1960	15	14	52	42
1961	15	14	50	40
1962	14	13	50	39
1963	14	13	50	38
1964	14	13	49	36
1965	13	13	48	35
1966	12	11	48	34
1967	13	11	48	34
1968	13	11	48	34
1969	13	11	47	33
1970	13	12	47	33
1971	13	11	46	32
1972	13	12	45	32
1973	13	11	45	31
1974	13	11	45	31
1975	13	11	45	31
1976	13	11	45	31
1977	13	11	44	30
1978	13	11	44	30

Source: Statistical Office and own calculations.
[a]Excluding housing.

$$(5.1) \qquad A_z = \frac{1}{L} \int_0^L e^{-\rho u} du = \frac{1}{\rho L} \left(1 - e^{-\rho L} \right),$$

where L is the asset life for tax purposes and ρ is the company's discount rate.

Declining balance depreciation is allowed on equipment at three times the straight-line rate, up to a maximum of 30 percent of the initial cost of the asset. Table 5.7 illustrates the development of these "accelerated" depreciation rates since the 1950s. Accelerated depreciation was reduced in 1960 from 2.5 to 2.0 times the straight-line rate and increased again in 1977 to 2.5 times and in 1981 to 3 times. To reduce short-term demand pressure, accelerated depreciation was, however, not permitted during two short periods in the 1970s (6 May 1970–31 January 1971 and 9 May 1973–30 November 1973). Table 5.6 shows the development of the aver-

Table 5.7 **Development of Average Service Lives Rates of Accelerated Depreciation**
(first-year allowance)

Period of Investment	Average Tax Life of Equipment[a] (years)	Maximum First-Year Allowance Corresponding to Average Tax Life[b] (%)
1960	14	17.86[c]
1961	14	14.28
1962	13	15.38
1963	13	15.38
1964	13	15.38
1965	13	15.38
1966	11	18.18
1967	11	18.18
1968	11	18.18
1969	11	18.18
1970	12	16.66[d]
1971	11	18.18
1972	12	16.16
1973	11	18.18[e]
1974	11	18.18
1875	11	18.18
1976	11	18.18
1977	11	18.11[f]
1978	11	22.73
1979	(11)	22.73
1980	(11)	22.73
1981	(11)	27.27[g]

Source: Tax laws in Germany.
[a]From table 5.6 (rounded figures).
[b]From tax law in individual years.
[c]17.86 until 8 March 1960, followed by 14.28.
[d]16.66 until 5 July 1970, and zero until 31 January 1971.
[e]18.18 until 8 May 1973, zero until 30 November 1973, followed by 18.18.
[f]18.11 until 31 August 1977, followed by 22.73.
[g]22.73 until 29 June 1981, followed by 27.27.

age actual and tax service lives as implied in the official capital stock calculations and also the corresponding maximum depreciation rates.

As for buildings in the United States, it is optimal to switch from declining balance to straight-line depreciation after a certain portion of the asset has been depreciated. The concept of the "switchover point" is discussed in detail in section 6.2.3 for the United States. The present value of depreciation allowances for equipment (A_z) is given by

(5.2)
$$A_z = a' \int_0^{L_s} e^{-(\rho + a')u} du$$

$$+ (e^{-a' \cdot L_s}) \cdot \left(\frac{1}{L - L_s}\right) \cdot \int_{L_s}^{L} e^{-\rho u} du,$$

where

    B is the declining balance rate (equal to 2.0 for double declining balance and equal to 3.0 since 1981) in Germany

    L is the tax life of the asset

    L_s is the switchover point

$$a' = \frac{B}{L}.$$

    The switchover point occurs at time L_s, where the straight-line depreciation rate $1/(L - L_s)$ exceeds the declining balance rate B/L on the remaining basis, that is, when

(5.3)
$$L_s = \left(\frac{B - 1}{B}\right) L.$$

Integrating (5.2), we obtain

$$A_z = \left(\frac{a'}{\rho + a'}\right)(1 - e^{-(\rho + a')L_s})$$

(5.4)
$$+ \frac{e^{-a'L_s}}{(L - L_s)\rho} \cdot (e^{-\rho L_s} - e^{-\rho L}) \cdot$$

    As an alternative to straight-line depreciation over an average of thirty years, declining balance depreciation over fifty years is granted on buildings constructed after 31 August 1977. The rates are 5 percent in the first eight years, 2.5 percent from the ninth to the fourteenth year, and 1.25 percent from the fifteenth to the fiftieth year.[12] The present value is

$$A_z = \left(0.05 \int_0^8 e^{-\rho u} du\right) + \left(0.025 \int_8^{14} e^{-\rho u} du\right)$$

(5.5)
$$+ \left(0.0125 \int_{14}^{50} e^{-\rho u} du\right)$$

$$= \frac{1}{\rho} \cdot \{0.05 - 0.025 e^{-8\rho} - 0.0125(e^{-14\rho} + e^{-50\rho})\}.$$

12. Before 29 June 1981 the rates were 3.5 percent in the first twelve years, 2 percent from the thirteenth to the thirty-second year, 1 percent from the thirty-third to the fiftieth year.

The present position concerning depreciation allowances is summarized in table 5.6. We have assumed a tax life (L) of eleven years for machinery, and since $B = 3.0$ the switchpoint is $L_s = 7.27$ (from equation 5.3). Since the straight-line tax life for buildings is considerably shorter than that specified by these "accelerated" depreciation provisions, we have assumed that companies employ straight-line depreciation with a tax life of thirty years. For both equipment and buildings, $f_1 = 1$ and $f_2 = 0$ for all sectors.

Turning to the tax treatment of inventories, it is interesting that German tax law disallows, with a few exceptions, the use of either LIFO (last in, first out) or FIFO (first in, first out).[13] The most common practice is to use a weighted average of the prices of the goods acquired during the year (*Durchschnittliche Anschaffungskosten*). To compute the effective proportion of the increase in the value of inventories taxed according to FIFO, we assumed that the real value of the inventory is constant, that there is continuous turnover during the year, and that inventories fully turn over in one year. The value of the taxable portion of inventories under these assumptions will, at the margin, be half that taxed according to the FIFO principle. Therefore $v = 0.5$, $f_1 = 1$, and all other depreciation parameter values are zero.

It is also possible for special reserves to be set aside when the replacement cost of purchased raw materials and work in progress has increased by more than 10 percent in the course of a year.[14] The reserves must be added back to taxable income no later than the sixth year following the end of the taxable year in which the allocation to reserves is made.

The value of the deferral of tax may be considerable at high rates of inflation. If we let π define the nominal increase in the price of inventories, the present value of the deferred taxes on the increase in price in excess of 10 percent is equal to $\tau(\pi - 0.1)e^{-6\rho}$, where τ is the rate of corporation tax and ρ is the discount rate. Hence total taxes on the increase in inventory values are given by the tax on the first 10 percent increase in price (0.1τ) plus the deferred taxes:

$$(5.6) \qquad \tau\{0.1 + (\pi - 0.1)e^{-6\rho}\}.$$

The value of this deferral possibility will depend on the comparison with the usual method of inventory accounting. We have not incorporated deferral into our estimates because the average level of price increases was lower than 10 percent. This provision may nonetheless be important for some firms in order to smooth out large changes in relative prices.

---

13. LIFO is allowed if a taxpayer can *prove* it is his established practice to sell first the goods most recently produced or acquired.

14. There are also tax-free reserves for commodities that fluctuate on world markets.

5.2.4   Estimates of Economic Depreciation

The calculation of the rate of true economic depreciation is always problematic. The formulas in chapter 2 employ a declining balance rate that is not readily available from German statistics. It was therefore necessary to resort to some simplifying assumptions.

First we calculated the average economic useful lives used by the Statistical Office in capital stock computations. Second, we estimated depreciation rates as follows. With straight-line economic depreciation, the average rate of economic depreciation can be found by dividing the annual flow of depreciation by the gross capital stock. We tested the accuracy of the computed average depreciation rates (which were calculated by using gross capital stock figures) by building up the capital stock time series for past years. The values thus obtained were very close to the official capital stock figures. The estimated depreciation lives are shown in table 5.6 for both equipment and buildings.

The straight-line rate of economic depreciation was translated into an equivalent declining balance rate by assuming that (as derived in chap. 2)

$$(5.7) \qquad \frac{L}{2} = \frac{1}{\delta},$$

where L is now the economic life of the asset. Based on information from the Statistical Office, we have assumed that $L = 12.77$ for equipment, which gives δ as 0.1566. For buildings $L = 43.9$, which implies that δ is 0.0456.

The assumption that the economic life is on average longer than the tax service life is confirmed by a recent survey in which, out of 1,900 firms in manufacturing, 43 percent claimed economic life was longer, 46 percent stated that they were roughly equal, and only 11 percent reported that economic life was shorter than the tax service life (see Uhlmann 1981).

5.2.5   Investment Grants and Incentives

A special law (*Investitionszulagengesetz*) encourages three types of investment by offering nontaxable cash grants. Eligible investment includes:

1. investment in the eastern border areas (with a grant of 10 percent) and other less developed regions (8.75 percent). The subsidy is confined to the acquisition of new investment goods if they are part of a new establishment, an enlargement, or a rationalization of a factory. Furthermore, investment goods must stay in the factory for at least three years.[15]

---

15. For investment in the eastern border area, additional special depreciation allowances are granted for the first five years (50 percent for equipment investment and 40 percent for buildings). In exceptional cases it is also possible to set aside tax-free reserves (*Zonenrandförderungsgesetz*).

2. Research and development investment (20 percent, up to an investment of DM 500,000; 7.5 percent in the case of higher investment).

3. Certain types of investment in the energy sector (7.5 percent).

In addition to the nontaxable cash grants in less developed areas, there are taxable cash grants that range between 2.5 and 17.5 percent of initial cost. Substantial tax incentives are provided for investment in Berlin. The program includes favorable depreciation allowances (up to 75 percent in the first five years); tax-free cash grants (*Investitionszulage*) ranging from 10 to 30 percent; a 30 percent (22.5 percent) reduction of the income tax rate (corporate tax rate) on income from activities in Berlin; a reduction of the value-added tax (VAT) liability of Berlin suppliers (in general 4.5 percent of the amount received from its VAT liability for deliveries to a West German business) and of West German customers (4.2 percent of the amount payable from the tax liability, provided the goods were manufactured in West Berlin and shipped to West Germany).[16]

Table 5.8 shows the development of investment grants since 1960. In order to compare tax-free and taxable grants, all rates have been expressed as an equivalent rate of tax-free grant. These grants are particularly significant for the mining and energy sector and the sector "other industry." In this latter case, however, the figures are dominated by payments to public corporations, which are excluded from our study. For this reason we do not use this column of data. The last column of table 5.8 includes construction (part of our "other industrial" sector) and services (part of our commercial sector). We use this column for investment grants in both sectors. Table 5.9 shows investment grants by type given to the manufacturing sector. For our calculations only regional policy measures were included (25 percent of the total), because other grants are discretionary and to a large extent are also intramarginal. Our procedure here is the same as that followed in the United Kingdom chapter. For our estimate of g, therefore, we used not the 8.5 percent figure shown in table 5.8 but a rate of (0.25×0.085), which equals 2.1 percent. A lower figure of 0.7 percent was used for the other two industry groups (final column of table 5.8). The same rates of grant apply to equipment and buildings, but no grants are available for investment in inventories.

5.2.6 Local Taxes

There are two local taxes on companies in Germany, a local business tax (*Gewerbesteuer*) and a local land tax (*Grundsteuer*). These taxes are regulated by federal legislation but are levied by local authorities who are free to determine the rate of tax. Both local taxes are deductible against corporation tax, since they are considered a business expense.

---

16. In addition, the promotion of Berlin includes tax-free cash grants to employees amounting to 8 percent of their salaries, which may be increased by DM 49.50 for each child.

Table 5.8   **Investment Grants as a Percentage of Investment**
                              (subsidy values)

Year	Agri-culture	Mining, Energy	Manu-facturing	Other Industry[a]	Other Sectors[b]
1960	6.5	7.5	1.1	3.3	4.5
1961	5.9	7.5	1.3	5.4	2.4
1962	6.1	6.8	1.3	3.7	0.6
1963	7.2	9.7	1.6	7.1	0.6
1964	6.2	5.9	1.5	8.6	0.6
1965	11.2	6.0	1.6	9.0	0.6
1966	11.8	5.8	1.7	12.1	0.6
1967	14.9	5.7	2.8	5.9	2.4
1968	17.7	10.4	2.8	5.7	0.7
1969	16.5	13.2	3.0	9.4	2.6
1970	21.0	16.3	2.4	16.7	1.5
1971	17.6	12.7	4.0	11.5	1.4
1972	13.7	13.6	5.4	11.3	1.0
1973	12.7	12.1	7.4	11.7	1.0
1974	13.3	12.7	10.5	13.9	1.7
1975	12.5	14.3	15.9	22.4	5.4
1976	9.2	9.7	7.9	15.3	1.5
1977	8.0	11.9	7.8	17.9	0.8
1978	8.1	12.9	8.1	20.6	0.7
1979	8.4	13.3	8.5	25.4	0.7

Source: Teschner (1981).
[a]Includes public transport and excludes construction.
[b]Includes construction (part of our "other industrial" sector) and services (part of our commercial sector).

Gewerbesteuer

The local business tax has two bases—profits and capital stock.[17] The base for the local profits tax (*Gewerbeertragsteuer*) is equal to taxable income as defined for the corporation tax except that interest payments on long-term debt are not deductible. It is further adjusted by excluding a pro rata share (0.12) of the value of land.[18] The tax rate for the Gewerbe-ertragsteuer is calculated as the product of a basic rate (*Messzahl*), M, of 0.05 and a multiplicative coefficient (*Hebesatz*), H. The *Hebesatz*, which at present varies between 3 and 5, is set each year by the local municipality. The tax is computed on a tax-exclusive basis, which means that the effective tax-inclusive rate (τ_L) on earnings above the exemption level limits is given by

17. Until 1979 some states used payroll as a third tax base.
18. The latter is excluded in order to avoid double taxation of land from the land tax.

Table 5.9   **Investment Grants to Manufacturing**
                     (share of total grants from each type of grant, %)

Year	Sectoral Aids	Environ-mental Protection	Regional Policy (Including Promotion of Berlin)	Anticyclical Measures[a] and Special Labor Market Measures	Total
1960	15	39	41	5	100
1961	19	32	34	15	100
1962	18	34	34	14	100
1963	30	31	30	9	100
1964	27	32	30	11	100
1965	25	37	27	11	100
1966	16	46	25	13	100
1967	30	40	20	10	100
1968	31	40	20	9	100
1969	36	31	28	5	100
1970	20	33	43	6	100
1971	27	26	45	2	100
1972	26	21	49	4	100
1973	39	17	40	4	100
1974	36	14	32	18	100
1975	21	7	18	54	100
1976	30	15	35	20	100
1977	33	17	34	16	100
1978	33	16	35	16	100
1979	23	22	25	30	100

Source: Teschner (1981).
Note: Investment grants equal subsidy values.
[a]1974–75.

$$(5.8) \qquad \tau_L = \frac{M \cdot H}{1 + M \cdot H}.$$

For our calculations we have taken the average value of 3.25 for H from the 1979 statistics of the *Hebesatz*. From (5.8) this gives an average local tax on adjusted profits of $\tau_L = 0.14$.

It is now possible to compute the parameter value for τ, the tax rate on corporate profits, given the deductibility of local taxes. Its value is given by

$$(5.9) \qquad \tau = c_u(1 - \tau_L) + \tau_L,$$

where c_u is the rate of federal corporation tax on undistributed profits. For $c_u = 0.56$ and $\tau_L = 0.14$, the value of τ is equal to 0.62.

The basis of assessment for the local capital tax (*Gewerbekapitalsteuer*) is the capital stock as estimated for wealth tax purposes (see below) but inclusive of the value of long-term debt.[19] The value of buildings is deducted from the tax base so the local capital tax applies only to equipment and to inventories. As with the local profits tax, there is a basic rate of tax (0.002) that is multiplied by a local multiplier (3.25). This yielded in 1979 a local tax rate of 0.0065. Since the tax is deductible from both the local profits tax and the corporation tax, the effective overall local wealth tax on equipment and inventories is equal to 0.0026, or 0.26 percent. Addition of the federal wealth tax is described below.

Grundsteuer

The local land tax is paid on agricultural wealth (land tax A), on the value of land and buildings in general use (land tax B), and on land and buildings used for business purposes (either land tax A or land tax B). The base for the land tax is the "standard value" (*Einheitswert*), which is assessed at irregular periods and adjusted to take account of price changes (see section 5.2.7). It is widely held that at present the valuation is considerably below actual replacement cost. Estimates made by the Ministry of Finance suggest that the *Einheitswert* is approximately a quarter of the true replacement cost of assets. The computation of the tax rate is similar to that for other local taxes. A local multiplier (the average for 1979 being 2.75 for land tax B) is applied to a base rate of 0.0035 for industrial buildings and land.[20] The tax rate is therefore equal to 0.0096, which in turn is deductible from the local profits tax and the corporation tax. Allowing for the deductibility of the tax and the low valuation, the effective local tax on buildings is equal to 0.09 percent.[21] Although this is a tax on wealth, this figure is clearly very small. The federal wealth tax is added to this figure below.

5.2.7 Wealth Taxes

In contrast to the Anglo-Saxon countries, federal taxes on wealth have long been a feature of the German tax system. In 1981 the wealth tax rate was 0.5 percent of taxable wealth for individuals and 0.7 percent for corporations. As can be seen from table 5.10, these rates have changed frequently during the past decade.

All assets are valued according to a set of rules incorporated in the Fiscal Code. Buildings and land are assessed separately from other assets on special dates and with reference to definite periods of time. These

19. The exemption level (*Freibetrag*) has been successively raised from DM 6,000 (1977) to DM 60,000 (1978) and to DM 120,000 (1981).

20. The base rate varies according to type of asset. Other representative rates are 0.006 for agricultural land, 0.0026 to 0.0035 for one-family houses, and 0.0031 for two-family houses.

21. Note that $0.0009 = (2.75 \times 0.0035)(1 - .62) \times 0.25$.

Table 5.10   **Development of Nominal Wealth Tax Rates**
                              (%)

	Until 1973	1974	1975	1976	1977	Since 1978
Personal wealth tax	1.0	0.7	0.7	0.7	0.7	0.5
Corporate wealth tax	1.0	0.7	1.0	1.0	1.0	0.7
d_1 (= 1 if wealth tax deductible from corporate income tax, = 0 otherwise)	1	1	0	0	0	0

Source: Tax laws in Germany.

"standard" or "ratable" values (*Einheitswert*) have not been regularly computed in recent years, and, as was mentioned above, buildings and land are widely believed to be considerably undervalued. In 1981 the valuation was based on assessments made in 1964, which were increased by 40 percent in 1974. Official estimates suggest that the *Einheitswert* was only 25 percent of actual values. The valuation of equipment is based on the so-called *Teilwert*, which the tax law defines as the value a potential buyer of the enterprise would place on the individual piece of equipment. This rule is obviously difficult to apply in practice. The tax administration has therefore set an upper limit equal to replacement cost and a lower limit equal to scrap value. In general it uses acquisition cost less accumulated depreciation up to a minimum value (*Anhaltewert*) as the tax base.[22] The base for the valuation of inventories is normally taken to be replacement cost.

For individuals, certain amounts of wealth are tax free (DM 70,000 for the taxpayer and DM 70,000 for the spouse and each child). In 1979 total wealth tax revenues amounted to DM 4.5 billion, or 1.4 percent of total tax revenues. Although the tax rates are low, the wealth tax burden may be substantial for individual enterprises, particularly since the wealth tax cannot (since 1975) be deducted from the income, corporate, or local business tax bases.

The wealth tax burden for a given investment depends on the source of finance. Since the tax is based on net worth, a corporate investment financed by debt does *not* increase the corporate wealth tax base.[23] The federal wealth tax rate of 0.7 percent (in addition to the local capital tax) applies to equity-financed investment in machinery and inventories. Making allowance for the favorable valuations used, a rate of 0.2 percent

22. These minimum values were, in general, 15 percent of acquisition cost for equipment acquired before 31 December 1969 and 30 percent for assets acquired after that date.
23. In fact, because of a favorable valuation formula, gross taxable wealth may be increased by less than the additional debt employed to acquire the land, since borrowings are fully deductible.

was assumed for investment in buildings (in addition to the local land tax).

We may summarize our assumptions as follows. Including both local and federal wealth taxes, for debt-financed investment $w_c = 0.09$ for buildings and 0.26 for machinery and inventories. For equity-financed investment, we add the 0.26 percent local tax and 0.7 percent federal tax to obtain $w_c = 0.96$ percent for all machinery and inventories. We add the 0.09 percent local tax and 0.2 percent federal tax to obtain $w_c = 0.29$ percent for buildings. Because these calculations already account for the deductibility of the local tax at the federal level, $d_1 = 0$ in both cases. The wealth tax rate on households is $w_p = 0.5$ percent for all types of financial security.

5.2.8 Household Tax Rates

Estimates of the marginal tax rate on capital income accruing to households have been based on the distribution of capital income as given in the income tax statistics. Unfortunately, the most recent statistics available to us refer to 1974. Table 5.11 shows the distribution of capital income from 1961 to 1974 and the corresponding marginal income tax rates in the various income brackets from 1961 to 1979. Because of inflation and increases in real income, in 1979 the income distribution was weighted more heavily toward the higher brackets than it was in 1974. On the other hand, the marginal tax rates shown in table 5.11 are those applying before taking account of income splitting (see section 5.2.1). They imply, therefore, an overstatement of the average marginal income tax rates on recipients of capital income as a whole.

To estimate the average marginal capital income tax rate in 1979, we used the 1974 income weights. Our assumption is that the change in the income distribution since 1974 is offset by the opportunities created by income splitting. The average marginal tax rate on interest and dividend income in 1979 (a separation of the two was not possible) was 48 percent. It is, however, widely believed that the taxation of interest income is often evaded. To allow for this possibility, in one of the simulations reported below, the marginal tax on interest income was taken to be equal to 20 percent.

Finally, we account for the corporate interest that accrues to individuals in the form of tax-free banking services. Banks use sight deposits to buy corporate debt but use the interest receipts to provide banking services to depositors rather than to pay interest. We calculate a weighted average household tax rate on interest income, where a 48 percent marginal rate applies to direct ownership and bank holdings through time deposits, and a zero marginal tax rate applies to bank holdings through sight deposits. Using data from section 5.3.5 on the ownership of corporate debt, we find a weighted-average 39.8 percent tax rate is used for

Table 5.11   Distribution of Gross Capital Income and Marginal Personal Income Tax Rates
(%)

Income Groups (DM)[a]	1961 Distribution of Capital Income	1961 Marginal Tax Rate	1965 Distribution of Capital Income	1965 Marginal Tax Rate	1968 Distribution of Capital Income	1968 Marginal Tax Rate	1971 Distribution of Capital Income	1971 Marginal Tax Rate	1974 Distribution of Capital Income	1974 Marginal Tax Rate	Marginal Tax Rate after 1974 1975-78	Marginal Tax Rate after 1974 1979
Below 1,500	0.1	0	0.1	0	0.1	0	0.1	0	0.1	0	0	0
1,500–2,900	0.6	20	0.5	19	0.5	19	0.4	19	0.3	19	0	0
3,000–4,999	1.8	20	1.6	19	1.6	19	1.2	19	0.9	19	22	22
5,000–7,999	3.4	20	3.2	19	3.5	19	2.8	19	2.2	19	22	22
8,000–11,999	4.5	28	4.3	22	4.7	22	3.9	22	3.3	22	22	22
12,000–15,999	4.2	31	4.9	27	4.5	27	3.7	27	3.2	27	22	22
16,000–24,999	8.3	35	8.2	34	8.9	34	7.8	34	6.7	34	35	29
25,000–49,999	14.8	42	15.2	43	16.8	43	17.0	43	16.2	43	46	45
50,000–74,999	8.6	47	9.1	48	9.4	48	10.0	48	10.6	48	51	51
75,000–99,999	5.8	52	6.2	51	6.4	51	6.6	51	6.9	51	54	54
100,000–249,999	16.5	53	17.5	53	17.4	53	18.3	53	18.7	53	56	56
250,000–499,999	9.4	53	10.0	53	9.2	53	9.4	53	10.4	53	56	56
500,000–999,999	7.4	53	7.5	53	}17.0	53	7.0	53	7.0	53	56	56
1,000,000 and above	14.6	53	11.7	53		53	11.8	53	13.5	53	56	56
Weighted marginal tax rate	(100.0)	45	(100.0)	46	(100.0)	45	(100.0)	46	(100.0)	46	49	48

Source: Income Tax Statistics, tax laws, and own calculations.

[a]Annual taxable income.

households' direct and indirect holdings of corporate debt. This rate is used for household interest income, and 48 percent is used for dividend income.

5.2.9   Tax-Exempt Institutions

The ownership category "tax-exempt institutions" includes pension funds, many of which are public pension funds, and the so-called *Gemeinnützige Institutionen*—religious organizations, foundations, and trade unions. The description of all these organizations as tax-exempt relates only to their investment activities under the new corporate tax system. These tax-exempt institutions are *not* allowed to impute the corporate tax that has been paid on distributions, so these shareholders bear a corporate tax at a rate of 36 percent on distributions and a dividend withholding tax of 25 percent. This implies a total tax burden of 52 percent (0.36 + 0.25 (1 − 0.36)). The dividend withholding tax is, however, refunded either totally (to charitable or religious institutions) or by one-half (to other institutions such as trade unions). In these cases dividends pay tax at either 36 percent or 44 percent. Capital income other than dividends is, with a few exceptions, tax free. We have assumed that the marginal tax rate on interest income is zero and on dividend income is 40 percent.[24]

5.2.10   Insurance Companies

In 1981 there were approximately 430 major insurance companies in Germany. Of this group, 46 percent were corporations, 20 percent were mutual insurance companies, 11 percent were "enterprises under public law" (regulated companies known as *Unternehsmen des Öffentlichen Rechts*), and 23 percent were foreign companies. The market shares were distributed among these enterprises as follows: corporations 60 percent; mutual insurance companies 26 percent; enterprises under public law 10 percent; and foreign companies 4 percent. Corporations concentrate on life insurance, mutual insurance companies on health insurance, and enterprises under public law on insurance against damage to tangible (fixed) assets. With premiums of about DM 26 billion and about DM 13 billion, respectively, life insurance and automobile insurance companies are the largest individual insurance branches. Apart from insurance, these companies are heavily engaged in financial investment activities (leasing, building and loan associations, etc.).

Besides the private insurance companies, there exists an extensive system of public social security including the old-age pension system, unemployment insurance, health insurance, and accident insurance. In 1978 total expenditure of the whole public social security system amounted to DM 403 billion or 31 percent of GNP, which is rather high by international standards.

---

24. This rate may be on the high side since, in practice, some of these institutions have created companies that act as intermediate institutions so that the imputation credit can be received.

In general, savings made through contributions to insurance companies must be made from net of tax income, and the proceeds are tax free to the beneficiaries.[25] Insurance companies are subject to the corporate tax, the corporate wealth tax, and the local business tax. But there are some special concessions. The accumulation of tax-free reserves is possible up to certain limits (*Deckungsrückstellung*). In 1978, life insurance companies placed 95.6 percent of their cash flow (before taxes) into reserves. Since these reserves were tax free, interest income would have borne an effective tax of 2.7 percent (0.62 times 0.044). Dividend income bears no additional tax at the insurance company level when allocations to reserve are taken into account. Because of the imputation system, the 95.6 percent allocation to reserves implies a rebate of 19 percent.[26]

National accounts statistics also give evidence of a relatively low tax burden on the capital income of insurance companies. In 1979 private insurance companies paid DM 630 million in direct taxes and earned DM 18,250 million of income from property and entrepreneurship, implying an average direct tax rate of 3.5 percent. Since wealth tax payments are included in these direct taxes, the effective corporate tax rate has been somewhat lower. For our calculations, we have assumed that the effective income tax rate of insurance companies was 2.7 percent, as derived above.

5.3   The Structure of the Capital Stock and Its Ownership

5.3.1   Data Limitations

The major sources of data for the present study were the Statistics of the Bundesbank and the national accounts statistics of the Statistical Office. Many adjustments were made to the data in order to obtain the various matrixes of parameters used in our calculations. Although precise numbers are presented in the following tables, it should be borne in mind that various figures had to be estimated. This is especially true for those data refering to the structure of the ownership of debt. As far as equity ownership is concerned, we carried out our own investigation into the pattern of ownership of German corporations.

---

25. There are exceptions: If proceeds of life insurance policies are paid in the form of pensions, part of this income (the so-called *Ertragswert*, which amounts to 30 percent of the pension) is liable to income tax. Furthermore, for private pension funds it can generally be assumed that premiums are lower than the maximum allowances (*Sonderausgabenhöchstbetrag*), so that at the margin they are deductible from taxable income. In turn, pensions paid by these institutions are taxable.

26. The computation is given by the following formula:

$$0.62 \left(1 + \frac{36}{64} - 0.956\right) - \frac{36}{64} = -0.186.$$

Because of legal restrictions concerning the capital structure of these companies, dividend income is only a small share (5–10 percent) of total capital income.

5.3.2   Capital Stock Weights

Data on the size of capital stock are published by the Statistical Office both for the total business sector and for major industrial sectors.[27] These figures were adjusted to obtain the breakdown among the three sectors: manufacturing, other industry, and commerce, as defined in chapter 2. From the manufacturing (*Verarbeitendes Gewerbe*) sector, the automobile repair and services sector was reallocated to the commercial sector. The commercial sector, in addition to wholesale and retail trade (*Handel*), contains the private part of social and personal services. Since no capital stock data were available for this latter subgroup, estimates were obtained by using the share of total sales of this group as a proxy for the share of the capital stock.

The sector "other industry" includes electricity, gas, and water, construction, transport, and communication. Since the electricity, gas, and water sector is either directly or indirectly owned by the public sector, or is at least regulated by public administration, it has been excluded. Public railroads and postal services that are included in official data of the transport and communication sector were also excluded. These estimates were based on capital stock statistics provided by the DIW-Institute for Economic Research (Görzig and Kirner 1976). The official data on inventories are less detailed than those for machinery and buildings. The levels of inventories for the sector other industry and for the service part of the commercial sector were estimated separately.

Since official data by the Statistical Office refer to the business sector as a whole—that is, to the corporate and noncorporate sectors—we made our own estimates to provide data for the corporate sector alone. Bundesbank statistics provide data for the breakdown of fixed assets (book values) by corporate and noncorporate enterprises in manufacturing, construction, and trade.[28] Our estimates are based on these relationships. Table 5.12 presents the resulting matrix of the proportions of the total net capital stock by asset and industry in the total business sector and in the corporate sector. We use these 1978 proportions for the capital stock weights in 1980.

5.3.3   Sources of Financial Capital

Data concerning the structure of business financing are published by the Statistical Office and the Bundesbank. The major drawback of both these sources is that they are based on book values. It was therefore necessary to adjust the raw figures to obtain the proportions needed for our calculations. Both sources were used at different stages.

The Bundesbank provided statistics on the aggregate balance sheets

---

27. Volkswirtschaftliche Gesamtrechnungen, tables on "Sachvermögen."
28. Jahresabschlüsse der Unternehmen.

Table 5.12   **Proportion of Capital Stock by Asset and Industry, 1978**
(at replacement costs)

	Sector			
Asset	Manufacturing	Other Industry	Commercial	Total
A. Corporate and Noncorporate Enterprises				
Machinery	0.2454	0.0559	0.0537	0.3550
Buildings	0.1794	0.0637	0.1315	0.3746
Inventories	0.1687	0.0166	0.0851	0.2704
Total	0.5935	0.1362	0.2703	1.0000
B. Corporate Enterprises Only				
Machinery	0.3648	0.0243	0.0281	0.4172
Buildings	0.2069	0.0266	0.0641	0.2975
Inventories	0.2378	0.0060	0.0414	0.2853
Total	0.8096	0.0569	0.1335	1.0000

Source: Own estimates based on Statistisches Bundesamt, 1980, Bundesbank, 1976, and updatings provided by the Bundesbank.

for different types of legal entities operating in manufacturing, trade, and construction. Although the original sources do not cover all enterprises, the Bundesbank adjusted the figures to be representative of the whole economy.[29]

The values of the gearing ratio (debt to total market value) were computed for each sector in several steps (see tables 5.13 to 5.15).

1. Book values of the capital stock were adjusted by the ratio of the capital stock at replacement cost to the capital stock at historical cost implied by the aggregate capital data published by of the Statistical Office, and also by a factor that reflects the depression of recorded book values owing to the use of accelerated tax depreciation. In this way the capital stock at replacement cost was calculated for the corporate manufacturing, construction (other industry), and trade (commerce) sectors (see table 5.13). These capital stock figures are repeated in the first row of table 5.14.

2. Financial assets and liabilities were taken directly from Bundesbank statistics, as shown in rows 2–6 of table 5.14. Net financial liabilities are shown in row 7.

3. The next step was to compute the tax-adjusted value of the capital stock as the difference between the capital stock and the deferred tax liability. The latter was computed by a "backward-looking" measure as τ times the difference between the replacement cost value of the capital

29. Bundesbank statistics are based on balance sheets of about 9,800 corporations (*Kapitalgesellschaften*), 24,500 unincorporated firms (*Personengesellschaften*), and 14,100 other firms (*Einzelkaufleute*).

Table 5.13   **Capital Stock Figures at Replacement Costs**
                        (RC) and Book Values (BV)
                             (billion DM)

	Manufacturing	Other Industry	Commerce
Machinery			
RC	99.17	2.79	7.13
BV	66.11	1.86	4.75
RC/BV	1.50	1.50	1.50
Buildings			
RC	79.29	2.56	16.09
BV	44.05	1.42	8.94
RC/BV	1.80	1.80	1.80
Inventories			
RC = BV	99.36	0.96	21.32
Total			
RC	277.82	6.31	44.54
BV	209.52	4.24	35.01
RC/BV	1.33	1.49	1.27

Source: Own calculations as described in the text.

Table 5.14   **Computation of Market Value of Equity**
                             (billion DM)

	Manufacturing	Other Industry	Commerce
1. Capital stock (at replacement cost)[a]	277.82	6.31	44.54
2. Financial assets	165.10	20.95	39.17
3. Short-term financial liabilities	140.23	18.50	45.89
4. Long-term financial liabilities	55.03	1.25	7.22
5. Reserves (pensions, etc.)	85.88	3.03	7.42
6. Total gross financial liabilities (3 + 4 + 5)	281.14	22.77	60.53
7. Net financial liabilities (6 − 2)	116.04	1.83	21.36
8. Deferred tax liability .62 × [replacement cost of capital stock − book value]	42.35	1.28	5.91
9. Tax-adjusted capital stock (1 − 8)	235.47	5.03	38.61
10. Market value of equity [$q \times (9 - 7)$]	150.48	4.03	21.74
11. Debt as a proportion of (debt + market value of equity)	0.4354	0.3123	0.4956

Source: Statistical Office, Bundesbank, and own calculations.
[a]From table 5.13.

stock and the tax written down value of the stock.[30] The deferred tax liability is shown in row 8 of table 5.14, and the tax-adjusted capital stock is shown in row 9.

4. Since no reliable figures were available for the aggregate market value of outstanding shares, it was necessary to compute the market value of equity indirectly by employing an equilibrium value of Tobin's "q" derived analytically. Personal taxation affects the value of equity, and hence "q," by capitalizing the tax penalty (or advantage) of any eventual distribution (see Auerbach 1979; Bradford 1981; King 1977). The value of q was estimated using the same procedure as that described in section 4.3.3 for Sweden. For our estimates, we used a weighted average marginal tax rate on dividends, computed by employing the table for "proportion of ownership by source of finance" (see section 5.3.4) and the values of m for the different owners. This weighted marginal tax rate on dividends equals 0.436. The market value of equity was then computed as q times the tax-adjusted capital stock net of financial liabilities. This market value of equity is shown in row 10 of the table. The market value debt/equity ratio is shown in row 11.

5. Finally, the weights for new share issues and retentions were computed by making use of flow of funds data as shown in table 5.15. That is, the equity share (unity minus the debt share from table 5.14) was multiplied by the ratio of new share issues to total equity (in table 5.15) to obtain the ratio of new shares to total finance. The final proportions for the different sources of finance are given in table 5.16.

5.3.4   The Ownership of Equity

There has been no recent comprehensive study of the ownership of equity in German industry. To determine the distribution of equity among the three sectors (private households, tax-exempt institutions, and the insurance sector), we carried out our own analysis based on statistics of the Commerzbank (1979). These statistics provide information on firms with a minimum share capital of DM 500,000. For each firm, this information includes the trade or industry code, the total outstanding shares, and the shareholdings of major shareholders. Where other companies were shareholders, we traced ownership back to the original owner. With this information about direct and indirect ownership, it was possible to attribute 65 percent of total share capital to four groups of owners: households, tax-exempt institutions, insurance companies, and foreigners. About 31 percent of share capital either was held by companies not included in these statistics or was widely distributed stock. For the residual 4 percent of share capital, no information was given about either direct or indirect ownership.

---

30. This correction is similar to that proposed by Flemming et al. (1976).

**Table 5.15   Ratio of New Share Issues in Total Equity
                      Finance of Corporate Industry**

1973	1974	1975	1976	1977	1978	1979	Average 1973–79
.091	.074	.128	.086	.082	.093	.058	.087

Source: Statistical Office and own calculations.
Note: Includes only *Aktiengesellschaften*.

Table 5.16   Weights for Sources of Finance by Industry

	Manufacturing	Other Industry	Commerce
Debt	0.4354	0.3123	0.4956
New share issues	0.0491	0.0599	0.0439
Retained earnings	0.5155	0.6278	0.4605
Total	1.0000	1.0000	1.0000

Source: Own estimates as described in text.

For the distribution of widely distributed share capital or holdings by companies that are not included in the statistics (the above-mentioned 31 percent of total share capital), we used as a second source Bundesbank statistics on the ownership of shares held in bank custody.[31] The residual share capital (the above-mentioned 4 percent) was distributed among the ownership groups in the same proportions as the allocated 96 percent.

Table 5.17 shows the resulting ownership pattern for the three business sectors under consideration. Private households own about 44 percent, tax-exempt institutions about 13 percent, insurance companies about 4 percent, and foreigners about 39 percent of total share capital of the business sector as defined in this study. Households own more than 40 percent of share capital in all three sectors, but their share reaches almost 50 percent in the other industrial sector. Foreign ownership is especially concentrated in the manufacturing and commercial sectors, with shares of about 44 percent and 41 percent of total share capital, respectively. In the other industrial sector, foreigners own only about 20 percent of total share capital. Tax-exempt institutions and insurance companies own about 10 and 3 percent of share capital in the manufacturing sector, but about 24 and 7 percent of share capital in the other industrial sector.

In our study of effective tax rates, we consider only domestic ownership. If foreign holdings are excluded, the share of private households increases to about 73 percent, the share of tax-exempt institutions to about 21 percent, and the share of insurance companies to about 6

31. In 1978, according to statistics on shares held in banks, 66.8 percent of these shares were held by private households, 9.3 percent by tax-exempt institutions, 8.9 percent by insurance companies, and 20.9 percent by foreigners.

Table 5.17   **Ownership of Equity in Each Industry**
                                      (%)

	Manu-facturing	Other Industry	Commerce	Total
A. Including Foreign Ownership				
Private households	42.6	49.1	44.6	44.1
Tax-exempt institutions	10.4	23.7	11.3	13.3
Insurance companies	3.1	6.8	3.6	3.9
Foreign ownership	43.9	20.4	40.6	38.6
Total	100.0	100.0	100.0	100.0
B. Excluding Foreign Ownership				
Private households	75.8	61.7	75.1	73.1
Tax-exempt institutions	18.6	29.8	18.9	20.7
Insurance companies	5.6	8.5	6.0	6.2
Total	100.0	100.0	100.0	100.0

Source: Own estimation on the basis of statistics of the National Bank and Commerzbank.

Table 5.18   **Liabilities of Aggregate German Enterprises in 1978**

	Billion DM	%
1. Short-term		
Bank credit	176.9	21.4
Money market paper	2.3	0.3
2. Long-term		
Bank credit	319.3	39.1
Loans from building and loan associations	0.7	0.1
Loans from insurance companies	37.5	4.6
Bonds	30.4	3.7
3. Other liabilities		
Domestic creditors[a]	107.4	13.1
Foreign creditors	142.7	17.5
Foreign trade credits	(52.5)	(6.4)
Total	817.2	100.0
Total without trade credits	(764.7)	(93.6)

Source: Bundesbank statistics.
[a]Excluding intrasectoral liabilities.

percent. Table 5.17 also shows the corresponding ownership pattern for the three industry groups.

5.3.5   The Ownership of Debt

Data from the Bundesbank were used to calculate the distribution of corporate liabilities among the four groups of creditors: private households, tax-exempt institutions, insurance companies, and foreign owners. The starting point for these calculations is table 5.18, which shows the aggregate liabilities of German enterprises. Tables 5.19 and 5.20 show

Table 5.19   Liabilities of German Enterprise in 1978, by Type and by Creditor Group

| | | Groups of Creditors | | | | | | | |
| | Total (Billion DM) | Private Households | | Tax-Exempt Institutions | | Insurance Companies | | Foreign Owners | |
Liabilities[a] (percentage figures in each row sum to 100.0)		%	Billion DM	%	Billion DM	%	Billion DM	%	Billion DM
1. Short-term									
a. Bank credit	176.9	66.3	117.3	16.2	28.6	6.5	11.5	11.0	19.5
b. Money market paper	2.3	66.3	1.5	16.2	0.4	6.5	0.1	11.0	0.3
2. Long-term									
a. Bank credit	319.3	59.3	189.3	18.7	59.7	5.8	18.5	16.2	51.7
b. Loans from building and loan associations	0.7	100.0	0.7	0.0	0.0	0.0	0.0	0.0	0.0
c. Loans from insurance companies	37.5	0.0	0.0	0.0	0.0	100.0	37.5	0.0	0.0
d. Bonds	30.4	52.2	15.9	16.5	5.0	16.2	4.9	15.1	4.6
3. Other liabilities									
a. Domestic creditors	107.4	0.0	0.0	100.0	107.4	0.0	0.0	0.0	0.0
b. Foreign creditors (without trade credit)	90.2	0.0	0.0	0.0	0.0	0.0	0.0	100.0	90.2
Total	764.7	42.5	324.7	26.3	201.7	9.5	72.5	21.7	166.3

Of which (percentage figures in each column sum to 100.0)							
Direct loans (2c, 3b above)	0.0	0.0	0.0	0.0	51.7	37.5	54.2	90.2
Through commercial bank loans (1a, 1b, 2a, 2b above)	95.1	308.8	44.1	88.7	41.5	30.1	43.0	71.5
Through direct and indirect bond holdings (2d above)	4.9	15.9	2.5	5.0	6.8	4.9	2.8	4.6
Direct		5.3		1.7		3.7		1.3
Indirect		10.6		3.3		1.2		3.3
Other sources[b] (3a above)		0.0		107.4		0.0		0.0

Source: Own calculations based on data from Duetche Bundesbank.
Note: Excludes housing.
[a]Without trade credits.
[b]Especially workers' pension funds and "special government lending."

Table 5.20   Liabilities of German Enterprises in 1978, by Creditor Group

	Total		Domestic	
	Billion DM	%	Billion DM	%
Private households	324.7	42.5	324.7	54.3
Tax-exempt institutions	201.1	26.3	201.1	33.6
Insurance companies	72.5	9.5	72.5	12.1
Foreign owners	166.3	21.7	—	—
Total	764.7	100.0	598.3	100.0

Source: Own estimation, as described in the text.
Note: Excludes housing; liabilities are without trade credits.

the distribution of these liabilities among the four groups—private households, tax-exempt institutions, insurance companies, and foreigners—and also the corresponding structure for domestic creditors only. These estimates have been based on Bundesbank data.

The distribution of direct industrial bondholdings has been estimated on the basis of statistics on total bondholdings. Indirect debt holdings (via the banking sector and investment funds) have been estimated on the basis of bank deposits and special statistics on investment funds. Direct (both long- and short-term) bank credits and money market paper have also been distributed on the basis of the bank deposit structure. Loans from building and loan associations have been fully attributed to the private household sector.

"Other" domestic liabilities in table 5.19 include pension reserves and direct public loans but do not include domestic trade credits. These liabilities have been totally attributed to tax-exempt institutions. Foreign liabilities as in table 5.19 also exclude trade credits.

The share of debt finance directly and indirectly provided by private households amounts to about 43 percent according to these estimates. About 26 percent is provided by tax-exempt institutions, about 10 percent by insurance companies, and about 22 percent by foreigners. Of the domestic ownership of debt finance, 54 percent is provided by private households, while 34 percent and 12 percent are provided by tax-exempt institutions and by insurance companies, respectively.

5.4   Estimates of Effective Marginal Tax Rates

In this section the tax parameters described in section 5.2 and the weights described in section 5.3 are employed together to compute the effective tax rate on capital income originating from the corporate sector in West Germany. In section 5.4.1 we describe the results of the "standard case," which represents our best estimates of the tax parameters and of the weights in 1980. It also describes the sensitivity of the results to an alternative assumption about the marginal capital income tax rate of households. In section 5.4.2 the effect of the 1981 increase in accelerated depreciation is analyzed. Section 5.4.3 compares the effective tax rates in 1980 with the corresponding rates in 1960 and 1970. Section 5.4.4 compares our estimates of marginal tax rates with the average tax rate on companies implied by tax payments.

5.4.1 Principal Results

We consider the fixed-p and fixed-r cases in turn. Using as weights the structure of the capital stock by asset and by industry, and the structure of ownership and business financing, and with the average German inflation rate of the past ten years (4.2 percent), then for a real return before tax of 10 percent (fixed-p case) the average marginal tax wedge in 1980 was 4.8 percent and the average marginal tax rate ($p - s/s$) was 48.1 percent. By coincidence 48 percent is also the average marginal tax rate for capital income of private households, so the result suggests that overall the German tax system is close to a comprehensive income tax. But the breakdown of this effective tax rate in table 5.21 by asset, by industry, by source of finance, and by owner reveals striking differences.

Table 5.21   **Effective Marginal Tax Rates,**
West Germany, 1980, Fixed-p Case
(%)

	Inflation Rate		
	Zero	10%	Actual (4.2%)
Asset			
Machinery	38.1	46.6	44.5
Buildings	42.7	31.2	42.9
Inventories	57.7	60.8	59.0
Industry			
Manufacturing	44.7	46.8	48.1
Other industry	50.8	57.9	57.0
Commerce	44.6	36.6	44.4
Source of finance			
Debt	12.1	−33.3	−3.1
New share issues	56.1	65.7	62.6
Retained earnings	72.0	111.5	90.2
Owner			
Households	59.7	82.0	71.2
Tax-exempt institutions	17.6	−17.9	6.3
Insurance companies	14.6	−38.9	−3.8
Overall	45.1	46.1	48.1

The breakdown by assets shows that investment in inventories bears the highest tax burden (59 percent), while for machinery and buildings the effective tax rates are similar (44 and 43 percent, respectively). This difference reflects the inventory valuation scheme, which is relatively unfavorable compared with depreciation allowances for fixed investment. As regards the various industries, the other industrial sector has the highest and the commercial sector the lowest effective tax rate. The main reason is the difference in debt/equity ratios. The debt/equity ratio is relatively low in the other industry sector and relatively high in the commercial sector. Concerning the various sources of finance, there are also striking differences. For debt financing the marginal effective tax rate is slightly negative, whereas it amounts to 63 percent for investment financed by new share issues and to 90 percent for financing by retained earnings. With debt finance, corporations may deduct nominal interest payments against the corporate tax rate, which is considerably higher than the average rate at which recipients of interest pay tax. In addition, debt finance is not liable to the federal corporate wealth tax. The higher effective tax rate for retained earnings compared with new share issues results from the imputation system: the average marginal income tax rate of owners is lower than the corporate tax rate, which implies that the opportunity cost of keeping the money in the firm (retentions) is higher than the opportunity cost of raising new capital (new share issues).

The savings of private households bear an effective tax rate of 71 percent at the margin, while for investment financed by tax-exempt institutions and insurance companies the effective tax rates are much lower (6 percent and -4 percent, respectively).

Table 5.21 shows that (at least in the fixed-p case) there is no significant relation between the rate of inflation and the overall effective marginal tax rate. There are obviously some factors that lead the tax rate to increase with inflation, but there are others that tend to reduce the effective tax rate as inflation rises. This can be seen from the disaggregated result. The effect of inflation differs significantly for the various types of assets, industries, sources of finance, and groups of owners. The effective tax rate increases with inflation in the case of machinery and also for inventories, but it declines for buildings. This seems to reflect the fact that the adverse effect of historic cost valuation is more than offset by the significantly shorter service life compared with life for buildings.

Inflation increases the effective tax rate for retained earnings and for new share issues but reduces it for debt finance. With higher inflation the deductibility of nominal interest payments against the corporate tax rate of 62 percent outweighs the taxation of nominal interest receipts at lower income tax rates. The effect of inflation on the effective tax rate in the case of debt financing explains the differences in the impact of inflation among the industry groups. In the commercial sector, which has a relatively high debt/equity ratio, the effective tax rate declines with inflation.

For the fixed-*r* calculations (described in chap. 2) with our standard tax parameters and the actual average inflation rate, the overall effective tax rate is 64.8 percent, as shown in table 5.22. This can be interpreted as follows: if the real rate of return before personal tax were 5 percent, if the inflation rate were 4.2 percent, and if the savings of all owners were increased by 1 percent, then the present value of the expected tax would be 64.8 percent of the additional real return. It is shown in table 5.22 that, in the fixed-*r* case, the effective tax rate increases slightly with inflation. With zero inflation the German tax system would provide an overall effective tax rate of 57.4 percent, and with 10 percent inflation a rate of 68.2 percent. The same pattern of the tax rates for asset, industry, source of finance, and owner can be seen in the fixed-*r* case as in the fixed-*p* case.

As mentioned in section 5.2.8, it is widely believed that taxes on interest income are often evaded by households. To analyze the sensitivity of the results to the assumed marginal tax rate of households, we have replaced the standard parameter of 39.8 percent by a lower rate of only 20 percent. The overall marginal effective rate would then (in the fixed-*p* case and with actual inflation) be 41.1 percent; that is, seven percentage

Table 5.22   **Effective Marginal Tax Rates,**
West Germany, 1980, Fixed-*r* Case
(%)

	Inflation Rate		
	Zero	10%	Actual (4.2%)
Asset			
Machinery	53.0	68.9	63.4
Buildings	51.5	56.1	59.9
Inventories	66.3	74.6	70.4
Industry			
Manufacturing	57.4	68.8	65.0
Other industry	60.5	73.8	69.5
Commerce	56.1	60.7	61.3
Source of finance			
Debt	16.3	−211.3	−17.9
New share issues	63.1	83.8	73.2
Retained earnings	73.4	94.0	85.4
Owner			
Households	68.6	94.0	82.4
Tax-exempt institutions	32.9	7.5	26.5
Insurance companies	30.5	−32.6	9.1
Overall	57.4	68.2	64.8

points lower than with the standard assumption. The reduction of the effective tax rates of the three assets and three industries would be of a similar order of magnitude. The subsidy for debt financing would increase considerably from 3.1 percent to 23.6 percent, and the effective tax rate on households would decline from 71.2 percent to 59.6 percent.

5.4.2   Recent Changes in Tax Legislation

As part of our standard set of parameters, we have included the new rate of accelerated depreciation for machinery of three times the straight-line rate. Although this was increased from 2.5 times the straight-line rate in 1981, the change was felt to be important enough to be included in the standard case. To examine the effects of the change, we show in table 5.23 the marginal tax rates under the old regime in the fixed-r case. The table shows that this measure reduced the effective marginal tax rate for machinery by 4.8 percentage points from 49.3 percent to the 44.5 percent figure mentioned above. Other assets were unchanged. The effect on machinery was sufficient to reduce the overall rate by 2.1 percentage points, from 50.2 to 48.1 percent.

Table 5.23   **Effective Marginal Tax Rates, West Germany, with 250 Percent of Declining Balance for Machinery, Fixed-p Case**
(%)

	Inflation Rate		
	Zero	10%	Actual (4.2%)
Asset			
Machinery	41.7	52.7	49.3
Buildings	42.7	31.2	42.9
Inventories	57.7	60.8	59.0
Industry			
Manufacturing	46.4	49.5	50.3
Other industry	52.1	60.2	58.9
Commerce	45.3	37.9	45.4
Source of finance			
Debt	14.3	−29.6	−0.1
New share issues	57.5	68.1	64.5
Retained earnings	72.9	113.1	91.5
Owner			
Households	60.9	84.0	72.8
Tax-exempt institutions	19.6	−14.5	9.1
Insurance companies	16.9	−35.0	−0.6
Overall	46.6	48.6	50.2

5.4.3 Comparison with 1960 and 1970

As mentioned in section 5.1, various attempts have been made since the mid-1970s to establish a "better general framework" for investment activity. In terms of the tax parameters used for this study, the following measures were especially important:

1. The introduction of the new corporate tax system (1977), which abolished the double taxation of distributed earnings.

2. Depreciation allowances were increased in various steps. In 1960 and also in 1970 only double declining balance (DDB) was possible for machinery, but the accelerated rate of depreciation was increased in 1977 to 2.5 and in 1981 to 3.0 times the straight-line rate (see table 5.5). Furthermore, there was on average a moderate reduction in actual service lives and a larger reduction in tax lives during the 1960s and 1970s (see table 5.6).

3. During the 1970s there were some changes in wealth taxes. Rates were first increased (1975) and then lowered again (1978), and the income deductibility of this tax was abolished (1975; see table 5.10).

4. Investment grants were increased during the 1960s and also during the 1970s (see tables 5.8 and 5.9).

5. Owing to the interaction between a progressive income tax and inflation, the marginal rate on households increased over the period (see table 5.11).

6. The estimated effective marginal tax rates for 1960 and 1970 are shown in tables 5.24 and 5.25, respectively. Between 1960 and 1970, the overall marginal tax rate fell by 2.6 percentage points from 52.5 to 49.1 percent.

The various policy measures between 1970 and 1980 did not bring about a fundamental change in the effective taxation of capital income, but the overall rate fell by one more percentage point. In comparison with the other countries in this study, the German experience has been one of stability with relatively high marginal tax rates on capital income.

The various measures combine into an overall effect as follows:

1. The improvement in depreciation allowances reduced the effective tax rate for machinery between 1970 and 1980 by 5.2 percentage points. A similar reduction (by 5.3 percentage points) also occurred between 1960 and 1970.

2. Owing to the introduction of the imputation system with full imputation of corporate tax payments at the recipient level, the effective tax rate on new share issues declined by 16.8 percentage points between 1970 and 1980.

As mentioned above, these reductions did not bring about a substantial reduction in the overall effective tax rate between 1970 and 1980/81. One reason for this is the low weight of new share issues as a source of finance.

Furthermore, there were offsetting effects. With the new corporate tax system, tax-exempt institutions are not allowed to benefit from the imputation of corporate tax paid on distributions. This tax rule implied a substantial increase in the marginal dividend income tax rate for this group of owners as compared with the "old" system. This is in sharp contrast to the United Kingdom, where tax-exempt institutions are allowed to benefit from imputation relief and, in consequence, receive substantial refunds from the tax authorities.

5.4.4   Comparison with Average Tax Rates

The calculations in the present study refer to the marginal effective tax burden on capital income, and it is interesting to compare these results with the average tax burden on companies, particularly since this usually plays an important role in public discussions.

The numerator of such an average tax rate should include the actual tax revenues from corporate tax, the local business tax, the wealth tax, and taxes on dividend receipts and interest receipts from the corporate sector. The denominator should reflect actual operating profits defined to include distributed and retained profits and interest payments of the corporate sector. We based our estimate on the national accounts statistics,

Table 5.24   **Effective Marginal Tax Rates,
West Germany, 1960, Fixed-p Case**
(%)

	Inflation Rate		
	Zero	10%	Actual (4.2%)
Asset			
Machinery	47.5	57.3	55.0
Buildings	48.1	33.7	46.4
Inventories	53.4	57.6	55.2
Industry			
Manufacturing	49.7	51.9	53.2
Other industry	52.1	55.4	56.8
Commerce	46.5	38.7	46.1
Source of finance			
Debt	19.7	−19.9	6.9
New share issues	68.7	94.1	81.4
Retained earnings	72.7	105.8	88.4
Owner			
Households	65.9	89.4	77.8
Tax-exempt institutions	15.5	−26.5	1.8
Insurance companies	24.0	−20.0	9.5
Overall	49.4	50.4	52.5

which provide profits data (distributions and retentions) for the nonfinancial corporate sector. The other elements in our calculation had to be estimated by using information provided by Bundesbank statistics on balance sheets of corporations and by tax statistics.

In table 5.26 real operating profits are defined to consist of net interest and net dividend payments, corporate taxes (including corporate local taxes and corporate wealth taxes), and retained earnings. During 1978–80 the average corporate tax rate on real corporate profits amounted to 57.8 percent. Tax, interest, and dividend payments were larger than operating profits, which implied negative retained earnings. The negative sign for retained earnings in table 5.26 cannot be fully explained by a relatively depressed profit level; it seems also to reflect statistical errors. There are indications that during the envisaged national accounts revisions, estimates of operating profits of nonfinancial corporations will be revised upward. Since tax payments will not be revised, the average tax rate in table 5.26 will decline somewhat. In table 5.27 we show taxes on interest and dividend payments paid by the owners of the securities, and also the corresponding personal wealth taxes. For the taxation of interest payments, an average of owners' tax rates was used. These rates were 30 percent for households, zero for tax-exempt institutions, 3 percent for

Table 5.25   **Effective Marginal Tax Rates, West Germany, 1970, Fixed-*p* Case**
(%)

	Inflation Rate		
	Zero	10%	Actual (4.2%)
Asset			
Machinery	43.2	50.7	49.7
Buildings	44.2	28.3	42.2
Inventories	54.5	56.6	55.4
Industry			
Manufacturing	46.9	47.2	49.8
Other industry	49.9	52.2	54.3
Commerce	44.2	34.0	43.0
Source of finance			
Debt	13.7	−32.2	−1.5
New share issues	67.1	91.4	79.4
Retained earnings	72.8	107.5	89.2
Owner			
Households	64.5	87.6	76.3
Tax-exempt institutions	10.5	−36.4	−5.2
Insurance companies	18.8	−30.4	2.3
Overall	46.7	45.7	49.1

Table 5.26   **Corporate Profits and Their Appropriation, Germany, 1978–80**
(billion DM in current prices)

	1978–80 Average
Real operating profits	55.7
Corporate taxes	32.2
Interest payments	10.8
Dividend payments	16.2
Real retained earnings	−3.5

Source: National Accounts Statistics, Deutsche Bundesbank, and own estimates.

Table 5.27   **Average Tax Rate on Real Corporate Profits**
(billion DM in current prices)

	1978–80 Average	Percentage of Profits
Total taxes	37.5	67.32
Corporate taxes	32.2	57.81
Taxes on		
Interest payments	2.5	4.49
Dividend payments	2.0	3.59
Real retained earnings	—	—
Personal wealth	0.8	1.44
Real operating profits	55.7	
Average tax rate (%)	67.3	
Average profit rate (%)		
Gross of tax	16.9	
Net of tax	5.5	

Source: Own calculations as described in text.

insurance companies, and 15 percent for dividends to foreigners, which are also included here. The ownership of debt in section 5.3.5 was used to weight the tax rates. For additional taxes on dividends at the recipient level, corresponding estimates have been made using our own estimates on the ownership of equity and marginal tax rates of the different ownership groups.

With these assumptions, the estimated average tax rate on real operating profits amounts to 67.3 percent for the period 1978–80. Taxes therefore reduced the average profit rate from 16.9 percent before tax to 5.5 percent after tax (see table 5.27). With the above-mentioned forthcoming statistical revisions to the profits data, the average tax rate as calculated in table 5.27 will be reduced. It may therefore come somewhat closer to the marginal effective tax rate as described above.

Nevertheless, the average tax rates do not depart significantly from the estimated marginal rates, especially in the fixed-r case, which is the estimate more closely related to the comparison with actual tax payments.

6   The United States

6.1 Introduction

In early United States history, tariffs and excise taxes were the major sources of government revenue. Because of constitutional constraints on direct taxation at the federal level, an income tax could not be enacted until the Sixteenth Amendment was passed in 1913. Since that time the personal income tax has become the single most important tax, growing to more than 35 percent of total revenue and to more than 45 percent of federal revenue (see the annual *Economic Report of the President*).

The importance of the corporate income tax also grew in the first part of this century, but the past thirty years have seen a decline in its share of federal revenue, from about 25 percent to 15 percent. Major policy shifts have reduced the corporate tax by introducing investment tax credits and by speeding up allowances for depreciation. Under the Economic Recovery Tax Act of 1981, as amended by the Tax Equity and Fiscal Responsibility Act of 1982, corporate revenues are expected to fall still further. The decline in corporate revenues has, however, been more than offset by the increase in social insurance taxes. From 18 percent of federal revenues in 1960, payroll taxes increased by one percentage point per year before leveling off at 33 percent in 1975. Finally, the proportions above leave only about seven percentage points for the recent share of other federal sources, including excise taxes. Thus revenue sources have experienced a major reversal in the seventy years since 1913.

Trends in revenue between 1960 and 1979 are shown in table 6.1 (which may be compared with the corresponding tables in the other country chapters). The rising shares of personal and payroll taxes are evident in this table, as are the falling shares of corporate and excise taxes. As a proportion of GDP, taxes grew from about 7 percent to 24 percent over the first half of this century. The bottom of table 6.1 shows that this

Table 6.1   Sources of Tax Revenue, United States, 1960–79

Revenue Source	Share of Total Receipts (%)			Total Receipts ($ billion)
	1960	1970	1979	1979
Taxes on personal incomes	32.7	35.2	36.5	254.772
Federal income tax		29.4	30.0	209.541
State and local income tax		3.5	5.1	35.524
Capital gains (federal, state, and local)		2.3	1.4	9.707
Taxes on corporate incomes	17.2	12.7	11.1	77.874
Social security contributions[a]	14.4	19.3	25.4	177.441
By employers		10.5	15.0	105.099
By employees		8.1	9.6	67.309
By self-employed		0.7	0.7	5.033
Property taxes	12.4	12.1	9.3	64.943
By households		7.5	5.8	40.265
By others		4.6	3.5	24.678
Estate, inheritance, gift, and transfer taxes	1.9	1.8	1.2	8.267
Value-added tax	—	—	—	—
Taxes on goods and services	21.5	18.9	16.5	115.501
General sales tax		5.6	6.7	46.558
Alcohol (federal, state, and local)		2.1	1.2	8.079
Tobacco (federal, state, and local)		1.6	0.9	6.265
Motor fuels (state and local)		2.2	1.4	10.080
Other (federal, state, and local)		7.4	6.4	44.519
Total receipts	100.0	100.0	100.0	698.798
Gross domestic product ($ billion)	502.9	985.4	2,370.1	
Share of taxes in GDP (%)	26.6	29.2	29.5	

Source: Revenue Statistics of OECD Member Countries, 1965–1980 (Paris, 1981).

[a]Employee shares exactly match employer shares for Old-Age, Survivors, Disability, and Health Insurance (OASDHI), but only employers pay for unemployment insurance and workmen's compensation.

growth has continued since 1950, although at a slower rate, to about 30 percent of GDP in 1979.

One trend not evident in table 6.1 is the growth of state and local tax revenues in the 1960s. These revenues were 8.6 percent of GDP in 1960 and just over 11 percent in both 1970 and 1980 (see *Economic Report of the President*). When this revenue is coupled with grants from the federal government, it is clear that the funds available to subfederal governments have increased dramatically. Federal grants to the state and local governments were 1.3 percent of GDP in 1960, 2.5 percent in 1970, and 3.3 percent in 1980. The revenues retained at the federal level have thus declined as a percentage of GDP.

Within the United States, different levels of government use a variety of separate instruments for the taxation of income from capital. Income in the corporate sector is subject to the federal corporate income tax, state corporate income or franchise taxes, local property taxes, and the personal income tax of the ultimate recipients. Federal corporate and personal income taxes are not integrated, though there is a small dividend deduction of up to $100 at the personal level ($200 for joint returns). Though there has been considerable discussion of integration in academic circles,[1] actual policy proposals that would affect taxation of capital income tend to involve changes in accelerated depreciation, investment tax credit rates, interest exemptions, or the various forms of savings deductions for individual retirement accounts.

Aside from being a major source of revenue in the United States, the corporate tax system has been used for stabilization and as an incentive. The rate of tax, the rate of investment tax credit, and the allowances for depreciation have all been changed in response to macroeconomic conditions. Depreciation for tax purposes, known as "capital consumption allowance" in the United States, is accelerated to a different degree for each asset. Accelerated allowances have been used to provide incentives for investment in particular kinds of assets such as pollution-control equipment and low-cost housing.

Another concern has been the effect of inflation on the taxation of income from capital. Because depreciation is based on historical cost, inflation reduces the real value of nominal depreciation deductions in later years. This problem was not important in the 1950s and 1960s when inflation was running at about 2 percent per year, but from 1970 to 1980 the deflator for gross private domestic product increased at an average annual rate of 6.77 percent. This inflation rate averages consumption and investment goods, and it is the measure used for expected inflation in this chapter. Because of inflation, there have been frequent proposals to shorten asset lives for tax purposes. The recently enacted Accelerated Cost Recovery System (ACRS) not only shortens lives but simplifies administration by aggregating diverse assets into only a few categories of service lives. Other discussion has centered on reestimation of economic service lives (e.g., Hulten and Wykoff 1981) and indexing depreciation for inflation (e.g., Auerbach and Jorgenson 1980).

The fifty states have different systems for taxing income in the corporate sector. Thousands of local jurisdictions impose further taxes on commercial and industrial property, each with its own statutory rate and its own ratio of assessed value to market value. Capital income taxation is further complicated at the individual level, where taxes depend on considerations such as the proportion of dividend recipients with less than $100 of dividends, the dividend/retention policies of firms, the determi-

---

1. Charles McLure (1979) provides a comprehensive discussion of integration proposals in the United States, and Fullerton et al. (1981) provide some estimates of welfare effects attributable to several such proposals.

nants of tax-exempt status, the ceilings on individual retirement accounts, and the interaction of inflation with the nominal brackets of a graduated personal tax system.

Because of the variations of personal tax rates among income recipients, property tax rates among state and local jurisdictions, depreciation lives among different assets, and means of finance among different industries, an overall evaluation of United States effective marginal tax rates is a particularly useful but difficult exercise.

The outline for this chapter is the same as that of the other country chapters in this study: section 6.2.1 describes salient features of the personal income tax in the United States, including both federal and state tax provisions. While the 1980 law is used for comparison with other countries, the two new tax laws of 1981 and 1982 are also described and evaluated. Section 6.2.2 describes federal and state income tax provisions, but it defers discussion of depreciation allowances to section 6.2.3 and discussion of investment tax credits to section 6.2.5. Economic depreciation appears in section 6.2.4, and property taxes are described in section 6.2.6. Effective personal tax rates for our three ownership categories are provided in sections 6.2.8, 6.2.9, and 6.2.10. The various parts of section 6.3 provide information on the amount of investment flowing from each owner to each location, and the parts of section 6.4 provide final estimates of the total effective marginal tax rates in the United States.

6.2   The Tax System

6.2.1   The Personal Income Tax

Because personal taxes started primarily as taxes on income, and because departures from comprehensive income taxation have tended to involve various types of income from capital, many individuals view these departures as loopholes for wealthy taxpayers that significantly reduce the progressivity of the overall tax system. For example, capital gains taxation has been a more prominent feature in the United States than in the other three countries in this study, yet many view as a loophole the fact that the tax base includes only 40 percent of long-term capital gains (those resulting from assets held more than twelve months). Some recent proposals would increase this partial exclusion, while others would tax all capital gains. Still other proposals would broaden the tax base in other ways and replace the graduated rate structure with a flat rate of tax that is relatively low. On the other hand, the 40 percent inclusion refers to *nominal realized* long-term capital gains, an amount that might be greater than or less than real accrued capital gains, depending on the rate of inflation and on the asset.

Other departures from comprehensive income taxation include the nontaxation of state and local bond interest, the imputed rents from owner-occupied homes, and the income from saving through pension funds and life insurance. As the untaxed proportion of investment income has increased, and as discussion about the switch to a consumption-based tax has continued, fewer of these features have come to be viewed as loopholes. Yet, as pointed out by Bradford (1980) and others, having half of all assets on a consumption-tax basis is not like being halfway between an income tax and a consumption tax. Because of the dispersion of tax rates on different investments, this hybrid system has many disadvantages not associated with either pure extreme.

Table 6.2 documents some of the changes in the personal income tax base since 1950. The National Income and Product Accounts' definition of personal income is the starting point in the first row of table 6.2. This definition is equivalent to an economic definition of income minus unrealized capital gains and minus the imputed rents of owner-occupied homes. The basic income concept for personal tax purposes in the United States is called adjusted gross income (AGI). It can be obtained from personal income by subtracting 60 percent of realized long-term capital gains, all of interest from state and local bonds, transfer receipts, pension contributions of employers, moving expenses, alimony, and the income from saving through life insurance. The second row of table 6.2 reveals that these exclusions have increased steadily as a fraction of personal income since 1950.

Table 6.2 also reveals that the illegally unreported fraction of income diminished from 1950 to 1970, before turning back up again. The fraction of personal income on taxable returns increased from 70 percent in 1950 to 76 percent in 1970, and it fell back to 72 percent by 1978.

"Taxable income" in the United States refers to reported AGI after personal deductions and exemptions. Personal deductions can include charitable contributions, interest paid, state and local taxes, medical

Table 6.2   **Taxable Income as a Percentage of Personal Income**

	1950	1960	1970	1978
Total personal income	100.0	100.0	100.0	100.0
Adjusted gross income (AGI)	89.4	86.4	84.1	81.6
Reported AGI	79.2	78.9	78.8	75.6
Reported AGI on taxable returns	70.1	74.4	76.2	72.1
Taxable income on taxable returns	37.3	42.9	50.0	59.7

Source: Own calculations from data in the *Survey of Current Business* (Commerce Department) and *Statistics of Income, Individual Income Tax Returns* (Treasury Department). See Pechman (1977) or Steurle and Hartzmark (1981) for further tables.

Note: Adjusted gross income is the basic accounting measure for tax purposes in the United States and is further described in the text.

expenses above 3 percent of AGI, and some casualty losses. Each tax-payer can elect to "itemize" these deductions—that is, to list all deductions, add them up, and subtract the total from AGI before paying tax. As an alternative, taxpayers can take the "standard deduction" of $2,300 (or $3,400 for joint returns), also called the zero-bracket amount. The personal exemption is $1,000 per taxpayer, spouse, and each dependent. As shown in table 6.2, these deductions and exemptions made up over 30 percent of personal income in 1950, fell gradually to 26 percent in 1970, but then fell dramatically to only 12.4 percent in 1978. Inflation has eroded the real value of these nominal amounts in spite of occasional legislative increases, and as a result the taxable portion of personal income has risen from 37 to 60 percent since 1950.

The taxable portion of income in the United States is subject to the federal rate schedules of table 6.3 for joint returns. To show the zero-bracket amount, "income" in this table is defined as AGI less exemptions and less any itemized deductions over $3,400. The schedules for single and married taxpayers differ in such a way that a couple with sufficiently unequal incomes can reduce their total taxes by being married, while a couple with similar incomes would suffer a tax penalty by being married. Although marginal rates ranged from 14 percent to 70 percent in 1980,

Table 6.3   **Federal Tax Rates for Joint Returns**

		Marginal Tax Rate	
Income	Percentage of All 1979 Returns Taxed at or Below Marginal Rate	1980 Law	New Law after Phase-in (1984)
$ 0–3,400	21.3	.00	.00
3,400–5,500	29.2	.14	.11
5,500–7,600	35.8	.16	.12
7,600–11,900	48.6	.18	.14
11,900–16,000	63.5	.21	.16
16,000–20,200	75.2	.24	.18
20,200–24,600	83.8	.28	.22
24,600–29,900	90.7	.32	.25
29,900–35,200	95.3	.37	.28
35,200–45,800	97.9	.43	.33
45,800–60,000	99.1	.49	.38
60,000–85,600	99.7	.54	.42
85,600–109,400	99.8	.59	.45
109,400–162,400	99.9	.64	.49
162,400–215,400	100.0	.68	.50
Over 215,400	100.0	.70	.50

Source: Revenue Act of 1978, Economic Recovery Tax Act of 1981, and Steurle and Hartzmark (1981).

table 6.3 shows that three-fourths of all returns were taxed at a 24 percent marginal rate or less.

Tax rates under the Economic Recovery Tax Act are also shown in table 6.3. This 1981 law specifies a phased reduction of personal tax rates over three years starting with 1981. The top bracket is reduced from 70 percent to 50 percent, and if there were no inflation other rates would be reduced by 23 percent. Much of this reduction just offsets the effects of inflation since the last adjustment in 1978, however, and further inflation is expected to erode the value of these tax cuts by the time they take full effect in 1984. This law specifies automatic inflation adjustments to the income brackets and exemptions, starting in 1985.

Low-income taxpayers with dependents can qualify for the "earned income credit." This credit is equal to 10 percent of earned income up to $5,000, and it is reduced thereafter to the point where no credit is received with $10,000 of earned income. However, this credit is unusual in that it is refundable, which means that the government will send a check to the household if the credit exceeds their normal tax liability. A joint return with two dependents receives a credit in excess of tax liability up to an AGI of $8,483. Thus, the United States system includes a type of negative income tax. At the other end of the spectrum, earned income in 1980 was ostensibly subject to a maximum tax of 50 percent.[2]

For all qualified private retirement plans, both employee and employer contributions are deductible, while all benefits are taxable. If the individual's marginal tax rate does not change upon retirement, then this treatment is equivalent to that of a consumption tax.[3] Employees not covered by a pension plan in 1980 could deduct savings of 15 percent of earned income up to a $1,500 maximum ($1,750 for joint returns) through an individual retirement account (IRA). The 1981 Tax Act removed the percentage limitation and increased the maximum to $2,000 ($2,250 for joint returns). It also made IRAs available to those already covered by pension plans of their employers. Self-employed persons could deduct savings of 15 percent of earned income up to $7,500 under a Keogh retirement plan, increased to $15,000 by the new law.

Social security taxes and subsequent benefits could be viewed as another savings vehicle, an alternative to the various retirement savings vehicles just described. Because these social security payments are man-

2. For an exposition of how earned income could be effectively taxed at more than 50 percent at the margin, see Lindsey (1981). The Economic Recovery Tax Act of 1981 reduced all marginal rates to a maximum of 50 percent.

3. See chapter 2. *Blueprints for Basic Tax Reform* (U.S. Department of the Treasury 1977) describes a consumption tax that operates like a comprehensive income tax but allows deductions for savings through "qualified accounts." Since income minus savings leaves only consumption in the tax base, a normal graduated schedule can be applied to it. Qualified retirement plans operate in this manner, except that they have contribution ceilings and withdrawal constraints.

datory, however, they are not included in our calculations of the effective tax on a marginal increase of savings. To the degree that social security is an actuarially fair way to save, this vehicle would receive favored status relative to an income tax or even a consumption tax. While employee contributions are taxable, the employer contributions and all social security benefits go tax free.

Business income of unincorporated enterprises is taxed under the personal tax system. Depreciation allowances are the same as those described in section 6.2.3 for corporations, and investment tax credits are the same as those described in section 6.2.5 for corporations.

Because of the various exclusions and deductions, tax revenue from high-income individuals can sometimes be small. Income from capital is more readily sheltered than income from labor, particularly through exclusion of imputed rents and 60 percent of long-term capital gains. To take another example, a combination of debt finance and accelerated depreciation means that an investor can often claim first-year allowances greater than the initial capital investment. These considerations have led to two kinds of provisions. First, Congress has passed rules that prevent the investor from taking depreciation allowances beyond the amount of the investment for which he is at risk. That is, the investor cannot use nonrecourse debt and still qualify for fully accelerated allowances. Second, Congress passed "minimum tax" provisions in 1969, strengthened them in 1976, and weakened them again in 1978. These provisions operate as a floor to tax liability, designed to ensure that at least some tax is paid at high income levels. A 15 percent rate is applied to "preference income," defined as the excluded 60 percent of long-term gains, itemized deductions that are over 60 percent of AGI, and parts of depletion deductions, intangible drilling costs, and accelerated depreciation. State and local interest is not included here as a preference income item.

Finally, at the federal level, we should mention the averaging provisions that are designed to help avoid the payment of extra tax that is due solely to the interaction of a volatile income stream and a graduated tax system. However, income must exceed the average of the previous four years by at least one-third, this excess must be more than $3,000, and no allowance is made for falling incomes.

Of the forty-one states with personal income taxes, thirty-two make use of the AGI concept from the federal tax calculations. States differ with respect to exemptions and deductions and with respect to the applicable rate structure. Most state systems have graduated rates, and several have top marginal rates as high as 11 percent. Only Alaska, Delaware, Iowa, and New York have top marginal rates above 11 percent. Also, state taxes paid are deductible at the federal level if the taxpayer itemizes deductions.

Several local governments collect personal income taxes. New York City and Washington, D.C., obtain more than 20 percent of their revenues from this source, while Philadelphia gets a full half. In total, however, local income taxes collected only $3.75 billion in 1977. When compared with $25.5 billion at the state level and $156.7 billion at the federal level, this $3.75 billion of local tax can be ignored for present purposes.

Effective marginal tax rates at the household level are estimated using the tax simulation (TAXSIM) model of the National Bureau of Economic Research (NBER). This model is described in Feldstein and Frisch (1977) and in Feenberg and Rosen (1983). The data base for this model includes 25,000 tax return records from the Internal Revenue Service (IRS) for each year. TAXSIM has information not only on adjusted gross income, but also on wages, dividends, interest, capital gains, other types of income, and on various tax deductions taken for each return in the sample. The state of residence is also available for each return. The federal tax law and each of the fifty states' tax laws are specifically programmed into the model. To calculate the effective marginal tax rate on a given type of income, such as interest income, the TAXSIM model raises all individuals' receipts of that income type by 1 percent, recalculates their tax liabilities, and sums the additional tax to be paid. It is thus a weighted-average marginal tax rate, where the weights are the shares for the type of income under consideration.

To obtain federal rates, the TAXSIM model need not account for the deductibility of any additional state taxes. For combined state and federal tax rates, however, there is a simultaneous deductibility in states that allow a deduction for federal taxes. These deductions are simulated for the same tax year, though actual federal (state) practice allows a deduction for one year's state (federal) taxes in the following tax year. Deductions are allowed only for those who itemize.

Because tax law does not require the separate specification of corporate bond interest and bank deposit interest, the tax-return data show only total interest receipts. Thus we can calculate an overall marginal tax rate on interest income but not a separate weighted-average marginal tax rate on corporate interest alone. The most recent data available are for 1977, a problem that is discussed further below.

If a marginal dollar of wage income were distributed in proportion to all wage income, the simulated extra tax would be about 27 cents at the federal level, 5 cents on average at the state level, and about 32 cents overall. Similar overall weighted-average marginal tax rates for dividend and interest incomes are 47.5 percent and 32.5 percent, respectively. These estimates reflect the fact that dividends are more highly concentrated in high income brackets than are taxable interest receipts.

Finally, data in TAXSIM can be used to estimate the elasticity of personal income taxes to changes in the tax base. This "liability" measure of progressivity is equal to one for proportional taxes and is larger than one for progressive taxes. For the United States personal income tax, the estimated elasticity is 1.66, including state and federal taxes.[4] This estimate is similar to the 1.76 estimate found by Ott and Dittrich (1981).

6.2.2   The Corporate Tax System

The federal corporate income tax started in 1913 at a rate of 1 percent. The marginal rate varied around 12 percent from 1918 to 1935. The United States instituted a surcharge on retained earnings in 1936 and 1937 and thus experimented briefly with a form of corporate integration. It reverted to a classical system, however, and the top rate varied around 40 percent until 1945. The top marginal rate after 1946 has varied around 50 percent, as shown in table 6.4.

In 1980 the federal corporate tax had a graduated rate structure, with percentage rates of 17, 20, 30, and 40 applied to four brackets of $25,000 each. The 1981 law reduces the first two brackets' rates to 15 and 18 percent, respectively. Above $100,000 of taxable income under both laws, corporations pay a flat 46 percent marginal tax rate.

For the federal part of τ, the statutory corporate rate, the relevant concept is the additional tax on profits resulting from a dollar of marginal investment allocated in proportion to existing capital. While most corporations do not reach the top marginal rate of 0.46, the great bulk of corporate capital is held by firms that do.[5] Thus we can safely ignore investment in firms with less than $100,000 of profits and take 0.46 as the federal part of τ.

The corporate income tax applies to all corporate profits net of depreciation, interest payments, and other expenses, whether those profits are retained or distributed. The payment of dividends does not affect the corporate tax as it does in Germany or the United Kingdom. Thus, since 1938, the United States corporate tax is a classical system. If the corporation retains another dollar, it gives up a dollar of dividends that are gross of the personal income tax. Thus 1.0 is the value for θ, the opportunity cost of retained earnings in terms of gross dividends.

The corporation may deduct all dividends it receives from subsidiaries and 85 percent of dividends from other corporations. Long-term capital gains are fully taxed under both the old law and the new law, but at a reduced rate of 0.28 instead of 0.46. Capital losses may be used only to offset capital gains within the previous three or following five years. On the other hand, net operating losses may be carried back for three years or forward for seven. The 1981 Tax Act extends this carryover to fifteen years.

4. I am grateful to Daniel Feenberg, who performed all TAXSIM calculations.
5. See Musgrave and Musgrave (1980).

Table 6.4   **Top Marginal United States Corporate Income Tax Rates**

Tax Years	Top Rate (%)	Tax Years	Top Rate (%)
1946–49	38	1965–67	48
1950	42	1968	52.8[a]
1951	50.75	1969	49.2[a]
1952–63	52	1970–78	48
1964	50	1979–82	46

Source: Facts and Figures on Government Finance, Tax Foundation, 1981.
[a]In 1968 and 1969 the basic rate was 48 percent, but there were surcharges of 10 percent and 2.5 percent, respectively, applied to tax liabilities.

Before 1969, oil and gas producers could deduct 27.5 percent of gross receipts as an allowance for the depletion of reserves. Total depletion was not limited to the cost of the asset. Since exploration and drilling costs were immediately expensed, however, these depletion allowances were generally recognized as a preferential treatment. In 1969 these allowances were reduced to 22 percent, and in 1975 they were cut to 15 percent for small producers and eliminated for large producers.

Several other features of the federal tax code are worth mentioning at this point. First, immediate expensing is allowed for intangible investments such as advertising and R&D. Since neither corporate "goodwill" nor research and development capital is considered an asset in this study, this tax break is ignored. Second, certain tax credits are allowed for the hiring of new employees. Third, earnings of foreign subsidiaries are taxed only upon repatriation to the United States parent corporation. A credit on United States taxes is allowed for any foreign taxes already paid on those earnings. Finally, a domestic international sales corporation (DISC) can be organized to handle export business of a United States corporation. Part of the DISC earnings are also untaxed until returned to the parent corporation.

With respect to subfederal corporate income taxes, forty-five states and the District of Columbia levy rates varying from 2 percent to 12 percent. Most systems define corporate income in a manner similar to the federal system, but adjustments vary from state to state. Most also have a graduated structure. A significant problem arises, however, in determining what portion of the corporation's total profits were generated in the state. Most corporate income is apportioned among states through the use of a formula based on the proportion of the corporation's total property located in the state, the proportion of total wages paid in the state, and the proportion of the corporation's sales in the state. Each state can choose its own formula. An interesting result of this procedure is that the sum of a corporation's tax base across the taxing states can exceed its total profits, if each state chooses a formula that is advantageous to its own base. Many states use the "Massachusetts formula," giving equal weight to each of the three factors mentioned above.[6]

For our marginal statutory tax rate τ, we would like to include a weighted average of state marginal tax rates and account for deductibility at the federal level. The top marginal rate in each state is available in *Facts and Figures on Government Finance* (Tax Foundation 1981), but the choice of weights is more difficult. A 1 percent increase in all corporate capital holdings would be distributed among the states in proportion to existing capital holdings, but state taxes on the income would also depend on where those corporations paid wages and made sales. Since states adopt different apportionment formulas, a "correct" set of weights is virtually impossible. We use personal income in each state to weight statutory marginal tax rates, since this is highly correlated with payroll and with sales. Since it is based on residence, however, personal income may be less well correlated with corporate property. These data are available for the first quarter of 1980 in the July 1980 *Survey of Current Business*. The personal-income-weighted average of state marginal corporate tax rates, including a zero rate for states without a corporate tax, is 6.55 percent. If we multiply this rate by $(1 - 0.46)$ to account for deductibility at the federal level, we get a net rate of 3.54 percent. Adding 0.46 for the federal tax itself, we have 0.495 for the value of τ.[7]

6.2.3 Tax Allowances for Depreciation and Inventories

Because provisions related to depreciation are relatively less straightforward, we first discuss provisions related to inventories. United States corporations are allowed to use any of a number of consistent accounting methods, including last in, first out (LIFO) and first in, first out (FIFO).[8] Unlike other countries in this study, however, the United States requires firms to use the same method for profits reported to shareholders as they use for profits reported to taxing authorities.

With recent increases in the rate of inflation, many firms have been switching from FIFO to LIFO accounting. Because first-bought inventory items have a lower nominal cost than the last-bought items, FIFO profits are larger than LIFO profits for a given sales price. Firm managers might like to report FIFO profits to shareholders, especially if executive

6. McLure (1980) argues that these apportionment formulas change the effect of a particular state's corporate income tax from a tax on income to an excise tax on sales, payrolls, or property. We have a national perspective, however. Our marginal investment is made in proportion to existing capital with its existing allocation among assets, industries, and states. The earnings from such an investment would incour additional state corporate income tax liability at the weighted-average rate.

7. This calculation ignores the deductibility of federal corporate taxes in some state tax systems.

8. Other allowable methods include an "average cost" method, a "standard cost" method, and an "actual cost" method. See Shoven and Bulow (1975) for further discussion of these accounting choices.

salaries or bonuses are based on reported profits. On the other hand, taxes can be reduced by reporting relatively smaller LIFO profits to the IRS. It is thus surprising that only 30 percent of manufacturing inventories and only 22 percent of retail trade inventories were on a LIFO basis in 1979.[9] Most large corporations are on LIFO accounting, so perhaps small businesses find it easier to remain on FIFO.

Two possibilities exist for our parameter v, the proportion of inventories on FIFO accounting. In our standard case, we set v to zero and assume that firms act so as to minimize taxes in this regard. (This assumption is consistent with the use of minimum lifetimes and maximum acceleration in the depreciation of assets discussed below.) As an alternative, we report results for the case where v is set to 0.7, the actual proportion of manufacturing inventories on FIFO in 1979.

We turn now to look at depreciation allowances for tax purposes. Tax law, government data, and United States studies typically divide assets into "equipment" and "structures," but these categories correspond to our "machinery" and "buildings" categories. All assets received straight-line allowances with the beginning of the personal and corporate income taxes in 1913, but considerable choice was available on tax lifetimes. The Treasury Department first published a set of suggested lifetimes in its *Bulletin F* of 1931, and depreciation allowances were still based on those estimates in 1980. Tightening and controversy followed with the lengthening of suggested lifetimes in the 1942 edition of *Bulletin F.*

Reversing this trend in 1954, Congress decided to allow accelerated methods of depreciation. In particular, both equipment and structures were allowed double declining balance (DDB) or sum-of-the-years'-digits (SYD) methods of depreciation.[10] The actual adoption of acceler-

9. Data are from the United States Commerce Department publication *Current Industrial Reports* (Manufacturers' Shipments, Inventories and Orders) and from *Current Business Reports* (1979 Retail Trade).

10. This footnote describes each depreciation scheme in more detail. For straight-line depreciation, the law specifies a lifetime for tax purposes L, and it allows the taxpayer to deduct $1/L$ of the purchase price of the asset each year for L years. The asset is fully depreciated after L years. For sum-of-the-years'-digits (SYD), the taxpayer starts by calculating a SUM, equal to $\Sigma_{i=1}^{L}\ i$. The purchase price is multiplied by $L/$SUM for depreciation in the first year, $(L-1)/$SUM for depreciation in the second year, down to $1/$SUM for depreciation in the last year. If $L = 3$, for example, the purchase price is allocated as 3/6, 2/6, and 1/6 across the three years, and again the asset is fully depreciated. With double declining balance (DDB), the taxpayer can take twice the straight-line rate, but on a declining balance basis. That is, first-year depreciation is $2/L$ of the purchase price, but second-year depreciation is $2/L$ of the remaining basis $(1 - 2/L)$. As described in the text, some assets receive less than twice the straight-line rate. With "150 percent of declining-balance," for example, taxpayers can deduct $1.5/L$ of the purchase price in the first year and $1.5/L$ of remaining basis in later years. We refer to the numerator of this ratio as B in our equations below. Under declining balance methods, however, the asset is never fully depreciated. The United States law allows taxpayers to switch from the declining balance method to one of the other methods to complete depreciation deductions. The optimal times to make such switches are described in the text below.

ated methods has, however, been gradual. Jorgenson and Sullivan (1981) estimate that the proportion of assets using these methods jumped from 0.30 to 0.52 between 1954 and 1955, but then grew more slowly to 0.85 in 1978. Adjustment costs and traditional accounting practices are the major available explanations for the continued use of less accelerated methods.

At least partly in response to taxpayer practices of using shorter asset lives for tax purposes, in 1962 the Treasury issued "Guidelines" with a 30 to 40 percent shortening of suggested *Bulletin F* lives. These changes were accompanied by the 1962 introduction of the investment tax credit (ITC) discussed in the next section. Although the "Long Amendment" specified that the basis for depreciation was to be net of the ITC, this amendment was repealed in 1964, and investors were allowed to increase the basis of assets bought in 1962 and 1963.

Later changes included the 1969 elimination of double declining balance for structures other than public utility structures. New nonresidential structures were reduced from 200 percent to 150 percent of declining balance, while used nonresidential structures were reduced from 150 percent to straight-line.

In 1971 the Asset Depreciation Range (ADR) system further liberalized depreciation allowances for equipment and public utility structures by permitting lifetimes that were 20 percent above or below the Guideline lifetimes (which were themselves 30–40 percent lower than those of *Bulletin F*). Taxpayers did not always adopt the shortest lifetimes available, because longer lifetimes made some assets eligible for higher rates of investment tax credit. In particular, the asset's life must be at least seven years to qualify for the full 10 percent credit, at least five years to qualify for two-thirds of that credit, and at least three years to qualify for one-third of the credit.

The law also includes a requirement that assets not be depreciated below their ultimate scrap values. However, the assumed scrap value as a proportion of asset value has been considerably reduced in recent years. The reduction in allowances comes at the end of the depreciation stream for the declining balance methods, and the present value effect of the scrap value provisions must be very small. As a result, this complication can be ignored.

We now turn to a detailed examination of depreciation allowances as they stood in 1980 (the "old law"), to be followed by an examination of the Economic Recovery Tax Act of 1981 and the Tax Equity and Fiscal Responsibility Act of 1982. We assume that the hypothetical project under study is one undertaken by a corporation using the most favorable depreciation method, and we assume that the investment under consideration is a new asset, not a used one.

For the old law, Guideline lifetimes are specified for hundreds of different assets. To reduce this number to more manageable proportions, several studies have provided information on an aggregation to the thirty-four asset types listed in table 6.5. For example, Hulten and Wykoff (1981) have estimated economic depreciation rates based on this aggregation. These estimates, shown in column 1 of table 6.5, are discussed in the next section. The first twenty assets are types of equipment and will ultimately be aggregated into a single asset for the purposes of this study. The following fourteen assets are types of structures, also to be aggregated for this study. Inventories are treated elsewhere.

These thirty-four assets are used in different proportions by each of our three industries (manufacturing, other industry, and commerce). To obtain the relevant thirty-four by three matrix, we aggregated more detailed capital stock data provided by Dale Jorgenson.[11] As described below, these 1977 capital stocks are used in weighting depreciation rates of column 1 and investment tax credit rates of column 2 to obtain industry-specific values for δ and g.

We also use these capital stocks to obtain industry-specific values for tax depreciation allowances, but this procedure is considerably more complicated for two reasons. First, United States tax law does not specify any exponential depreciation rate suitable for use as the parameter a, defined in chapter 2. Instead, tax lifetimes and depreciation formulas are used directly to calculate A_z, defined as the present value of depreciation allowances for a dollar of investment, in each of the thirty-four assets under each law. Multiplication by τ provides A_d, defined in chapter 2 as the tax saving from these depreciation deductions. Second, the law differs for each of the thirty-four assets. In particular, the "buildings" asset in this study includes public utility structures, which are allowed double declining balance like equipment, plus other structures, which receive only 150 percent of declining balance under the old law (175 percent under the 1981 and 1982 laws). We use the capital stock matrix to calculate a weighted average of the present value of depreciation allowances in each industry, first over the twenty types of equipment and then over the fourteen types of structures. In this case, however, capital stocks do not provide the correct weights by themselves. After we describe depreciations allowances below, we refer to Appendix D for a procedure to average allowances over the twenty types of equipment or fourteen types of structures in each industry.

To proceed, for the old law Jorgenson and Sullivan (1981) have aggregated the Guideline lifetimes for hundreds of assets into thirty-four

---

11. See Jorgenson and Sullivan (1981), Fraumeni and Jorgenson (1980), and section 6.3.2 for more detail.

Table 6.5   **Depreciation, Investment Tax Credit (ITC) Rates, and Tax Lifetimes by Asset Class**

Asset Class	Hulten/ Wykoff Depre- ciation Rates (1)	1980 Law		1981 and 1982 Laws	
		ITC Rate (2)	Life- time (3)	ITC Rate (4)	Life- time (5)
1. Furniture and fixtures	0.1100	0.100	8.00	0.10	5.0
2. Fabricated metal products	0.0917	0.100	10.00	0.10	5.0
3. Engines and turbines	0.0786	0.100	12.48	0.10	5.0
4. Tractors	0.1633	0.067	5.00	0.10	5.0
5. Agricultural machinery	0.0971	0.100	8.00	0.10	5.0
6. Construction machinery	0.1722	0.100	7.92	0.10	5.0
7. Mining and oilfield machinery	0.1650	0.100	7.68	0.10	5.0
8. Metalworking machinery	0.1225	0.100	10.16	0.10	5.0
9. Special industry machinery	0.1031	0.100	10.16	0.10	5.0
10. General industrial machinery	0.1225	0.100	9.84	0.10	5.0
11. Office and computing machinery	0.2729	0.100	8.00	0.10	5.0
12. Service industry machinery	0.1650	0.100	8.24	0.10	5.0
13. Electrical equipment	0.1179	0.100	9.92	0.10	5.0
14. Trucks, buses, and trailers	0.2537	0.067	5.00	0.10	5.0
15. Autos	0.3333	0.033	3.00	0.06	3.0
16. Aircraft	0.1833	0.100	7.00	0.10	5.0
17. Ships and boats	0.0750	0.100	14.40	0.10	5.0
18. Railroad equipment	0.0660	0.100	12.00	0.10	5.0
19. Instruments	0.1473	0.100	8.48	0.10	5.0
20. Other equipment	0.1473	0.100	8.16	0.10	5.0
21. Industrial buildings	0.0361	0.0	28.80	0.0	15.0
22. Commercial buildings	0.0247	0.0	47.60	0.0	15.0
23. Religious buildings	0.0188	0.0	48.00	0.0	15.0
24. Educational buildings	0.0188	0.0	48.00	0.0	15.0
25. Hospitals	0.0233	0.0	48.00	0.0	15.0
26. Other nonfarm buildings	0.0454	0.0	30.90	0.0	15.0
27. Railroads	0.0176	0.100	24.00	0.10	15.0
28. Telephone and telegraph	0.0333	0.100	21.60	0.10	15.0
29. Electric light and power	0.0300	0.100	21.60	0.10	15.0
30. Gas	0.0300	0.100	19.20	0.10	10.0
31. Other public utilities	0.0450	0.100	17.60	0.10	10.0
32. Farm structures	0.0237	0.0	25.00	0.0	15.0
33. Mining, shafts, and wells	0.0563	0.0	6.80	0.0	5.0
34. Other nonresidential structures	0.0290	0.0	28.20	0.0	15.0

Source: Depreciation rates are from Hulten and Wykoff (1981). For public utility struc-tures (assets 27–31), Jorgenson and Sullivan (1981) provide estimates based on the Hulten/ Wykoff methodology. Investment tax credit rates and lifetimes are from Fullerton and Henderson (1981) and are described in the text.

lifetimes, based on the aggregations of table 6.5. These lifetimes provide estimates of the midpoints of the Asset Depreciation Range (ADR) system. Most structures are assigned these lives directly, but the ADR system allows 20 percent longer or shorter lives for equipment (assets 1–20) and public utility structures (assets 27–31). Because of our optimizing tax practice assumption, these assets are assigned lives that are 80 percent of ADR midpoints, except where the use of a longer life would reduce effective taxes through eligibility for a higher investment tax credit. In order to concentrate on tax law rather than on actual practices, we ignore the possibility of shorter lives substantiated by facts and circumstances. The resulting vector of lives, shown in column 3 of table 6.5, is consistent with the ITC vector in that three- and five-year assets get one-third and two-thirds of the full investment tax credit, respectively.[12] This vector of lives also appears in Fullerton and Henderson (1981).

For equipment (assets 1–20) and public utility structures (assets 27–31), the old law allows double declining balance (DDB), with a switch to sum-of-the-years'-digits (SYD). See footnote 10 for description of these schemes. This combination is used here as tax-minimizing practice because it can be shown to provide the earliest possible depreciation deductions.[13] Define L as the asset's lifetime for tax purposes, an integer number of years. Define L_s as the time of the optimal switch, and B as the "declining balance rate." The B parameter refers to the multiplier for the straight-line rate when depreciation is allowed on a declining basis. That is $B = 2.0$ for double declining balance, and $B = 1.5$ for 150 percent of declining balance. We can then define $a' \equiv B/L$ as the exponential rate for the first part of the asset's life. The prime distinguishes this parameter from the exponential rate that would apply to the asset's whole life. Since DDB starts out with higher depreciation allowances, and since SYD on the remaining basis must eventually exceed DDB, the optimal switching point can be found by equating depreciation under the two methods:

---

12. Lifetimes for many of the thirty-four assets are actually averaged over more diverse asset categories. As a result, only some of the assets in one of our categories may need their lifetimes adjusted to receive higher credits. Since the aggregation to thirty-four assets provides considerable detail, however, it seems appropriate to treat each asset as individually homogeneous. One example where this treatment may be less appropriate is in mining, shafts, and wells. The 6.8 year life here reflects an average of intangible drilling with a zero life and other structures with a longer life.

13. See Shoven and Bulow (1975). If a firm expects a steady stream of positive taxable profits, as assumed, it would always take depreciation allowances as early as possible. In other circumstances, however, the firm may prefer later deductions. Under the old law, the firm could delay its depreciation by delaying the switch or by using straight-line. The 1981 and 1982 laws are less flexible, however, because they mandate the switchover time that would be optimal for the firm wanting the earliest deductions. All laws allow the flexibility to combine just straight-line depreciation with longer tax lives, but this decision can be made only at the time of acquisition.

(6.1)
$$\frac{L - L_s}{F(L - L_s)} = \frac{B}{L},$$

where the F function is defined by

(6.2)
$$F(x) = \sum_{j=0}^{x} (x - j)$$

if x is an integer. As seen below for cases where x is not an integer, the summation goes from zero to the integer part of x.

For such equipment, the firm would use DDB in the first year, would be indifferent in the second year, and would switch to SYD by the third year of the asset's life. However, tax laws make use of the half-year convention, assuming that all assets were bought on 1 July. The firm thus uses DDB for $L_s = 1.5$ years, and SYD afterward. Take, for example, a one-dollar asset with $L = 5$, $B = 2$, and $a' = 0.40$. Then the firm would deduct 0.2 (half of a') in the year of purchase and 0.32 (a' times 0.8) in the first full taxable year. Switching to SYD for the 0.48 remaining basis over 3.5 years, the firm would use numerators of 3.5, 2.5, 1.5, and 0.5 respectively. The sum of those figures for the denominator is 8.0, as defined by $F(L - L_s)$ in equation (6.2), where $L - L_s$ is not an integer. Because allowances are on a historical cost basis, these nominal future depreciation deductions are discounted at the nominal (after-tax) discount rate ρ. Since A_z was defined as the present value of depreciation allowances on a current dollar of investment, the general expression under 1980 law for equipment and public utility structures is:[14]

$$A_z = a \int_0^{.5} e^{-\rho u} du + a'\left(1 - \frac{a'}{2}\right) \int_{.5}^{1.5} e^{-\rho u} du$$

(6.3)
$$+ \left(1 - \frac{a'}{2}\right)(1 - a') \cdot \sum_{J=2}^{L} \frac{L - (J - .5)}{F(L - L_s)}$$

$$\cdot \int_{J - .5}^{J + .5} e^{-\rho u} du.$$

To save space, the integration is not performed here.

For structures (assets 21–26 and 32–34), the old law specifies a 150 percent declining balance rate ($B = 1.5$) with a switch to straight-line.

---

14. This expression avoids assuming a continuously declining basis, which would inaccurately leave $e^{-a'L_s}$ remaining at the time of the switch. Instead, we follow the law by specifying yearly adjustments to basis. Also, because we discount continuously, depreciation deductions at the beginning of the year are worth more than those at the end of the year. This procedure explicitly recognizes that depreciation deductions are "coincident" with the associated earnings and tax liability.

The switch time L_s is again found where the two methods provide the same deductions. Since continued exponential deductions would allow a rate B/L on remaining basis, and since straight-line would allow $1/(L - L_s)$ on the same remaining basis, we can set these two expressions equal to each other and solve for L_s as:

$$(6.4) \qquad L_s = \left(\frac{B-1}{B} \right) L.$$

Thus the firm would switch after one-third of the asset's life, but it must begin straight-line at the start of a tax year. For a twenty-five year asset, for example, L_s would be 8.33 years. If we assume midyear purchase dates on average, the firm actually switches after 8.5 years. The general present value expression for structures is then:

$$
A_z = a' \int_0^{.5} e^{-\rho u}\, du + a' \left(1 - \frac{a'}{2} \right)
$$

$$
\cdot \sum_{J=0}^{L_s - 1.5} (1 - a')^J \cdot \int_{J+.5}^{J+1.5} e^{-\rho u}\, du
$$

$$(6.5) \qquad + \left(1 - \frac{a'}{2} \right) (1 - a')^{(L_s - .5)} \cdot \frac{1}{L - L_s} \cdot \int_{L_s}^{L} e^{-\rho u}\, du.$$

The Economic Recovery Tax Act of 1981 changed both the investment tax credit, as described in the next section, and depreciation allowances. It introduced the Accelerated Cost Recovery System (ACRS), under which any depreciable asset falls into one of four classes and is given a tax life of three, five, ten, or fifteen years. The ACRS lifetimes for our thirty-four assets are shown in column 5 of table 6.5. The law assigns a three-year life to autos, light trucks, R&D equipment, certain race-horses, and personal property with an ADR midpoint of four years or less. Our level of aggregation shows autos with a three-year life, but none of the other assets has an (average) ADR midpoint of four years or less. All other equipment gets a five-year life.

A ten-year life is granted to any public utility structure with an ADR midpoint between eighteen and twenty-five years. Since the "gas" and "other public utility" categories have ADR midpoints of less than twenty-five years, we assign a ten-year life to these two assets under ACRS. Finally, a fifteen-year life is assigned to public utility structures with an ADR midpoint of more than twenty-five years, and to all other structures except mining, shafts, and wells, which we reduce from 6.8 years to a five-year life. Thus, all thirty-four assets receive lifetimes that are shorter than the minimum allowable under the old law, and tax lives are no longer based on estimates of expected useful lives.

Although these shorter lives were effective immediately, the 1981 law specifies a depreciation schedule that is less accelerated during a five-year phase-in period. In 1981, purchases of equipment and public utility structures were allowed only 150 percent of declining balance, switching to straight-line, and from 1982 to 1985 they were scheduled to receive 175 percent, switching to SYD. They were scheduled to receive double declining balance again starting in 1986. We will investigate only the posttransition allowances that were scheduled to start in 1986.

Under the ultimate 1981 law, equipment and public utility structures receive DDB switching to SYD as before, so we could almost get away with substituting the new lifetimes into equation (6.3) from the old law to obtain A_z, the present value of allowances. However, the 1981 law moves up depreciation from the last half-year. As a result, the three-year class is depreciated in only 2.5 years, the five-year class in 4.5 years, and the ten-year class in 9.5 years. For the five-year asset example, depreciation deductions are 0.2 in the first half-year (half of B/L) and 0.32 in the first full year (B/L times 0.8), but the remaining 0.48 basis is given SYD treatment over only three remaining years. Also, the taxpayer is not given the choice of when to switch. If the firm selects a five-year life for equipment, the law actually provides a table requiring deductions of 0.2, 0.32, 0.24, 0.16, and 0.08, starting in the year of purchase. We thus have a general expression for A_z under the 1981 Economic Recovery Tax Act for equipment and public utility structures in 1986:

$$
A_z = a' \int_0^{.5} e^{-\rho u} du + a' \left(1 - \frac{a'}{2}\right) \int_{.5}^{1.5} e^{-\rho u} du
$$

(6.6)

$$
+ \left(1 - \frac{a'}{2}\right)(1 - a') \cdot \sum_{J=2}^{L} \frac{L - J}{F(L_s - G - .5)} \int_{J-.5}^{J+.5} e^{-\rho u} du .
$$

This formula is essentially that used to calculate the depreciation amounts specified in the tables of the law.

Other structures have no transition but immediately increase from 150 to 175 percent of declining balance. They still switch to straight-line, however, and the last half-year is not moved up. As a result, we can set B to 1.75 and use formulas from the old law for structures. Equation (6.4) implies that the switch point is 3/7 of L. For a fifteen-year asset purchased 1 July, L_s is set to 6.5 years, and equation (6.5) provides the present value of depreciation allowances, A_z.

The 1981 act represented a dramatic tax change, but not only because of the business provisions described here. Personal tax cuts and many other features of the act are described in section 6.4.2. While the Reagan administration may have planned commensurate cuts in government expenditures, the 1981–82 recession served both to reduce revenue and to increase required expenditures relative to planned amounts. In light of high deficit projections, growing concern over deficits, and claims that the 1981 tax cuts were tilted in favor of business, Congress passed the Tax Equity and Fiscal Responsibility Act of 1982. This act retains the personal tax cuts, the ACRS lifetimes, and the ITC rates of the 1981 act, but it repeals the last two phases of the transition for equipment and public utility structures. These assets are left with 150 percent of declining balance (switching to straight-line) rather than progressing to 175 and 200 percent of declining balance (switching to SYD). Further, the 1982 act reduces the depreciation basis by half of the investment tax credit.

Operationally, for equipment (assets 1–20) and public utility structures (assets 27–31), we set B equal to 1.5 and use equations (6.4) and (6.5) to calculate A_z. We then multiply by $(1 - g/2)$ to get the present value of allowances per dollar of investment.[15] Other structures are unchanged from the 1981 law, using $B = 1.75$ and the same equations.

For any law, we now have A_z for each of the thirty-four assets. This A_z was defined as the present value of depreciation allowances for a dollar of current investment, but we want the present value of allowances for a dollar of maintained capital stock. A distinction arises because reinvestment in later years also receives accelerated allowances (at historical cost). For this reason, each A_z is weighted not by capital stocks alone, but by existing capital plus the present value of reinvestment required to replace capital in each asset and industry. A short-lived asset receives relatively more weight because it requires more reinvestment qualifying for depreciation deductions A_z. This procedure is fully described in Appendix D.

The correctly averaged A_z for equipment or structures in each industry, called $\overline{A_z}$ in Appendix D, is multiplied by τ to obtain A_d, the present value of tax savings from these future depreciation deductions. These tax savings thus depend in a very nonlinear manner on ρ, and they cannot be calculated until this nominal after-tax discount rate is available. In the fixed-r case this requirement presents no obstacle. In the fixed-p case, however, equation (2.23) of chapter 2 shows that A_d is required before the discount rate can be calculated. This simultaneity cannot be resolved by an analytical solution for ρ. Instead, we iterate to find an interest rate ρ that is consistent with both sets of equations.

Finally, for the United States data set, the f_2 parameter is set to zero, indicating no immediate free depreciation of investment. The f_1 param-

---

15. Tables in the 1981 and 1982 laws specify actual percentages of purchase price to be depreciated each year for each asset. These percentages can all be derived from our formulas, with one exception. For five-year equipment in 1981, B is 1.5, and the optimal switch to straight-line would occur after one-third the life of the asset. With the half-year convention L_s would be 2.5. Because of early-year revenue constraints, however, the 1981 tables require a switch to straight-line after only the first half-year. These amounts were multiplied by $(1 - g/2)$ to provide tables for the 1982 law. We capture this effect by specifying $L_s = 0.5$ for five-year assets under the 1982 law.

eter is set to one, indicating that all equipment and structures depreciate for tax purposes according to the formulas above. Inventories receive no depreciation allowances.

6.2.4   Estimates of Economic Depreciation

The most recent and most comprehensive estimates of economic depreciation in the United States are found in Hulten and Wykoff (1981). They use prices observed from secondhand asset markets to infer the declines in asset values that occur with age, taking inflation into account. To avoid "censored sample bias," a problem associated with the fact that prices would not be available for retired assets, they use separate data on retirements to obtain survival probabilities. The "average" price for an asset of a particular vintage is then its observed price times its survival probability (plus zero times its retirement probability). A potential difficulty is that assets appearing in the secondhand markets may be systematically inferior to those retained by original owners. If buyers cannot distinguish between normal assets and these inferior assets, called "lemons" by Akerlof (1970), then market prices would understate the average value of a particular vintage. Hulten and Wykoff argue that this problem is not serious for business resale markets. Since buyers are sophisticated specialists, sellers cannot expect to gain from offering only their inferior assets. Furthermore, assets such as construction machinery are often bought for particular jobs and sold afterward.

Hulten and Wykoff use "blue book" and other business asset price data directly for eight asset categories. They test alternative assumptions about the time profile of depreciation, and they conclude that exponential decay is much more data-compatible than straight-line or one-horse-shay depreciation. The weakest link in their procedure is the derivation of thirty-two depreciation rates from the eight directly estimated rates. For each of these thirty-two assets, the Commerce Department provides an estimate of actual economic life, assuming that depreciation is straight line. Call this economic life L (but note that this concept differs from the tax lifetime discussed in the previous section).

If each asset does decay exponentially, and if each has an associated lifetime L, then each depreciation rate can be described by

$$(6.7) \qquad \delta = \frac{B}{L},$$

where B is the "declining balance rate" for economic depreciation. Again, this concept differs from the legal B of the previous section, but $B = 2$ would imply that actual depreciation was on a declining basis at twice the straight-line rate defined by L. Since they have δ and L for their six directly estimated equipment types, Hulten and Wykoff use (6.7) to find an average B of 1.65 for equipment. They use this B with other lifetimes

Table 6.6   Economic Depreciation Rates by Asset and Industry

Industry	Machinery (Equipment)	Buildings (Structures)	Inventories
Manufacturing	.1331	.0343	.0
Other industry	.1302	.0304	.0
Commerce	.1710	.0247	.0

Source: Own calculations from Hulten and Wykoff (1981) depreciation rates and Jorgenson's unpublished capital stock matrix, as described in the text.

in equation (6.7) to get a δ for each type of equipment. Similarly, they find an average B of 0.91 for their two directly estimated structure types, and they use this B with other lifetimes in equation (6.7) to get a δ for each type of structure. These rates are shown in column 1 of table 6.5. They range from a low of 0.0176 for railroad structures to a high of 0.3333 for automobiles.

Since each industry's capital stock in each asset is available from the unpublished Jorgenson data, we can calculate separate weighted averages for each of our three industry groups. These rates are shown in table 6.6, based on the Hulten-Wykoff depreciation rates. They do not depend on the discount rate.[16]

Equipment (or machinery in the terminology of this study) depreciates at about 13 percent per year except in the commercial industry, with its high weight on autos and trucks. Structures (or buildings) depreciate at rates between 2.5 and 3.4 percent per year, as shown in the table.

6.2.5   Investment Grants and Incentives

The investment tax credit (ITC) was introduced in 1962 at a 7 percent rate on equipment and a 3 percent rate on public utility property. It was repealed in 1969 but was reintroduced in 1971 at a 7 percent rate on equipment and a 4 percent rate on public utility property. A 1975 act temporarily increased the credit to 10 percent for both types of assets and eliminated the 50 percent limit on the amount of tax liability that could be offset. In 1978 the 10 percent credit was made permanent, and taxpayers were allowed to offset all of the first $25,000 of tax liability and 90 percent of any remaining liability.

The 1980 statutory rate of credit is 10 percent for all qualifying equipment and special-purpose structures, but the latter definition has been

16. To see that the capital stocks are the correct weights for economic depreciation rates, we could perform an exercise similar to that performed for tax depreciation in Appendix D. Take the present value of actual depreciation on a dollar of current investment in each of the disaggregate assets, and add the present value of depreciation on the reinvestment necessary to maintain a dollar of real capital. Take a capital-weighted average of those present values, then ask what depreciation rate δ on an aggregate maintained asset would yield the same value of depreciation. The answer for δ reduces to a K-weighted average of δ_j.

broadened to include more than half of our total structures category.[17] As mentioned, the credit was only two-thirds effective for assets with lives less than seven years, one-third effective for assets with lives less than five years, and not effective for assets with lives less than three years. Furthermore, owing to inadequate taxable profits, some credits had to be carried forward and some were never able to be used. As a result of all these considerations, Jorgenson and Sullivan (1981) estimate that the effective 1980 tax credit rates for equipment and structures were 0.078 and 0.045, respectively.

In this study, however, we focus on a company with sufficient profits to enable it to use the statutory rates of credit. The 1980 statutory ITC rates for each of our thirty-four assets are shown in column 2 of table 6.5 above. These rates are the same as those in Fullerton and Henderson (1981).

We use Jorgenson's capital stocks separately for each industry in weighting the investment tax credits over the twenty types of equipment and the fourteen types of structures. Here again, however, capital stocks by themselves do not provide correct weights. If an asset depreciates faster than average, it will have more than the average amount of reinvestment associated with maintaining it. Because replacement investment also qualifies for the ITC, the weight on such an asset should be larger than its current stock.

Appendix D describes our procedures for calculating $\bar{g}$, the average of investment grant rates g, for each asset and industry. Weights are equal to capital plus the present value of replacement investment. As a result, $\bar{g}$ cannot be expressed as raw data but must be calculated for each ρ and π combination. One set of $\bar{g}$ for 1980 is shown in table 6.7. The 0.07833 discount rate for this example corresponds to debt finance in the fixed-r case with the actual United States inflation experience. Rates for equipment are close to 0.10, as would be expected by looking at the rates in column 2 of table 6.5. Only tractors, trucks, and autos have statutory rates less than 0.10. These assets have large weights in commerce and in other industry, so their $\bar{g}$ values are 0.0852 and 0.0897, respectively. Manufacturing gets a 0.0957 effective rate. Structures receive no investment credit, except for the 0.0978 rate in other industry, which includes public utility structures.

Table 6.8 shows ITC rates under the Economic Recovery Tax Act of 1981. These are very similar to those for 1980, except that the statutory credit for autos has been increased from 0.033 to 0.06, and that for trucks and trailers has been increased from 0.067 to 0.10, as shown in column 4 of table 6.5.

The value of $\bar{g}$ for inventories is always zero. Finally, the f_3 parameters

---

17. Special-purpose structures are those that "are replaced contemporaneously with the equipment that they . . . house, support, or serve" (U.S. Department of the Treasury, 1962 Guidelines).

Table 6.7   Investment Tax Credit Rates in 1980, by Asset and Industry

Industry	Machinery (Equipment)	Buildings (Structures)	Inventories
Manufacturing	.0957	.0	.0
Other industry	.0897	.0978	.0
Commerce	.0852	.0	.0

Source: Own calculations from data in Fullerton and Henderson (1981) and Jorgenson's unpublished capital stock matrix. The values in this table are based on a 0.07833 nominal discount rate, as obtains for debt finance in the case where r is fixed at 0.05, $\bar{m}$ is 0.3559, and inflation is at the 0.0677 actual United States rate.

Table 6.8   Investment Tax Credit Rates under the Economic Recovery Tax Act of 1981, by Asset and Industry

Industry	Machinery (Equipment)	Buildings (Structures)	Inventories
Manufacturing	.0984	.0	.0
Other industry	.0988	.0978	.0
Commerce	.0941	.0	.0

Source: Own calculations from data in Fullerton and Henderson (1981) and Jorgenson's unpublished capital stock matrix. The values in this table are based on a 0.07833 nominal discount rate, as obtains for debt finance in the case where r is fixed at 0.05, $\bar{m}$ is 0.3559, and inflation is at the 0.0677 actual United States rate.

are all set to one, indicating that all investments qualify for effective credit rates $\bar{g}$.

6.2.6   Local Taxes

Personal and corporate income taxes at the local level were discussed in sections 6.2.1 and 6.2.2. Local governments also collect considerable revenue from sales taxes, business and occupation taxes, license fees, and gross receipt taxes on public utilities. These taxes are not relevant for this study, since we are concerned with taxes for which the base is capital or capital income. Some states do collect a "corporate franchise" or "net worth" tax, however, with capital assets as the tax base. These were incorporated into the statutory state corporate income tax rates, discussed above.

The major remaining tax on capital is the property tax, providing at least a quarter of total state and local revenues. Thousands of local jurisdictions each set their own statutory rate, and they each have their own assessment practices. A given asset may be subject to interjurisdictional differences in statutory rates or interjurisdictional differences in average assessed-value/market-value ratios. In addition, assets can be treated differently within a jurisdiction if some assets have not been reassessed recently and have assessment ratios different from the average. Generally, the statutory rates differ for real property (buildings and land) and for personal property (machinery, inventory, livestock, motor vehicles, furniture, etc.).

We would like to estimate the average effective rate of property tax on each asset in each industry. Because Jorgenson's 1977 capital stock matrix is available, we could divide 1977 property taxes in each category by the corresponding stock of capital. Unfortunately, however, property tax payments are not generally broken down by both asset and industry. Because there are substantial rate differentials between equipment and structures, we will disaggregate by asset, not by industry.

Table 6.9 summarizes the calculation of effective property tax rates. The first row presents data from the Advisory Commission on Intergovernmental Relations (ACIR), available only for 1972. This row shows that 28.6 percent of property taxes were paid on business realty (land and structures) and that 11.8 percent were paid on business personalty (equipment and inventories). No further disaggregation is available. These figures include both the corporate and the noncorporate sectors but exclude public utility taxes, which were not divided between realty and personalty. Data from the Commerce Department's Bureau of Economic Analysis show that a total of $62.535 billion of state and local property taxes was paid in 1977. If we assume that the allocation of these

Table 6.9   **Derivation of Property Tax Rates by Asset**

	Nonbusiness (Household) Sector		Business Sector	
	Realty	Personalty	Realty (land and structures)	Personalty (equipment and inventories)
1. Proportion of total 1972 property tax	0.501	0.019	0.286	0.118
2. Estimated 1977 tax (multiply (1) by $62.535 billion)	31.330	1.188	17.885	7.379
3. Jorgenson's 1977 capital stocks in $ billion			1,588.516	960.382
4. Estimated rate of tax (divide (2) by (3))			0.01126	0.00768

Source: Proportions in row 1 are from the Advisory Commission on Intergovernmental Relations (ACIR), as found in Harriss (1974). They exclude the 0.075 proportion of 1972 property taxes paid by public utilities. The 1977 property tax figure in row 2 is from the Commerce Department's Bureau of Economic Analysis. Capital stocks in row 3 are from Dale Jorgenson's unpublished data. We have excluded public utility capital in order to match the available tax data.

taxes was the same as in 1972, then $17.885 billion was paid on business realty and $7.379 billion on equipment and inventories, as shown in row 2.

The appropriate denominator for realty is the aggregate of Jorgenson's corporate and noncorporate capital stocks over land and all types of structures in all industries except public utilities ($1,588.5 billion, as shown in row 3 of table 6.9). For personalty, the appropriate denominator is the aggregate of Jorgenson's corporate and noncorporate capital stocks over inventories and all types of equipment in all industries except public utilities ($960.4 billion, also shown in the table). Division, in row 4 of the table, provides 0.01126 as the effective property tax rate on realty, applied to buildings in this study, and 0.00768 as the effective rate on personalty, applied to machinery and inventories in this study.

Though our study does not include residential capital explicitly, it is nevertheless interesting to compare the 0.01126 business realty rate to a household realty rate. Table 6.9 shows $31.33 billion of 1977 property taxes on household realty, including rented and owner-occupied housing. The February 1981 *Survey of Current Business* shows $1,705.7 billion as the appropriate denominator, providing 0.01837 as the effective property tax rate on housing. Thus the United States, in contrast to the United Kingdom, for example, imposes higher effective property tax rates on households than on business. Houses are sold more often than business realty, so there are longer lags in the reassessment of business property. In addition, jurisdictions often compete for incoming businesses by offering temporary tax abatements.

In fact, because a firm can bargain with a number of cities before deciding where to locate, a city might provide a ten-year tax holiday for the buildings of that firm alone. These property tax abatements lower the payments of only new entrants, implying that the marginal property tax rate could be less than the average tax rate calculated here.

Finally, because of the mobility among the many taxing jurisdictions, followers of Tiebout (1956) might argue that the local property tax payments must be exactly offset by the value of local public goods in each jurisdiction. As with other tax calculations in this study, however, our property tax calculation ignores the possibility of offsetting benefits on the expenditure side.[18]

18. The property tax in each jurisdiction is used to finance local public expenditure benefits that can offset any disincentive effects of the tax. Fischel (1975) and White (1975) argue, for example, that communities compete to obtain commercial and industrial property, implying that a community would be indifferent to the entry of a marginal firm in equilibrium. If we sought net budget incentive effects, and if this argument were correct, then the effective property tax rate should be set to zero. The use of nonzero rates can be taken as a rejection of this argument, or as an attempt to measure purely tax effects rather than net effects of government activity. See Fullerton and Gordon (1983) for further discussion and alternative simulations with and without distorting property taxes.

6.2.7 Wealth Taxes

Various forms of state and local net wealth taxes and property taxes have already been reviewed. At the federal level, article I, section 9 of the United States Constitution prohibits direct taxation. Since the Sixteenth Amendment specifically introduced a federal income tax, the constitutionality of a federal wealth tax is left in doubt. There is a federal estate tax, and this section describes some of its features. As specified in chapter 2, however, the estate tax does not enter our calculations.

In 1980 the federal estate tax had a graduated structure with the equivalent of a $175,000 initial exemption. The marginal tax rate reached 70 percent for estates over $5 million. Half of an estate was not taxable if left to a spouse. Estate tax returns were filed for only about 9 percent of deaths, and only 40 percent of those filing returns had to pay any tax. These taxes amounted to less than 2 percent of federal revenue.

The Economic Recovery Tax Act of 1981 specifies a transition period during which the exemption equivalent is increased and the top marginal tax rate is decreased. After 1987 there will be no tax on estates up to $600,000, and the top marginal rate will be 50 percent. Also, unlimited property can be left to a spouse without tax. These provisions will essentially eliminate estate taxes as a source of revenue.

For purposes of this study, the personal wealth tax rates of all three ownership categories are set to zero. The vectors of wealth tax rates for each asset are given by the effective property tax rates of the preceding section. These parameters are summarized in table 6.10.

6.2.8 Household Tax Rates

To estimate weighted-average personal tax rates on marginal increases in various types of income, we use the tax simulation (TAXSIM) model of the National Bureau of Economic Research (NBER). The model and our estimation procedures are described in section 6.2.1, and the estimates based on these procedures are shown in table 6.11. These marginal rates apply to 1977, the most recent year for which TAXSIM calculations are available. Inflation would have pushed many households into higher marginal rate brackets by 1980, but the Revenue Act of 1978 readjusted the nominal boundaries of the brackets. While explicit recalculation of

Table 6.10   Wealth Tax Rates

	Households	Tax-Exempt Institutions	Insurance Companies
Personal Wealth Tax			
w_p	0	0	0
Corporate Wealth Tax	Equipment	Structures	Inventories
w_c	.00768	.01126	.00768

Source: Own calculations as described in the text.

Table 6.11   Personal Marginal Tax Rates for 1977

	Federal Only	State and Federal
1. Wages	.270	.324
2. Dividends	.410	.475
3. Interest	.271	.325
4. Statutory capital gains	.260	.280
5. Realized capital gains	.130	.140
6. Accrued capital gains	.065	.070

Source: Calculations from NBER's tax simulation (TAXSIM) model. As described in the text, the statutory capital gains rates of row 4 are halved (because of the increase of basis at death) to obtain row 5. These rates are approximately halved again (because of deferred realizations) to obtain row 6.

1980 rates is desirable, we have no procedure that rivals the quality of the TAXSIM procedures for 1977. Thus, the table 6.11 rates are employed for our 1980 calculations.

For wage income, the federal marginal tax rate from this model is 27 percent, while the combined state and federal rate is about 32 percent. For interest income, these rates are also 27 percent and 32 percent, respectively.[19] For dividend income, the federal and combined rates are 41 percent and 47.5 percent. To account for the dividend deduction, these calculations assign a zero tax rate to the dividends received by those with less than $100 of dividends ($200 for joint returns). These estimates correspond closely to the dividend rates estimated by Brinner and Brooks (1981). Their combined state and federal tax was 43.2 percent for 1953–79 and 49 percent for 1979 alone.

Retained earnings are taxed by the personal income tax only to the extent that they induce share appreciation over historical cost, and then only when realized. This deferral advantage clearly depends on the average length of the holding period or the proportion of gains to be realized each year. Furthermore, about half of gains are never realized because of the increase of basis at death. (No capital gains taxes are paid out of the estate, but the basis for calculating capital gains of the new owner is set equal to market value at the time of inheritance.) These considerations reduce the present value of expected taxes on current accrued capital gains.

With only 40 percent of realized gains taxable in 1979–80, and with a top marginal rate of 70 percent, the highest nominal rate of tax on capital

19. Feldstein and Summers (1979) report a 25 percent federal rate on interest income from the TAXSIM model but use a 35 percent rate on corporate bond interest to account for its greater concentration in high-income brackets. Without a breakdown of interest receipts in each bracket, it is appropriate to take the 32 percent combined state and federal tax rate for use in this study.

gains would be 28 percent. NBER's TAXSIM model places the federal capital gains rate at 26 percent, reflecting a very high concentration of capital gains in the high-income brackets. To account for state taxes, we use 28 percent as the combined nominal statutory rate.[20]

In other studies of taxes in the United States, a common assumption is that this nominal rate is halved owing to the deferral advantage and halved again owing to the increase of basis at death. It is sometimes argued that the resulting 0.07 effective tax rate on accrued capital gains is still too high, because investors can selectively realize their losses and hold onto their gains.

To account for deferral in this study, we multiply the capital gains rate by the effective accrued tax (EAT) ratio found in chapter 2:

$$(6.8) \qquad \text{EAT ratio} = \frac{\lambda}{\lambda + \rho_p},$$

where λ is the proportion of accrued gains realized each year and ρ_p is the investor's rate of discount. Suppose that λ is set to 0.1, reflecting an average lag of ten years between accrual and realization. The proper discount rate is the investor's nominal after-tax interest rate, a rate that depends on the combination under consideration. As an illustration, consider the fixed-r case. For the particular calculation where inflation adds $\pi/(1 - \bar{m})$ to nominal interest rates, r is 0.05, and π is 0.0677, the nominal interest rate is 0.155 before tax. If the investors are households with the 0.325 marginal tax rate on interest income, their interest rate is 0.105 after tax. With this discount rate, the EAT ratio is 0.539, and the capital gains rate is still approximately halved owing to deferral. In our calculations the ratio is endogenous because it depends on ρ_p, the personal discount rate, which depends on inflation and the ownership category.

In this study we further halve the capital gains rate to account for the increase of basis at death and the selective realization of losses. This adjustment cannot be justified on solid empirical grounds, but it does make our procedures comparable to those of other United States tax studies that have adopted the same assumption.[21]

We turn now to the treatment of banks. In general, we assume that banks are financial intermediaries through which households hold part of their ownership of corporate capital. Since bank holdings of corporate equities are small enough to be safely ignored, we use the personal tax rates described above for all household dividend income and capital gains.

20. Because the TAXSIM model has complete tax return information with complete tax law specifications, the estimated nominal rate would reflect the alternative tax limitations and the inclusion of untaxed gains in the minimum tax calculations.

21. See, for example, Feldstein and Summers (1979), Fullerton et al. (1981), and Feldstein, Poterba, and Dicks-Mireaux (1983).

Households' purchases of bonds, however, account for only part of their ultimate ownership of debt-financed corporate investment. They also make deposits at banks, which, in turn, use those funds for loans to corporations in the forms of mortgages, commercial paper, acceptances, and bond purchases. If all of these corporate interest payments flowed through the intermediaries to households in a taxable form, then we could just add bank holdings of corporate debt to the household sector and tax it all at the 0.325 combined household rate on interest receipts. Since individuals in 1980 received no interest on demand deposits (checking accounts) and sometimes received low interest rates on time deposits, we could imagine three alternative treatments of the taxation of interest payments made by companies to banks. The first alternative represents a strict adherence to the general procedures of chapter 2, intended for use by all four countries. The second alternative follows the spirit of those procedures but accounts for interest ceilings on time deposits, found primarily in the United States. The third alternative follows a different view taken by Feldstein and Summers (1979).

Bank assets such as corporate debt are not tied to particular liabilities such as time deposits or demand deposits. As a result, all three alternatives employ information on total time and demand deposits for a breakdown of bank holdings of corporate debt. In the first alternative, time deposits are a conduit through which all corporate returns are paid out in the form of interest that is fully taxable at the household level. This procedure ignores the differential between the rate earned on corporate loans and the rate paid to depositors. Demand deposits, on the other hand, are a conduit through which all corporate returns are used by the bank not to pay interest, but to provide services to depositors. Households receive liquidity in the form of check writing and other banking services, but they are not taxed on this form of return to their investment. We thus assign a zero tax rate to the return on the share of households' corporate debt held through demand deposits, and a 0.325 rate to all other holdings of corporate debt.

For specific estimates, we use statistics on the ownership of corporate debt from table 6.18 of the next section. Of the $528.7 billion held by households in 1980, $285.6 billion was in commercial banks and $83.6 billion in savings institutions. Essentially all of the last category represents time deposits, taxed at the household rate. For commercial banks, *Flow of Funds* data reveal that their $1,306.2 billion total liabilities included $306.4 billion (or 23.5 percent) in demand deposits, $462.0 billion (or 35.4 percent) in small savings and time deposits, and the rest (or 41.1 percent) in other large accounts with no ceilings. We apply these percentages to the bank holdings of corporate debt. Following the first alternative, the overall household rate is calculated as 0.325, the tax rate on interest, times the proportion of debt not in demand deposits:

$$(6.9) \qquad m = .325 \left[\frac{528.7 - (.235)(285.6)}{528.7} \right] = .284 \, .$$

The second alternative recognizes that regulatory ceilings affect the interest paid by both commercial banks and savings institutions. Each maturity has a separately assigned ceiling, but the average rate paid on savings and small-denomination time deposits was 7.88 percent in 1980.[22] Since the unconstrained money market rates were about 12 percent in 1980, there existed a considerable interest differential that was ignored by the first alternative. In the spirit of the first alternative, however, we can treat these small savings deposits as generating nontaxable services for depositors. They might not receive check-writing services, but there are few withdrawal constraints, and the banks provide other liquidity services. In this view the interest differential does not generate pure profits for the bank, because competition for customers would encourage banks to extend their hours, open more branches, or provide gifts for new depositors. Since demand deposits and the interest differential on savings deposits represent nontaxable returns to households, the figures above can be used to calculate the overall household rate.

$$(6.10) \qquad m = \frac{.325 \left[\left(\frac{7.88}{12} \right)(184.6) + 277.2 \right]}{528.7} = .245 \, ,$$

22. In 1980, the maximum interest rates payable on time and savings deposits at federally insured institutions were:

Type of Deposit	Savings Institutions	Commercial Banks	$ Billion at Commercial Banks
Savings	5.50	5.25	196.1
90 days to 1 year	6.00	5.75	17.2
1 to 2.5 years	6.50	6.00	11.1
2.5 to 4 years	6.75	6.50	7.6
4 to 6 years	7.50	7.25	27.9
6 to 8 years	7.75	7.50	17.8
8 years or more	8.00	7.75	2.5
6 month money market certificates			152.8
2.5 year variable ceiling deposits under $100,000			28.5

The ceiling on six-month money market time deposits was the auction average from most recently issued six-month United States Treasury bills. This rate varied throughout the year but reached 15 percent in December 1980. The ceiling for 2.5 year deposits was fifty basis points below the 2.5 year Treasury rate. This long-term rate varied around 11 percent during the year, substantially less than the short-term rate just mentioned. These regulations were in a state of transition, owing to the March enactment of the Depository Institution Deregulation and Monetary Control Act of 1980. This new law imposes more consistent reserve requirements, broadens the powers of savings institutions to invest in corporate securities and to offer checking services, and orders a phaseout and ultimate elimination of interest rate ceilings. The authorities to impose ceilings on deposits by any of the federal financial institutions regulatory agencies are repealed as of 31 March 1986.

where $184.6 = 83.6 + (.354)(285.6)$ is the part of households' corporate debt held in savings accounts, and $277.2 = 528.7 - [184.6 + (.235)(285.6)]$ is the part not in savings or checking accounts.

The third alternative corresponds to the procedures used in Feldstein and Summers (1979). They argue that corporate interest receipts of the bank, when not paid out to depositors, are taxed as equity income to the bank's shareholders. In other words, banks earn monopoly profits that are not competed away either in the form of interest or in the form of additional services. The assumption of monopoly profits is left unexplained. For the combined rate of tax on banking income, Feldstein and Summers used an estimate of 0.561, reflecting the statutory corporate tax rate plus additional personal taxes on dividends paid to bank shareholders. With this estimate, the total tax on household and bank receipts of corporate bond interest is another weighted average:

$$(6.11) \quad m = \frac{.325\left[\left(\dfrac{7.88}{12}\right)(184.6) + 277.2\right] + .561\left[\left(\dfrac{12 - 7.88}{12}\right)(184.6) + (.235)(285.6)\right]}{528.7} = .383.$$

In this equation the household rate is applied to the interest actually paid on time deposits, and to direct ownership, while the bank's shareholders' rate is applied to the retained interest differential on time deposits plus all interest earned on funds in demand deposits.

The different approaches may be further explained as follows. A marginal tax rate measures the increased tax associated with a marginal dollar of income. However, interest income iK can increase either because of an increase in the interest rate i or because of increased investment in assets K. In this study we are concerned with a marginal increase in corporate capital K, financed in the same proportions as existing net capital. With this assumption, a proportion of additional savings is deposited in banks that use the funds for loans to corporations. Some of the ensuing interest must be used to pay interest on the additional time deposits (with a 0.325 tax rate on household interest receipts), some must be used to service the additional time and demand deposits (with a zero tax rate), and some might be retained as monopoly profits to the owners of the banks (with a 0.561 corporate tax rate).

Feldstein and Summers, however, were concerned with a different margin. They measured the additional tax associated with increases in inflation and resulting increases in the nominal interest rate. Without any additional dollar deposited, there is no need for the bank to incur costs through services on the extra deposit. Furthermore, interest-rate ceilings prevented banks from paying higher interest themselves. As a result of the monopoly power assumption, all of the extra interest represents additional income to the banks and is taxed at the banks' corporate rate.[23]

Finally, this study is concerned with the total tax wedge on a *nonfinancial* corporate investment. While monopoly profits of the bank might be part of the wedge between the gross return on the nonfinancial investment and the net return of the ultimate saver, it is not clear that any of this monopoly wedge should be counted in our tax wedge. Any tax on these profits could be described as a tax on the financial activity rather than on the nonfinancial corporate investment.

Still, all three views have something to recommend them. We will take the central estimate of 0.284 as our household tax rate on interest income in the standard case. The lower rate of 0.245 will be used with an alternative "low tax" set of parameters, and the 0.383 rate will be used with an alternative "high tax" set of parameters.

6.2.9 Tax-Exempt Institutions

A deduction from personal tax is allowed for all employer and employee contributions to "qualified" retirement accounts, including Keogh and IRA accounts. A qualified pension must be nondiscriminatory and must meet certain other legal requirements for tax-exempt status. Not more than 20 percent of an employee's gross earnings may be placed in such an account and deducted from taxable income. The earnings of these pension reserves are also untaxed, but all retirement income is taxed when paid out. If the individual's marginal tax rate is unchanged after retirement, then this treatment is equivalent to that of a consumption tax. Thus the appropriate personal rate on this form of saving is zero.

Contributions to nonqualified pension plans, on the other hand, are not deductible in determining taxable income. The earnings on these nonqualified pension funds are untaxed until retirement benefits are paid, however, so these earnings have the advantage of tax deferral. One could think of the deferred personal income tax as an element in the taxation of nonqualified pension reserves. This treatment would require a

---

23. The two margins for effective marginal tax rates have different implications for behavior. To determine desired investment, individuals presumably want to know the extra tax associated with the marginal investment. Corporations receive investment tax credits and accelerated depreciation at historical cost on this marginal investment, and banks must pay the going rate of interest on the marginal deposit. By contrast, the extra tax associated with a marginal change in the interest rate does not involve any new credits or depreciation, or any new deposits. Bank interest might not increase, because of the ceilings. However, it is not clear that individuals can do anything about the extra tax associated with a marginal change in the inflation rate and the interest rate. Rather, if the inflation rate changes, individuals want to know the *new* extra tax associated with the marginal investment, including the ITC, accelerated depreciation at historical cost, and taxes on the interest of the new deposit.

present value calculation for retirement taxes, including a figure for the average time between pension earnings and pension benefits. A long postponement of tax and a high discount rate would imply a low effective tax on these pension earnings. Furthermore, the relative size of these nonqualified pensions is extremely small. Feldstein and Summers (1979) use zero for the effective personal rate on all pension income, and we make the same assumption here.

Nonprofit institutions also pay no tax on interest or dividend receipts. The m and z parameters for these groups are zero. Unfortunately, the *Flow of Funds* data include nonprofit institutions in the household sector. Sections 6.3.4 and 6.3.5 discuss ways of moving nonprofit institutions from the household category to the tax-exempt category.

6.2.10   Insurance Companies

Households receive investment income indirectly through insurance companies, and this income is taxed through a complicated set of provisions. In order to make sense of these provisions, this section breaks them down into corporate taxes on life insurance companies, corporate taxes on nonlife insurance companies, and personal taxes on amounts paid out by insurance companies. The particularly complicated, and seemingly arbitrary, taxation of life insurance companies is explained below by describing it in historical context.

First consider only the personal taxes on individual saving through life insurance. Individuals use after-tax income to pay insurance premiums, but no personal tax is due on accruals of interest to the reserves or on benefits paid on the death of the insured. If there were no corporate tax, then this treatment would correspond to the prepayment plan of a consumption tax.[24] If benefits are taken before the death of the insured, there is the possibility of a personal tax liability on earnings of the account— that is, benefits in excess of paid-in premiums. In this case insurance savings get the same deferral advantage as the nonqualified pension discussed in section 6.2.9. As mentioned there, a long postponement of tax, high discount rate, and/or a low personal rate after retirement can justify ignoring this personal tax as well.

For these reasons, we set the personal tax on insurance saving at zero. Insurance companies do, however, pay a corporate income tax. Consider the taxation of dividends and capital gains, followed by the taxation of interest income.

Since 85 percent of intercorporate dividends are excludable, the effective tax on insurance company dividend receipts is 0.15×0.46, or 6.9

---

24. See *Blueprints for Basic Tax Reform* (U.S. Department of the Treasury 1977) for thorough descriptions of prepayment plans and qualified accounts.

percent.[25] On realized capital gains, insurance companies pay the corporate statutory rate of 28 percent. We assume that insurance companies expect to realize 10 percent of their gains each year, and we use equation (6.8) above to calculate the effective rate on accrued capital gains. This rate depends on the discount rate and thus on the insurance company's marginal tax rate. However, when the EAT ratio of equation (6.8) is about one-half, the effective rate on accrued capital gains is about 14 percent.[26]

For interest income, insurance companies other than life insurance companies basically are taxed like other corporations. Feldstein and Summers (1979) take this to mean that these companies pay the 0.46 corporate rate on all interest income, and that their stockholders pay dividend taxes if the income is distributed or capital gains taxes if it is retained. Feldstein and Summers use 0.561 as the combined corporate and personal tax on insurance company income. Again, however, this procedure assumes that the extra capital income is generated by an unanticipated increase in the nominal interest rate. The relevant margin for our purposes is an increase in capital assets. The extra tax then depends on how the (nonlife) insurance company obtained the additional assets.

In our international comparison of marginal tax rates, we take a 1 percent increase in the existing capital stock, used wherever capital is currently used and owned wherever capital is currently owned. In general, individuals proportionately increase their holdings through all conduits, including direct ownership, banks, pensions, and insurance companies. Since insurance companies are a category of ownership, we posit an increase in their capital assets. If they make such investments out of their net earnings, without any additional reserves or expenses to deduct, then a tax of 0.561 might well be paid on the resulting income. However, the personal tax (associated with the difference between 0.561 and 0.46) would have to be paid on those earnings in any case. The only extra tax associated with this additional investment is the 0.46 corporate rate. If, instead, we explain the additional assets by suggesting an overall increase in the insurance business, then insurance companies would finance investments out of premiums but would incur additional reserves and expenses. They might pay no additional tax if there are no excess profits on their new operations. In light of all these considerations, the simplest

25. Note that here we use the 0.46 federal corporate tax rate rather than the 0.495 combined corporate tax rate. State and local governments typically impose premium taxes (on the consumer's purchase of life insurance services) rather than income taxes (on the investment income of the life insurance corporation).

26. For individuals, we cut the statutory capital gains rate of 0.28 in half to account for the increase of basis at death. We used the resulting 0.14 rate in (6.8) to get effective rates of about 7 percent. Since insurance companies do not have that advantage, their 0.28 statutory rate is used directly in (6.8) to get effective rates of about 14 percent.

and probably most appropriate marginal tax rate for nonlife insurance interest income is the 0.46 corporate rate. This rate is used with our standard parameters for the small portion of corporate debt held by nonlife insurance companies. The lower rate of zero will be used with our alternative "low tax" set of parameters, and the 0.561 rate will be used with our "high tax" set of parameters.

The taxation of life insurance companies is more complicated because of two special factors that exist only for life insurance companies or that become particularly acute only for them.[27] First, annual accounting would provide a particularly bad measure of life insurance income. While the income and expenses of most businesses are fairly close to concurrent, the life insurance transaction earns premiums many years before it is terminated. At the same time, long-run profitability of the insurance transaction can be accurately predicted by using mortality tables, and reserves can be set aside for those future death benefits. For these reasons, reserves are counted as a liability, income on the reserves is counted as a required expense for those future benefits, and annual tax calculations can use income on required reserves as a current deduction. Without legally specified allowances for reserves, however, life insurance companies could greatly affect their own taxable income through their choice of mortality and interest assumptions.

Second, the taxation of life insurance companies is complicated by the perceived need for maintaining the competitive balance between stock and mutual companies. The measured income of a stock company might be taxed at corporate rates before distribution of net earnings to shareholders, but the mutual company has no owners other than the policyholders who mutually insure each others' lives. Mutual companies would receive an unfair advantage if they were allowed to describe distributions as premium reductions and thus avoid corporate taxes.

The history of life insurance taxation reflects various attempts to embrace these special factors. From the beginning of the corporate tax until 1920, life insurance companies were subject to ordinary principles of taxation. That is, they included premiums and investment income, and they deducted operating expenses, sums paid out on insurance contracts, and net additions to policy reserves. Reserves were self-determined, and dividends were deductible if applied to current premiums. Capital gains were made nontaxable in 1921, and reserve interest requirements were limited to a uniform 4 percent rate. The company's actual interest requirements were not considered, but the 4 percent allowance changed several times since 1921. Mutual and stock companies were made comparable by eliminating the deduction for policyholder dividends.

27. The following discussion derives largely from the thorough treatment of the taxation of life insurance companies provided by McGill (1967). For more recent discussion, see Aaron (1982, 1983).

After 1942 the Treasury determined the excludable portion of investment income for each company, the "secretary's ratio," based on a weighted average of the company's actual interest requirements and an assumed interest rate of 3.25 percent. At various times when actual interest rates fell, the secretary's ratio exceeded one, and no taxes were paid by life insurance companies. The fixed 3.25 percent rate was dropped in 1949 so that reserve allowances could reflect the low actual rates then in effect. Reserve allowances were dropped altogether in 1951, but the statutory rate was reduced such that taxes would be the same as if the previous rates had applied with a secretary's ratio of 87.5 percent for all companies.

The Life Insurance Company Income Tax Act, passed in 1959, reverted to a modified version of the total income approach used before 1921. The major features of this act are still in effect. Premiums, investment income, and capital gains are all includable, while expenses, dividends to policyholders, and special reserve allowances are all deductible. Dividends to shareholders are not deductible. The company's tax is calculated in four "phases," but we assume that the firm is taxed under phase I. (Phase II taxes part of the underwriting gains, phase III taxes distributions not already taxed under phase II, and phase IV separates capital gains so that their tax is not offset by operating losses.)

Phase I calculates the investment yield as the difference between gross investment income and deductions for expenses, state and local taxes, depreciation, and depletion. Call this investment yield iK, the product of an interest rate and assets owned by the life insurance company. Reserve interest requirements are determined for each company in a formula with several steps. First, the "adjusted reserve rate" (arr) is found as the lesser of the company's current rate of return (i) and the average rate of return for the past five years. Next, the "average reserve interest rate" for all companies is derived from various assumptions. This average rate assumption has remained close to 0.03 and has not changed in response to inflation. Finally, the "adjusted life insurance reserves" are calculated by assuming that each percentage point by which the company's adjusted reserve rate (arr) exceeds the average interest rate (0.03) implies a 10 percent reduction in required reserves. If actual reserves are denoted R, then adjusted reserves are $R[1 - 10(arr - .03)]$. This formula is often called the "ten-to-one rule," or the "Menge formula" after its instigator. The company can deduct the adjusted reserve rate on these adjusted reserves.

(6.12)   Taxable income $= iK - (arr)R[1 - 10(arr - .03)]$.

Thus, if our margin is an increase in K with no change in actual reserves, the interest rate i, or the adjusted rate arr, then the additional capital income is taxed at the 0.46 corporate rate, and that is the end of it. As in the case of nonlife insurance, we could use 0.46 as the extra tax, assuming that the additional assets were financed out of net earnings (and that any additional personal tax would have had to be paid on those earnings in any case). Or again, as in the case of nonlife insurance, we can explain the additional assets by suggesting an overall increase in the life insurance business. The life insurance company finances investments out of premiums but incurs additional expenses in obtaining and servicing the additional policies. It must hire more salesmen, clerks, and investment analysts, and it might pay no additional tax if there are no excess profits on its new operations. Thus a tax rate of zero will again be used with our "low tax" set of parameters.

Suppose instead that all assets are held only for reserves, including the marginal increase in K. Suppose also that the adjusted reserve rate equals the actual interest rate. Since $R = K$ and $arr = i$, equation (6.12) can be multiplied by 0.46 and simplified.

$$(6.13) \qquad \text{Tax} = 4.6(i - .03)iK.$$

This simpler formula is used by Feldstein and Summers (1979) and others to compute life insurance taxes. When those authors calculate the extra tax for a change in i, they differentiate (6.13) with respect to i and obtain $4.6(2i - .03)$ as the extra tax on K. They use $i = 0.07$ to get a tax rate of 50.6 percent, but at the 1980 interest rates of approximately 0.12, this tax rate would be 96.6 percent.[28]

The problem, of course, is that regulatory authorities have not changed the 0.03 average reserve rate in response to inflation and higher interest rates. The increase in i serves to increase both the taxable income iK and the effective tax rate $4.6(i - .03)$.

Our margin, however, concerns not an increase in the interest rate i, but an increase in the capital stock K. From (6.13), the tax rate on interest income iK is equal to $4.6(i - .03)$. With $i = 0.07$ this rate is 18.4 percent, and with $i = 0.12$ this rate is still only 41.4 percent. For 1980 interest rates and actual inflation rates, we could just use this tax of 41.4 percent. Another problem arises, however, when we calculate effective tax rates under assumptions of different inflation rates: How would inflation affect the nominal yield?

Suppose first that $i = r + \pi/(1 - \bar{m})$ such that real after-tax returns are constant by assumption. Where r is fixed at 0.05, our model assumes that nominal interest rises by the increase in inflation rate divided by unity minus the average personal tax rate over debt and equity (0.3559). In this case, the $4.6(i - .03)$ tax rate becomes $(.092 + 7.14\pi)$, equal to 0.092 with no inflation, 0.5755 with the actual United States inflation, and

28. This description of Feldstein and Summers (1979) is only slightly different from their actual procedures, because they used the then-current corporate rate of 0.48, and took the difference between the tax at $i = .07$ and the tax at $i = .08$, rather than differentiating.

0.8062 with 10 percent inflation. The tax rate skyrockets because inflation adds more than point-for-point to the nominal interest rate within the effective tax rate formula. These rates will be used with our "high tax" set of parameters.

On the other hand, we might not believe that counterfactual scenario. In particular, the fixed 3 percent allowance is not consistent with a ceteris paribus change in π. With 10 percent inflation and 20 percent nominal interest rates, insurance companies would successfully lobby for a change in the law or at least a change in the fixed 3 percent allowance. Furthermore, Summers (1982) finds that actual interest rates hardly rise with inflation, if they rise at all. Our assumption of constant after-tax returns requires that inflation adds more than point for point to interest rates, but Summers finds evidence that a point-for-point relation is a high upper bound. Indeed, $r = 0.05$, $\pi = 0.0677$, and $i = r + \pi$ provides a 0.1177 nominal interest rate, very close to the 12 percent figure mentioned above for 1980. In this case, the $4.6(i - .03)$ tax rate becomes $(.092 + 4.6\pi)$, equal to 0.092 with no inflation, 0.403 with actual inflation, and 0.552 with 10 percent inflation. These rates will be used with our "standard" set of parameters.[29]

Insurance companies have recognized that their taxes rise with inflation. Partly in response to this effect, insurance companies have discovered and increased their use of tax loopholes such as "modified coinsurance." Under this arrangement, the life insurance company can reinsure its policies with another company while retaining the assets associated with those policies. Money changes hands in complicated ways, but the funds left with the original insurer are not called investment income. As a result, they are taxed at a lower rate. Table 6.12 shows recent revenues from life insurance companies in the last column. These revenues are generally increasing through the early 1970s but increase faster in the late 1970s with inflation. After 1979, when modified coinsurance was discovered, revenues suddenly fall.

Finally, the pension fund business of life insurance companies is not

29. We do not use the 0.46 rate that results from the assumption that life insurance companies invest out of net earnings with no change in actual reserves. Instead, the authors of all four country chapters agreed to assume that the additional investment comes from individuals saving through new life insurance policies. This assumption implies that the tax is zero if expenses exhaust the income from the new policies, or that it is from equation (6.13) if we ignore expenses other than the allowance for adjusted reserves. Still, however, the 0.46 rate might be justified from the $4.6(i - .03)$ formula if all assets are held for reserves and if the interest rate is a fixed 13 percent at any inflation rate. The use of a 0.46 tax rate on interest income would also be more compatible with the rates on dividends and capital gains discussed above. All forms of investment income enter the "yield," and the Menge formula determines the assumed split between the company and the policyholders. The fraction attributable to the company is multiplied by total dividends, and the company can exclude only 85 percent of its resulting share of total dividends. Thus the tax on dividends should really be 15 percent of whatever rate comes out of the Menge formula.

Table 6.12   Selected Data on Pensions and Life Insurance
($ billion in current prices)

| Year | Private Pension Reserves | Life Insurance Companies | | |
		Pension Reserves	Life Insurance Reserves	Federal Income Taxes
1965	59.2	27.3	98.9	0.741
1966	66.2	29.4	103.5	0.883
1967	74.2	32.0	108.2	1.040
1968	83.1	35.0	112.9	1.174
1969	90.6	37.9	117.8	1.237
1970	97.0	41.2	123.1	1.232
1971	106.4	46.4	129.4	1.451
1972	117.5	52.3	136.1	1.544
1973	126.5	56.1	143.5	1.803
1974	133.7	60.8	150.1	1.915
1975	145.2	72.2	158.6	1.910
1976	160.4	89.0	166.8	2.209
1977	181.5	101.5	178.1	2.526
1978	202.2	119.1	189.8	2.994
1979	223.5	139.2	202.0	3.269
1980	256.9	165.8	213.5	2.551

Source: *Flow of Funds* and *Life Insurance Fact Book.*

taxable. Table 6.12 shows not only the very rapid growth of private pension reserves in the first column, but also the rising pension reserves of life insurance companies in the second column. These pension reserves made up 22 percent of total life insurance reserves in 1965, 25 percent in 1970, 31 percent in 1975, and 44 percent in 1980. These assets of pension funds administered by life insurance companies are included in the tax-exempt category when we look at holdings of each group in section 6.3.5.

The final step is the averaging of the tax rate for life insurance with the tax rate for other insurance. As shown in section 6.3.5, all insurance companies hold $133.1 billion of corporate debt that is not attributable to pensions. Life insurance companies hold 84.4 percent of this total, and other insurance companies hold the remaining 15.6 percent. Table 6.13 summarizes our tax rate findings for all our ownership categories. For insurance companies, we use a weighted average of life insurance and other insurance companies found in the two preceding rows. The "low tax" parameter for both types of insurance is a zero rate, so the average is a zero rate. The "standard" tax rate for life insurance is $(.092 + 4.6\pi)$ and for other insurance is 0.46, so the weighted average is $(.149 + 3.88\pi)$. The "high tax" rate for life insurance is $(.092 + .714\pi)$ and for other insurance is 0.561, so the weighted average is $(.165 + 6.03\pi)$.

Table 6.13   Summary of Tax Rates by Ownership Category

	Interest Income				
Owner	Low-Rate Alternative	Standard Parameters	High-Rate Alternative	Rate on Dividends	Rate on Realized Capital Gain
Households	.245	.284	.383	.475	.14
Tax-exempt institutions	0	0	0	0	0
Insurance					
Life	0	$.092 + 4.6\pi$	$.092 + 7.14\pi$	.069	.28
Other	0	.46	.561	.069	.28
Total	0	$.149 + 3.88\pi$	$.165 + 6.03\pi$	.069	.28

Source: Derived and described in the text.

Finally, note that the tax rate for exempt institutions is always zero and that the tax rate for households has standard, low, and high alternatives given by equations (6.9), (6.10), and (6.11), respectively. All of these tax rates are listed in table 6.13.

6.3   The Structure of the Capital Stock and Its Ownership

6.3.1   Data Limitations

With the statutory tax parameters of section 6.2, we can calculate effective tax rates for each of the eighty-one combinations involving three assets, three industries, three sources of finance, and three ownership categories. Then, with the proportion of capital stock attributable to each of the eighty-one combinations, we can calculate various types of weighted averages. This section derives the weights for averaging these effective marginal rates. Section 6.3.2 describes a three-by-three matrix for the amount of each asset used in each industry. These nine numbers derive from Jorgenson's more detailed capital stock data that were used in sections 6.2.3, 6.2.4, and 6.2.5 to average depreciation and investment grants over thirty-four assets for each of our three industries. Section 6.3.3 describes another three-by-three matrix for the sources of finance used in each industry. While *Flow of Funds* data do not provide an industry breakdown of retained earnings, new equity, and new debt issues, we use data on the market value of debt and equity in each industry to derive these nine separate numbers.

Section 6.3.4 describes the ownership of corporate equity, and section 6.3.5 describes the ownership of corporate debt. A number of studies discuss the corporate shares, dividends, capital gains, and interest income of institutions and households in different income brackets, but none traces that ownership through to the industry or asset of origin.[30] Indeed, such a study for the United States would face enormous difficulties dealing with the ownership of conglomerate corporations and with inter-corporate shareholdings. (The chapter for Germany describes a study of the ownership of financial claims by industry, made possible by the lesser degree of conglomeration.) In any case, when we take the three own-ership proportions for debt in the United States and apply the three equity ownership proportions to both retained earnings and new equity issues, we have another three-by-three matrix of ownership for each source of finance. Finally, the three matrixes can be appropriately multi-plied together to produce eighty-one proportions. In doing so, we assume that all assets in a particular industry are financed in the same way, that all owners hold debt from the different industries in the same proportions, and that all owners hold equity from the different industries in the same proportions.

6.3.2   Capital Stock Weights

The most thorough and detailed capital stock data available for the United States are those described in Jorgenson and Sullivan (1981) and Fraumeni and Jorgenson (1980).[31] Their basic procedure starts with gross investment in the 1963 and 1967 "capital flows tables" from the *Survey of Current Business*. Though these matrixes are not available on an annual basis, the Commerce Department does provide enough information to construct a vector of investment by industry and a vector of investment by asset for each year. These vectors can be taken as row sums and column sums of underlying annual capital flow tables. For every year back to 1929, they take the 1963 gross investment matrix and scale each row so that its total equals the investment for that industry in that year. They then scale each column so that its total equals the investment for that asset in that year, and they iterate between row and column scaling until they have an investment matrix for that year that is consistent with the

---

30. See, for example, the 1962 *Survey of Consumer Finances*, done for the Federal Reserve Board by Projector and Weiss, and the 1974 *Survey of Current Business* study of stockownership trends, done by Blume, Crockett, and Friend.

31. Alternative published capital stock data are available in Kendrick (1976). He in-cludes much detail on industry, government, and personal wealth, but corporate capital is not segregated, and 1973 is the most recent year. Since machinery, buildings, and invento-ries make up the only three assets considered in this study, we effectively ignore investments in land, investments in R&D, and investments in goodwill through advertising. Since manufacturing, other industry, and commerce make up the only three industries considered in this study as described in chapter 2, we effectively ignore all investments in agriculture, mining, crude petroleum, financial business, real estate, and government enterprises. Trade and services fall into the commercial category, while construction, transportation, com-munications, and utilities are aggregated into other industry.

two investment vectors. This procedure of iterative row and column scaling is described in Bacharach (1971).

From this procedure they obtain gross investment for each asset in each industry back to 1929. They then use Hulten-Wykoff depreciation rates for each of the thirty-four assets, found in table 6.5, to calculate a capital stock matrix by the perpetual inventory method. For each asset-industry cell, they add gross investment from each year and subtract depreciation in each year up through 1977 to get net capital stock in that year. These capital stock data are particularly well suited for our purposes not only because of the great asset and industry detail, but also because they are designed to be consistent with Hulten-Wykoff depreciation rates used elsewhere in this study.[32]

The 1977 capital stock matrix, aggregated to our assets and industries, is shown in table 6.14. The total corporate capital in these categories (excluding land) is $1,702 billion, as shown in the fourth row of the table. Of this total, $746 billion or 44 percent is in manufacturing, $530 billion or 31 percent is in other industry, and $426 billion or 25 percent is in commerce. Of the capital in manufacturing, most is in buildings, but a surprisingly high proportion is held in the form of inventories. Since other industry includes utilities, the predominant share of capital is in buildings, followed by machinery. Our commercial category includes retail and wholesale trade, so the predominant share of capital is in buildings, followed by inventories. The proportion of capital in each of these nine cells is shown in parentheses in the table, and we assume that these proportions were the same in 1980 as in 1977.

6.3.3 Sources of Financial Capital

Data from the *Flow of Funds* are used in table 6.15 to estimate the proportions of corporate investment financed through retained earnings, new equity, and debt. The sector is defined as "nonfinancial corporate business," which would include not only manufacturing, but other industry and commerce as well. This data source does not disaggregate by industry. The first column gives gross internal funds on a national income accounting basis for 1970 to 1979. This definition corresponds to a measure of cash flow in the corporate sector, not a measure of economic profits.

The second column of table 6.15 provides net new equity issues for 1970–79. The third column shows the net increase in liabilities from debt instruments, including corporate bonds, mortgages, acceptances, commercial paper, finance company loans, United States government loans, bank loans not elsewhere classified, and tax-exempt bonds. The proportions at the bottom of table 6.15 are remarkably similar to those for the

---

32. The land and inventory figures were obtained somewhat differently by Dale Jorgenson and his colleagues but are still based ultimately on Commerce Department data.

Table 6.14   **Corporate Capital Stock by Asset and Industry**
($ billion in 1977; proportions in parentheses)

Asset	Manufacturing	Other Industry	Commerce	Total
		Sector		
Machinery	147.65	164.32	70.60	382.57
	(.0867)	(.0965)	(.0415)	(.2247)
Buildings	368.92	335.39	212.44	916.75
	(.2167)	(.1970)	(.1248)	(.5385)
Inventories	229.79	29.94	143.33	403.06
	(.1350)	(.0176)	(.0842)	(.2368)
Subtotal	746.36	529.65	426.38	1,702.39
	(.4384)	(.3111)	(.2502)	(1.000)
Land	52.83	23.44	33.65	109.91
Total	799.19	553.09	460.02	1,812.30

Source: Aggregation from unpublished data described in Jorgenson and Sullivan (1981) and in Fraumeni and Jorgenson (1980).

Table 6.15   **Sources of Finance for Nonfinancial Corporate Business, 1970–79**
($ billion in current prices; proportions in parentheses)

Year	Gross Internal Funds	Net New Equity Issues	Debt Instruments	Total
1970	58.9	5.7	35.0	99.6
	(.59)	(.06)	(.35)	
1971	68.6	11.4	33.8	113.8
	(.60)	(.10)	(.30)	
1972	80.8	10.9	47.2	138.9
	(.58)	(.08)	(.34)	
1973	83.8	7.9	65.2	156.9
	(.53)	(.05)	(.42)	
1974	75.7	4.1	78.0	157.8
	(.48)	(.03)	(.49)	
1975	106.8	9.9	28.0	144.7
	(.74)	(.07)	(.19)	
1976	125.3	10.5	50.2	186.0
	(.67)	(.06)	(.27)	
1977	139.9	2.7	77.2	219.8
	(.64)	(.01)	(.35)	
1978	148.8	2.6	92.2	243.6
	(.61)	(.01)	(.38)	
1979	158.3	3.5	110.1	271.9
	(.58)	(.01)	(.40)	
Average	(.602)	(.048)	(.349)	

Source: Flow of Funds Accounts, Board of Governors of the Federal Reserve System, Sector Statements of Savings and Investment.

other countries in this study. In the United States, 60 percent of corporate investments are financed by internal funds, 35 percent by debt, and only 4.8 percent by new share issues.

Because "internal funds" in this table is just a measure of cash flow, it takes no account of the fact that inflation reduces the real value of outstanding debt. In table 6.15, the sum of "internal funds" and "new equity issues" understates equity finance by the amount of this inflation-induced gain to equity holders. However, while inflation affects the validity of the debt–equity breakdown in table 6.15, it does not affect the validity of the relation between retained earnings and new share issues. Thus we use table 6.15 for the equity breakdown, but we obtain debt/equity ratios elsewhere.

An industry breakdown for debt and equity is available with data from the COMPUSTAT tape of the Standard and Poor's Corporation. This data tape contains balance sheet information on 2,484 publicly traded corporations, including firms with securities traded on the New York Stock Exchange, the American Stock Exchange, and over the counter. This tape was used by Gordon and Malkiel (1981) to estimate the economy-wide ratio of the market value of debt to the market value of debt plus equity. Since the information on each corporation also includes its primary industry of operation, we can reproduce the Gordon and Malkiel procedures to get a similar ratio for each of our three sectors. For each corporation on the tape, we first determine the industry with which it is associated. Most of these disaggregated industries fall into one of our three sectors, while firms in agriculture, mining, finance, or real estate are excluded. We are left with 1,201 firms in manufacturing, 298 in our "other industry" category, and 395 in commercial enterprises. Only the book value of debt is reported on the COMPUSTAT tape. For each firm on the tape, we construct a figure for the market value of debt by using its disaggregated industry's average ratio of market value of debt to book value of debt, available in von Furstenberg, Malkiel, and Watson (1980). When the ratio of the market value of debt to the book value of debt was not available for a specific industry, we applied the economywide ratio to the firms in that industry.

The resulting debt/capital ratios are 0.1981 for manufacturing, 0.4847 for other industry, and 0.3995 for commercial enterprises. The high proportion for debt in other industry reflects the high proportion of public utilities in that sector. The remaining fractions in each industry, attributable to equity, can now be divided into new shares and retained earnings by using the average division found in table 6.15. For all industries combined, the ratio of new shares to total equity is 0.0738. Applying this fraction to the remaining equity/capital ratio for each of our three industrial sectors, we obtain the three-by-three matrix in table 6.16 for source of finance by industry.

Table 6.16   **Source of Finance Proportions for Each Industry**

Industry	Debt	New Share Issues	Retained Earnings	Total
Manufacturing	.1981	.0592	.7427	1.000
Other industry	.4847	.0381	.4772	1.000
Commerce	.3995	.0443	.5562	1.000

Source: Derived and described in the text.

6.3.4   The Ownership of Equity

Proportions for equity ownership are obtained from *Flow of Funds* data. Neither this source nor any other source can be used to determine the industrial mix of each owner's debt or of each owner's equity.

The household sector in the *Flow of Funds* includes both individuals and nonprofit institutions such as hospitals and universities. Since we want these institutions to be grouped with the tax-exempt category, we must impute a division to the data. For this purpose we follow Feldstein and Summers (1979) and Feldstein, Poterba, and Dicks-Mireaux (1983) in assuming that 7 percent of household equity is held by nonprofit institutions. This percentage, applied to all years, is the figure estimated for 1975 by the Securities and Exchange Commission (1977). The resulting individual holdings are shown in the first line under households in table 6.17, and the resulting nonprofit holdings are shown in the last row under tax exempt. Tax-exempt ownership also includes private pensions and state and local government retirement funds that are fully funded pensions.

Insurance company equity must also be divided into the part attributable to the companies' insurance business and the part attributable to their pension business. The latter holdings must also be moved into tax exempt. Table 6.12 showed that pension reserves made up 22 percent of total life insurance reserves in 1965, 25 percent in 1970, and 44 percent in 1980. These proportions are applied to 1960, 1970, and 1980 life insurance holdings of equity to obtain their pension holdings, shown in the second row under tax-exempt holdings.

Table 6.17 shows that the proportion of equity held by our household category has declined from 86.8 percent in 1960, to 81.5 percent in 1970, and to 74.3 percent in 1980. It is still higher than the corresponding 43.5 percent figure for Britain or the 60.4 percent figure for Sweden, but it is comparable to the several industry-specific figures for Germany.

Inspection of annual data in the *Flow of Funds* reveals that the decline across time in the United States was nearly monotonic, but that most of it took place in the first half of the past decade. The household proportion was already down to 74 percent by 1975. Bank and insurance company

Table 6.17   Ownership of Corporate Equity in 1960, 1970, and 1980
(\$ billion in current prices; proportions in parentheses)

	1960	1970	1980
1. Households	368.1	676.8	1,117.9
	(.868)	(.815)	(.743)
Individuals	351.9	634.1	1,071.1
Commercial banks	0.0	0.1	0.1
Savings institutions	1.3	2.8	4.2
Mutual funds	14.8	39.7	42.4
2. Tax-exempt institutions	44.7	128.8	324.0
	(.105)	(.155)	(.215)
Private pensions	16.5	67.1	175.8
Life insurance pensions	1.1	3.9	23.3
S&L government retirement	0.6	10.1	44.3
Nonprofit	26.5	47.7	80.6
3. Insurance companies	11.3	24.7	61.9
	(.027)	(.030)	(.041)
Life	3.9	11.5	29.6
Other	7.5	13.2	32.3
Total	424.1	830.2	1,503.9
	(1.000)	(1.000)	(1.000)
4. Addenda			
Rest of the world	9.3	27.2	64.5
Brokers and dealers	0.5	2.0	3.9

Source: Flow of Funds Accounts: Assets and Liabilities Outstanding, Board of Governors of the Federal Reserve System, various issues.

holdings have increased slightly over the two decades, but they remain inconsequential. The big increase since 1960 is to be found in various pension plans, including private plans, those operated through insurance companies, and the funded pension plans of state and local governments. These and other ownership trends are further discussed in Blume, Crockett, and Friend (1974). The final equity ownership proportions, those from 1980, are 0.743 for households, 0.215 for tax-exempt institutions, and 0.041 for insurance companies.

6.3.5   The Ownership of Debt

Nonfinancial corporate borrowing can also be obtained from the *Flow of Funds* data, but the lenders in each case cannot be traced directly. We will trace these owners of corporate debt indirectly by first looking at all the forms of corporate net liabilities and then looking at financial assets in the portfolios of each ownership category. This procedure essentially replicates for 1960, 1970, and 1980 the procedures used by Feldstein and Summers (1979) for 1976 alone.

For each year, we have data on the financial assets and liabilities of nonfinancial corporate business. Debt instrument assets include demand deposits, time deposits, security repurchase agreements (RPs), government securities, commercial paper, consumer credit, net trade credit, and miscellaneous assets. Debt instrument liabilities include bonds, mortgages, bank loans, more commercial paper, bankers' acceptances, finance company loans, United States government loans, and miscellaneous liabilities. If all these amounts were listed vertically with assets included negatively, the column would sum to net corporate indebtedness. In this study, however, we exclude government securities, government loans, and net trade credits. Then, for each item in this column, we construct a row that determines its distribution among creditors or debtors. For example, each ownership category has a table in the *Flow of Funds* that shows its holdings of corporate and foreign bonds but does not show its holdings of United States nonfinancial corporate bonds separately. We assume that the latter are distributed among owners in the same proportions as the former.

Similarly, we assume that United States nonfinancial corporate mortgage liabilities are distributed among owners in the same proportions as total holdings of mortgages shown in the tables. Bonds and mortgages are the only two forms in which pensions and life insurance companies hold any corporate debt. Next, nonfinancial corporate liabilities in the form of bank loans or bankers' acceptances are allocated entirely to commercial banks, and those in the form of finance company loans are allocated entirely to finance companies.

Similar assumptions are made about corporate assets. Demand deposits and security RPs are allocated to commercial banks, while time deposits are split between commercial banks and savings institutions in proportion to their total liabilities in that form. Net assets in the form of commercial paper are allocated entirely to finance companies because these are the largest single issuers of open-market paper. Consumer credit is allocated entirely to households. The result is a matrix for the distributional ownership of each corporate asset (listed negatively) or liability. The sum of each column gives the net corporate liabilities in the hands of each owner. As in the case of equity, however, the part of life insurance holdings that are attributable to pension business are moved to the tax-exempt category.

The resulting ownership of corporate debt is shown in table 6.18 for 1960, for 1970, and for 1980. Unlike equity, the trend seems to be an increasing proportion of debt held in the household sector. Most of this debt is attributable to banks and finance companies. Holdings of tax-exempt institutions are diminishing slightly over time, but most of the decline is found in the proportional holdings of insurance companies. The proportion of total corporate debt held for the pension business of life insurance companies is actually increasing.

A comparison of debt and equity and in tables 6.17 and 6.18 demon-

Table 6.18   **Ownership of Nonfinancial Corporate Net Debt in 1960, 1970, and 1980**
($ billion in current prices; proportions in parentheses)

	1960	1970	1980
1. Households	40.4	150.6	528.7
	(.365)	(.505)	(.609)
Individuals and nonprofit institutions	8.6	23.8	70.1
Commercial banks	15.0	81.4	285.6
Savings institutions	8.6	28.4	83.6
Mutual funds	1.0	2.9	6.2
Finance companies	5.7	12.4	78.4
Real estate investment trusts	—	1.8	2.3
Mortgage pools	—	0.0	2.4
2. Tax-exempt institutions	30.6	77.0	205.7
	(.277)	(.258)	(.237)
Private pensions	13.5	25.6	44.0
Life insurance pensions	10.8	21.2	88.3
S&L government retirement	6.3	30.3	73.4
3. Insurance companies	39.7	70.9	133.1
	(.359)	(.237)	(.153)
Life	38.2	63.6	112.4
Other	1.5	7.3	20.7
Total	110.6	298.7	867.6
	(1.000)	(1.000)	(1.000)
4. Addendum			
Miscellaneous (largely rest of the world)	1.5	6.1	29.8

Source: Flow of Funds Accounts: Assets and Liabilities Outstanding, Board of Governors of the Federal Reserve System, various issues.

Note: Net debt equals (bonds + mortgages + bank loans + commercial paper issued + bankers' acceptances + finance company loans) minus (demand deposits + time deposits + security repurchase agreements + consumer credit + commercial paper owned).

strates the portfolio effects of differential tax treatments. Individuals in 1980 own the smallest part of debt (8.1 percent) and the largest part of equity (71.2 percent). However, banks and other household intermediaries hold 52.8 percent of debt and 3.1 percent of equity. Finally, insurance companies own a larger share of debt (15.3 percent) than of equity (4.1 percent). These patterns are not surprising in light of comparative tax advantages.

Also, as in the case of equity, *Flow of Funds* data do not separate the debt held by nonprofit institutions from the debt held by taxable individuals. This aggregation causes less of a problem here in that individual plus nonprofit debt holdings are miniscule compared with their equity holdings. But it causes more of a problem in that no estimates are available for the breakdown of this debt. As in the case of equity, we could assume that 7 percent of this debt is held by nonprofit institutions, but portfolio responses to taxation suggest that much more of the equity would be held by individuals and much more of the debt would be held by nonprofits. Since the numbers in the case of debt are small, we proceed by using two sets of parameters. The standard set of parameters come directly from table 6.18 and are shown in the top half of table 6.19. We use the 1980 proportions of 0.609 for households, 0.237 for tax-exempt institutions, and 0.153 for insurance company holdings of corporate debt in all industries.

The "low tax" set of parameters are obtained from table 6.18 by assuming that all of the debt holdings of individuals and nonprofit institutions are actually in the hands of the nonprofit institutions. These parameters, as shown in the bottom half of table 6.19, are 0.529 for households, 0.318 for tax-exempt institutions, and 0.153 for insurance companies.

6.4 Estimates of Effective Marginal Tax Rates

6.4.1 Principal Results

With the fixed-p calculations described in the methodology chapter, our standard assumptions about tax parameters, and the actual inflation rate of 6.77 percent, the overall weighted average of the marginal effective tax rate on capital income in the United States is 37 percent. The interpretation is that if all assets started with a gross return of 10 percent, and if all capital of all owners were increased by one dollar, then the present value of the expected tax would be 37 percent of the additional return. It is noteworthy that this effective rate is less than the 46 percent statutory corporate tax rate, but the effective rate incorporates many factors that tend to offset or increase overall taxes. Some of these factors are discussed as we look at the breakdown of this effective tax rate in table 6.20.

The numbers in this table are calculated such that the overall rate of 37 percent is obtained by taking a weighted average of rates over the three

Table 6.19	Ownership Proportions for Corporate Net Debt		
	1960	1970	1980
Standard parameters			
Households	.365	.505	.609
Tax-exempt institutions	.277	.258	.237
Insurance companies	.359	.237	.153
"Low tax" parameters			
Households	.288	.425	.529
Tax-exempt institutions	.354	.337	.318
Insurance companies	.359	.237	.153

Source: Derived and described in the text.

Table 6.20   Effective Marginal Tax Rates, United States, 1980, Fixed-*p* Case
(%)

	Inflation Rate		
	Zero	10%	Actual (6.77%)
Asset			
Machinery	3.9	22.8	17.6
Buildings	35.4	41.8	41.1
Inventories	50.9	45.5	47.0
Industry			
Manufacturing	44.2	55.0	52.7
Other industry	10.0	15.8	14.6
Commerce	37.9	37.5	38.2
Source of finance			
Debt	−2.0	−22.2	−16.3
New share issues	61.0	104.6	91.2
Retained earnings	48.4	66.5	62.4
Owner			
Households	44.1	61.9	57.5
Tax-exempt institutions	4.0	−37.2	−21.5
Insurance companies	4.0	44.3	23.4
Overall	32.0	38.4	37.2

assets, or over the three industries, or over the three sources of finance, or over the three owners. A glance down any column of this table reveals considerable dispersion among these combinations, however, and this dispersion increases with the rate of inflation. This first column shows rates for zero inflation that vary from −2 to +61 percent, while the second column shows rates for 10 percent inflation that vary from −37 to +105 percent. (Because we use the same capital stock weights for different inflation rates, we abstract from the possibility that patterns of investment might shift in response to a change in the rate of inflation.) The distribution of 1980 tax rates is further discussed in chapter 7.

The bottom row of this table shows that overall taxes increase somewhat with inflation, from 32 percent at zero inflation, to 37 percent with 6.77 percent inflation, and to just over 38 percent with 10 percent inflation. This very moderate rise with inflation may be surprising to those who are accustomed to thinking about depreciation at historical cost, FIFO inventory accounting, and the taxation of purely nominal capital gains. Feldstein and Summers (1979) found that these factors combined to increase taxes significantly with inflation. They found no offsetting effect through the deductibility of nominal interest payments, because the tax rate at which individuals included interest receipts (42%) was as high on average as the rate at which corporations deducted interest payments (40.4%).

Here, by contrast, we find that the combined federal and state corporate rate for nominal interest deductions is 49.5 percent. For nominal interest receipts, when we use weights for debt in table 6.18 to average the owners' marginal tax rates in table 6.13, we obtain an overall rate of 23.6 percent. Our procedures improve on earlier ones by using more recent data, by treating some of the return from banks as tax-free services, by moving the pension business of insurance companies into the tax-exempt category, and by looking at a marginal increase in capital rather than in the interest rate. (These differences are further explored in Fullerton 1983.) Thus corporations can deduct nominal interest at a 49.5 percent rate, significantly higher than the 23.6 rate at which recipients must include it, and the row for debt in table 6.20 shows a subsidy that increases with inflation. This effect offsets some of the other effects of inflation. In table 6.20, we also assume that all firms use the tax-minimizing practice of LIFO accounting, so no extra inflation tax exists for that reason.[33]

We do, however, include the effect of inflation on the nominal allowances for depreciation. This effect is pronounced for machinery, where the effective rate changes from 4 percent at no inflation to 18 percent at 6.77 percent inflation and 23 percent at 10 percent inflation. The tax on buildings increases slightly with inflation, as shown in the table, but the tax on inventories falls from 51 percent with no inflation to 45.5 percent with 10 percent inflation. This asset receives no depreciation allowances, so the disadvantage of historical cost depreciation does not offset the advantages of nominal interest deductions.

The effective tax rate includes the taxation of purely nominal capital gains, but at the reduced statutory rate applicable to capital gains. The row for retained earnings in table 6.20 shows a rate that increases from 48

---

33. As an alternative, we recalculate effective tax rates with the assumption that the proportion of inventories on FIFO is $v = 0.7$, the actual fraction for manufacturing inventories in 1979 as discussed in section 6.2.3. Fixed-p results are summarized in the accompanying table.

Overall Effective Tax Rate	Inflation Rate		
	Zero	10%	Actual (6.77%)
No FIFO (standard case)	32.0	38.4	37.2
70% FIFO	32.0	47.2	43.2

Clearly, with no inflation, the choice for inventory accounting is irrelevant. Also, as can be seen from the detailed results, the choice has no effect on machinery or buildings. It has a large influence on inventories, however, producing the overall effect shown here. FIFO accounting adds six percentage points to the effective tax rate at 6.77 percent inflation, and almost nine percentage points at 10 percent inflation.

to 67 percent with inflation. More important, we include the effect of inflation on the taxation of insurance companies. As described in section 6.2.10, we find that their interest income is taxed at a rate equal to (.149 + 3.88π), where π is the rate of inflation. Because the allowance for reserves is based on a fixed nominal interest rate, inflation tends to increase insurance companies' effective rate of tax as well as their nominal taxable income. The effect is dramatically demonstrated in the row for insurance companies in table 6.20, where the overall tax increases from 4 percent to 44 percent as inflation changes from zero to 10 percent.

The rates in table 6.20 include state corporate income taxes, state and local property taxes, complicated nonlinear depreciation schedules, and an asset-specific investment tax credit. As described in section 6.2.6, state and local property tax rates are lower on machinery and inventories than on buildings. Furthermore, as described in section 6.2.5, the investment tax credit is available only for machinery and for public utility structures. Table 6.20 shows effective tax rates that are substantially lower for machinery than for other assets, and substantially lower for "other industry" (including public utilities) than for manufacturing or commerce.

Table 6.21 shows results for the fixed-r calculations described in the methodology chapter. If the real interest rate with no inflation were 5 percent, if inflation at rate π added $\pi/(1 - \bar{m})$ to the nominal interest

Table 6.21   Effective Marginal Tax Rates, United States, 1980, Fixed-r Case
(%)

	Inflation Rate		
	Zero	10%	Actual (6.77%)
Asset			
Machinery	− 33.0	37.3	26.4
Buildings	43.2	56.0	54.1
Inventories	55.2	54.0	54.5
Industry			
Manufacturing	48.9	64.2	61.2
Other industry	9.2	27.3	24.4
Commerce	44.6	49.0	48.8
Source of finance			
Debt	− 1.2	− 166.5	− 72.5
New share issues	62.2	85.9	81.8
Retained earnings	50.3	70.2	66.5
Owner			
Households	50.3	80.7	73.4
Tax-exempt institutions	11.9	− 42.7	− 21.3
Insurance companies	10.2	49.3	22.4
Overall	39.1	52.3	49.9

rate, if the expected rate of inflation were 6.77 percent, and if all capital of all owners were increased by one dollar, then the present value of the expected tax would be 50 percent of the additional return. As explained in chapter 2, averaged effective tax rates are higher than in the fixed-p case, but the same essential patterns exist. Overall rates are still slightly increasing with inflation, debt is still subsidized at rates that grow with inflation, insurance company taxes still increase dramatically with inflation, machinery is still taxed at rates lower than buildings, and other industry is still taxed at rates lower than our manufacturing or commercial sectors.

At several points in the derivation of parameter values, we described alternative arguments in favor of different procedures. Rather than claim that any single treatment is the only appropriate one, we often decided to select "standard" parameters as best estimates and to present high and low alternatives to that treatment. In the taxation of banks in section 6.2.8, for example, we reviewed one argument that depositors receive tax-free services in lieu of interest and another argument that bank owners pay a corporate rate of tax on the interest differential. The various arguments gave us 0.245 for the "low" tax rate on the household sector's interest income, 0.284 as the standard rate, and 0.383 as an alternative high rate.

For insurance companies, the "low" tax rate is zero, the standard rate is $(.149 + 3.88\pi)$, and the "high" rate is $(.165 + 6.03\pi)$. These alternatives are reviewed in table 6.13 above. Finally, the standard parameters use 0.609 and 0.237 for the proportions of debt held by households and tax-exempt institutions, respectively, allocating all of the individuals plus nonprofit category to households. As an alternative, the "low" tax parameters allocate all of these holdings to nonprofit institutions and use 0.529 and 0.318 for the same parameters.

Table 6.22 shows our fixed-p results with the "low tax" assumptions. Relative to the standard parameters, for the actual inflation rate, the overall fixed-p tax rate falls from 37 percent to 32 percent. Thus the net result is fairly robust to these assumptions. (In the fixed-r case, not shown, the overall tax falls from 50 percent to 47 percent with the use of low tax parameters.) Some interesting differences exist, however, as the overall rate is no longer monotonically increasing with inflation. Since the proportion of debt held by tax-exempt institutions has increased, and since individuals are taxed on nominal interest at a lower rate, inflation provides more of a subsidy through the deductibility of nominal interest payments at the corporate level. Because the effects of historical cost depreciation diminish as inflation increases, and since the effects of nominal interest deductions do not diminish, the latter eventually overtake the former, and the effective tax rate turns down at some inflation rate. That point is reached earlier with the low tax parameters than with

Table 6.22   **Effective Marginal Tax Rates, United States, 1980,**
with "Low Tax" Parameters, Fixed-*p* Case
(%)

	Inflation Rate		
	Zero	10%	Actual (6.77%)
Asset			
Machinery	1.0	13.2	10.6
Buildings	33.4	33.3	35.2
Inventories	49.8	39.7	43.1
Industry			
Manufacturing	43.7	53.3	51.4
Other industry	6.1	0.5	3.9
Commerce	35.8	27.1	31.1
Source of finance			
Debt	− 10.4	− 59.8	− 42.0
New share issues	61.0	104.6	91.2
Retained earnings	49.8	74.0	67.3
Owner			
Households	45.0	66.0	60.3
Tax-exempt institutions	1.8	− 37.8	− 23.1
Insurance companies	− 7.7	− 57.2	− 39.3
Overall	30.0	30.3	31.6

the standard parameters, but the effective tax rate still turns down if inflation becomes high enough.[34]

Table 6.23 shows our results with the "high tax" assumptions. In this case, the overall fixed-*p* tax rate is 41 percent. In light of these results, we can be fairly sure that the correct tax rate (given the methodology and our whole approach to the problem) is between 32 percent and 41 percent, with a best estimate of 37 percent. (In the fixed-*r* case, not shown, this rate falls between 47 and 52 percent, with a best estimate of 50 percent.) Household nominal interest is taxed at a 0.383 rate in the high tax case, much closer to the corporate rate at which nominal interest is deducted. Thus, table 6.23 shows that the average debt financed asset is no longer subsidized. More important, insurance companies are assumed to get reserve allowances at only a 3 percent nominal rate even as their actual nominal interest rate increases by more than the rate of inflation. Table 6.23 shows an effective rate for this ownership category that increases

---

34. Figure 7.1 of the next chapter shows tax rates for inflation rates up to 15 percent. The curve for the United States rises before leveling off. The curve for Germany, which has similar depreciation allowances and interest deductibility, rises and then falls.

Table 6.23   Effective Marginal Tax Rates, United States, 1980,
with "High Tax" Parameters, Fixed-p Case
(%)

	Inflation Rate		
	Zero	10%	Actual (6.77%)
Asset			
Machinery	6.4	29.7	22.8
Buildings	37.2	47.9	45.5
Inventories	51.8	49.5	49.9
Industry			
Manufacturing	44.5	55.9	53.4
Other industry	13.6	27.0	22.9
Commerce	39.8	45.0	43.5
Source of finance			
Debt	6.0	6.4	4.2
New share issues	61.0	104.6	91.2
Retained earnings	46.8	60.2	57.9
Owner			
Households	47.0	67.2	62.2
Tax-exempt institutions	2.6	−43.1	−25.6
Insurance companies	4.6	86.6	46.9
Overall	33.7	44.2	41.4

from 5 percent to more than 86 percent as inflation changes from zero to 10 percent.[35]

Returning to the standard parameter tax rates, we next attempt to determine the relative contributions of different tax instruments. That is, we decompose the effective tax rates of table 6.20 by calculating alternative tax rates that would exist were it not for property taxes, or corporate taxes, or personal taxes. To see how much of the 37 percent effective rate is due to the state and local property tax, table 6.24 reports fixed-p results for a simulation with no such tax. The overall tax rate falls from 37 percent to 31 percent, so the property tax contributes an average of six points to the overall effective rate. The property tax is deductible from the corporate income tax, however, so a calculation with a property tax and no other taxes would show an effective tax rate of more than 6 percent. By comparing table 6.24 with table 6.20, we can see that the

35. The reader might also notice that effective tax rates in some categories are raised by the use of "low tax" parameters or reduced by the use of "high tax" parameters. In particular, the effective tax rate on retained earnings is 67 percent with the low-tax assumptions, 62 percent with the standard assumptions, and only 58 percent with the high-tax assumptions. Because this phenomenon is general to all four countries, it is fully explained in chapter 7 (pp. 289–90).

Table 6.24   Effective Marginal Tax Rates, United States, with No Property Tax, Fixed-p Case (%)

	Inflation Rate		
	Zero	10%	Actual (6.77%)
Asset			
Machinery	−2.0	17.0	11.7
Buildings	28.2	34.5	33.8
Inventories	46.8	41.3	42.9
Industry			
Manufacturing	39.0	49.7	47.4
Other industry	2.1	8.1	6.8
Commerce	32.1	31.6	32.3
Source of finance			
Debt	−11.0	−30.8	−25.1
New share issues	57.5	101.0	87.6
Retained earnings	43.6	61.4	57.3
Owner			
Households	39.0	56.6	52.2
Tax-exempt institutions	−4.7	−46.4	−30.6
Insurance companies	−4.6	38.3	16.5
Overall	25.8	32.2	31.0

deductible property tax adds 7.3 percent to the tax on buildings, 5.9 percent to the tax on machinery, and 4.1 percent to the tax on inventories.

Table 6.25 reports fixed-p results of a simulation with no corporate tax. Depreciation allowances are irrelevant, and for consistency we have also set the investment tax credit rates to zero. This case is different from full integration of the corporate and personal tax systems in that it does not attempt to measure corporate income for personal tax purposes. Rather, personal tax applies just to interest paid, dividends paid, and realized capital gains. Under these assumptions, t falls from 37 percent to 35 percent. Again, this difference is affected by the deductibility of the property tax: a calculation with corporate taxes and no other taxes would show an effective rate larger than 2 percent. Still, however, it is clear that the investment tax credit, accelerated depreciation allowances, and the deductibility of interest payments and property taxes have all served to greatly diminish the incremental impact of the corporate tax system. Although t falls for buildings and inventories with the elimination of the corporate tax, the combination of credits and accelerated depreciation implies that the effective tax on machinery would rise were it not for the corporate tax. Similarly, as shown in the table, debt would no longer be subsidized.

Finally, table 6.26 portrays a world with corporate taxes and property taxes, but with no personal tax on any of our ownership categories.[36] Both m and z are set to zero so that no owners are taxed on interest receipts, dividend receipts, or capital gains. Now the effective tax rate is 7.7 percent as shown in table 6.26, almost thirty points lower than before. While interrelations (such as the deductibility of property taxes at the corporate level) destroy the additivity of our decomposition, it is clear that the personal tax system contributes the bulk of effective taxes in the United States. Without the personal tax, machinery would be subsidized, other industry would be subsidized, the subsidy for debt would increase from 16 to 73 percent, and the average rate on households would fall from 58 to 13 percent.[37]

6.4.2 Recent Changes in Tax Legislation

The Economy Recovery Tax Act of 1981 (ERTA) represented a major departure from recent tax history. It specified a 23 percent reduction in personal tax rates, phased in over a period of three years, and it introduced the first indexation of marginal rate brackets in the graduated personal income tax system, scheduled to start in 1985. It introduced tax-free "all savers' certificates" for individuals, charitable deductions for those who do not otherwise itemize their deductions, and a reduction in the marriage penalty mentioned in section 6.2.1.[38] For businesses, ERTA entirely removed the complex set of depreciable lifetimes for various assets and replaced them with only four categories of lives. It expanded the investment tax credit, extended the period for carryover of losses, introduced tax credits for new research and development, changed the tax rates in low corporate brackets, and created a "safe harbor" for a

---

36. Since insurance company taxes are actually part of the corporate tax system, we might have eliminated them along with the corporate tax rather than with the personal tax. However, these simulations are intended to provide intuition rather than evaluation of real policy proposals.

37. This decomposition was performed for both the fixed-p and the fixed-r methods, with the following summary results:

	Fixed-p Case		Fixed-r Case	
	Overall Effective Tax Rate	Decrease	Overall Effective Tax Rate	Decrease
With all tax instruments	37.2		49.9	
With no property taxes	31.0	6.2	41.7	8.2
With no corporate tax or ITC	35.3	1.9	48.1	1.8
With no personal taxes	7.7	29.5	25.7	24.2

38. Starting in 1983, joint filers are able to deduct 10 percent of the earnings of the lower-earning spouse, up to a maximum of $3,000. With a top marginal rate of 50 percent, the maximum tax saving is $1,500. If two individuals with similar incomes were to marry, however, they would still pay a higher total tax than they did under the single schedules.

Table 6.25   Effective Marginal Tax Rates, United States,
                      with No Corporate Tax, Fixed-p Case
                      (%)

	Inflation Rate		
	Zero	10%	Actual (6.77%)
Asset			
Machinery	23.2	39.2	34.0
Buildings	26.2	42.0	36.9
Inventories	23.0	37.4	32.8
Industry			
Manufacturing	24.1	36.4	32.7
Other industry	25.6	44.6	38.2
Commerce	24.9	41.8	36.3
Source of finance			
Debt	27.4	58.3	47.0
New share issues	41.8	77.4	65.9
Retained earnings	22.0	27.4	26.4
Owner			
Households	36.9	62.7	54.8
Tax-exempt institutions	−8.6	−36.4	−26.7
Insurance companies	11.5	58.1	37.8
Overall	24.8	40.3	35.3

leasing arrangement designed primarily to extend the benefits of credits and accelerated depreciation deductions to firms without enough tax liability to take advantage of them otherwise. Here we look at the ultimate version of the 1981 law, scheduled to start in 1986, where machinery receives five-year services lives and is depreciated at the double declining balance rate. Detailed provisions of the 1981 law are described in sections 6.2.3 and 6.2.5.

Several of these business tax provisions will not be evaluated here. First, changes to the tax rates in low corporate brackets do not affect the use of 0.46 as the top marginal rate. Second, the extension of the period for loss carryovers and the introduction of safe-harbor leasing pertain only to companies with insufficient tax liability to use all their deductions. In this study we abstract from actual practices and concentrate on a hypothetical project undertaken by a taxable firm that exhibits tax-minimizing behavior in this regard. Finally, business tax changes such as the new R&D credit do not relate primarily to income from capital.

A personal tax change that does relate to the taxation of income from capital is the phased reduction of personal marginal rates. While the top marginal rate falls from 70 percent to 50 percent immediately, all other rates are reduced by 23 percent over three years. The important issue for our purposes is to estimate the weighted-average personal marginal tax rate on interest income at the end of this transition. This rate was 0.325 for individuals in 1980, and it would fall to $0.325(1 - 0.23) = 0.250$ by 1985 if there were no inflation. Because indexation does not start until 1985, however, inflation will push many individuals into higher nominal brackets with higher marginal rates. What rate of inflation from 1980 to 1985 would be enough to completely negate the effects of the 23 percent cut? A lengthy footnote finds that the required inflation rate would be very close to our actual inflation rate, and so we use the 1980 personal tax rates for 1985.[39]

Other personal tax provisions of the Economic Recovery Tax Act are ignored. The new all savers' certificates provide tax-free interest, but at rates 30 percent below the corresponding taxable government bond rate. Finally, changes to the marriage penalty and to charitable deductions do not relate primarily to income from capital.

Effective tax rates under the ultimate 1981 law, presented in table 6.27, can be compared with rates under the old law in table 6.20. With these legal developments, the overall rate in the fixed-p case falls from 37 percent to 26 percent, with actual inflation. The rate is still only moderately related to inflation, while debt is still highly subsidized. Under the 1981 law every category of industry, owner, or source of finance has a tax rate that is lower than under the 1980 law, at any inflation rate. Every category of asset has a tax rate no higher than before, but inventories are taxed exactly the same way, since they receive no investment tax credit and no depreciation allowances.

---

39. If nominal incomes were unchanged when all marginal rates were cut by 23 percent, then revenue and average rates would also fall by 23 percent. The same holds for a tax schedule of the form

$$T = CY^\alpha,$$

where T is total tax collected, Y is nominal taxable income, α is the elasticity of T with respect to Y, and C is an arbitrary constant. The TAXSIM model of NBER has been used to estimate that α is 1.66 in the United States. Because $\partial T/\partial Y$ is equal to $\alpha T/Y$, the marginal rate is always 166 percent of the average rate. Thus when ERTA first cuts the marginal rate from 0.325 to 0.250, the average rate falls from 0.196 to 0.151. Revenues initially fall from CY_0^α to $(1 - .23)CY_0^\alpha$. Suppose, however, that inflation at rate π for five years increases nominal incomes and prices by the factor $e^{5\pi}$. Nominal tax revenue after five years would then be $.77C(Y_0e^{5\pi})^\alpha$. Dividing by the price index $e^{5\pi}$, we find that real revenue after five years is $.77CY_0^\alpha e^{5\pi(\alpha - 1)}$. We want to find the value π such that the increase in real revenues is equal to 23 percent of the prechange revenue:

$$.77CY_0^\alpha e^{5\pi(\alpha - 1)} - .77CY_0^\alpha = .23CY_0^\alpha.$$

Dividing both sides by $.77CY_0^\alpha$ and substituting for α, we have

$$e^{5\pi(.66)} - 1 = .23/.77,$$

and π is equal to 7.92 percent. If the time period were six years, π would only have to be 6.60 percent. Finally, because the marginal rate equals $\alpha T/Y$ and real income is unchanged by assumption, the restoration of real revenue also restores the marginal rate.

Table 6.26   Effective Marginal Tax Rates, United States,
with No Personal Taxes, Fixed-*p* Case
(%)

	Inflation Rate		
	Zero	10%	Actual (6.77%)
Asset			
Machinery	−16.7	−18.6	−16.5
Buildings	21.1	4.6	12.0
Inventories	40.1	11.6	20.8
Industry			
Manufacturing	32.4	26.7	29.8
Other industry	−10.1	−32.4	−23.4
Commerce	24.1	−2.3	7.5
Source of finance			
Debt	−26.8	−98.5	−73.2
New share issues	39.5	51.8	48.9
Retained earnings	39.5	51.8	48.9
Owner			
Households	19.9	7.5	12.9
Tax-exempt institutions	15.7	−2.2	5.0
Insurance companies	−3.9	−46.6	−31.1
Overall	17.1	1.0	7.7

If the phased increases in depreciation were continued to 1986, machinery would become subsidized on an overall average basis. This 5.5 percent subsidy results from the combination of investment tax credits, very short depreciable lives, and the use of double declining balance. Autos, for example, receive a 6 percent credit and a three-year life. With double declining balance and the half-year convention, as described in section 6.2.3, the investor could write off 33 percent of the asset in the year of purchase, and an additional 45 percent in the first full year of ownership. The net result is a subsidy at the corporate level alone, a subsidy that is augmented if the ultimate owner is a tax-exempt institution or if debt is used to finance the investment. The overall 5.5 percent subsidy for machinery in table 6.27 includes the average amount of personal taxes on interest or dividend receipts.

Buildings are taxed at an overall 30 percent rate, while inventories have not changed from their 47 percent rate under the 1980 law. As pointed out by Fullerton and Henderson (1981), the Economic Recovery Tax Act implies significantly disparate tax treatments of depreciable assets on the one hand, and of land and inventories on the other. For actual inflation in the fixed-*p* case, effective tax rates change from a dispersion of −21 to +91 percent in 1980 to a dispersion of −38 to +85 percent under ERTA.

Table 6.27   **Effective Marginal Tax Rates, United States, with the**
                       Economic Recovery Tax Act of 1981, Fixed-p Case
                       (%)

	Inflation Rate		
	Zero	10%	Actual (6.77%)
Asset			
Machinery	− 16.1	− 0.9	− 5.5
Buildings	24.1	31.8	30.2
Inventories	50.9	45.5	47.0
Industry			
Manufacturing	35.7	46.0	43.5
Other industry	− 2.9	2.0	0.7
Commerce	26.7	27.5	27.5
Source of finance			
Debt	− 17.6	− 37.1	− 31.9
New share issues	55.1	98.4	84.9
Retained earnings	40.2	57.7	53.4
Owner			
Households	35.4	52.7	48.2
Tax-exempt institutions	− 11.0	− 53.0	− 37.6
Insurance companies	− 10.8	33.9	11.2
Overall	21.4	27.7	26.2

The fixed-r case is not shown, but the overall tax falls from 50 percent to 41 percent under the 1981 law, when expected inflation is equal to the actual rate of 6.77 percent. As in the fixed-p case, the taxation of inventories is unchanged, while other rates are all lower than before. Debt and tax-exempt institutions would be subsidized more than before, and machinery would become subsidized at a 17 percent rate. Variations among the rates are again greater under ERTA than they were in 1980.

These calculations pertain to the ultimate version of the 1981 law, not scheduled to start until 1986. Equipment actually received the new five-year lives and 150 percent of declining balance in 1981, but Congress never allowed the phased changes to 175 and 200 percent of declining balance. In the Tax Equity and Fiscal Responsibility Act of 1982, the 150 percent declining balance rate was made permanent for equipment, and the depreciation basis was reduced by half the investment tax credit. Section 6.2.3 described these provisions in more detail. The 1982 law also changed safe-harbor leasing and excise taxes, but these provisions do not affect our calculations.

The resulting overall fixed-p effective tax rate, which fell from 37 percent to 26 percent with the ultimate 1981 law, now rises back to 31.5 percent. Table 6.28 shows the breakdown of fixed-p effective tax rates by asset and other combinations. For machinery, the tax rate fell from 17.6

Table 6.28   Effective Marginal Tax Rates, United States, with the
Tax Equity and Fiscal Responsibility Act
of 1982, Fixed-*p* Case
(%)

	Inflation Rate		
	Zero	10%	Actual (6.77%)
Asset			
Machinery	−0.3	15.7	11.0
Buildings	27.4	34.7	33.2
Inventories	50.9	45.5	47.0
Industry			
Manufacturing	38.4	49.0	46.4
Other industry	7.9	12.4	11.4
Commerce	29.6	30.5	30.5
Source of finance			
Debt	−8.9	−29.1	−23.5
New share issues	57.8	101.2	87.7
Retained earnings	43.9	61.7	57.3
Owner			
Households	39.7	57.2	52.7
Tax-exempt institutions	−3.5	−45.3	−29.8
Insurance companies	−3.0	39.2	17.3
Overall	26.7	33.0	31.5

to −5.5 percent under the ultimate 1981 law but rises back to 11 percent under the 1982 law. Inventories are unchanged at 47 percent. Most buildings are unaffected by the 1982 law, but public utility structures were grouped with equipment for phased changes that were cut off by the 1982 law. Thus table 6.28 also shows a rate for buildings that rises from 30 to 33 percent, and a rate for "other industry" (including utilities) that rises from 0.7 to 11.4 percent. Sources of finance and owners show somewhat higher tax rates as a result of these changes for equipment and public utility structures.

In the fixed-*r* case, not shown, the overall effective tax rate fell from 50 to 41 percent but now rises back to 45 percent. The rate for machinery fell from 26 to −17 percent but now rises back to 19 percent. Although the weighted-average fixed-*r* tax rates are higher than the fixed-*p* tax rates, patterns among combinations are very similar. In either case the 1982 changes for equipment reverse about half of the overall tax cut associated with the 1981 law.

Finally, we note a surprising and dramatic result of these changes in corporate taxation. With personal and property tax rates unchanged, the overall fixed-*p* effective tax rate falls from 37 percent in 1980 to 31.5

percent in 1982. Yet table 6.25 shows that these personal and property taxes alone yield an overall effective rate of 35 percent. Thus, while elimination of the corporate tax under 1980 law would subtract two percentage points, repeal of the corporate tax after 1982 would *raise* the overall effective tax rate from 31.5 percent to 35 percent. Taxes will still be collected on the income from old investments, but the combination of new grants, accelerated depreciation, and interest deductions more than offsets any corporate tax on the marginal investment. If firms can make use of these tax benefits, then the corporate system amounts to a net subsidy to marginal investments after 1982.

6.4.3   Comparison with 1960 and 1970

Although histories of the personal and corporate income taxes were provided in sections 6.2.1 and 6.2.2, particular parameter values for use in calculating 1960 and 1970 effective tax rates were not specified. By referring back to those sections, and particularly to a few tables, we can now specify the tax parameters that were different in those years. In order to compare only the tax systems in the three periods, however, we do not recalculate capital stock weights or inflation rates in earlier years. Rather, we try to determine the effect of 1960 law were it to exist in 1980.

Since 1938, the United States corporate income tax system has been a classical (nonintegrated) system in the terminology of chapter 2, so the θ parameter is unity in all years. Table 6.4 shows some historical variation in the federal statutory tax rate on all corporate profits, however, including a 0.52 rate for 1960 and a 0.48 rate for 1970. In addition we need to adjust for state corporate taxes, as in section 6.2.2, where the 1980 federal rate of 0.46 was augmented by $(1 - .46)(.0655)$ to account for the weighted-average state marginal rate of 0.0655 and the deductibility of state corporate taxes at the federal level. We cannot calculate the weighted-average state corporate tax rates for 1960 and 1970 the same way we did for 1980, but we adjust the 1980 rate by factors that reflect the growth of state corporate taxes. In particular, data in Feldstein, Poterba, and Dicks-Mireaux (1983) show that the 1979 ratio of the marginal federal corporate rate to the average federal corporate rate (.46/.317) was 1.22 times the ratio of the marginal state corporate rate to the average state corporate rate (.0655/.055). If the same relationship existed in earlier years, then the 1960 and 1970 state marginal rates would have been 0.0245 and 0.0460, respectively. The total 1960 statutory rate is then $[.52 + (1 - .52)(.0245)] = 0.532$, and the total 1970 rate is $[.48 + (1 - .48)(.046)] = 0.504$. Thus the total rate fell from 53.2 to 49.5 percent from 1960 to 1980, even though the state rate rose from 2.45 to 6.55 percent.

Starting in 1954, all assets were depreciated by the double declining balance method with a switch to sum-of-the-years' digits, but since 1969 buildings have been depreciated by the 150 percent of declining balance method with a switch to straight-line. These methods and the tax-minimizing choices of firms are described in section 6.2.3. While Jorgenson and Sullivan (1981) found that firms have moved only gradually toward the more accelerated methods, we wish to look at changes in tax law rather than changes in actual practice. For this reason we assume that firms choose the most advantageous depreciation schedules in all years, and these are given by equations (6.1) through (6.6) above.

Tax law has been amended to allow shorter lifetimes, however. Table 6.29 is similar to table 6.5 in that it lists the same twenty types of

Table 6.29   Tax Lifetimes by Asset Class in 1960 and 1970

Asset Class	Bulletin F Lifetimes (1960)	Guideline Lifetimes (1970)
1. Furniture and fixtures	17.6	10.0
2. Fabricated metal products	21.2	12.5
3. Engines and turbines	24.7	15.6
4. Tractors	9.4	4.3
5. Agricultural machinery	20.0	10.0
6. Construction machinery	10.6	9.9
7. Mining and oilfield machinery	11.8	9.6
8. Metalworking machinery	18.8	12.7
9. Special industry machinery	18.8	12.7
10. General industrial equipment	16.5	12.3
11. Office and computing machinery	9.4	10.0
12. Service industry machinery	11.8	10.3
13. Electrical equipment	16.5	12.4
14. Trucks, buses, and trailers	10.6	5.6
15. Autos	11.8	3.0
16. Aircraft	10.6	6.3
17. Ships and boats	25.9	18.0
18. Railroad equipment	29.4	15.0
19. Instruments	12.9	10.6
20. Other equipment	12.9	10.2
21. Industrial buildings	31.8	28.8
22. Commercial buildings	42.3	47.6
23. Religious buildings	56.5	48.0
24. Educational buildings	56.5	48.0
25. Hospitals	56.5	48.0
26. Other nonfarm buildings	36.5	30.9
27. Railroads	60.0	30.0
28. Telephone and telegraph	31.8	27.0
29. Electric light and power	35.3	27.0
30. Gas	35.3	24.0
31. Other public utilities	30.6	22.0
32. Farm structures	44.7	25.0
33. Mining shafts, and wells	18.8	6.8
34. Other nonresidential structures	36.5	28.2

Source: Jorgenson and Sullivan (1981).

equipment and the same fourteen types of structures. *Bulletin F* lifetimes, in the first column, were in effect for these assets from 1942 until 1962, when the "Guideline" lifetimes of the second column were introduced. The Guideline lifetimes (for 1970) are all 30 to 40 percent less than the *Bulletin F* lifetimes (for 1960). Then, in 1971, the Asset Depreciation Range (ADR) system established Guideline lives as the midpoints for an allowed 20 percent increase or decrease in depreciation periods for equipment (assets 1–20) and public utility structures (assets 27–31). For 1980, we therefore use 80 percent of ADR midpoints as the shortest allowable lives for those assets, as shown in column 3 of table 6.5.

As mentioned in section 6.2.5, the investment tax credit was first introduced in 1962 and was repealed from 1969 to 1971. Thus the rate of grant was zero for all assets in both 1960 and 1970. The corporate rates, grant rates, and other parameter changes are summarized in table 6.30.

In section 6.2.6, the effective property tax rates for buildings and for other assets are found to be 0.01126 and 0.00768, respectively. These rates are estimated for 1977 and applied to 1980. We cannot, however, calculate separate property tax rates for 1960 and 1970 in the same manner as for 1977. As with the state corporate tax rates, we adjust the 1977 property tax rates by factors that reflect changes in state and local

Table 6.30   **United States Tax Parameters for 1960, 1970, and 1980**

Parameter	1960	1970	1980
θ	1.0	1.0	1.0
Federal corporate rate	0.52	0.48	0.46
State corporate rate	0.0245	0.0460	0.0655
τ	0.532	0.504	0.495
Investment tax credit rates, g	0.0	0.0	(table 6.5, col. 2)
Asset lifetimes, L	*Bulletin F* (table 6.29, col. 1)	Guidelines (table 6.29, col. 2)	ADR (table 6.5, col. 3)
Property tax rates, w_c			
Buildings	0.01126	0.01408	0.01126
Machinery and inventories	0.00768	0.00960	0.00768
Tax rate on dividends			
Households	0.431	0.413	0.475
Tax-exempt institutions	0.0	0.0	0.0
Insurance companies	0.078	0.072	0.069
Tax rate on capital gains, z_s			
Households	0.14	0.14	0.14
Tax-exempt institutions	0.0	0.0	0.0
Insurance companies	0.30	0.30	0.28
Tax rate on interest income			
Households	0.284	0.284	0.284
Tax-exempt institutions	0.0	0.0	0.0
Insurance companies	$(0.149 + 3.88\pi)$	$(0.149 + 3.88\pi)$	$(0.149 + 3.88\pi)$

Source: Derivations described in the text.

property taxation. Data in Feldstein, Poterba, and Dicks-Mireaux (1983) show that the overall property tax rate in 1960 was very close to the overall rate in 1977, and that the overall rate in 1970 was 1.25 times the rate in 1977. We therefore use 1980 rates for 1960 and scale them by 1.25 to obtain rates for 1970. Final property tax rates are shown in table 6.30.

For the weighted-average marginal tax rate on dividends in 1980, we use 0.475 as found by the TAXSIM model of NBER. Since that source is not available for earlier years, we turn to rates estimated by Brinner and Brooks (1981). The total federal and state tax rates on personal dividend receipts in 1960 and 1970 were 0.431 and 0.413, respectively. Tax-exempt institutions pay no tax on dividend receipts, while insurance companies, like other corporations, can deduct 85 percent of dividend receipts. Since the federal corporate tax rates were 0.52 in 1960, 0.48 in 1970, and 0.46 in 1980, their effective tax rates on dividends in those years were 0.078, 0.072, and 0.069, respectively.

We use 0.28 for the weighted-average statutory personal marginal tax rate on realized capital gains in 1980, a number found by the TAXSIM model. This time, however, we have no viable alternative source for earlier years. Although the Revenue Act of 1978 reduced the taxable proportion of long-term gains from 50 to 40 percent (and thereby set the top federal rate at 28 percent), prior law specified a maximum 25 percent rate on the first $50,000 of gains and an additional 10 percent tax on the excluded gains in some circumstances. Since we halve the 0.28 rate to account for the increase of basis at death, and since the resulting 0.14 rate is approximately halved again to account for deferral, the resulting rate is small, and variations over time would be small. For these reasons we use the TAXSIM personal rates in all years. Exempt institutions pay no tax on capital gains, while insurance companies paid the statutory corporate rate of 30 percent in 1960 and 1970, reduced by the Revenue Act of 1978 to 28 percent for 1980.

Finally, we turn to the tax on interest income. The TAXSIM model provides an estimate of 0.325 for the combined federal and state marginal personal rate in 1980, and again we have no viable alternative source for earlier years. There have been many adjustments to personal rates and brackets over the years, including a 1964 reduction in the top marginal rate from 90 to 70 percent, but most of these adjustments have only approximately offset the fact that inflation pushes individuals with un-changed real income into higher nominal brackets with higher marginal rates. Wright (1969) found that the average personal marginal tax rate on interest income in 1958 was 33.3 percent, very close to our number for 1980. As a result, we use the same personal rate for all years. When adjusted for interest receipts of banks, this figure is 0.284, as shown in table 6.30. Since the Life Insurance Company Income Tax Act of 1959 is still in effect, the tax rates for our third ownership category are also unchanged.

Table 6.31   **Effective Marginal Tax Rates, United States, 1960, Fixed-*p* Case** (%)

	Inflation Rate		
	Zero	10%	Actual (6.77%)
Asset			
Machinery	44.7	63.7	59.3
Buildings	41.7	44.3	45.0
Inventories	52.5	42.7	45.6
Industry			
Manufacturing	51.1	60.5	58.8
Other industry	37.3	37.1	38.4
Commerce	43.6	40.7	42.4
Source of finance			
Debt	16.9	−13.2	−3.6
New share issues	67.5	109.0	96.5
Retained earnings	58.6	77.3	73.1
Owner			
Households	54.0	68.1	65.3
Tax-exempt institutions	24.2	−17.0	−0.9
Insurance companies	23.2	56.5	37.6
Overall	44.9	48.3	48.4

When all of these 1960 parameters are substituted into the basic United States data to calculate effective tax rates using our standard methodology, the results are as shown in table 6.31. The overall fixed-*p* rate is 44.9 percent with no inflation, and 48.4 percent with 6.77 percent inflation. While the relation between inflation and the tax rate is not linear, it is clear that the tax rate in 1960 would be about 46 or 47 percent if very low rates of inflation were expected at that time. This rate falls in 1980 to 37 percent with 7 percent inflation, or 38 percent with 10 percent inflation. Many have suggested that accelerated depreciation and shorter lifetimes have been introduced in response to higher expectations of inflation, but these results indicate that legal changes have much more than offset any increases in inflationary expectations.[40]

Moreover, the bottom row of table 6.31 shows that the overall rate in 1960 is fairly insensitive to expected inflation and even falls as inflation increases from 7 to 10 percent. This result can be explained by the much

40. Since the pattern of investment responds to tax differentials, the weights would adjust over time. The rate on machinery fell the most, so investment would increase the most. Because we use the relatively high 1980 weight for machinery in all years, the high average rates from earlier years are somewhat overstated. Also, these calculations assume that firms minimize taxes by using LIFO inventory accounting. Footnote 33 summarizes some results with 70 percent FIFO accounting, and the tax rates in that case rise faster with inflation.

longer asset lifetimes in 1960, since depreciation deductions are less important. The fact that depreciation is on a historical cost basis when there is inflation cannot make real depreciation deductions much lower, while the fact that nominal interest is deducted against the corporate tax rate still substantially reduces the cost of debt finance. Indeed, the row for debt finance still shows a subsidy with 7 or 10 percent inflation, even though nominal interest receipts of individuals are included at the personal rate, and even though there are no investment tax credits or short lifetimes allowed on the assets that are financed by that debt.

Machinery, since it receives no credits, relatively long lives, and only historical cost depreciation, is taxed at a 59 percent effective rate in 1960. When compared with the 18 percent rate for machinery in 1980, this figure is striking. Table 6.29 shows that the lifetimes for some types of equipment were as long as twenty-five to thirty years, whereas the longest life in 1980 was fourteen years. Autos were depreciated over 11.8 years in 1960, compared with three years in 1970 and 1980. When we note that the economic depreciation rate for autos is measured to be 33.3 percent per year, it is clear that some assets were not receiving even economic depreciation write-offs in 1960. Since autos and machinery made up a relatively high proportion of total assets in commerce and manufacturing, those industries are taxed at rates of 42 and 59 percent respectively.

The overall tax rate in the fixed-r case is 59 percent for 1960, compared with 50 percent for 1980. As pointed out in chapter 2, the fixed-r tax rates are always higher than the fixed-p rates when there is a dispersion among the rates of individual combinations. Patterns between years and among assets in the fixed-r case are not shown, but they are similar to those in the fixed-p case.

The fixed-p results for 1970 are shown in table 6.32 with an overall rate of 47 percent. Thus, in the fixed-p case overall effective tax rates in 1960, 1970, 1980, under the ultimate 1981 law, and under the 1982 law, are equal to 48, 47, 37, 26, and 32 percent, respectively. In the fixed-r case the corresponding tax rates are 59, 57, 50, 41, and 45 percent. In either case the total taxation of income from capital falls substantially from 1960 to 1981, but some of this decline is reversed with the 1982 law. Since the fixed-p rate on machinery falls from 59 to 49 percent from 1960 to 1970, it is clear that the 1962 introduction of Guidelines did more to reduce equipment lives than building lives (see table 6.29 lifetimes). Since the rate on buildings rises from 45 percent to 47 percent, the elimination of double declining balance in 1969 had more effect than the shortening of lives in 1962. Most 1970 rates in table 6.32 are lower than the 1960 rates of table 6.31, but inventories reflect the higher property tax rate used in the later year.

Table 6.32   **Effective Marginal Tax Rates, United States, 1970, Fixed-*p* Case**
(%)

| | Inflation Rate | | |
	Zero	10%	Actual (6.77%)
Asset			
Machinery	36.7	52.6	48.5
Buildings	43.3	46.7	47.1
Inventories	51.8	44.0	46.3
Industry			
Manufacturing	51.1	59.9	58.3
Other industry	32.5	33.9	34.4
Commerce	45.1	42.3	43.8
Source of finance			
Debt	17.2	−7.8	−0.2
New share issues	65.6	104.8	92.9
Retained earnings	56.7	73.2	69.7
Owner			
Households	52.7	66.4	63.5
Tax-exempt institutions	23.4	−15.9	−0.7
Insurance companies	22.8	57.6	38.3
Overall	43.8	47.4	47.2

6.4.4 Comparison with Average Tax Rates

How do the 37 percent (fixed-*p*) and the 50 percent (fixed-*r*) marginal tax rates compare with other estimates of average tax rates? To maintain comparability in such a calculation, we look at only domestic nonfinancial corporate business, and we include all forms of capital taxation as a fraction of all forms of capital income. We also want the income measure to reflect economic rather than tax depreciation.

Table 6.33 summarizes the appropriation of corporate profits from 1978 to 1980. We average these years together because the series are fairly volatile. Since losses induce delayed rather than immediate tax offsets, the denominator of the average tax rate could be unusually low in a single year without a corresponding reduction in the numerator. Thus the average of several years could be expected to provide not just a more stable but a more accurate reflection of the normal tax on existing investments. Profits in table 6.33 are defined to include the "capital consumption adjustment," which corrects for economic rather than tax depreciation, and the "inventory valuation adjustment," which puts all inventories on a LIFO accounting basis. We also include interest pay-

Table 6.33   Corporate Profits and Their Appropriation, United States, 1978–80
                             ($ billion in current prices)

	1978–80 Average
Real operating profits	196.78
Federal and state corporate profits tax	73.10
State and local property tax	18.45
Interest payments	36.40
Dividend payments	36.90
Real retained earnings	31.93

Source: Various issues of the Survey of Current Business, plus calculations described in the text.

ments and property tax payments in the total gross profits figure. For domestic source income of only nonfinancial corporations, these profits were $196.78 billion.[41]

Corporate profits taxes at all levels of government totaled $73.10 billion for these corporations, as shown in the Survey of Current Business. This source also reports interest payments of $36.40 billion and dividend payments of $36.90 billion. Real retained earnings of $31.93 billion are obtained from their corrected profits figure less taxes, interest, and dividends.

The property tax payments are not shown separately for these corporations, however. To obtain an estimate for these taxes, we turn back to the effective rates estimated in section 6.2.6. The 0.01126 rate for buildings and the 0.00768 rate for machinery and inventories were estimated from total property taxes and total capital. When they are applied to Jorgenson's 1977 figures for only nonfinancial corporate structures, equipment, and inventories, $14.54 billion results. To approximate 1979 property taxes, we scale the 1977 amount by the ratio of the 1979 to the 1977 total nonfinancial corporate property tax base, as shown in Feldstein, Poterba, and Dicks-Mireaux (1983). The resulting estimate for 1979 is $18.45 billion, very close to the amount those authors find with their "equal rate" hypothesis.

These profit taxes and property taxes are included in the taxation of capital income, shown in table 6.34. Also in the table, we include estimates of personal taxes on interest, dividends, and real retained earnings. Interest payments from the previous table are multiplied by 0.236, the weighted average of debt holders' personal marginal rates on interest income. That is, the household rate of 0.284 (from table 6.13) is weighted by their 0.609 share of debt (from table 6.19), and the insurance company rate of $(.149 + 3.88\pi) = 0.412$ is weighted by their 0.153 share of debt.

41. We were unable to exclude agriculture, mining, and crude petroleum from these calculations of the average tax rate, since the Survey of Current Business does not show corporate interest payments or capital consumption adjustments separately by industry.

Table 6.34   **Average Tax Rate on Real Corporate Profits**
                        ($ billion in current prices)

	1978–80 Average	Percentage of Profits
Total taxes	115.11	58.50
Corporate taxes	73.10	37.15
Property taxes	18.45	9.38
Taxes on		
Interest payments	8.59	4.37
Dividend payments	13.13	6.67
Real retained earnings	1.84	0.94
Personal wealth	0.00	
Real operating profits	196.78	
Average tax rate (%)	58.50	
Average profit rate (%)		
Gross of tax	9.41	
Net of tax	3.91	

Source: Own calculations as described in the text.

Similarly, dividend payments are multiplied by 0.356, the weighted average of equity holders' personal marginal rates on dividends. Finally, each dollar of real retained earnings from table 6.33 is assumed to generate one dollar of real capital gains for shareholders. The household capital gains rate of 0.14 and the insurance company rate of 0.28 (from table 6.13) are first halved to account for deferral, then weighted by the 0.743 and 0.041 shares to obtain 0.058 as the effective rate on accrued capital gains. This rate is applied to the real retained earnings of table 6.33 to obtain $1.84 billion of tax, shown in table 6.34.

Total taxes are $115.11 billion, or 58.5 percent of gross corporate profits. The gross and net rates of return are 9.4 and 3.9 percent, respectively, derived by dividing gross or net profits by $2,091.0 billion, the total 1979 nonfinancial corporate stock from the Federal Reserve Board Balance Sheet data. Similar information, on average tax rates and profit rates, is available for a time series of thirty years in Feldstein, Poterba, and Dicks-Mireaux (1983).

Two questions arise. First, why is the 58.5 percent average tax rate lower than the 69.4 percent rate estimated for 1979 by Feldstein, Poterba, and Dicks-Mireaux (1983)? Second, why is the 58.5 percent average tax rate so much higher than the 37 to 50 percent marginal tax rate?

A number of differences exist between the two average tax rate estimation procedures. First, Feldstein, Poterba, and Dicks-Mireaux (1983) use 0.35 for the personal rate on interest. We found from the TAXSIM model that the total federal and state marginal rate on interest was 0.325, and we reduced that rate to 0.284 to account for the fact that some corporate interest reaches the hands of bank depositors in the form of tax-free services. Second, our calculations use weights from 1980 rather than 1976, and more recent data show more debt in the hands of tax-exempt institutions. Third, unlike those authors, we moved part of insurance company debt holdings into the tax-exempt group to account for their nontaxable pension business. For these reasons, our weighted tax rate on interest is 0.236 while theirs was 0.317. However, our 0.356 dividend rate is similar to their 0.349 rate, and our 0.058 capital gains rate is similar to their 0.044 rate for 1979. A final difference is that those authors include a capital gains tax on nominal gains, the product of an inflation rate and the capital stock. Chapter 2 describes our reasons for excluding this component.

The differences between average tax rates and marginal tax rates primarily involve distinctions between ex post taxes paid and ex ante expectations of taxes using current legislation. Several such distinctions can be suggested. First, unanticipated inflation reduces the real value of depreciation allowances on past investments without necessarily affecting the expected real value of depreciation allowances on the current marginal investment. Jorgenson and Sullivan (1981) argued that recent inflation rates have been higher than expected in the United States and have acted as a lump-sum tax on investments already in place. Second, the average tax rate mixes investments with different tax treatments. The rates from 1978 to 1980, for example, include taxes paid on some investments that were made before the 1971 liberalization of depreciation allowances, while the marginal rate in 1980 should reflect only the law then current. Third, transitory or windfall profits on past investments are subject to the statutory corporate tax rate, while the expected normal return to the marginal investment is also affected by investment tax credits and accelerated depreciation allowances. Fourth, monopoly profits receive the statutory rate. Fifth, initial corporate investments pay initial low-bracket corporate rates, while marginal investments were assumed to pay the 0.46 top bracket rate. Finally, firms may have reasons unrelated to the marginal investment for using charitable deductions, FIFO accounting, longer than minimum asset lives, and other features affecting the average tax rate without necessarily affecting the marginal tax rate.

It is thus not too surprising that when Fullerton and Henderson (1981) took different formulations for the marginal tax rates in eighteen United States industries, and different formulations for the average tax rates in the same eighteen industries, they obtained correlation coefficients that varied around zero and never exceeded 0.3. Furthermore, most of the reasons given above point to a marginal rate that is less than the average rate, as we found in this study. Fullerton (1983) includes much more discussion about the difference between average and marginal effective tax rates.

Table 6.35   Ratios of Total Capital Taxes to Total
               Capital Income from Two Different Studies

Industry	1953–59	1972–74
Included		
Manufacturing	.58	.58
Other industry	.58	.63
Commerce	.46	.57
Excluded		
Agriculture	.30	.35
Mining (including crude petroleum)	.35	.50
Real estate	.32	.39
Overall total	.47	.49

Source: The 1953–59 capital income, corporate taxes, and property taxes are from Rosenberg (1969). The imputation of personal taxes is based on assumptions of Harberger (1966), as corrected and disaggregated by Shoven (1976). The 1972–74 ratios are from the Fullerton/Shoven/Whalley model, using different personal tax imputations. See Fullerton et al. (1978, 1981).

Several other studies have estimated average tax rates by industry, including Rosenberg (1969) for 1953–59 and Fullerton et al. (1978, 1981) for 1972–74. Their results are summarized in table 6.35. In both of these studies, capital income is defined to include corporate profits, net interest paid, net rents paid, and corrections for economic depreciation. Several years are averaged in order to avoid problems with loss carry-forwards. Capital taxes are defined to include corporate income taxes, property taxes, and an imputation for the personal taxes paid on capital earned in each industry. In spite of these similarities, enough procedural differences remain so that we cannot attribute tax ratio differences to changes over time. However, it is fair to presume that the higher rate for mining and crude petroleum in the 1972–74 study reflects the phasing-out of oil depletion deductions. The higher rate for the commercial industry probably reflects increased incorporation.

Because personal and property taxes are included, we can also compare our corporate industries with three excluded noncorporate industries. These noncorporate industries clearly have lower average effective tax rates. In fact, the average tax rates in both of these studies have been used to estimate the capital misallocation and welfare effects from differential capital taxation.[42] Part of the point of this book is that our marginal effective tax rates might be better suited for measuring these investment incentive effects.

42. See Harberger (1966), Shoven (1976), and Fullerton et al. (1978, 1981).

7 Comparisons of Effective Tax Rates

One of the main purposes of our study is to examine the variations in effective tax rates among the four countries and to explain the main reasons for these differences. A summary of the major results for each country has been presented in the appropriate chapter. In section 7.1 we analyze the results more fully, placing particular emphasis on comparisons across countries. Such comparisons help to place the results for any one country in perspective and to shed light on some key relationships such as the effect of inflation on effective tax rates. As shown in section 7.2, this effect differs significantly from one country to another. In section 7.3 we also examine the extent to which differences in tax rates are attributable to differences in the tax systems or to differences in the importance of particular industries, assets, sources of finance, and owners.

In addition to these basic questions, we examine in section 7.4 the sensitivity of the estimated tax rates to the values of p (in the fixed-p case) and r (in the fixed-r case) at which they are evaluated. At different inflation rates, we evaluate the tax rates at constant average net of personal tax rates of return. The question of how sensitive our results are to this assumption is tackled in section 7.5. Finally, for each country we calculate the distribution of effective marginal tax rates.

7.1 Comparing Results under Standard Assumptions

Let us first summarize the results with the standard parameters for each country. Table 7.1 shows effective tax rates in the fixed-p case for the four countries. From the final row of table 7.1 we see that the highest overall effective marginal tax rate is the 48 percent rate in West Germany, followed by 37 percent in the United States, 36 percent in Sweden, and

Table 7.1   **Actual Effective Tax Rates for Each Country, Fixed-*p* Case**
(actual inflation, actual depreciation, actual weights)

	United Kingdom	Sweden	West Germany	United States
Asset				
Machinery	−36.8	0.2	44.5	17.6
Buildings	39.3	36.6	42.9	41.1
Inventories	39.5	68.8	59.0	47.0
Industry				
Manufacturing	−9.6	27.1	48.1	52.7
Other industry	−5.4	60.5	57.0	14.6
Commerce	36.2	39.2	44.4	38.2
Source of finance				
Debt	−100.8	5.0	−3.1	−16.3
New share issues	−4.2	90.4	62.6	91.2
Retained earnings	30.6	68.2	90.2	62.4
Owner				
Households	42.0	105.1	71.2	57.5
Tax-exempt institutions	−44.6	−51.8	6.3	−21.5
Insurance companies	−6.7	18.9	−3.8	23.4
Overall	3.7	35.6	48.1	37.2

only 4 percent in the United Kingdom. The overall rate for each country is an average of the effective marginal tax rates for the eighty-one combinations, weighted by the proportion of capital in each combination. These weights, together with all 1980 input parameters for each country, are shown in Appendix A, and the matrixes of tax rates for different combinations and inflation rates in the four countries are given in Appendix B.

Each row in table 7.1 shows a weighted average tax rate for a subset of combinations. For example, the first row shows the average tax rate over all combinations that include machinery. From this row we can see that immediate expensing of machinery is a major reason for the low overall rate in the United Kingdom. The effective tax rate on machinery is minus 37 percent, while other assets are taxed at over 39 percent. Britain has the lowest total tax on machinery and the highest share of machinery in its capital stock.[1] Sweden's exponential depreciation of machinery at a 30

1. The first matrix of weights in Appendix A shows the proportion of capital stock that is used in each combination of asset and industry. If we add across the three industries in each country, we find that machinery is 47 percent of total capital in Britain, 42 percent in West Germany, 32 percent in Sweden, and 22 percent in the United States. The high percentage in Britain can be explained by the tax advantages afforded machinery, and the low percentage in the United States can be explained by the fact that a larger proportion of utilities are private corporations in the United States than in Europe. Since there are more structure-intensive utilities in the "other industry" category, the United States has a lower relative total weight on machinery.

percent annual rate for tax purposes is considerably more than the 7 to 20 percent rates that we estimate for economic depreciation. This accelerated depreciation plus the 11 percent investment grant means that the total corporate and personal tax wedge on machinery in Sweden is zero. Accelerated depreciation plus a 10 percent grant in the United States implies that the total tax on machinery is 18 percent,[2] while tax lives of eleven years and only 2 percent credits in Germany result in a tax rate on machinery of 45 percent. The effective tax rate on investment in buildings is strikingly similar in all four countries, with rates ranging from 36 to 43 percent. The row for inventories demonstrates the importance of inflation accounting, since the lower tax rates are in the United Kingdom and United States, where FIFO accounting is not obligatory for tax purposes, while 59 and 69 percent tax rates are found in Germany and Sweden, where half of inventories and all of inventories, respectively, are on FIFO accounting.

Looking at the industry breakdown in the United Kingdom, the tax rate for manufacturing is lowest because of the high weight on machinery and because that industry receives extra grants for machinery. The "other industry" category, although qualifying for lower grants, has a higher relative weight on machinery. The more interesting aspect of the industry breakdown, however, is that in Germany and Sweden the tax rate in "other industry" is higher than the overall rate, and in the United Kingdom and the United States it is lower than the overall rate. The low United States rate reflects the availability of investment tax credits for both machinery and buildings in utilities. The higher tax rates in Germany and Sweden reflect larger weights on buildings and inventories, respectively. These assets receive less generous depreciation allowances and lower grants.

In the breakdown by source of finance, the United Kingdom again provides the most striking contrast. Debt-financed investments are heavily subsidized, since assets receive accelerated or immediate depreciation and corporate interest payments are fully deductible from taxable income. Investment financed by new share issues receives a small subsidy because of the tax credits for dividends afforded by the imputation system of corporation tax. Only investment projects financed by retained earnings are taxed at positive rates in Britain. In all four countries tax deductibility of interest payments keeps down the tax rate on debt finance. Because of the imputation system both in Germany and the

2. The overall rate on machinery is zero in Sweden and 18 percent in the United States, but we cannot infer that depreciation of machinery is more accelerated in Sweden. Indeed, as shown in table 7.5, the rate in Sweden exceeds the rate in the United States when we use a common set of weights. Instead, the zero rate for machinery in Sweden can be explained by the fact that Sweden has proportionately more of machinery in manufacturing and that this industry uses proportionately more debt than in the United States. All weights for each industry are shown in Appendix A.

United Kingdom, the tax rate on projects financed by new share issues is lower than that on projects financed by retained earnings. In Sweden and the United States, in contrast, the relative positions of the two sources of equity finance are reversed. The United States imposes both corporate and personal taxes on dividends, while Sweden's Annell deduction is not enough to offset a similar double tax.

Finally, table 7.1 shows effective tax rates by ownership category. These rates reflect the differences in personal rates on interest and dividends in each country that are shown in Appendix A. Households in Sweden and Germany have particularly high personal tax rates, and effective marginal tax rates on projects financed directly from households are 105 and 71 percent, respectively. In Germany, however, tax-exempt institutions do not receive refunds of dividend tax credits or withholding taxes, so that only in Germany is the tax wedge positive for projects financed by tax-exempt institutions.

In other countries tax-exempt institutions are subsidized because their receipts of income are tax free and the corporations in which they invest receive deductions for interest payments, accelerated depreciation, investment grants, and in certain cases credits for dividends paid. The position of insurance companies is rather different. Although they are, on average, subsidized in Britain and Germany, they are taxed at positive rates in Sweden and the United States. We discovered that in all four countries the taxation of insurance companies was an extremely complex matter. The effective tax rate depends critically on special provisions, such as the possibility of making tax-free allocations to reserves. These provisions imply that the tax may be quite different from the statutory corporate rate applying to insurance companies and can increase rapidly with inflation (see section 7.2).

The tax rates shown in table 7.1 refer to projects that are all assumed to earn a pretax rate of return of 10 percent per annum. These figures describe the incentives provided by the tax schedule but do not tell us what revenue we would expect to collect at the margin corresponding to a small increase in the capital stock as a whole. This is because we might expect investments to be pushed to the point at which all projects yield the same rate of return before deduction of personal taxes. This arbitrage equilibrium we call the fixed-r case. It gives greater weight to the more highly taxed combinations, because it is these combinations that require a higher pretax rate of return in order to generate funds to pay the given market rate of return. The results for the fixed-r case are shown in table 7.2. As mentioned above, the weighted-average tax rates in table 7.2 will generally be larger than those in table 7.1 for the fixed-p case.[3] The overall

---

3. If the tax system were linear, then the effective tax rate calculated for a particular combination would not depend on the choice of p or r in either the fixed-p or the fixed-r calculations. Since individual tax rates would then be the same in both cases, any weighted-

Table 7.2   **Actual Effective Tax Rates for Each Country, Fixed-*r* Case**
(actual inflation, actual depreciation, actual weights)

	United Kingdom	Sweden	West Germany	United States
Asset				
Machinery	−57.5	−0.7	63.4	26.4
Buildings	56.4	48.5	59.9	54.1
Inventories	45.9	72.5	70.4	54.5
Industry				
Manufacturing	10.7	45.1	65.0	61.2
Other industry	12.0	77.0	69.5	24.4
Commerce	55.0	53.7	61.3	48.8
Source of finance				
Debt	—	11.5	−17.9	−72.5
New share issues	−1.8	92.9	73.2	81.8
Retained earnings	48.2	89.6	85.4	66.5
Owner				
Households	104.6	141.0	82.4	73.4
Tax-exempt institutions	−34.5	−68.8	26.5	−21.3
Insurance companies	14.5	26.9	9.1	22.4
Overall	30.0	53.6	64.8	49.9

marginal tax rates in the fixed-*r* case are 30 percent in the United Kingdom, 50 percent in the United States, 54 percent in Sweden, and 65 percent in West Germany.

Although the absolute values of the tax rates shown in table 7.2 are higher than those in table 7.1, the patterns of variations of tax rates both among countries and across combinations remain the same. Investment in machinery is subsidized in the United Kingdom, pays virtually no tax in Sweden, and is taxed at higher positive rates in the United States and especially in West Germany. Tax rates on investments in inventories are highest in Sweden and Germany. Investment in the United Kingdom is taxed less heavily in manufacturing than in other industries, whereas in the United States manufacturing pays a higher tax rate than other sectors of the economy.

It is clear that investment financed by borrowing is much less heavily taxed than that financed by equity. In three of the four countries such

---

average in the fixed-*r* case must be greater than the corresponding weighted-average in the fixed-*p* case. The tax system is not linear, however, so the individual tax rates depend on the chosen *p* of 10 percent in table 7.1, and on the chosen *r* of 5 percent in table 7.2. Since the tax rates for individual combinations are not identical in the two cases, averages over tax rates in the fixed-*r* case do not necessarily exceed those in the fixed-*p* case. Indeed, when we average over all combinations involving a particular asset, industry, source, or owner, the fixed-*r* tax rate in table 7.2 is sometimes less than the corresponding fixed-*p* rate of table 7.1.

projects are subsidized, and in the exception, Sweden, they receive a tax rate of only 11.5 percent. In Britain the subsidy is sufficiently large that the required pretax rate of return, necessary to generate a 5 percent rate of return before personal taxes to savers, is actually negative. Thus the factor income net of depreciation that would be produced in arbitrage equilibrium is negative, and the use of this factor income as the denominator of an estimated tax rate would produce figures with a sign opposite from that corresponding to our intuition. The tax wedge on debt finance in the United Kingdom is negative, and in table 7.2 the implied tax rate would be positive because of the negative pretax rate of return. Hence this figure is omitted. One advantage of reporting the results in the form of the implied tax wedge ($p - s$) is that the sign of the wedge always corresponds to the effect of the tax system on the incentive to save and invest.

Finally, there are substantial differences in the effective tax rates levied according to the identity of the provider of the funds for the project. Tax-exempt institutions receive a net subsidy in all countries except Germany, whereas in all four countries projects financed directly by households pay extremely high tax rates.

7.2   Effects of Inflation on Marginal Tax Rates

Section 4 of each country chapter provides estimates of tax rates for inflation rates of zero, 10 percent per annum, and the estimated actual inflation rate during the period 1970–79. In this section we investigate more systematically the effect of inflation on marginal tax rates. Figure 7.1 shows the overall effective marginal tax rates in the fixed-p case for inflation rates varying from zero to 15 percent. The figure illustrates some major differences among the four countries. In particular, overall marginal tax rates in Germany and the United States are rather insensitive to the rate of inflation, whereas in Sweden and Britain the tax rate is much more dependent on the inflation rate. But the influence of inflation is in opposite directions for the latter two countries. At zero inflation both countries have an overall marginal tax rate of about 13 percent, but as inflation increases the tax rate rises in Sweden and falls in the United Kingdom.

To discuss figure 7.1 and the different net effects of inflation in each country, it is useful first to summarize four separate effects of inflation that might operate in any one country.[4] First, a marginal investment in 1980 typically has future depreciation allowances that are based on

4. We concentrate here on four effects of inflation because they serve to explain figure 7.1. Inflation might also (a) raise taxes on capital gains if the tax base is not indexed, (b) push taxpayers into higher brackets if the tax schedule is not indexed, and (c) reduce the real tax burden if payments are delayed relative to the time that liabilities are incurred.

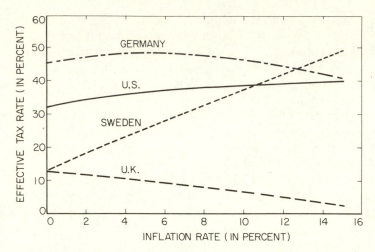

Fig. 7.1   Overall effective tax rate as inflation varies in each country.

historical cost (the 1980 purchase price for the asset). Since inflation reduces the real value of these fixed nominal deductions, it tends to increase effective tax rates. As inflation increases further, however, the real value of depreciation allowances falls at a reduced rate: only at an infinite rate of inflation does the real value of these deductions approach zero. For this reason the effect of historical cost depreciation becomes less important with successive increases in the rate of inflation. It is also less important in Britain, where machinery receives immediate expensing and hence inflation has no effect on the vector of such allowances.

Second, inflation increases the nominal interest rate. Where nominal interest payments are deductible from the corporate income tax, inflation tends to increase these deductions and decrease the overall tax rate. At the same time, where nominal interest receipts are included in the personal income tax base, inflation tends to increase these receipts and increase the overall tax. In combination, since the corporate rate is greater than the personal rate averaged over investors in all of our countries, inflation tends to decrease overall taxes.

Third, inflation increases the nominal value of inventories. Under FIFO inventory accounting, taxable profits are measured by the difference between nominal sales price and nominal costs. Thus, for given real magnitudes, inflation tends to increase taxable nominal profits and increase the effective tax rate. This effect depends on the proportion of assets held as inventories.

Fourth, tax rules for insurance companies can exacerbate the effects of inflation. In the United States and Sweden, insurance companies are allowed deductions for reserves that are based on fixed nominal interest rate assumptions. As inflation increases nominal interest receipts, it reduces the real value of deductions for reserves. The entire addition to the nominal return is taxed, even if it is needed to meet reserve obligations. As a result, inflation tends to increase the effective tax rate proportionately.

These four effects of inflation operate in different directions and with different magnitudes in each country, but the total effects are shown in figure 7.1. In Germany, for example, the tax rate starts at 45 percent with no inflation. It tends to increase because of historical cost depreciation and inventory accounting, but it tends to decrease because of nominal interest deductions at a corporate rate that exceeds the personal rate. The net effect is positive at first, but the effect of historical cost depreciation diminishes with further inflation. Nominal interest deductions become relatively more important at a 5 percent rate of inflation, and further inflation reduces the total tax.

The same general story applies to the United States, except that the effect of FIFO inventory accounting is replaced by the effect of nominal reserve allowances for insurance companies. Taxes increase with inflation, but at a diminishing rate as the effect of historical cost depreciation diminishes. The curve becomes almost flat at high rates of inflation, where the tax-increasing effects of insurance rules are almost exactly offset by the tax-reducing effects of nominal interest deductions at a corporate rate that exceeds the personal rate.

Most effects operate in the same direction for Sweden. First, depreciation is allowed on a historical cost basis. Second, Sweden requires FIFO inventory accounting. Third, insurance companies are allowed only a fixed nominal return for reserves. Finally, nominal interest is taxed at a weighted-average marginal rate that is almost as high as the corporate rate. (Sections 4.2.5 and 4.4.3 find that the effective corporate rate in Sweden was 35 percent in 1980.) The combination of these four effects for Sweden itself is dramatic, but the contrast with Britain in figure 7.1 is tremendous. Nominal interest in Britain is deducted at the 52 percent corporate rate, and it is received by households with an average 28 percent rate, tax-exempt institutions, or insurance companies with a 17 percent rate. This effect swamps that of historical cost depreciation. Although some buildings in Britain receive delayed depreciation at historical cost, other assets are expensed. Inflation does not operate to increase taxes through investment in inventories or saving through insurance companies. As a result, overall taxes start at about 13 percent of the pretax return, fall with inflation, and keep falling as inflation increases.

Figure 7.1 does not show differential effects of inflation among combinations in each country. To investigate differences among assets, industries, financial sources, or owners, we start with tax rates for zero inflation in table 7.3. These tax rates for each country are taken from the zero-inflation column of the first table of results in each country chapter. The

Table 7.3   Actual Effective Tax Rates for
Each Country with Zero Inflation, Fixed-p Case
(actual depreciation, actual weights)

	United Kingdom	Sweden	West Germany	United States
Asset				
Machinery	− 24.2	− 18.1	38.1	3.9
Buildings	41.5	28.9	42.7	35.4
Inventories	50.5	26.5	57.7	50.9
Industry				
Manufacturing	− 1.7	8.1	44.7	44.2
Other industry	4.6	29.6	50.8	10.0
Commerce	46.8	12.1	44.6	37.9
Source of finance				
Debt	− 29.6	− 12.9	12.1	− 2.0
New share issues	7.6	44.2	56.1	61.0
Retained earnings	23.5	40.9	72.0	48.4
Owner				
Households	26.6	57.1	59.7	44.1
Tax-exempt institutions	− 5.1	− 39.2	17.6	4.0
Insurance companies	8.7	− 16.0	14.6	4.0
Overall	12.6	12.9	45.1	32.0

columns for the United Kingdom and Sweden demonstrate that these two countries not only start at the same overall 13 percent effective tax rate with no inflation, but also start with very similar tax rates on particular combinations. Machinery is subsidized in both countries, because of accelerated or immediate depreciation, and other assets are taxed. Debt is subsidized in both countries, because of interest deductions at the corporate level, and other sources of finance are taxed. Tax-exempt institutions are subsidized, and households are taxed.

There, however, the similarity ends. Table 7.4 shows, for each combination in each country, the differential effect of inflation. Each entry shows the addition (or subtraction) to the tax rate in that combination for an increase of inflation from 6 percent to 7 percent. Almost all the entries for the United Kingdom are negative, and almost all the entries for Sweden are positive. One percentage point of inflation reduces British taxes by one percentage point for machinery, by five points for debt, and by three points for tax-exempt institutions. The one point of inflation *raises* Swedish taxes by four points for inventories, by four points for insurance companies, and by five full points for households. It even increases the tax rate on debt by two percentage points.

Finally, we might also be interested in the variance of the effects of inflation within each categorization. Among owners in the United States,

Table 7.4   **Change in Effective Tax Rates for a Change in the Inflation Rate from 6 Percent to 7 Percent, Fixed-p Case**
(actual depreciation, actual weights)

	United Kingdom	Sweden	West Germany	United States
Asset				
Machinery	−1.0	2.0	0.5	1.8
Buildings	−0.2	0.9	−1.9	0.4
Inventories	−0.8	4.1	0.3	−0.5
Industry				
Manufacturing	−0.6	1.9	−0.1	0.8
Other industry	−0.7	3.3	0.2	0.4
Commerce	−0.8	2.7	−1.3	−0.2
Source of finance				
Debt	−5.2	2.0	−5.1	−2.0
New share issues	−0.9	4.8	0.7	4.3
Retained earnings	0.5	2.6	3.7	1.5
Owner				
Households	1.1	5.0	2.0	1.6
Tax-exempt institutions	−3.0	−1.6	−4.1	−4.5
Insurance companies	−1.1	4.2	−5.9	5.0
Overall	−0.6	2.4	−0.2	0.4

for example, an extra point of inflation adds five points to the tax rate on insurance companies and subtracts 4.5 points from the tax rate on tax-exempt institutions. This difference of 9.5 points is larger than the difference among owners in any other country. Britain has the smallest difference among owners. Among sources of finance, Germany has the largest differences (−5.1 for debt and +3.7 for retained earnings, for a difference of 8.8), and Sweden has the smallest. Among industries, Germany has the largest differences, and Britain has the smallest. Finally, among assets in each country, Sweden has the largest differences, and Britain the smallest. Thus, we conclude that, although inflation reduces overall taxes in Britain, it does so on a comparatively uniform basis.

7.3   Differences among the Four Countries

While the United States, United Kingdom, Sweden, and Germany show obvious differences in the tax treatments of different assets, they also differ in the relative stocks of each asset. The weighted-average tax rates differ for both these reasons. Second, while we have found clear differences in the way inflation affects tax rates in each country, there are also differences in actual rates of inflation. Tax rates differ for both these reasons as well. Finally, while new investments receive different grants and allowances in each country, they also have different actual rates of depreciation. They thus have differences in the rates at which reinvestment qualifies for new grants and allowances. This section investigates how much of the overall tax rate differences is attributable to tax law and how much is due, instead, to differences in the measured weights, inflation rates, or actual depreciation rates.

To perform this decomposition, we first recalculate tax rates for each country, using its own parameter values everywhere except for a common set of weights. We recalculate tax rates again with own parameters everywhere except for a common inflation rate, and then with own parameters except for a common set of actual depreciation rates. Finally, we recalculate tax rates for each country using its own tax parameters, but using common weights, inflation rates, and actual depreciation rates.

The choices for the common weights, inflation rate, or depreciation rates are essentially arbitrary. We might select the weights or rates from any one of the four countries, or we might apply to each country an average set of weights or rates. We do not wish to introduce a fifth set of weights, however, even if it is an average of the four countries, because such parameters would not reflect any actual experiences. Instead, we select United States weights and rates for the standard of comparison.

Table 7.5 reflects results of the first simulation, which attempts to answer two questions. First, What would be the effective marginal tax rates in each country if they all had the United States mix of assets, industries, sources of finance, and owners? Second, or conversely, How much of existing tax rate differences are attributable to different weights on each category? If all countries provided the same relative tax treatments to different assets, industries, sources, or owners, then we would not expect taxes to cause differences in the distribution of capital among those components. If relative tax treatments differ, however, then we might expect substitution among production processes to allow relatively more use of a particularly tax-favored asset, more output of a tax-favored industry, more finance through a tax-favored source, or more savings channeled through a pension fund, insurance company, or other particularly tax-favored ownership category. Since there are these differences among countries, we might expect the switch to a common set of weights in each case to put less weight on particular tax-favored investments and thus to raise the overall average tax rate.[5]

The fourth column of table 7.5, for the United States, is identical to that of table 7.1. Since weights for the United States have not changed, the overall rate is still 37 percent in the fixed-p case. The overall rate for

5. Tax rates for Britain, Sweden, and Germany rise as expected in table 7.5 when those countries are given weights from the United States. In other experiments, however, this result does not hold. When other countries are assigned the debt-intensive weights from Sweden, for example, some effective tax rates fall.

Table 7.5 **Effective Tax Rates for Each Country, with United States Weights, Fixed-_p_ Case**
(actual inflation, actual depreciation)

	United Kingdom	Sweden	West Germany	United States
Asset				
Machinery	−45.5	25.7	54.6	17.6
Buildings	24.8	58.4	52.5	41.1
Inventories	35.8	87.6	71.5	47.0
Industry				
Manufacturing	22.0	66.6	69.2	52.7
Other industry	−13.6	44.4	43.6	14.6
Commerce	24.8	59.8	54.3	38.2
Source of finance				
Debt	−84.1	29.4	2.1	−16.3
New share issues	46.9	109.6	63.2	91.2
Retained earnings	61.5	69.6	87.5	62.4
Owner				
Households	48.3	103.0	73.3	57.5
Tax-exempt institutions	−82.6	−65.2	31.6	−21.5
Insurance companies	−46.5	7.7	−9.1	23.4
Overall	11.6	58.0	57.5	37.2

Britain, however, has increased from 3.7 to 11.6 percent. This overall change results primarily from the fact that the United States has a much lower weight for machinery than does the United Kingdom, where machinery is subsidized. It is somewhat offset by the fact that the United States has more weight on debt, which Britain also subsidizes.

The overall tax rate in Sweden increases from 36 to 58 percent when United States weights are employed. Zero-taxed machinery is given less weight, low-taxed debt is given much less weight, and the highly taxed households are given relatively more weight. Moreover, because United States statistics include more privately owned utilities in the other industry category, this highly taxed sector is also assigned more weight with the United States proportions. In West Germany, the overall tax rises from 48 to 58 percent when United States weights are employed. Again, the "other industrial" sector plays a major role, because it is the most highly taxed sector in Germany, and its weights are the largest in the United States. Also, debt changes from a net subsidy to a tax, because relatively more of it is held by households in the United States. Individual components can be further investigated by considering the individual country weights as shown in Appendix A.

Thus, as expected, overall tax rates of all countries increase when common weights are employed. The differences, however, remain intact.

The spread actually increases from forty-four percentage points (the difference between 48.1 for Germany and 3.7 for the United Kingdom) to forty-six percentage points (the difference between 57.5 and 11.6 for the same two countries). According to these experiments, then, differences in weights by themselves do not account for any of the overall tax rate differences.

Next we turn to inflation. How much of the actual tax rate differences would remain if all countries had the same rate of inflation? This question can be answered by looking at the zero inflation column of each country's 1980 results table (brought together in table 7.3) or by looking at the 10 percent column of each 1980 results table. For consistency, in table 7.6, we look at the tax rates that would exist in each country with 6.77 percent inflation, the actual United States rate of inflation.

Again tax rates in the United States are the same as they were before. Tax rates in other countries rise or fall, as can be seen from figure 7.1. Since taxes in Britain fall with inflation, and since the United States inflation rate is less the United Kingdom rate, the 3.7 percent tax rate for Britain in table 7.1 rises to 8.9 in table 7.6. This overall change reflects smaller subsidies on machinery, debt, and tax-exempt institutions, as well as higher positive taxes on other categories. Since taxes in Sweden rise with inflation, and since the United States inflation rate is

Table 7.6 **Effective Tax Rates for Each Country with 6.77 Percent Inflation, Fixed-p Case**
(actual depreciation, actual weights)

	United Kingdom	Sweden	West Germany	United States
Asset				
Machinery	−30.2	−5.2	46.3	17.6
Buildings	42.0	33.9	38.9	41.1
Inventories	45.5	58.6	59.8	47.0
Industry				
Manufacturing	−4.8	22.1	48.2	52.7
Other industry	0.2	51.7	58.3	14.6
Commerce	42.2	32.2	41.8	38.2
Source of finance				
Debt	−64.6	−0.6	−15.4	−16.3
New share issues	2.1	77.8	64.6	91.2
Retained earnings	27.9	61.8	100.1	62.4
Owner				
Households	34.8	92.1	76.5	57.5
Tax-exempt institutions	−23.8	−47.7	−3.4	−21.5
Insurance companies	1.9	6.6	−18.2	23.4
Overall	8.9	29.5	47.9	37.2

less than the Swedish rate, the 35.6 percent tax rate in table 7.1 falls to 29.5 in table 7.6. Finally, note that the figure 7.1 tax rate curve for Germany reaches its highest point at a 5 percent rate of inflation and then starts to decline. Since the German inflation rate is 4.2 percent and the comparison here is at a rate of 6.77 percent, the overall tax rate is hardly affected. The flatness of that curve incorporates offsetting effects, however, so there is a higher tax on inventories and a lower tax on debt.

According to these experiments, then, some of the actual tax rate differences can be attributed to inflation-rate differences. The forty-four point spread in table 7.1 falls to a thirty-nine point spread in table 7.6 (47.9 for Germany minus 8.9 for the United Kingdom). This conclusion is not robust, however, as can be seen from figure 7.1. For any two countries in that diagram, tax rates may become more similar at one common inflation rate and less similar at a different common inflation rate.

Finally, we ask, How much of the differences in tax rates may be attributed to differences in actual depreciation rates? We have two reasons for addressing this question. First, we want to isolate differences attributable solely to tax law. Of course, the tax law can induce producers to alter the maintenance or type of particular assets employed. Second, each of our country chapters uses its own procedures to derive estimates of actual depreciation. These methodological differences might contribute to apparent effective tax rate differences.

Table 7.7 shows calculations for all countries when we use only United States depreciation rates. As shown in Appendix A, these rates for buildings are greater than those for Britain and Sweden but less than those for Germany. The United States rates for machinery are approximately in the middle of those for other countries but depend on industrial location. Substitution of these parameters serves to reduce the overall tax rates in Britain and Germany and slightly increase that in Sweden. The spread between the low rate of Britain and the high rate of Germany is essentially unchanged.

While these factors sometimes greatly affect individual combinations, we conclude that none has a major impact on the differences in overall tax rates among countries. In table 7.8, however, we take all these factors together and calculate effective tax rates when all countries have the same weights, inflation rates, *and* depreciation rates. Because these factors are not independent, they have more of an effect together than they do separately. Taken together, these factors increase the tax in Britain for two reasons: we use less weight on Britain's subsidized machinery, and we use a lower rate of inflation. The overall rate in the United Kingdom increases from 3.7 to 18.9 percent, while that in Germany increases only from 48.1 to 52.6 percent. The spread thus falls from 44.4 to 33.7 percent. These remaining differences can be attributed solely to tax law.

All the calculations above referred to the fixed-p case. In table 7.9 we show comparable calculations for the fixed-r case. When all countries have all their own parameters, fixed-r tax rates vary between the 30 percent rate for Britain and the 65 percent rate for Germany (as shown in table 7.2). When all countries have their own tax parameters but United States weights, depreciation, and inflation, fixed-r tax rates vary between 42 percent for Britain and almost 70 percent for Sweden (as shown in table 7.9). The spread thus falls from thirty-five points to twenty-eight points. Changes in the individual components of any country can be explained by arguments similar to those for the fixed-p case above.

7.4   Sensitivity to Assumed Rates of Return

In general, the measured effective tax rate depends on the assumed value for p or r in the fixed-p or fixed-r calculations. Are our estimates relatively robust to these choices, or do they depend greatly on the assumed rate of return? This section discusses the possible reasons for this dependence and then calculates different effective tax rates for different rates of return.

In a linear system, the tax is a constant fraction of the pretax return.

Table 7.7   **Effective Tax Rates for Each Country, with United States Depreciation Rates, Fixed-p Case**
(actual inflation, actual weights)

	United Kingdom	Sweden	West Germany	United States
Asset				
Machinery	− 42.2	− 0.8	40.3	17.6
Buildings	39.7	38.3	35.4	41.1
Inventories	39.5	68.8	59.0	47.0
Industry				
Manufacturing	− 13.5	27.2	44.5	52.7
Other industry	− 5.1	61.2	51.3	14.6
Commerce	36.1	39.7	39.2	38.2
Source of finance				
Debt	− 104.2	5.4	− 8.9	− 16.3
New share issues	− 6.6	90.6	59.0	91.2
Retained earnings	28.5	68.3	87.8	62.4
Owner				
Households	40.0	105.3	68.1	57.5
Tax-exempt institutions	− 47.5	− 51.4	0.9	− 21.5
Insurance companies	− 9.2	19.2	− 9.9	23.4
Overall	1.3	35.9	44.2	37.2

Thus the tax *rate* is independent of the pretax or posttax rate of return. In general, however, tax systems are not linear. The tax rate depends on the present value of depreciation allowances, which depends nonlinearly on the rate of return used for discounting. The importance of this point justifies some algebraic elaboration. In chapter 2, equation (2.23) provides a complicated expression for the pretax return (p) as a function of the corporate tax rate (τ), the firm's discount rate (ρ), the depreciation rate (δ), the present value of allowances (A), and other parameters. In order to focus on the main issue and to avoid unnecessary complications, we consider the case with LIFO accounting ($v = 0$), no corporate wealth taxes ($w_c = 0$), and no inflation ($\pi = 0$ or, equivalently, complete indexation for inflation). In this simple case, (2.23) reduces to

$$(7.1) \qquad p = \frac{(1 - A)}{(1 - \tau)}(\rho + \delta) - \delta.$$

Also in chapter 2, equations (2.24) to (2.27) provide expressions for the firm's discount rates when finance is obtained by debt, new share issues (NSI), and retained earnings (RE). If we take a classical corporate tax system ($\theta = 1$) and ignore capital gains taxes ($z = 0$), then these equations reduce to

Table 7.8   **Effective Tax Rates for Each Country, with 6.77 Percent Inflation, United States Depreciation, and United States Weights, Fixed-p Case**

	United Kingdom	Sweden	West Germany	United States
Asset				
Machinery	−37.3	19.0	53.8	17.6
Buildings	31.7	56.0	42.0	41.1
Inventories	43.3	76.7	75.4	47.0
Industry				
Manufacturing	21.0	60.9	69.3	52.7
Other industry	1.1	40.2	32.5	14.6
Commerce	37.4	53.5	48.2	38.2
Source of finance				
Debt	−45.0	22.0	−20.3	−16.3
New share issues	40.4	96.4	59.2	91.2
Retained earnings	52.4	65.9	92.2	62.4
Owner				
Households	43.3	92.5	73.3	57.5
Tax-exempt institutions	−43.6	−52.4	19.3	−21.5
Insurance companies	−19.8	−3.6	−37.2	23.4
Overall	18.9	52.6	52.6	37.2

Table 7.9   Effective Tax Rates for Each Country,
with 6.77 Percent Inflation, United States Depreciation,
and United States Weights, Fixed-r Case

	United Kingdom	Sweden	West Germany	United States
Asset				
Machinery	−61.5	30.1	69.2	26.4
Buildings	51.7	69.5	59.2	54.1
Inventories	51.1	81.5	79.3	54.5
Industry				
Manufacturing	43.3	78.7	77.8	61.2
Other industry	25.0	55.9	51.4	24.4
Commerce	54.7	68.3	64.9	48.8
Source of finance				
Debt	−114.5	27.4	−125.5	−72.5
New share issues	55.0	93.5	71.4	81.8
Retained earnings	64.5	88.2	86.6	66.5
Owner				
Households	63.9	120.7	84.8	73.4
Tax-exempt institutions	−33.5	−65.2	39.7	−21.3
Insurance companies	−14.0	−6.0	−45.3	22.4
Overall	42.3	69.8	68.4	49.9

(7.2)
$$\begin{aligned}
\rho_{DEBT} &= r(1 - \tau)\\
\rho_{NSI} &= r\\
\rho_{RE} &= r(1 - m),
\end{aligned}$$

where m is the personal tax rate. The real interest rate r is equal to the nominal rate i, since inflation is assumed to be zero here. Finally, the saver's posttax real rate of return in equation (2.6) reduces to

(7.3) $s = r(1 - m).$

With these formulas, for any source of finance we can calculate the effective tax rate $t = (p - s)/p$. Starting with r, for example, we have s and ρ directly as linear functions. In general, however, the present value term A is not a linear function of ρ, so the tax is not linear in r. Similarly, if we start with a value for p, we can generally find a value for ρ that is consistent with equation (7.1). However, it also will depend nonlinearly on the initial p chosen. The tax rate remains a nonlinear function of p.

    Suppose, however, that there are no cash grants or immediate expensing ($f_2 = f_3 = 0$), and that depreciation allowances are equal to economic depreciation at replacement cost. In this case, the present value of allowances is

(7.4) $$A = A_d = \tau \int_0^{\infty} \delta e^{-(\delta + \rho)u} du = \frac{\tau \delta}{\delta + \rho},$$

and equation (7.1) reduces simply to

(7.5) $$p = \frac{\rho}{1 - \tau}.$$

Now the three effective tax rates reduce to

(7.6)
$$t_{\text{DEBT}} = m$$
$$t_{\text{NSI}} = \tau + m(1 - \tau)$$
$$t_{\text{RE}} = \tau.$$

That is, interest is deductible at the corporate level, so the return to debt is taxed only at the personal rate m. The return to equity is taxed only at the corporate rate τ if it is retained, but the after-tax profits are taxed again at the personal rate if the earnings are distributed.

Equations (7.6) make clear that these effective tax rates do not depend on p or r. The system is linear in that the tax is a constant fraction of any pretax return. Our effective tax rate formulas provide global estimates of the tax rate, in either the fixed-p case or the fixed-r case, for any initial p or r.

In our example above, linearity depends upon the assumption of economic depreciation at replacement cost.[6] Actual tax systems conform neither to an income tax on properly measured income nor to a consumption tax. In particular, depreciation allowances are often accelerated relative to economic depreciation. Because these tax advantages are delayed, the effective tax rate depends on their present value and thus nonlinearly on the rate of discount. For these reasons, there is no such number as *the* effective tax rate. Different estimates are obtained for different values of p and r. It is very important, therefore, to investigate the sensitivity of results to the initial p or r. For reasons of space, we limit this investigation to the standard 1980 parameters in each country. We also limit the investigation to one example, machinery in the manufacturing sector. Our sensitivity analysis should consider the most sensitive case, and machinery has differentially accelerated depreciation allowances. It is therefore expected to exhibit some of the greatest nonlineari-

6. Auerbach and Jorgenson (1980) suggest a "first-year recovery" system where the investor receives only an immediate deduction, equal to the present value of actual depreciation on the asset. All internally financed investments are then subject to a uniform tax rate τ, from equation (7.6). This is not the only linear tax system, however. At the other extreme, immediate expensing in our simple case provides a uniform rate of zero on all internally financed assets. Brown (1981) suggests that any uniform rate between zero and τ can be obtained by providing a common rate of grant that is proportional not to the purchase price of the asset, but to the purchase price minus the first-year deduction.

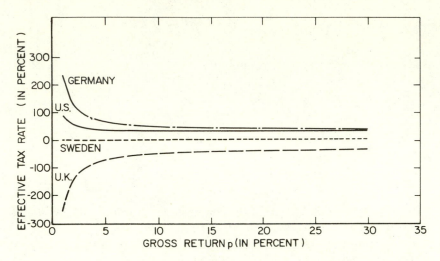

Fig. 7.2   Effective tax rate on machinery as p varies in each country.

ties. We weight over owners and sources of finance to calculate the total tax wedge or tax rate on the "average" investment in manufacturing machinery in each country.

Figure 7.2 plots, for each country, the effective tax rate on machinery as the pretax return varies from 1 to 30 percent. These calculations are for the fixed-p case, and the firm's discount rate is linked by our formulas to this pretax return. For machinery in the United Kingdom, immediate expensing means that the discount rate does not affect the present value of depreciation allowances, but additional grants ensure that the asset receives a subsidy at *any* pretax return. When this subsidy is expressed as a fraction of a 1 percent pretax return or less, the rate of subsidy becomes arbitrarily large. Because the rate of tax or subsidy is misleading in such cases, we also show the tax wedge in figure 7.3. As the pretax return becomes small, the negative wedge in Britain is reduced in absolute size, although it becomes a larger fraction of p.

In Sweden, as we see in table 7.1, the total tax on the average new investment in machinery is approximately zero. The wedge $(p - s)$ is zero, so the wedge as a fraction of p is also zero. As a result, the curves for Sweden in figures 7.2 and 7.3 are rather flat at a zero value for the tax rate.

To interpret the curves for Germany and the United States, consider first a hypothetical case with no inflation but with accelerated depreciation and investment grants. When the pretax return is relatively low, the discount rate is also relatively low, and the delayed depreciation allowances are more important. A subsidy may result in such a case, and it may be an arbitrarily high fraction of p. As p (or the discount rate) increases,

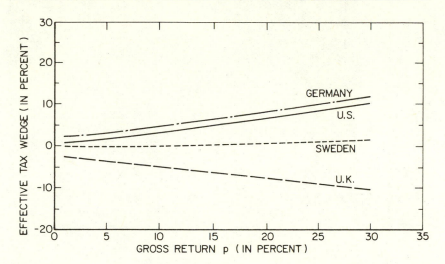

Fig. 7.3   Effective tax wedge ($p - s$) on machinery as p varies in each country.

depreciation allowances become less important, and the tax may rise to zero or above. In such a case, the curve would look like that of the United Kingdom.

With significant inflation, as in the United States, or with long asset lifetimes, as in Germany, depreciation allowances on historical cost may be less than economic depreciation at replacement cost. In such cases the tax wedge may be positive, and it may be an arbitrarily high fraction of a very small p. Moreover, as p (or the discount rate) increases, the disadvantageous depreciation allowances become less important, and the effective tax rate falls. Figure 7.3 shows that the tax wedges in the United States and Germany are small at low p, even if they are a high fraction of p as shown in figure 7.2.

An important aspect of figures 7.2 and 7.3 is that the curves do not cross. At actual inflation rates and standard 1980 parameters, the choice of p does not affect the conclusion that the highest tax rates are in Germany, followed by the United States, Sweden, and the United Kingdom. Moreover, while the amount of tax naturally increases with the earnings from the asset, as shown in figure 7.3, the tax rate curves of figure 7.2 have large segments that are fairly flat. Beyond some critical value of p, the tax rate is not much affected by further changes in p. Our standard calculations use a p of 10 percent, clearly beyond this critical point.

Similar analyses are performed for the fixed-r methodology in figures 7.4 and 7.5. Curves for Germany and the United States are very similar to those for the fixed-p case above. In Sweden, the fixed-r calculation

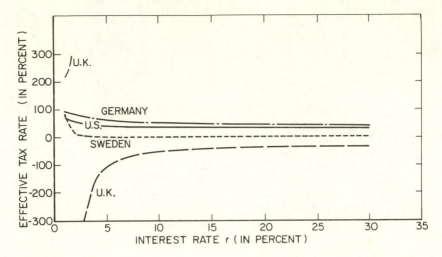

Fig. 7.4   Effective tax rate on machinery as *r* varies in each country.

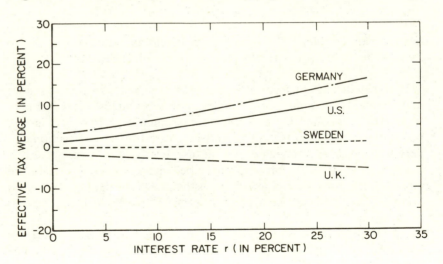

Fig. 7.5   Effective tax wedge ($p - s$) on machinery as *r* varies in each
                       country.

implies a small positive wedge for machinery in manufacturing.[7] When *r* is
1 percent in this case, the value of *p* is only 0.1 percent. A small denominator makes the tax rate misleadingly high.

For the United Kingdom, figure 7.5 demonstrates that machinery is
clearly subsidized at any value for *r*. As *r* is reduced to about 2 percent,
however, the subsidy ($p - s$) becomes equal to the whole return to the

7. Table 7.2 shows a small subsidy for machinery in Sweden when *r* is fixed at 5 percent,
but that calculation considers an average over all industries, sources, and owners. Here,
when we look at machinery only in manufacturing, we have a small positive tax at any value
for *r*.

saver (s). Since the government provides the saver's entire return, the asset need earn nothing. The pretax return p is zero, and the subsidy rate $(p - s)/p$ is not defined. At even lower values for r, the subsidy is even larger than the saver's return, and the asset can make a loss. A negative wedge $(p - s)$ divided by a negative p implies a positive rate in spite of the subsidy.

We need a common standard for comparing taxes on different assets or in different countries. The tax-inclusive effective rate $(p - s)/p$ is a logical candidate, because it corresponds to our general conception of a tax rate and because it reduces to the statutory rate in special cases. Because p can be zero or negative, however, this rate is sometimes not useful for drawing comparisons. The tax-exclusive rate $(p - s)/s$ is a logical alternative, but the next section describes cases where s can be zero or negative as well. Both rates are subject to misleadingly wide variations when their denominators are close to zero. The remaining alternative is to report the tax wedge $(p - s)$; in this case we do not have a denominator. This effective tax measure always has the "correct" sign, and it can be interpreted as a wealth tax rate, the percentage of the asset value paid in tax each year. As the earnings of the asset increase in figures 7.3 and 7.5, so does the amount of tax or subsidy. The tax wedge thus appears to be sensitive to higher rates of return, but this is a consequence of the fact that the tax *rates* level off in figures 7.2 and 7.4.

These diagrams demonstrate clearly the nonlinear aspects of our effective tax formulas. The tax rates in figures 7.2 and 7.4 are particularly nonlinear because p appears in the denominator. Even the tax wedges in figures 7.3 and 7.5 are nonlinear, however, because p is a nonlinear function of r. Both wedges and rates are sensitive to the choice of p or r, so care must be taken in their interpretation.

One other interesting result can be explained with the use of the equations given above. It turns out that the effective tax rate is related *inversely* to the personal tax rate m in some instances. In the United States, for example, the effective tax rates in some categories are raised by the use of "low tax" parameters or reduced by the use of "high tax" parameters. In particular, the effective tax rate on retained earnings is 67 percent with the low value for m, 62 percent with the standard value for m, and only 58 percent with the high value for m (see tables 6.20 and 6.23).

This result derives from the arbitrage assumption of chapter 2. In equilibrium, savers are assumed to require the same net-of-tax real return on any investment, in any asset or industry. Thus s is always given by the real net-of-tax interest rate, whatever source of finance is actually used. Consider an increase in the personal tax rate m on interest income. The value of s falls for a given r. Since equity does not actually pay the tax on interest income, however, the firm can earn a lower gross return on the asset and still provide a net return equal to that on interest income. In other words, the cost of capital for retained earnings falls. Whether the gross return p falls by more or less than the net return s depends on depreciation deductions. If depreciation allowances are not immediate, and the higher m implies a lower discount rate for the firm, then the present value of allowances rises. In this case the required return p falls by more than s, and the tax wedge is reduced. In effect, the increase in m raises the relative advantage of internal finance if capital gains are taxed at concessionary rates, and in some cases this can reduce the tax wedge on an investment project.

Consider, for example, the simple case with no inflation, no wealth taxes, no capital gains taxes, and no investment grants. Discount rates for this case are shown in equation (7.2), and the saver's return is shown in equation (7.3). With economic depreciation at replacement cost, the pretax return reduces to $\rho/(1 - \tau)$, as shown in equation (7.5). The total tax rate on debt is m, on new share issues is $\tau + m(1 - \tau)$, and on retained earnings is τ, as shown in equations (7.6). An increase in m thus raises effective tax rates for debt and new share issues but leaves unchanged the rate for retained earnings. With other than economic depreciation, however, the expression for the pretax return does not reduce to equation (7.5). To reduce the expression for p in a different way, suppose actual depreciation (δ) is zero. Then $A > 0$ represents "accelerated" depreciation, and a higher discount rate reduces the present value of depreciation allowances. With this alteration, the expression for the gross return p changes from (7.1) to

$$(7.7) \qquad p = \frac{\rho(1 - A)}{1 - \tau},$$

and the effective tax rate on retained earnings changes from τ to

$$(7.8) \qquad t = 1 - \frac{1 - \tau}{1 - A}.$$

Now a change in the personal tax rate m affects t for projects financed from retained earnings according to

$$(7.9) \qquad \frac{\partial t}{\partial m} = \frac{-(1 - \tau)}{[1 - A]^2} \cdot \frac{\partial A}{\partial \rho} \cdot \frac{\partial \rho}{\partial m}.$$

With $\rho = r(1 - m)$, the discount rate for retained earnings falls as m rises ($\partial \rho/\partial m \leq 0$). Since $\partial A/\partial \rho$ is negative, and τ is less than one, the effective tax rate also falls as m rises.

The effect on any single asset or industry depends on the share of retained earnings as a source of finance. In the countries studied here, other sources of finance are large enough that the overall effective tax rate does in fact increase with the personal tax rate.[8]

8. In an alternative methodology, Bradford and Fullerton (1981) assume that firms arbitrage between debt and real capital such that the net-of-tax return to the corporation is equalized. Since $r(1 - \tau)$ would be saved by retiring a unit of debt, the same must be earned

7.5 Sensitivity to Assumed Relation between Inflation and Interest Rates

In the fixed-r calculations above, we assume that arbitrage eliminates differences in net-of-tax interest rates, except for differences in personal tax rates among owners. In this case the same real interest rate r is earned on any investment. Because of tax differences, then, the pretax returns p must differ among investments. While we hold r constant across investments at any inflation rate, this assumption provides no guide to correct comparisons among inflation rates. There is no arbitrage story to be told here, and we are concerned simply with the choice of r at which to evaluate the tax rate. With a linear tax system the choice would not matter, but in practice nonlinearities necessitate an assumption to enable us to make comparisons for ceteris paribus changes in the rate of inflation. For this purpose we typically hold constant the average real rate of return to savers. (We could hold $i - \pi$ constant instead, but this real interest rate is relevant to only one saver, tax-exempt institutions.) This assumption implies a particular relation between the inflation rate and the nominal interest rate, and the purpose of this section is to investigate alternative assumptions about this relation.

In the fixed-r case, we may interpret r_F as the interest rate that would exist if there were no inflation. In such a case, the average posttax return to savers would be $\bar{s} = r_F(1 - \bar{m})$, where $\bar{m}$ is the weighted average of different owners' personal marginal tax rates. If inflation increased to the rate π, and the nominal interest rate rose to a value i, then in real terms the average saver would receive $\bar{s} = i(1 - \bar{m}) - \pi$. If the average real return to savers is to be constant across inflation rates, by assumption, then we must set these two expressions equal to each other and solve for the nominal interest rate as:

$$(7.10) \qquad i = r_F + \frac{\pi}{1 - \bar{m}}.$$

Because nominal interest is subject to tax, inflation must add more than point-for-point to the nominal interest rate for the real after-tax return to be constant. In our calculations above, we do not mean to claim that inflation does add more than point-for-point to nominal interest. Rather, equation (7.10) is a natural consequence of the standard we use for comparing across inflation rates.

Other standards might be employed, of course, and we now investigate their implications for our results. We stress, however, that the choice of

---

by a new investment in any asset using any source of finance. This net rate is always the firm's discount rate, so m cannot affect the gross return p. However, when the income from the asset is retained, distributed, or paid out in interest, different personal tax treatments imply that the net returns s must differ. Thus, when risk is ignored, one can assume either that individuals arbitrage away differences in s, or that firms arbitrage away differences in source of finance, but not both.

standard has nothing whatever to do with an empirical relationship between inflation and nominal interest rates. It merely determines the fixed value of r at which we evaluate effective tax rates. One alternative standard is to follow Fraumeni and Jorgenson (1980), who find a roughly constant real after-tax rate of return in the corporate sector. If corporations successfully arbitrage between bonds and real capital, then the real after-tax return they earn on an investment must be the same as the real net interest saved by retiring a bond, namely, $r_F(1 - \tau)$ with no inflation or $i(1 - \tau) - \pi$ with inflation at rate π. Assuming equality of these expressions across inflation rates implies

$$(7.11) \qquad i = r_F + \frac{\pi}{1 - \tau}.$$

Feldstein and Summers (1978), on the other hand, have estimated that inflation adds approximately point-for-point to nominal interest rates. This is described as the result of two countervailing forces within the tax system. Taxation of nominal interest tends to raise i by more than π to keep the real net return constant, while historical cost depreciation and taxation of nominal capital gains tend to reduce the real net return that can be earned. Summers (1981) makes a stronger statement, that nominal interest rates rise by at most the inflation rate, if at all. This empirical finding can be summarized as

$$(7.12) \qquad i = r_F + \pi.$$

In the absence of taxes, (7.12) would keep borrowing and lending opportunities independent of the rate of inflation. Since Irving Fisher originally considered the case without taxes, (7.12) has been referred to as "strict Fisher's law" (Bradford and Fullerton 1981). In a tax system where all nominal interest receipts are taxed at the rate τ and all nominal interest payments are tax deductible, (7.11) would keep real borrowing and lending opportunities independent of inflation. This relationship has been referred to as "modified Fisher's law." In the other relationship used above, equation (7.10), we account for varying tax rates on nominal interest income by keeping the average saver's opportunities independent of inflation. It can, of course, be thought of as a different modification to Fisher's law.

When inflation is zero, all versions of Fisher's law imply the same result. When inflation is positive, however, the choice among these standards has an effect on tax rate estimates. Table 7.10 shows overall tax rates for each country, using actual inflation and standard 1980 parameters (only the fixed-r case is presented). In the middle rows of table 7.10, where the standard assumption of equation (7.10) holds, the effective tax rates match those from table 7.2 above. In the bottom set of rows, where (7.11) holds, the effective tax rates in all countries are reduced. Because (7.11) holds constant the real return after corporate taxes, additional

Table 7.10   **Overall Tax Rates for Alternative Assumptions about the Effect of Inflation on Nominal Interest, Fixed-r Case**
(actual inflation, 1980 parameters, %)

		United Kingdom	Sweden	West Germany	United States
$i = r + \pi$	p	1.5	2.3	5.7	3.5
Equation (7.12)	s	0.7	−0.2	1.5	1.3
	$p - s$	0.8	2.6	4.2	2.2
	$(p - s)/p$	51.5	110.2	74.4	62.6
$i = r + \dfrac{\pi}{1 - \bar{m}}$	p	5.5	6.0	8.2	6.8
	s	3.9	2.8	2.9	3.4
Equation (7.10)	$p - s$	1.7	3.2	5.3	3.4
	$(p - s)/p$	30.0	53.6	64.8	49.9
$i = r + \dfrac{\pi}{1 - \tau}$	p	16.1	6.5	13.8	10.4
	s	12.1	3.2	6.0	5.8
Equation (7.11)	$p - s$	4.0	3.3	7.9	4.9
	$(p - s)/p$	24.9	50.8	56.9	45.7

inflation serves to *increase* the real return after personal taxes. To meet the higher required net return, assets must earn more before tax as well. The result is similar to consideration of figures 7.2 to 7.5, where higher rates of return imply lower tax rates.

In the top rows of table 7.10, where strict Fisher's law applies, effective tax rate estimates in each country are increased. Because inflation adds only point-for-point to nominal interest, and because nominal interest is fully taxable in these countries' tax systems, inflation reduces the real after-tax returns s (except for tax-exempt institutions). The assets need only earn a lower pretax return p. While the tax wedges ($p - s$) are all smaller, as shown in the table, division by small values of p implies higher tax as a proportion of gross returns. In fact, individual pretax returns are often negative under strict Fisher's law, so the use of effective tax rates presents more of a problem generally. We provide p and s separately in the table for this reason.[9]

With strict Fisher's law, the ordering of country tax rates is altered. Germany takes second place, and Sweden acquires the highest tax rate estimate. The inflation rate in Germany is low, however, so the taxation of nominal interest does not reduce s or p as much in that country as it does in Sweden. The high rate in Sweden reflects a low denominator, since the wedge is still higher in Germany.

To give an idea of how these assumptions might affect the breakdown of effective tax rates within a country, table 7.11 presents detailed results for the United States. For any individual combination, p is always lower

9. The choice among equations (7.10) to (7.12) also affects the relation between inflation and effective tax rates. While curves in figure 7.1 correspond to equation (7.10), similar curves could be plotted for each country under each alternative assumption.

Table 7.11 **Effective Tax Rates in the United States for Alternative Assumptions about the Effect of Inflation on Nominal Interest, Fixed-r Case** (actual inflation, 1980 parameters, %)

	$i = r + \pi$ Equation (7.12)			$i = r + \dfrac{\pi}{1 - \bar{m}}$ Equation (7.10)			$i = r + \dfrac{\pi}{1 - \tau}$ Equation (7.11)		
	p	s	t	p	s	t	p	s	t
Asset									
Machinery	2.0	1.3	32.9	4.7	3.5	26.4	7.9	5.9	25.6
Buildings	4.2	1.3	68.7	7.5	3.4	54.1	11.4	5.9	48.6
Inventories	3.2	1.2	62.1	7.3	3.3	54.5	12.0	5.7	52.1
Industry									
Manufacturing	4.4	1.1	75.3	8.2	3.2	61.2	12.5	5.5	55.9
Other industry	2.2	1.5	31.8	4.9	3.7	24.4	8.0	6.2	23.5
Commerce	3.3	1.4	58.6	6.9	3.5	48.8	11.0	6.0	45.7
Source of finance									
Debt	0.3	2.2	−769.9	2.7	4.6	−72.5	5.5	7.3	−32.7
New share issues	10.0	0.8	91.9	15.5	2.8	81.8	21.8	5.1	76.7
Retained earnings	4.7	0.8	82.7	8.4	2.8	66.5	12.7	5.1	60.1
Owner									
Households	3.6	0.1	98.0	7.1	1.9	73.4	11.1	3.9	64.5
Tax-exempt institutions	3.3	5.0	−49.8	6.7	8.1	−21.3	10.6	11.6	−10.1
Insurance companies	1.9	1.5	19.3	4.8	3.8	22.4	8.2	6.2	24.2
Overall	3.5	1.3	62.6	6.8	3.4	49.9	10.7	5.8	45.7

under strict Fisher's law (in the first column) than it is under either modified version of Fisher's law. The tax wedges ($p - s$) are also lower, but dividing by p provides tax rates that are higher. The subsidy for debt is so large that p is very close to zero, and the subsidy rate is misleadingly large. In fact, since further inflation reduces real net return still more under strict Fisher's law, calculations for 10 percent inflation imply that p is negative for the average debt-financed United States investment. The net return s is small but positive, so this subsidized investment would show a large positive tax "rate."

These sections have demonstrated that effective tax rates ($p - s$)/p may not be useful indicators of the total tax or subsidy on a given marginal investment. They are not very stable at low values of the pretax return, and they may even have the wrong sign. We recommend great care in their use and interpretation, and, in addition to the tax rate, we suggest using the tax wedge ($p - s$), which is more stable and always has the right sign.

7.6 Summary

We have tried in this chapter to present effective marginal tax rate calculations in a number of ways for each country. While these results depend fundamentally upon the basic methodology chosen for our study, they depend also on a number of additional assumptions. In particular, the results reflect our decision to look at the statutory provisions that determine the tax liability on a marginal investment in each combination of asset, industry, source of finance, and owner. The precise values of the estimated tax rates depend upon our choice of a given value for the pretax rate of return on all projects in the fixed-p case, and upon our choice for the interest rate earned on all projects in the fixed-r case.

Table 7.12 summarizes the major findings for each country. In the first row the tax rates refer to the fixed-p case, with a pretax annual return of 10 percent on all assets. In the second row they are based on a fixed real interest rate of 5 percent per annum for all assets. These fixed-r results are higher than the corresponding tax rates for the fixed-p case, but the ranking of the countries is the same. We find the highest overall effective tax rates in Germany, followed by Sweden, the United States, and the United Kingdom. As shown above, this ranking is unaffected by the values of p and r at which the tax rates are evaluated. As discussed in chapter 2, it is the fixed-p results that are more relevant for an analysis of the incentive to save and invest.

A major issue in all countries is the effect of inflation on effective tax rates. The overall effective tax rates for inflation rates between zero and 15 percent are plotted for each country in figure 7.1. The surprising result is that taxes in Sweden and the United Kingdom start out at a common 13

Table 7.12   **Summary of Overall Effective Tax Rates in Each Case**

Table Number	Case	United Kingdom	Sweden	West Germany	United States
7.1	Actual, fixed-p	3.7	35.6	48.1	37.2
7.2	Actual, fixed-r	30.0	53.6	64.8	49.9
7.3	Zero inflation, fixed-p	12.6	12.9	45.1	32.0
7.4	Change in t for change in π, fixed-p	−0.6	2.4	−0.2	0.4
7.5	With U.S. weights, fixed-p	11.6	58.0	57.5	37.2
7.6	With U.S. inflation, fixed-p	8.9	29.5	47.9	37.2
7.7	With U.S. depreciation rates, fixed-p	1.3	35.9	44.2	37.2
7.8	With U.S. depreciation, weights, and inflation, fixed-p	18.9	52.6	52.6	37.2
7.9	With U.S. depreciation, weights, and inflation, fixed-r	42.3	69.8	68.4	49.9

percent mean rate at zero inflation, but they diverge dramatically as inflation increases. Tax rates in Sweden rise with inflation, while those in Britain fall with inflation. In Germany, overall taxes rise initially because of historical cost depreciation, but they eventually fall as nominal interest deductions become more important at higher rates of inflation. The curve for the United States is similarly shaped, but tax rates level off only at a 15 percent inflation rate. At lower inflation rates, the effective marginal tax rates rise with inflation. The fourth row of table 7.12 shows the changes in taxes when inflation increases from 6 to 7 percent in each country.

We tried also to decompose tax rate differences into those attributable to differences in rates of inflation, the allocation of investment, and actual depreciation rates, as opposed to differences in tax parameters themselves. Table 7.12 summarizes these results, indicating that none of these differences taken by itself had a major influence on the spread of tax rates, but that in total they do have some influence. Effective tax rates are somewhat more equal among countries when only tax parameter differences remain.

A very important aspect of our study is not captured by any of these overall effective tax rate calculations. That is, the overall tax rates conceal a wide distribution of individual effective tax rates within each country. To summarize these differences in each country, figures 7.6 to 7.9 provide histograms for the actual inflation rate with 1980 parameters. For the height of each bar in the histogram, we add together the capital stock weights for any individual combinations that are taxed at effective rates falling in each 10 percent interval between −320 percent and +200 percent.

These bounds are chosen because at least one combination in the United Kingdom is taxed at a −312 percent rate. Appendix B shows the individual fixed-p tax rates for each combination, at each inflation rate, in each country. For actual inflation rates, the lowest tax rate anywhere is the −312 percent rate in Britain, for debt-financed machinery in the manufacturing sector, where the debt is held by tax-exempt institutions. At an annual inflation rate of 13.6 percent in the United Kingdom, a considerable inflation premium in the nominal interest rate is tax deductible at the corporate level, but for this combination it is not taxed at the personal level. Machinery receives immediate expensing and in addition qualifies for a cash grant. At the other extreme, Appendix B shows a +130 percent rate on an internally financed investment in other industrial buildings in the United Kingdom, where the equity is held by households. Buildings receive only straight-line depreciation, and other industry receives smaller grants than manufacturing. Because of disparate tax treatments of different assets, industries, sources, and owners, figure 7.6 shows a relatively flat distribution of tax rates in Britain. They extend from −312 to +130 percent, with no more than 12 percent of the capital stock taxed within a single ten-point interval. This implies a very high variance of marginal tax rates.

A similarly flat distribution is shown for Sweden in figure 7.7. Again, no more than 12 percent of the capital stock is taxed at rates falling within any ten-point interval. In this case, however, the rates range from −116 to +144 percent. The investment with the lowest tax rate is a machine in "other industry" financed by bonds sold to tax-exempt institutions. Although the 11.4 percent grant and 30 percent exponential depreciation allowances are the same for machinery in all sectors, machinery in other industry was found to have the highest true rate of economic deprecia-

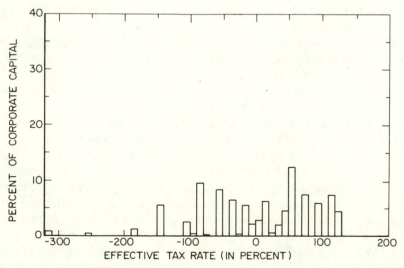

Fig. 7.6   Proportion of investment taxed at each rate in the fixed-*p* case for the United Kingdom.

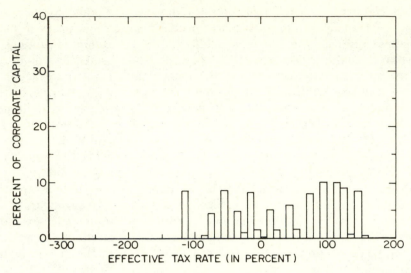

Fig. 7.7   Proportion of investment taxed at each rate in the fixed-*p* case
                     for Sweden.

tion. Reinvestment qualifies for grants at a faster rate, so this asset has the
lowest total tax rate. Other combinations with tax rates less than − 110
percent bring the total weight for that interval up to almost 10 percent of
total capital in Sweden. The investment with the highest total tax is a
building in other industry financed by issuing new shares to households.
The Annell deduction in Sweden did not fully mitigate double taxation of
dividends in 1980, so earnings on such an investment are taxed by both
the corporate and the personal tax systems.

West German investments are taxed at a much narrower spread of
rates, as shown in figure 7.8. The lowest tax rate is only − 59 percent, on a
building in manufacturing financed by debt issued to tax-exempt institutions. Machinery in Germany receives relatively long eleven-year tax
lifetimes, as well as a wealth tax rate that is higher than that on buildings.
Interest deductions make the lower building tax rates negative. At the
other end, the highest rate is "only" 102 percent, on inventories financed
internally through equity held by households. (This rate is identical for all
industries.) Inventories receive the highest tax rate because of unfavorable inflation accounting practices required for tax purposes, and internal
finance receives the highest tax rate because of taxation at both corporate
and personal levels. Dividends, on the other hand, receive imputation
credit at the personal level for corporate tax already paid.

Unlike the United Kingdom and Sweden, Germany and the United
States have most of their capital stock taxed at rates between zero and 100
percent. Figure 7.9 shows that nearly 30 percent of United States capital
is taxed at rates between 80 and 90 percent. Because another 30 percent

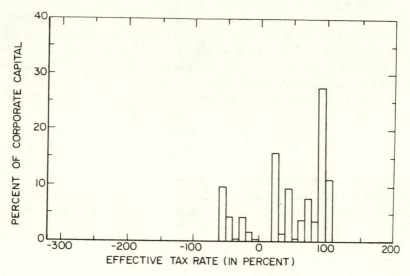

Fig. 7.8   Proportion of investment taxed at each rate in the fixed-p case
for West Germany.

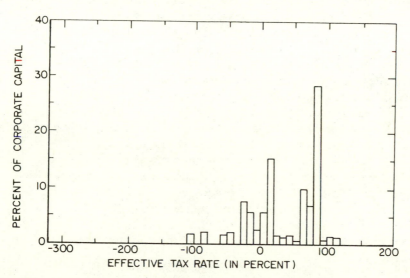

Fig. 7.9   Proportion of investment taxed at each rate in the fixed-p case
for the United States.

of United States capital is taxed at rates between -30 and $+20$ percent,
and because rates extend down to -105 percent, the weighted-average
marginal tax rate is found to be 37 percent in this fixed-p case. As in all
other countries, the least-taxed investment in the United States is
financed by debt sold to tax-exempt institutions, but in this case the asset
is machinery used in the commercial sector. This asset receives lower

grants in commerce and the same depreciation allowances in all sectors, but the faster actual depreciation rate in commerce means that reinvestment qualifies for those tax advantages more often. The highest tax rate in the United States is $+111$ percent, on buildings financed by new shares sold to households, in either manufacturing or commerce. Buildings receive less-accelerated depreciation allowances, while dividends are fully taxed at both corporate and personal levels.

In general, we find that the histograms in figures 7.6 to 7.9 provide much more useful information than individual overall tax rates in each of the four countries studied.

These disparate tax treatments in each country would be eliminated under a comprehensive income tax—that is, with full integration of corporate and personal tax systems, economic depreciation at replacement cost, no special grants or incentives, no wealth taxes, full indexing, and the full taxation of accrued real capital gains. In such a case, all investments would be taxed at the weighted-average personal tax rate. For comparison purposes, in table 7.13, we calculate this marginal personal tax rate in each country, taking weighted averages over household rates on debt and on equity. In order to capture a comprehensive tax concept, we do not include tax-exempt institutions or insurance companies, nor do we reduce personal rates to account for returns earned in the form of tax-free banking services. The United States, the United Kingdom, and West Germany are very close together, at 43–44 percent tax rates, and Sweden is at a 57 percent rate. Histograms under such a hypothetical comprehensive income tax would collapse to a vertical line at the country's single tax rate, applied to 100 percent of the capital stock. Under a comprehensive consumption or expenditure tax, the histograms would collapse to a vertical line at a tax rate of zero.

We do not mean to imply that countries could easily switch to a comprehensive income tax, or that to do so would be desirable. Rather, these calculations demonstrate another striking contrast: the overall effective rate in Britain is a full forty percentage points below the average marginal personal rate, the overall effective rate in Sweden is twenty-one points below the average personal rate, the effective rate in the United

Table 7.13   Comparison with a Comprehensive Income Tax
                    (%)

	United Kingdom	Sweden	West Germany	United States
Weighted-average personal rate on debt and equity (m)	44.0	57.3	44.4	43.1
Overall effective rate (t)	3.7	35.6	48.1	37.2
Difference ($m - t$)	40.3	21.7	−3.7	5.9

Source: Own calculations as described in the text.

States is six points below the personal rate, and the effective rate in West Germany is several points *above* the personal rate. Our four countries are quite different in this respect.

Finally, we might naturally ask about the implications of these effective tax rates for economic growth in each country. Clearly, this is not a study about comparative capital formation, income growth, or living standards in the four countries. We have attempted to measure effective marginal tax rates in each country in a number of ways, but we have not tried to use these estimates to measure effects on growth, excess burdens, or income distribution. Nevertheless, it is interesting to look at some summary growth statistics in light of our tax rate findings. To this end, the bottom row of table 7.14 reproduces our standard 1980 fixed-*p* overall effective tax rates, and the top rows show two average annual growth rates in constant dollars from 1960 to 1980 in each country. The first growth rate is for GDP, and the second is for the nonfinancial corporate capital stock, excluding inventories.

The results are surprising to say the least. If we rank the four countries by their average annual growth in GDP, we obtain exactly the same order as when we rank by 1980 effective tax rates. West Germany has the highest overall effective tax on income from capital *and* the highest growth rate. The United States is second in both categories, and Sweden is third. The United Kingdom has the lowest overall effective tax on income from capital *and* the lowest growth rate. If we look at growth of nonfinancial corporate capital, results are substantially the same. The United States and Sweden are reversed, but Germany is still the highest and Britain is the lowest.

Table 7.14   **Comparison with Alternative Growth Rates**
                               (%)

	United Kingdom	Sweden	West Germany	United States
Average annual growth of GDP in constant prices (1960–80)	2.3	3.2	3.7	3.5
Average annual growth of nonfinancial corporate capital in constant prices (1960–80)	2.6	4.7	5.1	3.7
Weighted standard deviation of 1980 tax rates	86.2	82.9	53.5	52.5
Coefficient of variation	2314.9	232.7	111.2	140.9
Overall effective tax rate				
1960	53.8	33.9	52.5	48.4
1970	33.6	41.6	49.1	47.2
1980	3.7	35.6	48.1	37.2

Source: United Kingdom: Blue Book. Sweden: National accounts. Germany: Bundesbank and Statistical Office. United States: *Survey of Current Business*.

Nothing here should be construed to imply causation in either direction. It is certainly possible that the slower-growing countries have reacted to their slow growth by providing more investment incentives that reduce overall effective taxes. As can be seen in the bottom three rows of the table, tax rates have changed over time, in some cases markedly. For example, tax rates in the United Kingdom were very high in 1960 but have fallen dramatically since then. This reduction in rates may lead to higher investment in the future than would otherwise have taken place. It is also possible that high growth is associated with high taxes on capital if these taxes are somehow less distorting than alternative taxes on labor income.[10]

Table 7.14 also shows the weighted standard deviation of 1980 effective tax rates in each country. This is a measure of the dispersion of rates that can be seen in each of the histograms discussed above. If this standard deviation is divided by the mean of the distribution (the overall effective tax rate) and expressed as a percentage, we have the coefficient of variation in the next row of the table.

Another startling result is the ordering of countries according to these coefficients of variation. Britain has the highest variation of tax rates on different combinations *and* the lowest growth from 1960 to 1980. Sweden is second for both parameters, and the United States is third. Germany has the lowest coefficient of variation and the highest overall growth.[11]

These correlations do not, of course, prove that diverse effective tax rates inhibit growth. Rather, the correlations in table 7.14 are interesting in themselves. They suggest many possible interpretations and hypotheses, some of which will, we hope, be investigated further and tested using the estimates of tax rates and data on individual countries that we have produced in the course of this study.

10. See Fullerton and Gordon (1983) for some elaboration and testing of the idea that replacement of capital taxes with a labor tax of equal yield can provide a welfare gain.
11. Harberger (1966), of course, suggests that varying effective tax rates cause capital misallocations and inefficient production. These could reduce overall growth. For this purpose, however, the standard deviations are more meaningful than the coefficients of variation.

8   Conclusion

The first seven chapters of this book have discussed at some length the tax systems of four industrialized Western countries. We have provided information on tax rates and tax rules applicable to different forms of investment in each country, a theoretical framework for organizing the analysis of these tax rates and rules, information on the allocation of capital in each country, and a summary of all this information in the form of effective rate calculations. Although we set out the goals of this exercise explicitly at the beginning of the book, it is easy for the reader to become lost in the detail of tax law and discussion of special cases. In this final chapter we place our results in perspective and reflect on the lessons of the project.

The objective of the study was descriptive: to characterize the taxation of income from capital in the four countries we studied. Our interest is in the way taxes affect the incentive to save and invest via the corporate sector. If the tax rules provided for an accounting system that measured "income" according to the economist's conception of the net return from investing, and if that income were taxed according to a single schedule, our task would have been easy. We need only have looked up the tax rates in the statute books.

Instead, the taxation of the return to investment is governed in all four countries by extremely complex rules. The primary basis for taxation is "income" in name only. Taxes intervene between the social yield on an investment and the return obtained by the saver, and these taxes are influenced by a variety of provisions that diverge widely from those required to tax real income. Some divergences are explicitly designed to encourage investment. Others reflect particular political interests. Still others arise from the sheer practical difficulty of identifying and measuring income, especially in a time of inflation.

8.1   Methodology

We conceive of the process of saving and investing in terms of double-entry accounts. Each act of investing must be associated with an act of saving (public or private) in equal amount. As assumed in this study, the relevant saving is restricted to private domestic sources. Under a genuine income-based system, the rate of tax applicable to a given "package" of saving and investment would depend at most upon the identity of the saver (because of graduated rates). In practice, however, the tax also depends upon the asset being acquired, the industry in which the asset is used, and the particular form of financing the transaction.

To deal with this complexity, we identified a relatively small number of types to represent the possible variations in each dimension. Thus, for example, assets are considered to be of three possible types that differ in the time path of associated cash flows. Each of the three types was chosen to approximate the actual characteristics of a practically important asset class (specifically machinery, buildings, and inventories).

Similarly, we defined three classes of industries (corresponding to manufacturing, commerce, and "other industry"), three types of finance (corresponding to debt, new share issues, and retained earnings), and three groups of savers (corresponding to households, tax-exempt institutions, and insurance companies). We can imagine a strand of transactions running from each type of saver via each financing mode to acquisition of each type of asset in each industry. We refer to each strand as a project type. The classification scheme thus depicts the corporate economy as a bundle of eighty-one distinct types of projects.

To describe the impact of taxation on each of the eighty-one projects, we employ an effective tax rate. One finds in the literature several different concepts of effective tax rates. In this study we use the term to describe the effect of taxes on a prospective or marginal investment (as distinguished from a measure of taxes paid on historically given capital stocks). The basic elements are a pretax rate of return on the project, denoted p, and the after-tax rate of return, s, received by the saver after all intervening taxes have been withdrawn from the flow. The difference between p and s is the effective tax "wedge," and the ratio of the difference to the pretax return is the notion of effective tax rate most widely used here. Because the measure takes into account all taxes on a marginal investment, a more precise term would be "marginal effective total tax rate."

8.1.1   The Fixed-p and Fixed-r Approaches

Chapter 2 describes in detail the procedures by which we determined the paired values of p and s for each of the eighty-one projects. We shall not attempt to summarize that discussion here; rather, let us remind the reader of the two basic conceptual approaches. The first, and probably easier to grasp, we called the "fixed-p" method. Here the starting point is an assumed value for p, the social rate of return on each hypothetical project. For this purpose we typically used a 10 percent real return per annum. The value of s for a project is the maximum return that could be provided to the specified saver in view of the tax provisions applicable to an asset of the specified type used in the specified industry and financed in the specified way.

The effective tax rates calculated in this way give a useful measure of the incentive or disincentive effect of taxes on the various investment projects. To have a measure that indicates the ratio of the tax wedge to the pretax return that actually obtains, however, it is necessary to take into account the response of investment and of pretax returns to the taxes themselves. An investment credit on one project type, for example, results in an incentive to pursue that type until its before-tax rate of return is below the level obtaining on other project types. In an actual equilibrium, then, we would not observe the same before-tax rate of return on all eighty-one projects. Because effective tax rates are typically sensitive to the magnitude of the before-tax rate of return, the picture we obtain of a tax system will depend somewhat on the extent to which we take into account such general equilibrium reactions.

The "fixed-r" approach represents an attempt to deal with this problem. The symbol r stands for the real rate of interest on debt. The fixed-r approach describes the values of p and s that would obtain if each saver received the same after-tax real return on each project as on a bond having a prespecified real interest rate (typically 5 percent per annum).

It is not clear, however, that this assumption is consistent with a general equilibrium based on individual optimizing behavior. When tax rates differ from one project to another, it may be necessary to impose some constraints to ensure that an equilibrium exists. The tax code contains many such constraints. For any particular set of constraints we may define an equilibrium. If the weights for each project implicit in that equilibrium correspond to the weights based on observed shares used here, then the tax rate in the fixed-r case is the tax rate relevant to an assessment of the welfare costs imposed by the tax system. To illustrate the difficulty of defining an arbitrage equilibrium, consider the following example.

There are differences in the tax treatment at the personal level between the return on an investment financed by retained earnings (which takes the form of capital gains) and the return on an investment financed by debt or new shares (which takes the form of interest or dividend income). These differences mean that if the after-tax returns are equal for one ownership category, they will not be equal for another. To illustrate, suppose a firm is providing a 12 percent return, on both its bonds and its common stock, to a tax-exempt saver. Suppose also that the common stock return is in the form of accruing capital gain. A different saver, one who is taxed at a higher rate on interest than on capital gains, will earn a higher after-tax return on that firm's stock than on its bonds. We would expect, therefore, that investors would specialize in particular securities according to their marginal tax rate, although we do not observe anything like complete specialization in practice.

The difficulties encountered here are representative of those facing the analyst equipped with an imperfect model of capital market equilibrium. The fixed-r analysis should be read as a measure of the additional taxes that will be paid taking into account the market response to incentives.

Most readers will probably find the fixed-p approach the easier to follow because it measures the tax schedule facing investors, and we have made most of our comparisons in terms of it. We should emphasize, however, that the effective tax rates differ under the two approaches. These differences suggest a degree of care when interpreting the results, and this warning is applicable to effective tax rate comparisons generally.

8.1.2   Behavioral Assumptions and Mean Rate Calculations

Recall that the essential objective is to *describe* tax systems. As long as we confine our attention to the individual project types, the analysis does not make severe demands on assumptions about the working of the economy. The effective tax rates tell us what rate of return could be provided to the saver, after all taxes, on an investment yielding a specified return before all taxes. To be sure, the relevance of such effective tax rates is dependent upon assumptions about the objectives of firms. The reason for studying effective tax rates is to understand the effect of tax laws on incentives and, through incentives, on behavior. It is at the stage of applying the effective tax rates that modeling assumptions become critical.

Applying the descriptive results presented in this study does require judgments or assumptions about the way the various projects—eighty-one of them—are tied together in the economy. To illustrate, one might be tempted to conclude that each class of saver would concentrate all of its savings in the single project type having the lowest effective tax rate. The implication would be a degree of portfolio specialization and investment composition that makes no empirical sense.

Comprehensive analysis of incentives challenges our understanding of capital markets. On the other hand, to confine our description to the eighty-one hypothetical projects would perhaps have been to be too agnostic about overall incentives. We resolved the issue by using weighted averages of the marginal effective tax rates. These averages answer a particular question: By how much would taxes increase if all the corporate assets in the economy were to increase by 1 percent? In posing the question this way we avoided the issue of whether such behavior would be economically sensible. We shall return briefly to this point below.

Based on this short recapitulation of our methodological approach, the reader who has begun with this chapter should be able to browse usefully through the book (with a little help from the glossary of notation at the front). Chapter 7 in particular contains summary comparisons of the four tax systems, together with brief explanations for the results displayed.

8.2   Principal Conclusions

What, then, are our major conclusions? The reader who is starting with this chapter may expect a summary judgment about the levels of taxation in each country as the most important result. In our view, however, the most significant acomplishment is the expression in reasonably manageable terms of the remarkably complex tax rules bearing on capital income in all four countries.

We knew at the outset that it would be difficult to develop a uniform method of comparing tax systems. We learned in the process that the matter is even more complex than we had expected. At the same time, substantial progress was made. The difficulty we anticipated was that of normalizing for nontax differences in the four economies. The tax systems in question are far from uniform in their treatment of particular transactions. Comparisons between tax systems are therefore potentially sensitive to the assumed projects to which the different tax rules are applied.

Our results confirm the importance of this point. In the fixed-p case, to take just one example, the overall average effective tax rates are: United Kingdom 3.7 percent, Sweden 35.6 percent, Germany 48.1 percent, and United States 37.2 percent when the four sets of national rules are applied to their own actual economic data. If, instead, we apply the tax laws of the four countries to the United States economy, we find the four overall tax rates to be: United Kingdom 18.9 percent, Sweden 52.6 percent, Germany 52.6 percent and United States 37.2 percent. Arguably the latter figures provide the better comparison of the tax rules by themselves, while the former give a better impression of the effect of the rules in action. The right figures to use depend upon the question being asked.

While our study indeed confirms the sensitivity of comparisons to assumptions, it also demonstrates the possibility of using the data we have collected to analyze alternative assumptions. The analytical framework makes it relatively simple to vary any assumed before-tax or after-tax return, any of the statutory provisions, or the size of any real or financial stock or flow.

It is natural for the reader to look for some summary statement about the levels of capital income taxation in the four countries. While we would emphasize that this depends upon the particular formulation of the question, we also bring away from the study the sense that capital income taxes are lowest on average in the United Kingdom at the same time that they are least uniform in the United Kingdom. Capital taxes are highest on average and most uniform in Germany.

More striking than any generalization about levels of taxation is the great variability observed across the eighty-one project types in any of the four countries. The variation can be grasped immediately by a glance at the histograms in figures 7.6 to 7.9. Economists will immediately recognize the potential for efficiency costs due to this lack of uniformity.

The country chapters describe the recent history of tax legislation in each country, finding considerable change over time in the tax rules applicable to various assets. The general trend in all four countries has been a "liberalization" of tax rules as applied to nominally defined income. This has typically taken the form of shortening asset lives on which depreciation allowances are based and enhancing investment grant provisions. Many observers have pointed to the interaction of inflation and an unindexed tax system as a possible rationale for these changes in tax law. This point is illustrative of the general proposition that the tax policy of a country needs to be seen in the context of prevailing conditions.

The 1980 effective tax rate calculations in this book should be viewed as a particular snapshot of the four tax systems. They reflect, of course, the particular tax rules in effect during that year. But their overall effect, as well as the objectives of their framers, can only be understood in relation to the particular expected inflation rate and the particular allocation of capital, both of which are in turn the outcome of historical forces.

Doubtless the effect of inflation on income accounting has much to do with the evolution of the four tax systems. The methods of this study allow us to see the practical importance of the proposition, well understood by economists, that ad hoc corrections are an imperfect substitute for indexing. The combined effect of inflation and tax rule change has generally been an increase in the dispersion of effective tax rates. Many rates have been dramatically lowered, while some have been just as dramatically raised. For all countries we found that an increase in inflation by itself would increase the dispersion of effective tax rates.

Because the various tax rules interact in significant ways, it can be very misleading to deal with a particular component in isolation. The corporate income tax, the personal income tax, and wealth and property taxes all impinge on the return to investment. Similarly, national, state, and local levies interact. Although the various layers tend to have an additive effect, sometimes one tax is ameliorated by its impact on another. For example, the effect of a wealth tax may be exaggerated if its deductibility under an income tax is neglected.

One particularly often encounters attempts to evaluate corporation income taxes in isolation. Our study shows clearly how misleading this may be. A low effective corporate tax wedge may be completely offset by a high effective personal tax wedge. A particularly interesting finding is that the corporate tax system, including investment tax credits and other incentives, often contributes little to the overall total effective tax wedge. In Britain, Sweden, and the United States after 1982, the corporate tax system actually reduces the overall wedge. At the same time it *does* contribute significantly to variations in effective tax rates among assets. In Britain,where machinery is allowed immediate expensing and interest is deductible, firms can use the resulting effective subsidy to offset any positive tax liability that is due on other investments. The result may be little combined revenue but considerable influence on the allocation of capital.

Some previous studies of different countries have compared the average tax rate—that is, the ratio of observed tax paid to observed capital income. Such a rate may be useful for measuring cash flow from capital owners to government, but it may not indicate much about the incentives for making new investment. Unanticipated inflation, for example, can increase the real cash flow of taxes on previous investments without necessarily affecting the expected tax on a new investment. Inflation acts as a lump-sum tax by reducing the real value of the depreciation allowances on existing capital. Furthermore, the cash flow of taxes paid in a given year reflects taxes on assets put in place in different years. If tax allowances have recently become more generous, for example, then the marginal tax rate can be expected to be less than the average tax rate. The United States chapter (section 6.4.4) summarizes some other reasons the marginal tax rate might differ from the observed average tax rate.

In making overall comparisons we looked at a marginal increase in the existing capital stock: a 1 percent increase in the existing allocation of assets, located among industries in the existing proportions of assets, financed in existing proportions for each source of finance and ultimately provided by ownership groups in proportion to existing holdings. It is for this reason that the four country chapters were careful to derive weights based on capital stocks, not on investment flows. Similarly, we looked at the market value of debt and the market value of equity to characterize the financial structure of our hypothetical increase in saving.

The margin we chose to analyze may not represent a realistic description of likely new investment in the four countries. The associated mean tax rates may not be the actual future taxes to be expected in a country which is changing the pattern of its capital stock. The data presented, however, especially the tables of effective tax rates for the eighty-one project types (in Appendix A), allow other analysts to substitute alternative investment weights and thereby answer other questions.

The tax rates calculated here, if used properly, can provide information about the misallocation of capital among assets within the corporate sector. In combination with other information on taxes in the noncorporate sector, our tax rates can be used to measure overall effects of taxes on the allocation of capital among all competing uses (corporate, other business, or residential). They can be used to shed light on the misallocation of savings among different vehicles (such as pensions, insurance, and direct ownership), and they can be used to help measure efficiency costs associated with the way taxes affect debt/equity choices, dividend payment decisions, and corporate financial policy in general. Because we have no explicit treatment of risk, however, these results cannot be used to measure other efficiency costs such as those associated with the allocation of risk bearing. They shed some light on intertemporal distortions, but because noncorporate investments are excluded our calculations do not by themselves provide information on the total or average wedge in the economy between the social marginal product of capital and the saver's ultimate return net of tax. The average social marginal product of capital in the economy would depend on the combination of corporate, noncorporate, public, and residential investments, while the saver's net of tax return, or rate of time preference, would have to be averaged over all those investments as well.

We might point out some particular complications that arise in using our effective tax rates or wedges (between the pretax return and the posttax return for each combination in a given country) to estimate the welfare costs of the misallocation of capital even within the corporate sector. Tax rates on different combinations are affected by different personal tax rates among different owners, and these differences do not necessarily imply anything about capital misallocations. To make the same point another way, the histograms in figures 7.6 through 7.9, if taken at a glance, probably overstate the differential effects of capital income taxation. Some of the variation just reflects the normal variation of rates among individuals.

If the corporate tax system did not discriminate among assets, industries, or sources of finance, and if there were ten ownership categories with equal holdings and ten different personal tax rates varying from zero to 90 percent, then the histograms would just show the uniform distribution of ownership among the ten ownership categories. Analysis of corporate capital misallocation (across asset types or industries) would, in such an instance, require controlling for differences in personal tax rates.

8.3   The Quest for Improved Equilibrium Models

The differences in personal tax rates found in this study are of a slightly different character from the ones in the example just described. While the ownership category "household" does have a different marginal rate from the ownership categories "tax-exempt institutions" and "life insurance companies," households are the indirect claimants on the other two. In the final analysis one would like to have an equilibrium theory rationalizing the picture of the economy revealed in the figures on asset composition, industry structure, financing methods, and ownership breakdown.

The development of such a theory is a matter requiring further study. The research reported here is intended as a contribution both to an increased awareness of how our tax systems actually work in practice and to the empirical modeling of taxes and the capital market. We hope that the results of our study will stimulate further theoretical analysis of equilibrium models with diverse tax rates, and that in turn this will lead to improved quantitative estimates of the impact of taxes. The interplay between theoretical and empirical investigation is crucial if research in this area is to shed light on the ways tax policy might be improved.

Appendix A

Standard Input Parameters for All Four Countries

Table A1 **Specific Tax and Inventory Parameters**

	United Kingdom	Sweden	West Germany	United States
τ	0.5200	0.349[a]	0.6200	0.4950
θ	1.4290	1.0000	2.2727	1.0000
π	0.1357	0.0940	0.0420	0.0677
v	0.0	1.0000	0.5000	0.0
Wealth tax rates (w_c)				
Machinery	0.0	0.0	0.0096	0.00768
Buildings	0.0246	0.0	0.0029	0.01126
Inventories	0.0	0.0	0.0096	0.00768

[a]Estimated at 9.4 percent inflation. See Swedish chapter, section 4.2.5.

Table A2   Tax Parameters, by Source of Finance

	United Kingdom			Sweden			West Germany			United States		
	Debt	New Shares	Retained Earnings	Debt	New Shares	Retained Earnings	Debt	New Shares	Retained Earnings	Debt	New Shares	Retained Earnings
Personal wealth tax rates (w_p)												
Households	0.0	0.0	0.0	0.006	0.017	0.017	0.005	0.005	0.005	0.0	0.0	0.0
Tax-exempt institutions	0.0	0.0	0.0	0.0	0.0	0.0	0.0	0.0	0.0	0.0	0.0	0.0
Insurance companies	0.0	0.0	0.0	0.0	0.0	0.0	0.007	0.007	0.007	0.0	0.0	0.0
Tax rates on interest (m)												
Households	0.3055	0.4500	0.4500	0.492	0.640	0.640	0.398	0.480	0.480	0.284	0.475	0.475
Tax-exempt institutions	0.0	0.0	0.0	0.0	0.0	0.0	0.0	0.400	0.400	0.0	0.0	0.0
Insurance companies	0.2328	0.1765	0.1765	$(.105 + 1.94\pi)$	$(.106 + 1.36\pi)$	$(.106 + 1.36\pi)$	0.028	0.028	0.028	$(.149 + 3.88\pi)$	0.069	0.069
Tax rate on capital gains (z_s)												
Households	0.2832	0.2832	0.2832	0.26	0.26	0.26	0.0	0.0	0.0	0.14	0.14	0.14
Tax-exempt institutions	0.0	0.0	0.0	0.0	0.0	0.0	0.0	0.0	0.0	0.0	0.0	0.0
Insurance companies	0.1765	0.1765	0.1765	$(.05 + 1.5\pi)$	$(.05 + 1.5\pi)$	$(.05 + 1.5\pi)$	0.0	0.0	0.0	0.28	0.28	0.28

Table A3 Parameters for Each Asset, by Industry

	United Kingdom			Sweden			West Germany			United States		
	Manufacturing	Other Industry	Commerce	Manufacturing	Other Industry	Commerce	Manufacturing	Other Industry	Commerce	Manufacturing	Other Industry	Commerce
Depreciation rates (δ)												
Machinery	0.0819	0.1535	0.0831	0.077	0.197	0.182	0.1566	0.1566	0.1566	0.1331	0.1302	0.1710
Buildings	0.0250	0.0250	0.0250	0.026	0.023	0.018	0.0456	0.0456	0.0456	0.0343	0.0304	0.0247
Inventories	0.0	0.0	0.0	0.0	0.0	0.0	0.0	0.0	0.0	0.0	0.0	0.0
Proportion immediate depreciation (f_2)												
Machinery	1.0	1.0	1.0	0.3	0.3	0.3	0.0	0.0	0.0	0.0	0.0	0.0
Buildings	0.5	0.5	0.01	0.0	0.0	0.0	0.0	0.0	0.0	0.0	0.0	0.0
Inventories	0.0	0.0	0.0	0.6	0.193	0.6	0.0	0.0	0.0	0.0	0.0	0.0
Proportion with later depreciation (f_1)												
Machinery	0.0	0.0	0.0	0.7	0.7	0.7	1.0	1.0	1.0	1.0	1.0	1.0
Buildings	0.5	0.5	0.04	1.0	1.0	1.0	1.0	1.0	1.0	1.0	1.0	1.0
Inventories	0.0	0.0	0.0	0.0	0.0	0.0	1.0	1.0	1.0	1.0	1.0	1.0
Lifetimes (L)												
Machinery	—	—	—	28	33	36	11	11	11	—	—	—
Buildings	12	12	12	—	—	—	30	30	30	—	—	—
Inventories	—	—	—	—	—	—	—	—	—	—	—	—

Table A3 (*Continued*)

	United Kingdom			Sweden			West Germany			United States		
	Manufacturing	Other Industry	Commerce	Manufacturing	Other Industry	Commerce	Manufacturing	Other Industry	Commerce	Manufacturing	Other Industry	Commerce
Type of depreciation[a]												
Machinery	0	0	0	0	0	0	2	2	2	4	4	4
Buildings	1	1	1	3	3	3	1	1	1	4	4	4
Inventories	0	0	0	0	0	0	0	0	0	0	0	0
Exponential tax depreciation rate (a)												
Machinery	—	—	—	0.3	0.3	0.3	—	—	—	—	—	—
Buildings	—	—	—	—	—	—	—	—	—	—	—	—
Inventories	0.0	0.0	0.0	0.0	0.0	0.0	0.0	0.0	0.0	0.0	0.0	0.0
Proportion with investment grant (f_3)												
Machinery	0.323	0.004	0.0	1.0	1.0	1.0	1.0	1.0	1.0	1.0	1.0	1.0
Buildings	0.821	0.007	0.0	1.0	1.0	1.0	1.0	1.0	1.0	1.0	1.0	1.0
Inventories	0.0	0.0	0.0	1.0	1.0	1.0	1.0	1.0	1.0	1.0	1.0	1.0
Rate of investment grant (g)												
Machinery	0.1946	0.1946	0.0	0.114	0.114	0.114	0.021	0.007	0.007	0.0959	0.0902	0.0857
Buildings	0.1476	0.1476	0.0	0.057	0.057	0.057	0.021	0.007	0.007	0.0	0.0978	0.0
Inventories	0.0	0.0	0.0	0.0	0.0	0.0	0.0	0.0	0.0	0.0	0.0	0.0

[a]*Key:* 0 = exponential; 1 = straight-line; 2 = declining balance/straight-line; 3 = straight-line with extra 2 percent for five years; 4 = United States only (see United States chapter).

Table A4 Weights

	United Kingdom			Sweden			West Germany			United States		
	Manu-facturing	Other Industry	Com-merce	Manu-facturing	Other Industry	Com-merce	Manu-facturing	Other Industry	Com-merce	Manu-facturing	Other Industry	Com-merce
Proportion of capital stock												
Machinery	0.298	0.090	0.080	0.2635	0.0253	0.0345	0.3648	0.0243	0.0281	0.0867	0.0965	0.0415
Buildings	0.171	0.022	0.139	0.2127	0.0662	0.0620	0.2069	0.0266	0.0641	0.2167	0.1970	0.1248
Inventories	0.135	0.005	0.060	0.1496	0.0957	0.0905	0.2378	0.0060	0.0414	0.1350	0.0176	0.0842
Proportion by source of finance												
Debt	0.193	0.193	0.193	0.405	0.812	0.625	0.4354	0.3123	0.4956	0.1981	0.4847	0.3995
New share issues	0.044	0.044	0.044	0.024	0.009	0.018	0.0491	0.0599	0.0439	0.0592	0.0381	0.0443
Retained earnings	0.763	0.763	0.763	0.571	0.179	0.357	0.5155	0.6278	0.4605	0.7427	0.4772	0.5562
Ownership shares												
Debt												
Households	0.718	0.718	0.718	0.252	0.750	0.482	0.543	0.543	0.543	0.6094	0.6094	0.6094
Tax-exempt institutions	0.137	0.137	0.137	0.672	0.199	0.476	0.336	0.336	0.336	0.2371	0.2371	0.2371
Insurance companies	0.145	0.145	0.145	0.076	0.051	0.042	0.121	0.121	0.121	0.1534	0.1534	0.1534
New shares												
Households	0.435	0.435	0.435	0.604	0.604	0.604	0.758	0.617	0.751	0.7433	0.7433	0.7433
Tax-exempt institutions	0.407	0.407	0.407	0.302	0.302	0.302	0.186	0.298	0.189	0.2154	0.2154	0.2154
Insurance companies	0.157	0.157	0.157	0.094	0.094	0.094	0.056	0.085	0.060	0.0412	0.0412	0.0412
Retained earnings												
Households	0.435	0.435	0.435	0.604	0.604	0.604	0.758	0.617	0.751	0.7433	0.7433	0.7433
Tax-exempt institutions	0.407	0.407	0.407	0.302	0.302	0.302	0.186	0.298	0.189	0.2154	0.2154	0.2154
Insurance companies	0.157	0.157	0.157	0.094	0.094	0.094	0.056	0.085	0.060	0.0412	0.0412	0.0412

Appendix B Effective Tax Rates in Each Combination for Each Country (%)

Asset	Indus-try	Owner	Source of Finance	United Kingdom Inflation Rates Zero	10%	Actual (13.57%)	Sweden Inflation Rates Zero	10%	Actual (9.4%)	West Germany Inflation Rates Zero	10%	Actual (4.2%)	United States Inflation Rates Zero	10%	Actual (6.77%)
1	1	1	1	-84.3	-129.0	-145.0	4.1	47.2	44.3	25.5	21.6	27.0	-22.1	-28.6	-24.9
1	1	1	2	-0.1	21.3	28.9	66.3	132.8	128.9	54.0	76.5	65.8	54.8	115.4	96.4
1	1	1	3	16.1	47.0	57.9	63.6	115.5	112.6	70.8	119.0	92.6	39.5	81.4	69.2
1	1	2	1	-165.4	-273.8	-312.4	-99.8	-111.4	-111.3	-32.1	-104.6	-57.3	-70.5	-119.2	-101.2
1	1	2	2	-82.1	-125.0	-140.3	-40.8	-33.8	-34.1	41.1	51.7	48.3	13.9	38.8	31.9
1	1	2	3	-52.5	-78.1	-87.6	-48.4	-81.9	-79.4	60.6	100.7	79.3	-15.1	-25.9	-20.0
1	1	3	1	-103.6	-163.5	-184.8	-79.2	-15.5	-21.0	-21.4	-89.1	-44.7	-45.1	52.2	9.5
1	1	3	2	-49.9	-67.6	-73.9	-26.3	25.4	21.6	11.6	-33.2	-2.8	19.8	49.9	41.3
1	1	3	3	-25.6	-29.0	-30.5	-33.1	-10.6	-12.7	43.1	46.2	47.4	-7.2	-10.3	-7.0
1	2	1	1	-45.3	-90.0	-105.9	-0.6	45.0	42.1	31.2	26.6	32.4	-21.4	-29.4	-25.2
1	2	1	2	21.1	42.5	50.1	65.4	132.3	128.4	58.2	80.2	69.8	55.1	115.1	96.3
1	2	1	3	34.5	65.8	76.7	61.0	114.1	111.2	73.7	121.4	95.3	39.9	81.0	69.0
1	2	2	1	-109.2	-217.5	-256.2	-109.0	-115.6	-115.5	-22.7	-96.4	-48.4	-69.5	-120.3	-101.7
1	2	2	2	-43.5	-86.4	-101.7	-43.2	-35.2	-35.5	46.0	56.0	52.9	14.4	38.2	31.6
1	2	2	3	-19.1	-44.1	-53.4	-55.5	-85.8	-83.3	63.8	103.6	82.4	-14.5	-26.7	-20.3
1	2	3	1	-60.5	-120.3	-141.7	-87.5	-18.4	-24.0	-12.2	-81.1	-36.0	-44.3	51.7	9.2
1	2	3	2	-18.2	-35.8	-42.2	-28.5	24.3	20.5	19.5	-26.3	4.7	20.3	49.4	41.0
1	2	3	3	1.9	-1.0	-2.4	-39.5	-13.5	-15.6	48.4	50.8	52.4	-6.6	-11.0	-7.4
1	3	1	1	-44.7	-89.4	-105.3	-0.1	45.3	42.4	31.2	20.6	32.4	-25.8	-30.8	-27.8
1	3	1	2	21.4	42.8	50.5	65.5	132.4	128.5	58.2	80.2	69.8	53.4	114.5	95.3
1	3	1	3	34.8	66.0	77.0	61.3	114.3	111.3	73.7	121.4	95.3	37.6	80.2	67.6
1	3	2	1	-108.3	-216.7	-255.3	-108.0	-115.1	-115.0	-22.7	-96.4	-48.4	-75.7	-122.4	-105.3
1	3	2	2	-42.9	-85.8	-101.1	-42.9	-35.1	-35.3	46.0	56.0	52.9	11.3	37.2	29.8

-22.9	-28.2	-18.8	82.4	103.6	63.8	-82.8	-85.4	-54.7	-52.9	-43.6	-18.6	3	2	3	1
7.1	50.7	-49.5	-36.0	-81.1	-12.2	-23.6	-18.1	-86.6	-141.0	-119.7	-59.8	1	3	3	1
39.3	48.4	17.4	4.7	-26.3	19.5	20.6	24.4	-28.2	-41.7	-35.4	-17.7	2	3	3	1
-9.7	-12.4	-10.6	52.4	50.8	48.4	-15.3	-13.2	-38.8	-2.0	-0.6	2.4	3	3	3	1
14.5	4.6	27.7	26.0	5.2	31.3	70.9	73.2	41.4	-58.2	-45.8	-17.7	1	1	1	2
111.0	127.6	73.2	65.0	64.2	58.3	143.7	147.4	85.2	76.1	66.5	36.0	2	1	1	2
89.8	99.1	64.7	92.1	110.8	73.7	129.8	132.5	83.5	99.6	86.9	47.3	3	1	1	2
-46.2	-72.9	-1.0	-59.0	-131.8	-22.4	-59.1	-60.4	-26.7	-187.5	-153.9	-69.6	1	1	2	2
59.7	62.2	49.0	47.4	37.6	46.1	7.1	6.7	11.7	-54.6	-42.8	-16.3	2	1	2	2
19.4	7.7	32.8	78.7	91.3	63.9	-31.5	-34.6	7.1	-11.8	-5.7	4.3	3	1	2	2
41.8	73.7	14.0	-46.4	-115.5	-12.0	15.8	19.8	-13.7	-88.9	-71.5	-30.1	1	2	2	2
67.1	71.7	52.6	-4.3	-56.1	19.7	52.7	55.6	20.8	-3.3	0.1	4.2	2	2	2	2
29.6	21.0	37.4	46.4	30.9	48.5	23.5	24.7	16.6	31.9	30.6	21.2	3	2	2	2
-13.4	-21.8	-1.7	27.7	6.8	33.2	71.3	73.5	42.6	-34.2	-21.0	10.6	1	2	2	2
100.6	117.9	62.3	66.3	65.4	59.7	143.9	147.6	85.8	89.1	79.9	51.5	2	3	2	2
75.2	85.0	49.9	93.0	111.6	74.7	130.0	132.7	84.2	111.0	98.7	60.5	3	3	2	2
-85.2	-109.8	-42.1	-56.1	-129.2	-19.3	-58.4	-59.8	-24.3	-153.0	-118.2	-28.7	1	1	2	2
40.0	43.6	28.2	48.9	39.0	47.7	7.7	7.2	13.4	-30.9	-18.3	11.7	2	1	2	2
-8.5	-19.0	4.5	79.7	92.2	65.0	-30.9	-34.1	8.9	9.1	15.8	28.1	3	1	2	2
18.9	56.6	-20.9	-43.6	-113.0	-9.0	16.3	20.2	-11.5	-62.5	-44.2	1.3	1	2	2	2
48.8	54.4	33.2	-1.8	-53.9	22.3	53.1	56.0	22.3	16.2	20.2	27.3	2	2	2	2
3.7	-3.9	11.1	48.0	32.4	50.3	24.0	25.2	18.3	49.1	48.3	40.8	3	2	2	2
14.5	3.3	31.2	27.7	6.8	33.2	70.8	73.0	42.5	4.8	20.6	64.8	1	3	2	2
111.0	127.2	74.5	66.3	65.4	59.7	143.7	147.4	85.8	110.3	102.6	80.9	2	3	2	2
89.8	98.4	66.5	93.0	111.6	74.7	129.7	132.4	84.2	129.7	118.4	84.9	3	3	2	2
-46.2	-74.7	3.9	-56.1	-129.2	-19.3	-59.4	-60.8	-24.5	-96.8	-58.3	49.3	1	1	3	2
59.7	61.3	51.5	48.9	39.0	47.7	7.0	6.6	13.3	7.6	22.8	65.2	2	1	3	2
19.4	6.4	36.1	79.7	92.2	65.0	-31.8	-35.0	8.8	42.9	51.7	72.5	3	1	3	2
41.8	72.8	18.2	-43.6	-113.0	-9.0	15.5	19.5	-11.7	-19.4	1.8	61.1	1	2	3	2
67.1	70.9	54.8	-1.8	-53.9	22.3	52.6	55.5	22.2	47.9	54.1	71.4	2	2	3	2
29.6	19.8	40.5	48.0	32.4	50.3	23.3	24.5	18.2	76.9	77.9	77.4	3	2	3	2
5.6	-7.9	33.9	45.0	39.6	48.9	94.4	97.7	36.2	-30.1	-14.1	30.6	1	3	1	3
107.7	123.0	75.5	79.2	89.9	71.4	153.6	158.0	81.3	91.3	83.7	62.3	2	3	1	3
85.2	92.4	67.8	101.6	128.0	82.5	144.9	148.5	80.8	113.1	102.0	69.6	3	3	1	3
-58.7	-90.3	7.7	-27.4	-74.7	6.8	-13.1	-12.4	-36.9	-147.0	-108.3	0.0	1	2	1	3

Appendix B (Continued)

Asset	Indus-try	Source of Owner	Source of Finance	United Kingdom Inflation Rates			Sweden Inflation Rates			West Germany Inflation Rates			United States Inflation Rates		
				Zero	10%	Actual (13.57%)	Zero	10%	Actual (9.4%)	Zero	10%	Actual (4.2%)	Zero	10%	Actual (6.77%)
3	1	2	2	31.4	-11.5	-26.8	0.7	36.0	34.7	61.3	67.2	63.8	53.4	53.4	53.4
3	1	2	3	44.7	21.8	12.7	-0.6	9.7	10.5	74.1	111.1	89.6	38.7	-4.9	10.5
3	1	3	1	23.3	-36.6	-57.9	-22.8	53.0	48.1	16.5	-60.0	-15.7	21.4	65.6	34.5
3	1	3	2	43.5	25.8	19.5	10.9	77.5	73.5	44.3	-8.2	22.2	56.6	63.5	61.3
3	1	3	3	54.4	53.2	52.1	9.8	57.9	55.3	65.0	63.0	64.2	42.9	9.2	21.3
3	2	1	1	30.6	-14.1	-30.1	50.2	102.3	99.2	48.9	39.6	45.0	33.9	-7.9	5.6
3	2	1	2	62.3	83.7	91.3	89.1	161.5	157.3	71.4	89.9	79.2	75.5	123.0	107.7
3	2	1	3	69.6	102.0	113.1	88.2	151.5	148.1	82.5	128.0	101.6	67.8	92.4	85.2
3	2	2	1	0.0	-108.3	-147.0	-9.5	-3.4	-3.6	6.8	-74.7	-27.4	7.7	-90.3	-58.7
3	2	2	2	31.4	-11.5	-26.8	22.5	45.9	44.9	61.3	67.2	63.8	53.4	53.4	53.4
3	2	2	3	44.7	21.8	12.7	20.0	18.0	19.2	74.1	111.1	89.6	38.7	-4.9	10.5
3	2	3	1	23.3	-36.6	-57.9	1.8	59.3	54.8	16.5	-60.0	-15.7	21.4	65.6	34.5
3	2	3	2	43.5	25.8	19.5	30.5	84.9	81.3	44.3	-8.2	22.2	56.6	63.5	61.3
3	2	3	3	54.4	53.2	52.1	28.3	64.1	61.8	65.0	63.0	64.2	42.9	9.2	21.3
3	3	1	1	30.6	-14.1	-30.1	36.2	97.7	94.4	48.9	39.6	45.0	33.9	-7.9	5.6
3	3	1	2	62.3	83.7	91.3	81.3	158.0	153.6	71.4	89.9	79.2	75.5	123.0	107.7
3	3	1	3	69.6	102.0	113.1	80.8	148.5	144.9	82.5	128.0	101.6	67.8	92.4	85.2
3	3	2	1	0.0	-108.3	-147.0	-36.9	-12.4	-13.1	6.8	-74.7	-27.4	7.7	-90.3	-58.7
3	3	2	2	31.4	-11.5	-26.8	0.7	36.0	34.7	61.3	67.2	63.8	53.4	53.4	53.4
3	3	2	3	44.7	21.8	12.7	-0.6	9.7	10.5	74.1	111.1	89.6	38.7	-4.9	10.5
3	3	3	1	23.3	-36.6	-57.9	-22.8	53.0	48.1	16.5	-60.0	-15.7	21.4	65.6	34.5
3	3	3	2	43.5	25.8	19.5	10.9	77.5	73.5	44.3	-8.2	22.2	56.6	63.5	61.3
3	3	3	3	54.4	53.2	52.1	9.8	57.9	55.3	65.0	63.0	64.2	42.9	9.2	21.3

Appendix C
Technical Aspects of the Swedish Tax System

Annell Deduction

The first point we discuss is the value of the Annell deduction for new share issues. In chapter 4 we argued that the deduction must be transformed into a tax saving per dollar of investment. The problem of transformation arises simply because assets depreciate. In deriving the cost of capital for a hypothetical investment project, we implicitly assumed that the financial capital raised to pay for new investment was repaid to the investors as the asset depreciated. In the light of this, it is not reasonable to interpret the Annell rules to imply that a firm that raises one hundred crowns worth of new equity capital to finance an asset that depreciates in, say five years' time would be able to deduct $h(100)$ annually for w years notwithstanding that after five years the original one hundred crowns are already repaid to the equity investors. Consider an all-equity firm that distributes all its after-tax economic profits, including real capital gains. This firm would issue new shares at time u of an amount, $N(u)$, equal to the change in the nominal value of its capital stock,

$$(C.1) \qquad N(u) = P_K \dot{K} + \dot{P}_K K,$$

where P_K denotes the price of capital goods and K the net capital stock.

Assuming geometric depreciation at the rate of δ so that $I = \dot{K} + \delta K$, we have

$$(C.2) \qquad N(u) = P_K I - (\delta - \pi) P_K K,$$

where $\pi = \dot{P}_K / P_K$. The flow of new equity capital therefore equals the amount required to finance gross investment minus the amount repaid to the owners to maintain the chosen equity/capital ratio (of unity) as the capital stock depreciates and the price level rises.

In the case of pure *debt* finance, the equation corresponding to (C.2) represents the net change in debt. The two terms appearing on the right-hand side of (C.2) then have a clear interpretation as borrowing to finance new investment and amortization of previously acquired debt to maintain the debt/capital ratio. Such a distinction is obviously difficult to make in the case of new issues, since it is hard to imagine that firms in practice would simultaneously raise and pay back new equity capital. For analytical purposes, however, we may look upon the flow of new share capital to the firm as the *net* of the amount raised to finance investment and the amount repaid to the owners. It is clear from (C.2) that, except for the case $\delta = \pi$, the amount of new share capital raised by the firm $N(u)$, and on which the firm claims Annell deductions, is not equal to gross investment. Let H be the present value of tax savings per dollar of new issue, as defined by equation 4.1 in chapter 4. The equivalent present value of tax savings per dollar of *investment*, A_A, can then be defined as

(C.3) $$\int_0^\infty A_A P_K I \cdot e^{-\rho u} du = \int_0^\infty H N(u) \cdot e^{-\rho u} du.$$

Integrating by parts, and assuming $K(0) = 0$, it can then be shown that

(C.4) $$A_A = \left(\frac{\rho}{\rho - \pi + \delta} \right) H,$$

where $\rho/(\rho - \pi + \delta)$ is interpreted as the amount of new issues that "on average" is required per dollar of gross investment. Hence the "net cost of investment," as defined in chapter 2, becomes

(C.5) $$1 - A = 1 - f_1 A_d - f_2 \tau - f_3 g - A_A.$$

Equation (C.4) assumes that fiscal depreciation coincides with economic depreciation. As explained in chapter 4, Swedish tax laws allow firms accelerated depreciation. The deferral of corporation tax brought about by accelerated depreciation is often compared to an interest-free loan from the Treasury. The deferred corporate tax may thus be regarded as a source of finance to the firm.

Let A_E represent the present value of the tax savings from true economic depreciation, taken to be replacement cost depreciation minus the nominal capital gain that accrues on fixed assets (cf. Bergström and Södersten 1981 and King 1977, p. 243),

$$A_E = \frac{\tau(\delta - \pi)}{\rho - \pi + \delta}.$$

The value of actual depreciation allowances may be written as

(C.6) $$A = A_E + f_3 g + (f_1 A_d + f_2 \tau - A_E),$$

where the last term (in parentheses) may be interpreted as the presented value of the tax savings from accelerated depreciation. The equation for MRR in chapter 2 (setting $w_c = d_2 = 0$ to simplify exposition) becomes

(C.7)
$$MRR = \delta - \pi + \frac{\rho}{1-\tau}$$
$$\left[1 - \left(\frac{\rho - \pi + \delta}{\rho}\right)(f_1 A_d + f_2 \tau - A_E)\right]$$
$$- \frac{f_3 g(\rho - \pi + \delta)}{1-\tau}.$$

To interpret (C.7), consider the case when there is no accelerated depreciation. In this case $f_2 = 0$, $f_1 = 1$, and $A_d = A_E$. Gross capital cost MRR then equals the rate of change in the nominal value of the asset ($\delta - \pi$) plus the required before-tax net rate of return. This net rate of return is the firm's pretax rate of discount $[\rho/(1 - \tau)]$ less the imputed gross return on the investment grant.

As can be seen from (C.7), the effect of accelerated depreciation is to reduce the weight attached to the firm's pretax rate of discount, and this effect has a clear economic interpretation. Consider a hypothetical situation where the Treasury, rather than providing accelerated depreciation allowances, offers to finance a fraction E of the acquisition cost of the investment by an interest-free loan, to be repaid at the rate of true economic depreciation $\delta - \pi$. In order for the firm to be indifferent between this arrangement and accelerated depreciation, E must be chosen such that the present value of the imputed interest on this loan equals the reduction in the present value of tax payments obtained by accelerating depreciation allowances. This condition means that:

(C.8)
$$\int_0^\infty \rho E e^{-(\delta - \pi + \rho)u} du = f_1 A_d + f_2 \tau - A_E.$$

Solving (C.8), we obtain

(C.9)
$$E = \left(\frac{\rho - \pi + \delta}{\rho}\right)(f_1 A_d + f_2 \tau - A_E).$$

This is exactly the term that appears in our expression for capital cost. E may be regarded as the proportion (in present value terms) of the investment that on average is financed by deferred taxes, and therefore $1 - E$ can be seen as the proportion financed by new equity (or debt or retained earnings).

We may now express the effects of the Annell deduction as

$$A_A = \left[\frac{\rho}{\rho - \pi + \delta}\right] H (1 - E) = \frac{\tau h [1 - e^{-\rho \omega}]}{\rho - \pi + \delta}$$

(C.10)
$$\left[1 - \left(\frac{\rho - \pi + \delta}{\rho}\right)(f_1 A_d + f_2 \tau - A_E)\right].$$

There is, finally, an empirical problem to take into account when analyzing the effects of the Annell deduction. In practice, few Swedish firms pay dividends on new share capital of as much as 10 percent, which is the maximum rate of Annell deduction. Available data suggest an average dividend yield of 6 percent for firms issuing new shares at the end of the 1970s, implying an Annell deduction of 6 percent after the new issues. It is reasonable to assume, however, that a successively higher rate of deduction—relative to the amount raised by the new issue—can be claimed for later years, since the amount of dividends paid by firms typically increases over time. Our numerical calculations actually assume that, starting at 6 percent, the rate of Annell deduction increases over time at the rate of inflation. A 10 percent rate of inflation means, therefore, that the maximum Annell deduction (10 percent) can be claimed on the sixth year after the new issue (assuming the initial deduction to be 6 percent). The firm then deducts 10 percent annually for an additional six years, after which time the sum of deductions taken equals the amount raised by the new issue. In the case of stable prices the annual deduction of 6 percent is taken for 16.7 years.

The Effects of Abolishing Corporate Income Tax

We examine here the relationship between the corporate tax rate and the tax wedge between savings and investment. Equation (2.17) of chapter 2 may be written as

$$(C.11) \qquad p = \frac{\rho}{1 - \tau}[1 - X] - \pi,$$

where

$$(C.12) \qquad X = \left[\frac{\rho - \pi + \delta}{\rho}\right][f_2\tau + f_1 A_d + f_3 g + A_A - A_E].$$

When the sum of the investment grant ($f_3 g$) and the present value of the tax savings from depreciation allowances and so on exceed the tax savings from true economic depreciation (A_E) $X > 0$. If the tax system allows immediate expensing of investment and no further deductions or grants ($f_2 = 1, f_1 = f_3 = A_A = 0$), equation (C.12) simplifies to $X = \tau$. We note also that the abolition of the corporate income tax implies $X = 0$.

For debt finance, the firm's after-tax rate of discount ρ is related to the nominal market interest rate i by equation (2.24) of chapter 2, which is

$$(C.13) \qquad \rho = i(1 - \tau).$$

Substituting into (C.11) yields

$$(C.14) \qquad i = \frac{p + \pi}{1 - X_D},$$

where the subscript D signifies that the discount rate ρ takes the value $i(1 - \tau)$. Equation (C.14) defines (in implicit form, since i appears as an argument of X_D) the maximum nominal interest i the firm can afford to pay on a loan acquired to finance an investment project with a pretax rate of return p (say 10 percent).

It is clear from equation (C.14) that if the tax laws provide for accelerated write-off ($X_D > 0$), the abolition of the corporation income tax (making $X_D = 0$) would reduce i. Through the fall in the nominal interest rate i, the posttax return to savings is reduced, increasing the wedge between the pre- and posttax rates of return p and s and therefore the effective tax rate.

In the case of an equity-financed investment project, equation (C.13) is replaced by $\rho = i/\theta$ for new share issues and $\rho = i(1 - m)/1 - z)$ for retained earnings. Since the corporate tax rate τ does not appear in these equations, the effect of abolishing the corporation tax can be inferred directly from equation (C.11). Inverting this equation yields

$$(C.15) \qquad \rho = (p + \pi)\left[\frac{1 - \tau}{1 - X}\right].$$

It is immediately clear that only if $X > \tau$ at the outset will ρ, and therefore i, fall as the corporation tax is abolished. Thus only if tax laws allow firms deductions (or grants) that reduce tax payments by more than would immediate expensing will the wedge between the pre- and posttax rates of return p and s (and therefore the effective tax rate) increase upon abolishing the corporation income tax.

Appendix D
Technical Aspects of the United States Tax System

This appendix describes a procedure to take A_z, the present value of depreciation allowances on a dollar of investment, and average it over different assets. Capital stocks by themselves do not provide correct weights, because short-lived assets require relatively more reinvestment that also qualifies for depreciation deductions. In particular, a dollar of asset type j can be maintained in real terms by reinvesting, at time u, a nominal amount equal to $\delta_j e^{\pi u}$, where δ_j is the jth asset's economic depreciation rate and π is the inflation rate. Each dollar of that reinvestment receives A_{zj} of depreciation allowances in present value terms at time u. Discounting those nominal amounts by ρ, the nominal discount rate, provides

$$PV(A_{zj}) = A_{zj} + A_{zj} \int_0^\infty \delta_j \, e^{\pi u} \, e^{-\rho u} \, du$$

(D.1)
$$= A_{zj} \left[1 + \frac{\delta_j}{\rho - \pi} \right]$$

as the present value of depreciation on a maintained real dollar of capital. Note that $[1 + \delta_j/(\rho - \pi)]$ is the present value of expenditures necessary to keep a real dollar of capital stock. These present values can be averaged over the twenty equipment types or fourteen structure types, weighting by capital stock in each type, K_j, to get the present value of depreciation for an aggregate asset in each industry:

(D.2)
$$\overline{PV}(A_z) = \sum_{j=1}^N K_j \, PV(A_{zj}) / \sum_{j=1}^N K_j,$$

where N is twenty for equipment and fourteen for structures (industry subscripts are suppressed for simplicity, but K is actually a thirty-four-by-three matrix). We can now ask the following question: Suppose a maintained real dollar of a single aggregate asset (either equipment or structures) had an aggregate economic depreciation rate $\bar{\delta}$ and was allowed exponential tax depreciation at rate $\bar{a}$. What rate $\bar{a}$ would provide the same present value of allowances as (D.2) above?

The present value of depreciation for a current dollar of investment in this aggregate asset is

$$(D.3) \qquad \overline{A}_z = \int_0^\infty \bar{a} e^{-\bar{a}u} \, e^{-\rho u} \, du = \frac{\bar{a}}{\bar{a} + \rho}.$$

The present value of depreciation for a maintained real dollar of this aggregate asset is

$$(D.4) \qquad PV(\overline{A}_z) = \frac{\bar{a}}{\bar{a} + \rho} \left[1 + \frac{\bar{\delta}}{\rho - \pi} \right].$$

Setting (D.4) equal to (D.2) implies that

$$(D.5) \qquad \overline{A}_z = \frac{\bar{a}}{\bar{a} + \rho} = \frac{\sum\limits_{j=1}^{N} K_j \, A_{zj} \left[1 + \dfrac{\delta_j}{\rho - \pi} \right]}{\sum\limits_{j=1}^{N} K_j \left[1 + \dfrac{\bar{\delta}}{\rho - \pi} \right]}.$$

The right-hand side of (D.5) is used to calculate $\overline{A}_z$ from the disaggregate A_{zj} described in the text. Since $\bar{\delta}$, derived in section 6.2.4, is just the capital-weighted average of δ_j, the denominator of equation (D.5) can be written as $\Sigma \, K_j[1 + \delta_j/(\rho - \pi)]$. Thus the desired aggregate present value $\overline{A}_z$ is just a weighted average of the A_{zj}, but the weights are $K_j[1 + \delta_j/(\rho - \pi)]$ rather than K_j. These weights can be interpreted as capital plus the present value of economic depreciation. Assets that depreciate faster than the average are given more weight because they will require more than the average amount of reinvestment receiving A_{zj} in future years. Or, if depreciation rates δ_j were the same for all assets, then A_z would be a simple capital-weighted average of the A_{zj}.

Now consider the averaging of g_j, the rate of grant for the jth asset. For the same permanent one-dollar increase in the stock of this asset, nominal replacement investment at time u is $\delta_j e^{\pi u}$. These nominal amounts receive credits at rate g_j and can be discounted by the nominal rate ρ to obtain $PV(g_j)$, the present value of credits for the original investment as well as for the subsequent reinvestment:

$$PV(g_j) = g_j + g_j \int_0^\infty \delta_j \, e^{(\pi - \rho)u} \, du$$

$$(D.6) \qquad = g_j \left[1 + \frac{\delta_j}{\rho - \pi} \right].$$

These present values can be weighted by K_j, the stock of capital in the jth asset, to obtain,

(D.7)
$$\overline{PV}(g) = \sum_{j=1}^{N} K_j \, PV(g_j) / \sum_{j=1}^{N} K_j,$$

where N is twenty for equipment and fourteen for structures. If an aggregate asset of all equipment or of all structures were to depreciate at rate $\bar{\delta}$ and receive a credit at rate $\bar{g}$, then the present value of its credits would be:

$$PV(\bar{g}) = \bar{g} + \bar{g} \int_{0}^{\infty} \bar{\delta} e^{(\pi - \rho)u} \, du$$

(D.8)
$$= \bar{g} \left[1 + \frac{\bar{\delta}}{\rho - \pi} \right].$$

Set (D.7) equal to (D.8) and solve for $\bar{g}$ as:

(D.9)
$$\bar{g} = \frac{\sum K_j g_j \left[1 + \dfrac{\delta_j}{\rho - \pi} \right]}{\sum K_j \left[1 + \dfrac{\bar{\delta}}{\rho - \pi} \right]}.$$

Since $\bar{\delta}$ is the capital-weighted average of δ_j, equation (D.9) just weights g_j by $K_j[1 + \delta_j/(\rho - \pi)]$, the capital stock plus present value of actual depreciation.

References

Aaron, H. 1982. *A report: Taxation of life insurance companies.* [Washington, D.C.]: American Council of Life Insurance.

―――. 1983. *The peculiar problem of taxing life insurance companies.* Washington, D.C.: Brookings Institution.

Akerlof, G. 1970. The market for lemons. *Quarterly Journal of Economics* 84:488–500.

American Council of Life Insurance. 1981. *Life insurance fact book.* Washington, D.C.: American Council of Life Insurance.

Auerbach, A. J. 1979. Wealth maximization and the cost of capital. *Quarterly Journal of Economics.* 93:433–46.

Auerbach, A. J., and Jorgenson, D. W. 1980. Inflation-proof depreciation of assets. *Harvard Business Review* 58:113–18.

Auerbach, A. J., and King, M. A. 1983. Taxation, portfolio choice, and debt-equity ratios: A general equilibrium model. *Quarterly Journal of Economics*, in press.

Bacharach, M. 1971. *Bi-proportional matrices and input-output change.* Cambridge: Cambridge University Press.

Bentzel, Ragnar, and Berg, Lennart. 1983. The role of demographic factors as a determinant of savings. In *National savings and wealth*, ed. F. Modigliani and R. Hemming. International Economic Association. London: Macmillan.

Bergström, Villy, and Södersten, Jan. 1976. *Double taxation and corporate capital cost.* Working Paper no. 9. Stockholm: Industriens Utredningsinstitut.

―――. 1981. Inflation, taxation and capital cost. In *Business taxation, finance and firm behavior*, ed. Gunnar Eliasson and Jan Södersten. IUI Conference Reports. Stockholm: Industriens Utredningsinstitut.

Blume, M. E.; Crockett, J.; and Friend, I. 1974. Stockownership in the United States: Characteristics and trends. *Survey of Current Business* 54:16–40.

Board of Inland Revenue. 1953. *Income tax wear and tear allowances for machinery and plant*. London: Her Majesty's Stationery Office.

———. 1977–78. *Survey of personal incomes*. London: Her Majesty's Stationery Office.

———. 1980. *Inland revenue statistics*. London: Her Majesty's Stationery Office.

Boman, Ragnar. 1982. Ägarstrukturen i börsföretagen. In *Löntagarna och kapitaltillväxten 9*. Statens offentliga utredningar (SOU), 1982:28. Stockholm: Ekonomidepartementet.

Bradford, D. F. 1980. The economics of tax policy toward savings. In *The government and capital formation*, ed. G. M. von Furstenberg. Cambridge, Mass.: Ballinger.

———. 1981. The incidence and allocation effects of a tax on corporate distributions. *Journal of Public Economics* 15 (1):1–23.

Bradford, D. F., and Fullerton, D. 1981. Pitfalls in the construction and use of effective tax rates. In *Depreciation, inflation, and the taxation of income from capital*, ed. C. R. Hulten. Washington, D.C.: Urban Institute.

Brinner, R. E., and Brooks, S. H. 1981. Stock prices. In *How taxes affect economic behavior*, ed. H. Aaron and J. Pechman. Washington, D.C.: Brookings Institution.

Brown, E. Cary. 1981. The "net" versus the "gross" investment tax credit. In *Depreciation, inflation, and the taxation of income from capital*, ed. Charles R. Hulten. Washington,D.C.: Urban Institute.

Carlsson, Bo; Bergholm, Fredrik; and Lindberg, Thomas. 1981. *Industristödspolitiken och dess inverkan på samhällsekonomin*. Stockholm: Industriens Utredningsinstitut.

Carlsson, Torsten. 1976. *Aktiemarknadens roll*. Aktiespararnas skriftserie no. 7. Stockholm: Sveriges Aktiesparares Riksförbund.

Cederblad, Carl Olof. 1971. *Realkapital och avskrivning*. Urval no. 4. Stockholm: Statistiska Centralbyrån.

Central Statistical Office. 1980*a*. *Economic trends*. London: Her Majesty's Stationery Office.

———. 1980*b*. *Financial statistics*. London: Her Majesty's Stationery Office.

———. 1980*c*. *National income and expenditure*. London: Her Majesty's Stationery Office.

Commerzbank. 1979. *Wergehörtzuwern: A guide to capital links in West German companies*. Hamburg: Commerzbank.

Corporation tax. 1982. Command Paper 8456. London: Her Majesty's Stationery Office.

Feenberg, D. R., and Rosen, H. S. 1983. Alternative tax treatment of the family: Simulations, methodology, and results. In *Behavioral simulation methods in tax policy analysis*, ed. M. S. Feldstein. Chicago: University of Chicago Press.

Feldstein, M., and Frisch, D. 1977. Corporate tax integration: The estimated effects on capital accumulation and tax distribution of two integration proposals. *National Tax Journal* 30:37–52.

Feldstein, M.; Poterba, J.; and Dicks-Mireaux, L. 1983. The effective tax rate and the pretax rate of return. *Journal of Public Economics*, in press.

Feldstein, M., and Summers, L. 1978. Inflation, tax rules, and the long-term interest rate. *Brookings Papers on Economic Activity* 1:61–109.

————. 1979. Inflation and the taxation of capital in the corporate sector. *National Tax Journal* 32:445–70.

Fischel, W. A. 1975. Fiscal and environmental considerations in the location of firms in suburban communities. In *Fiscal zoning and land use controls*, ed. E. S. Mills and W. E. Oates. Lexington, Mass.: Lexington Books.

Flemming, J. S., et al. 1976. Trends in company profitability. *Bank of England Quarterly Bulletin* 16, no. 1 (March):36–52.

Fraumeni, B. M., and Jorgenson, D. W. 1980. The role of capital in U.S. economic growth, 1948–76. In *Capital, efficiency, and growth*, ed. G. M. von Furstenberg. Cambridge, Mass.: Ballinger.

Fullerton, D. 1983. *Which effective tax rate?* Working Paper no. 1123. Cambridge, Mass.: National Bureau of Economic Research.

Fullerton, D., and Gordon, R. H. 1983. A reexamination of tax distortions in general equilibrium models. In *Behavioral simulation methods in tax policy analysis*, ed. M. S. Feldstein. Chicago: University of Chicago Press.

Fullerton, D., and Henderson, Y. K. 1981. *Long run effects of the Accelerated Cost Recovery System*. Working Paper no. 828. Cambridge, Mass.: National Bureau of Economic Research.

Fullerton, D.; King, A. T.; Shoven, J. B.; and Whalley, J. 1981. Tax integration in the U.S.: A general equilibrium approach. *American Economic Review* 71:677–91.

Fullerton, D.; Shoven, J. B.; and Whalley, J. 1978. General equilibrium analysis of U.S. taxation policy. In *1978 compendium of tax research*, ed. U.S. Treasury Department. Washington, D.C.: U.S. Government Printing Office.

Furstenberg, G. M. von; Malkiel, B. G.; and Watson, H. S. 1980. The distribution of investment between industries: A microeconomic application of the "*q*" ratio. In *Capital, efficiency, and growth*, ed. G. M. von Furstenberg. Cambridge, Mass.: Ballinger.

Gordon, R. H., and Malkiel, B. G. 1981. Corporation finance, In *How taxes affect economic behavior*, ed. H. Aaron and J. Pechman. Washington, D.C.: Brookings Institution.

Görzig, B., and Kirner, W. 1976. *Anlagenivestitionen und Anlatevermögen in den Wirtschaftsbereichen der Bundes Republik Deutschland.* Beiträge zur Strukturforschung, no. 41. Berlin: Deutsches Institut für Wirtschaftsforschung (DIW).

Griffin, Tom. 1975. *Revised estimates of the compensation and stock of fixed capital.* Economic Trends, no. 264 (October). London: Her Majesty's Stationery Office.

————. 1976. *The stock of fixed assets in the United Kingdom: How to make the best use of the statistics.* Economic Trends, no. 276 (October). London: Her Majesty's Stationery Office.

Gumpel, Henry J., and Boettcher, Carl. 1963. *Taxation in the Federal Republic of Germany.* Chicago: Commerce Clearing House.

Harberger, A. C. 1966. Efficiency effects of taxes on income from capital. In *Effects of corporation income tax*, ed. M. Krzyzaniak. Detroit: Wayne State University Press.

Harriss, C. L. 1974. *Property taxation in government finance.* Research Publication no. 31. Washington, D.C.: Tax Foundation, Inc.

Häuser, K. 1966. West Germany. In *Foreign tax policies and economic growth.* New York: Columbia University Press.

Hulten, C. R., and Wykoff, F. C. 1981. The measurement of economic depreciation. In *Depreciation, inflation, and the taxation of income from capital*, ed. C. R. Hulten. Washington, D.C.: Urban Institute.

Jakobsson, Ulf, and Normann, Göran. 1974. *Inkomstbeskattningen i den ekonomiska politiken.* Stockholm: Industriens Utredningsinstitut.

Jorgenson, D. W., and Sullivan, M. A. 1981. Inflation and corporate capital recovery. In *Depreciation, inflation, and the taxation of income from capital*, ed. C. R. Hulten. Washington, D.C.: Urban Institute.

Kay, John A., and King, Mervyn A. 1983. *The British tax system.* 3d ed. Oxford: Oxford University Press.

Kendrick, J. W. 1976. *The national wealth of the United States.* New York: Conference Board.

King, Mervyn A. 1977. *Public policy and the corporation.* London: Chapman and Hall.

King, Mervyn A., and Mairesse, J. 1982. *Profitability in Britain and France: A comparative study, 1956–75.* Working Paper. Paris: INSEE.

Körner, J. 1981. Trenzen der Steurbelastung erreicht? *Schnelldienst* 16/17:19–43. (Munich: Institute for Economic Research).

Lindsey, L. 1981. Is the maximum tax on earned income effective? *National Tax Journal* 34:249–55.

Lodin, S. O. 1976. *Progressive expenditure tax—an alternative?* Stockholm: LiberFörlag. (English translation published 1978.)

McGill, D. M. 1967. *Life insurance*. Rev. ed. Homewood, Ill.: Richard D. Irwin.

McLure, C. E. 1979. *Must corporate income be taxed twice?* Washington, D.C.: Brookings Institution.

————. 1980. The state corporate income tax: Lambs in wolves' clothing. In *The economics of taxation*, ed. H. J. Aaron and M. J. Boskin. Washington, D.C.: Brookings Institution.

Meade Committee, 1978. *The structure and reform of direct taxation*. London: Allen and Unwin.

Miller, M. H. 1977. Debt and taxes. *Journal of Finance*, May, 261–75.

Musgrave, R. A., and Musgrave, P. B. 1980. *Public finance in theory and practice*. 3d ed. New York: McGraw-Hill.

Normann, Göran. 1978. Bruttobeskattning och skatter på produktionsfaktorer. In *Skattepolitisk resursstyrning och inkomstutjämning*, ed. G. Normann and J. Södersten. Stockholm: Industriens Utredningsinstitut.

————. 1981. Sweden. In *The value-added tax: Lessons from Europe*, ed. H. J. Aaron. Washington, D.C.: Brookings Institution.

Orhnial, F., and Foldes, L. P. 1975. Estimates of marginal tax rates for dividends and bond interest in the United Kingdom, 1919–1970. *Economica* 42:79–92.

Organization for Economic Cooperation and Development. 1981. *Revenue statistics of OECD member countries, 1965–80*. Paris: OECD.

Ott, A. F., and Dittrich, O. L. 1981. *Federal income tax burden on households: The effects of tax law changes*. Washington, D.C.: American Enterprise Institute.

Pechman, J. A. 1977. *Federal tax policy*. 3d ed. Washington, D.C.: Brookings Institution.

Projector, D. S., and Weiss, G. S. 1966. *Survey of financial characteristics of consumers*. Washington, D.C.: Board of Governors of the Federal Reserve System.

Redfern, P. 1955. Net investment in fixed assets in the United Kingdom, 1938–53. *Journal of the Royal Statistical Society*, ser. A, 118:35–53.

Rosenberg, L. G. 1969. Taxation of income from capital, by industry group. In *The taxation of income from capital*, ed. A. C. Harberger and M. J. Bailey. Washington, D.C.: Brookings Institution.

Rundfelt, Rolf. 1981. Capital gains taxation and effective rates of return. In *Business taxation, finance and firm behavior*, ed. G. Eliasson and J. Södersten. IUI Conference Reports no. 1. Stockholm: Industriens Utredningsinstitut.

————. 1982. Några av bolagsbeskattningens principer. Stockholm: Sveriges Industriförbund. Mimeographed.

Securities and Exchange Commission. 1977. *Statistical Bulletin* (June).

Shoven, J. B. 1976. The incidence and efficiency effects of taxes on income from capital. *Journal of Political Economy* 84:1261–83.

Shoven, J. B., and Bulow, J. I. 1975. Inflation accounting and nonfinancial corporate profits: Physical assets. *Brookings Papers on Economic Activity* 3:557–611.

Södersten, Jan. 1975. Företagsbeskattning och resursfördelning. Ph.D. diss., University of Uppsala.

————. 1978. Bolagsbeskattningens verkningar. In *Skattepolitisk resursstyrning och inkomstutjämning*, ed. G. Normann and J. Södersten. Stockholm: Industriens Utredningsinstitut.

————. 1982. Accelerated depreciation and the cost of capital. *Scandinavian Journal of Economics* 84(1):111–15.

Spånt, Roland. 1979. Den svenska förmögenhetsfördelningens utveckling. In *Löntagarna och kapitaltillväxten 2*. Statens Offentliga Utredningar (SOU), 1979:19. Stockholm: Ekonomidepartementet.

Statens Offentliga Utredningar. 1969. *Kapitalbeskattningen*. SOU 1969:54. Stockholm: Finansdepartementet.

————. 1977. *Beskattning av företag. Bilagor*. SOU 1977:87. Stockholm: Finansdepartementet.

Statistiska Meddelanden. 1981*a*. *Inkomstfördelningsundersökningen 1978:1*. SM N 1981:1. Stockholm: Statistiska Centralbyrån.

————. 1981*b*. *Nationalräkenskaper*. SM N 1981:2.5. Stockholm: Statistiska Centralbyrån.

Steurle, E., and Hartzmark, M. 1981. Individual income taxation, 1947–79. *National Tax Journal* 34:145–66.

Summers, Lawrence. 1982. *The non-adjustment of nominal interest rates: A study of the Fisher effect*. Working Paper no. 836. Cambridge, Mass.: National Bureau of Economic Research.

Sutherland, A. 1981. Capital transfer tax: An obituary. *Fiscal Studies* 2:37–51.

Tax Foundation, Inc. 1981. *Facts and figures on government finance*. 21st biennial edition. Washington, D.C.: Tax Foundation.

Teschner, St. 1981. Sektorale Besteuerung der Produktion: Ungunstige Struktureffekte offensichtlich. *Schnelldienst* 16/17:44–60 (Munich: Institute for Economic Research).

Tiebout, C. 1956. A pure theory of local expenditures. *Journal of Political Economy* 64:416–24.

Uhlmann, L. 1981. *Konsum- und investitionsverhalten in der Bundesrepublik seit den fünfziger jahren*. Vol. 2. *Das Investitionsverhalten in der Industrie im Spiegel von Investorenbefragungen*. Berlin-München: Schriftenreihe des Ifo-Instituts.

U.S. Board of Governors of the Federal Reserve System. 1980. *Flow of funds accounts: Assets and liabilities outstanding*. Washington, D.C.: Board of Governors of the Federal Reserve System.

————. 1980. *Flow of funds accounts: Sector statements of saving and investment.* Washington, D.C.: Board of Governors of the Federal Reserve System.

U.S. Council of Economic Advisers. 1981. *Economic report of the president.* Washington, D.C.: U.S. Government Printing Office.

U.S. Department of Commerce. 1981. *Current business reports.* Washington, D.C.: U.S. Government Printing Office.

————. 1981. *Current industrial reports.* Washington, D.C.: U.S. Government Printing Office.

————. 1981. *Survey of current business.* Washington, D.C.: U.S. Government Printing Office.

U.S. Department of the Treasury. 1977. *Blueprints for basic tax reform.* Washington, D.C.: U.S. Government Printing Office.

————. 1981. *Statistics of income, individual income tax returns.* Washington, D.C.: U.S. Government Printing Office.

Waldenström, Erland, ed. 1976. *Företagsvinster, kapitalförsörjning, löntagarfonder.* Stockholm: Sveriges Industriförbund, Svenska Arbetsgivarföreningen.

Wallander, Jan. 1962. *Verkstadsindustrins maskinkapital.* Stockholm: Industriens Utredningsinstitut.

Wallmark, Kerstin. 1978. Planenkäten 1978. In *Industrikonjunkturen våren, 1978.* Stockholm: Sveriges Industriförbund.

White, M. 1975. Firm location in a zoned metropolitan area. In *Fiscal zoning and land use controls*, ed. E. S. Mills and W. E. Oates. Lexington, Mass.: Lexington Books.

Wilson Committee. 1980. *Committee to review the functioning of financial institutions: Report.* Command Paper 7937. London: Her Majesty's Stationery Office.

Winfrey, Fobley. 1935. *Statistical analysis of industrial property retirements.* Bulletin 125, Iowa Engineering Experiment Station. Ames, Iowa: Iowa State College of Agriculture and Mechanical Arts.

Wright, C. 1969. Saving and the rate of interest. In *The taxation of income from capital*, ed. A. C. Harberger and M. J. Bailey. Washington, D.C.: Brookings Institution.

Contributors

Julian Alworth
Bank for International
  Settlements
CH-4002 Basel
Switzerland

David F. Bradford
Woodrow Wilson School
Princeton University
Princeton, New Jersey 08544

Don Fullerton
Woodrow Wilson School
Princeton University
Princeton, New Jersey 08544

Mervyn A. King
Department of Economics
Faculty of Commerce and
  Social Science
University of Birmingham
P.O. Box 363
Birmingham, B15 2TT
England

Willi Leibfritz
Institut für Wirtschaftsforschung
Poschingerstrasse 5
Postfach 86 04 60
80000 Munich 86
West Germany

Thomas Lindberg
Industriens Utrediningsinstitut
Grevgatan 34, S-11453
Stockholm
Sweden

Michael J. Naldrett
Woodrow Wilson School
Princeton University
Princeton, New Jersey 08544

James M. Poterba
Department of Economics
Massachusetts Institute of
  Technology
Cambridge, Massachusetts 02139

Jan Södersten
Industriens Utredningsinstitut
Grevgatan 34, S-11453
Stockholm
Sweden

Author Index

Subject Index